Yale Agrarian Studies Series
James C. Scott, *Series Editor*

"The Agrarian Studies Series at Yale University Press seeks to publish outstanding and original interdisciplinary work on agriculture and rural society — for any period, in any location. Works of daring that question existing paradigms and fill abstract categories with the lived-experience of rural people are especially encouraged."
James C. Scott, *Series Editor*

Brian Donahue, *Reclaiming the Commons: Community Farms and Forests in a New England Town* (1999)

James C. Scott, *Seeing Like a State: How Certain Schemes to Improve the Human Condition Have Failed* (1999)

Tamara L. Whited, *Forests and Peasant Politics in Modern France* (2000)

Peter Boomgaard, *Frontiers of Fear: Tigers and People in the Malay World, 1600–1950* (2001)

James C. Scott and Nina Bhatt, eds., *Agrarian Studies: Synthetic Work at the Cutting Edge* (2001)

Janet Vorwald Dohner, *The Encyclopedia of Historic and Endangered Livestock and Poultry Breeds* (2002)

Deborah Fitzgerald, *Every Farm a Factory: The Industrial Ideal in American Agriculture* (2003)

Stephen B. Brush, *Farmers' Bounty: Locating Crop Diversity in the Contemporary World* (2004)

Brian Donahue, *The Great Meadow: Farmers and the Land in Colonial Concord* (2004)

J. Gary Taylor and Patricia J. Scharlin, *Smart Alliance: How a Global Corporation and Environmental Activists Transformed a Tarnished Brand* (2004)

Raymond L. Bryant, *Nongovernmental Organizations in Environmental Struggles: Politics and the Making of Moral Capital in the Philippines* (2005)

Edward Friedman, Paul G. Pickowicz, and Mark Selden, *Revolution, Resistance, and Reform in Village China* (2005)

Michael Goldman, *Imperial Nature: The World Bank and Struggles for Social Justice in the Age of Globalization* (2005)

Arvid Nelson, *Cold War Ecology: Forests, Farms, and People in the East German Landscape, 1945–1989* (2005)

Steve Striffler, *Chicken: The Dangerous Transformation of America's Favorite Food* (2005)

Lynne Viola, V. P. Danilov, N. A. Ivnitskii, and Denis Kozlov, eds., *The War Against the Peasantry, 1927–1930* (2005)

Parker Shipton, *The Nature of Entrustment: Intimacy, Exchange, and the Sacred in Africa* (2007)

Parker Shipton, *Mortgaging the Ancestors: Ideologies of Attachment in Africa* (2009)

For a complete list of titles in the Yale Agrarian Studies Series, visit www.yalebooks.com.

Mortgaging
the Ancestors

Ideologies of Attachment
in Africa

Parker Shipton

Yale University Press   NEW HAVEN & LONDON

Published with assistance from the Mary Cady Tew Memorial Fund.

Set in Ehrhardt and The Sans types by Tseng Information Systems, Inc.
Printed in the United States of America.

Library of Congress Cataloging-in-Publication Data
Shipton, Parker MacDonald.
Mortgaging the ancestors : ideologies of attachment in Africa / Parker Shipton.
p. cm. — (Yale agrarian studies series)
Includes bibliographical references and index.
ISBN 978-0-300-11602-1 (cloth : alk. paper) 1. Land tenure—Africa. 2. Mortgages—Social aspects—
Africa. 3. Economic anthropology—Africa. 4. Economics—Sociological aspects. I. Title.
HD968.S55 2009
333.3'23096—dc22

2008017706

A catalogue record for this book is available from the British Library.

This paper meets the requirements of ANSI/NISO Z39.48-1992 (Permanence of Paper).
It contains 30 percent postconsumer waste (PCW) and is certified by the Forest Stewardship
Council (FSC).

10 9 8 7 6 5 4 3 2 1

TO
Polly

Contents

Preface

Human attachment—to other humans or to things—is an idea that always contains a question. What, really, is a bond, a tie, or a connection . . . and if it is invisible, impalpable, something just in the minds of the ones who feel attached, or those who speak or write of them, then is it any less real than a piece of sisal rope?

This is a study about human attachments that have no feel or texture like twine but that would seem somehow to tie persons to other persons, warm and breathing; and to soil and sand that have color, taste, and smell. It is about attachments between people, and between people and things—and what these two kinds of ties have to do with each other. In short, it is about belonging.

People in East Africa have lately used use sisal not just to make rope but also as a growing plant, to mark boundaries and corners of fields. They use it not just to connect, that is, but also to divide. Some are going further and fencing off their fields. Whether they ought to be doing this, and whether those who lend them money ought to be attaching their land in a way that might let them yank it away from them, is a matter of much local uncertainty and debate. The mortgage, a new practice in the area, threatens to separate people in rural areas from home, from kith and kin, and from ancestral graves, with all that these mean. This is not just a local issue; it also reaches between continents.

This is one volume of an informal trilogy written to be readable in any sequence. *The Nature of Entrustment,* the first published, presents the Luo people, and the topic I call fiduciary culture, describing the part that local borrowing and lending, and deeper, longer-lasting entrustments and obligations, play in their lives. Sketching previous anthropological work on entrustment (usually published only in fragments and in other terms), it directs attention to a neglected borderland between anthropology and political economy—one that runs from the mundane and material to the spiritual and abstract. Fiduciary thought and action appear not just economic or political, but deeply cultural. Land, animals, food, money, human labor, and even humans themselves are moved around the countryside, and back and forth between town and country, in not just reciprocal transactions but also ones involving serial entrustment. Land transfers between families, and invitations to live among the people on that land and their kin, are powerful ways of defining social identities in the Luo country and elsewhere in western Kenya.

This volume, the second in the set, explores further the attachments perceived between people and land—expressions of enduring trust, among other things, between people themselves. I attempt to show how the processes of titling and finance, combined in the institution of the mortgage, represent a threat to these attachments, and to peaceful social relations.

Credit Between Cultures, as the third volume is tentatively titled, discusses people who call their work development, and the effects of some of their hands-on agricultural credit projects on Luo farming. It examines three kinds of aid programs: a series of state-sponsored, internationally funded "green revolution" attempts, a lucrative private tobacco-growing venture, and some small-scale programs organized privately by charitable agencies for self-help. The financial and fiduciary interventions that volume discusses do not depend on property reform and are a bit more technical in nature, allowing more concrete suggestions for practitioners.

The checkered history of credit programs for small-scale farming casts further doubt on the most widely held assumptions about the roles of individual property and long-distance financial assistance in economic life and in human social development—or whatever is so deemed. With or without mortgage credit, I suggest, intercontinental lending has proved an inadequate central strategy for alleviating rural poverty or for improving lives.

Together, the trilogy is meant to depict a diverse and adaptive African way of life, and to offer a suggestion for outsiders who wish their involvements in the African countryside to fit in better—with hard local realities,

and with African aspirations for dignity—than those of the past half-century
have done.

The topic of this volume cuts across several academic disciplines in the
social studies and humanities, and it bears on several professions beyond the
academy that have their own specialized training. It ought to be admitted at
the outset that these pages freely traverse some other boundaries too, particularly the one that conventionally separates the secular from the sacred.
I suggest, for instance, that land tenure and attempts to change or "reform"
it cannot be understood without knowing who is buried on that land, and
what sorts of kin groups or other entities claim attachment to those meaning-
laden graves. Some people in East Africa speak as though they compare debts
between persons with those between persons and spiritual beings and forces,
including divinity or what is so perceived. Debts and trespasses can be two
aspects of the same idea. One connotes money or finance and the other land
or territory, but in a more abstract way they are similar in suggesting in-
fringements or implying obligations.

It is precisely the tie between finance and landholding—whether or how
they are or ought to be interlinked—that is at issue in the mortgage system
now on trial in East Africa, and that lies right at the heart of this study. The
knot that foreign financiers and Kenyan development planners have sought
to tie between the two—private new land titles negotiable as security for
loans, and able to be seized in case of default—bears directly on what many
Luo and other western Kenyans perceive as sacred or otherwise special. That
connection, the freehold-mortgage process, challenges the attachments of
rural-dwelling people to their kin, to ancestral lands, and through ancestors
to divinity. For this and other reasons, land in East Africa has often been
the subject of violence. Blood and soil mix, and compete, symbolically and
materially. People make metaphors and analogies between sacred and secular
spheres all the time, knowingly or not. I hope the pages that broach these
delicate topics herein, revealing some cultural misunderstandings involved,
respect the dignity of the people involved and will not offend other readers'
feelings about whatever they may revere.

To venture along the thin rope bridge between anthropology and political
economy is to feel oneself trespassing in philosophy too. Looking into the
depths of Luo entrustments and obligations, an outsider can feel his or her
deepest ontological assumptions shaken. Distinctions between persons and
things begin to seem less clear, less immutable: in the rural Kanyamkago

community of Luo country you *are* your land (and your cows too) in ways you might not be, say, in Boston, Moscow, or Sydney. Distinctions between persons themselves, too, may begin to seem less clear. Where monetary debts are heritable, as they are in Luo country, a son is considered to *be* his father— and his own son too—in a way most Bostonians might not admit to being. Also called into question is the link between being and acting. Not in every culture, on the one hand, does signing a loan contract make you subject to removal from your patrimonial homestead in the case of a loan default, as it does in Boston and across North America as a matter of course. Not in every culture, on the other hand, may being a land client or tenant determine whether you are welcome to speak up at local headmen's meetings, as it does in Luo country. What counts as intimacy, too, varies from one cultural context to another. Whether your next-of-kin is your spouse or your clansman may be something you thought you knew. But if you entrust your dead body both to them and to the courts in Kenya, as did, for instance, one cosmopolitan Luo lawyer when he died intestate, the question of where it ought to be buried may become an international cause célèbre.

Surely the ethnographer's shaken sense of naturalness resembles the historian's. Whereas one travels in distance, the other does in time, gaining perspective on what is mutable and immutable in human nature, just as when looking back from Old Sturbridge Village to a time of debtors' imprisonment—or from present-day Rome to an era of debtors' rack dismemberment—claims and measures that seem perfectly normal and reasonable in one context are seen in the other as an abomination, and vice versa. Alterability means recurring possibility. What seemed safely over the horizon, or buried in the past, becomes something to contemplate, as dream or nightmare, for the future. If the skeins of intercontinental indebtedness that now entangle African nations and demoralize African people were not always there, there is hope for a time when they will somehow be cut loose.

Whether one travels across the map like an ethnographer or over time like a historian, seeing how much fiduciary custom can differ raises the question whether anyone is ultimately in control of it. Who, for instance, can legitimately and effectively regulate marriage dues, reset interest rates, or lay down a moratorium on farmland mortgage foreclosure? Seldom is it just individual or society, church or state, World Bank or rural populace. More often it is some shifting mix of groups, networks, and categories that will never fit any easy description. If control is neither certain nor static, one who wishes to relay sensitive information that might help in some small way to improve a people's chances of life and livelihood in the places they call home (or the chances of others somehow like them) cannot be quite sure to whom to pass it, beyond those people themselves. Still less can one be sure how the information will be used. Accordingly, this study is addressed: To whom it may concern, with trust.

Acknowledgments

Now some words of thanks. In any study that takes as long as this one, the debts incurred, and the kinds of people and institutions to whom they are owed, become too many and various to be properly listed. All those acknowledged in *The Nature of Entrustment* may consider themselves thanked again here; and there are more to come in the next round. But particular mention must be made here of people whose work and cooperation particularly on land, belonging, and property issues made special contributions to this work.

This study has been generously funded by a mix of institutions. They include the British Marshall Aid Commemoration Commission; St. John's College, Cambridge and its Warmington Research Studentship; Cambridge University; the Wenner-Gren Foundation for Anthropological Research; the Royal Anthropological Institute of Great Britain and Ireland; the Social Science Research Council; and the American Council of Learned Societies. A grant from the United States Agency for International Development (no. PDC-0068-G-SS-6197-00) allowed a period of comparative research and some responses to preliminary ideas from practitioners. Research fellowships at the University of Virginia's Carter G. Woodson Institute of African-American and African Studies and at Yale University's Agrarian Studies Program afforded the serene settings, strong support, and exciting colleagueship for research and writing that are every scholar's dream.

In Kenya, the Office of the President kindly granted research clearance, endorsed also by the Ministries of Lands, Agriculture, and Cooperative Development. At the University of Nairobi, my research affiliations at the Institute of African Studies and the Institute of Development Studies have provided both valuable colleagueship and practical support of many kinds.

Officers of the World Bank and the Agricultural Finance Corporation helped me gain insight into not only land matters but also the workings and concerns of their agencies.

I also thank the Survey of Kenya, the former EcoSystems Limited, and the Lake Basin Development Authority for some of the aerial land survey data briefly alluded to herein. Far more extensive data were kindly made available to me, in the overzealous collecting I did in the early years of this study, from cadastral registries, aerial survey headquarters, and other repositories than I have been able to put to full use or to represent here. The same is true of the genealogies and survey forms my hardworking assistants collected to match up with them. I am no less grateful for the favors and the confidences.

All the institutions named above, and all the individuals named below, deserve my thanks.

John Beattie and Ray Abrahams were foremost among the many who worked from Oxford and Cambridge, respectively, to make this research come about in its early stages and helped guide it from afar over the years. Peter Rivière and Africanists Jack Goody, Keith Hart, Polly Hill, Wendy James, Godfrey and Peter Lienhardt, John Lonsdale, John Middleton, David Parkin, Sandy (A. F.) Robertson, Malcolm Ruel, Migwe Thuo, and Michel Verdon did much in those centers and elsewhere for me, while John M. Roberts and Andrew Macintosh helped me thread through ancient labyrinths. Patrick Alila, Asenath Bole Odaga, and Joseph Ssenyonga all helped me arrange field and library research from their Nairobi bases. Joseph Fitzsimons from the Rapogi Mission, and Ben Ogallo, Peter Otieno, and Selemiah Ouma helped me adjust to lake basin country living.

My deep and enduring gratitude goes to the hosts and the many friends who opened their homes and lives to me and to mine—in Kanyamkago (my longest-visited base), Kagan, Sakwa, Uyoma, and Isukha in western Kenya, and not least Nairobi. Here I can name just a few. Rispa Akech, Esther Akinyi, Ulda Ayier, Janes Athiambo Omolo, Charles Opon, Hezron Oriedo, Agnes Azangu Tizika, and Ladan Madegwa variously provided shelter, sustenance, guidance, or a mix of these as only elders could, and Jeremiah and Jedidah Okumu did likewise as welcoming neighborly peers. Ismael Owiro, Joash Songa, and Hudson Azangu all helped keep me housed when I was not living with families. Joseph Obura Opon and Emin Ochieng' Opere provided steady companionship and cultural training in my earlier visits and beyond; Dan Odhiambo Opon, Meshack Magack Opon, Everlyn Millicent

Adhiambo Odhiambo, Ben Omondi, Elly Owino Nyanje, and Fred M. Shijenje all similarly kept me supplied with family, friendship, and insights in their home neighborhoods. My continuing thanks to them all, and to their kith and kin.

John and Jennifer Coope, Abraham Goldman, Mark Harris, Roger Kirby and Anne Stroud, Roiko Fukunaga, David Salter, Thomas Downing, and Joseph Valadez, among others, hosted or arranged intermittent stays in Nairobi and Maragoli, as did Patrice Haffeman, Kazuo Udagawa, and Valerie Smith in Kisumu and Maragoli, and David and Weisu Nugent during a writing spell in New Haven. Ray Abrahams, Patrick Alila, Frank Fitch, Richard Leakey, and Elijah Mugo all set me up with rugged transport, among all else they did. Others who sacrificed in one way or another in keeping the wheels of this work rolling, in ways figurative and literal—deserve thanks no less heartfelt.

While we learned simultaneously in different parts of western Kenya, Michael Dietler and Ingrid Herbich shared their quickly growing expertise on matters related to homesteads and spatio-temporal ordering in particular; David Anderson and Richard Waller, to herding and grazing; JoAnn Paulson and Benjamin Polak, to mortgage finance institutions; and Patrick Alila and Peter Little, to development encounters—along with all the other experiences we shared. Insights gained from simultaneous research in central Kenya by Philip Amis, David Throup, and Angelique Haugerud (one of those who kindly read an early draft) allowed explicit or implicit comparisons with westerly settings. Michael Norton-Griffiths helped make available aerial survey data. Nancy Schwartz, Maria Cattell, and some of the others mentioned above have generously helped keep me up to date with news on scores of topics.

My colleagues at Harvard and more recently at Boston University have provided more kinds of support and encouragement than I can name. In particular, Harvard's Department of Anthropology, Institute for International Development, and John Winthrop House; and Boston University's Department of Anthropology and African Studies Center; have kept me fueled with intellectually stimulating company, ideas, and collegial friendship. Among the many who generously shared their hard-earned understanding of land matters in Africa in those places and elsewhere over the years, special mention must go to John M. Cohen, Allan Hoben, Calestous Juma, Christian Lund, Shem Migot-Adholla, and Pauline Peters; all have been most helpful. Much have I learned about land, legal process, and what they have to do with each other from H. W. O. Okoth-Ogendo and Sally Falk Moore, who have helped steer me around many rocks. Among my other senior colleagues, Margaret Jean Hay, Robert and Sarah LeVine, David H. P. Maybury-Lewis, and Marguerite Robinson have also been unflagging in their encouragement over decades, as has Walter Sangree for many years too — with readings, referrals, and you name it. Department chairs Thomas Barfield and Robert Weller have helped me strategize to dovetail research and teaching, and Fredrik Barth helped clear a logjam of competing projects. Africanists including Barbara Brown, Edouard Bustin, James McCann, Michael DiBlasi, John Hutchison, Judith Mmari, James Pritchett, Diana Wylie and others have, on the corridor and around the coffee pot, made the late stages of writing and rewriting not only instructive but warming. My students over the years have taught me more than I suspect they realize. And Benzburg Nyakwana, Isaiah Nengo, Herine Ogutha, Arthur Omondi, Lisasa Opuka, and Elizabeth Siwo are among those who have continued educating me about western Kenya in eastern Massachusetts.

For sharing office life and cyber-tasking so cheerfully and effectively, Rebecca New, Margaret Nipson, Bradley Nixon, John Pollard, Sarah Potok, Suzanne Sloan, Kathleen Taffel, and Katherine Yost deserve special thanks. Anne Bellows, Magdalena Goodwin, Joanne Hart, Kathy Kwasnica, and Mark Palmer have all kindly exercised their managerial know-how on my behalf at Boston University, as have Kay Mansfield at Yale and longer ago, Geraldine Cully at the Marshall Commission. Kathleen Hanson, Anne Lewinson, Antonia Lovelace, and Clancy Pegg worked hard processing survey data for this study and the one to follow. The librarians of Oxford's Rhodes House and Institute of Social Anthropology libraries and Cambridge's African Studies Center library mined their collections on my behalf, and Henry West opened up his. In later library research, able assistance by Michael Katz, Fred Klaits, Anne Lewinson, Thomas Schaub, Michael West, and a few others all dug rare and valuable sources from Harvard's libraries. Gene DeVita and his fellow librarians in Harvard's Tozzer Library, and Boston University's African Studies librarians Loumona Petroff, Gretchen Walsh, and David Westley have done likewise. Karyn Nelson's mapmaking and Michael Hamilton's photo processing have provided the helpful visuals. Adam Kuper helped me settle on a title.

For kind permission to reproduce material from publications I have previously authored — expanded, updated, rewritten, and combined with other materials — I thank the following: The journal *Ethnology* for my article

"Lineage and Locality as Antithetical Principles in East African Systems of Land Tenure" (1984); Wiley-Blackwell for my article "Strips and Patches: A Demographic Dimension in Some African Landholding and Political Systems" (1984) in *Man* (Journal of the Royal Anthropological Institute); Edinburgh University Press [www.eupjournals.com] for my three articles in *Africa* (Journal of the International African Institute) titled "Understanding African Land-holding: Power, Wealth, and Meaning" (co-authored with Mitzi Goheen, 1992), "Debts and Trespasses: Land, Mortgages, and the Ancestors in Western Kenya" (1992), and "Luo Entrustment: Foreign Finance and the Soil of the Spirits in Kenya" (1995); and the University Press of New England for my chapter, "The Kenyan Land Tenure Reform: Misunderstandings in the Public Creation of Private Property," in S. P. Reyna and Richard Downs, eds., *Land and Society in Contemporary Africa* (1988).

Then the publishing itself. To series editor James C. Scott, and to in-house senior editor Jean Thomson Black, go my hearty thanks for not only showing enough continuing confidence in the potential value of this and the companion works (in Jim's case over many years as they grew) to make this come about, but also making the publishing process so easy, inspiring, and fun throughout. Would that every author could be so lucky as to work with editors like them. Two anonymous referees from outside, too, lent excellent suggestions for the tailoring, as did Jean Hay later, arriving with Occam's razor in the nick of time. Joyce Ippolito made the text editing easy, and Annie Imbornoni ably oversaw the production. Others at the Press who lent their skills in editing and production include Laura Davulis, Matthew Laird, Mary Valencia, and Maureen Noonan. Thanks to Bob Land for creating the index.

James Shipton, Elizabeth Cornu Shipton, and Susannah Shipton have, in their readings and much-needed distractions, struck just the right balance between the tenderly kind and the teasingly critical support that a writer in my generation needs from theirs.

To Polly Steele, who watched this project germinate decades ago, shared in the intercontinental adventures that have brought it about, and kept on adding more to my education and the bigger project than one could ever have hoped from any partner and spouse, I lovingly dedicate this work.

To acknowledge the efforts of all these people takes at least three tongues. *Ero kamano, asanteni,* thanks . . . and a space of silence for the ones who have not lived to see these words.

CHAPTER 1

Introduction

What we call land is an element of nature inextricably woven with man's institutions. To isolate it and form a market out of it was perhaps the weirdest of all undertakings of our ancestors.
— KARL POLANYI

"When you find a diamond that belongs to nobody, it is yours," proclaimed a character in Antoine de Saint-Exupéry's short novel *The Little Prince*. He went on, "when you discover an island that belongs to nobody, it is yours. . . . So with me: I own the stars, because nobody else before me ever thought of owning them" (Saint-Exupéry 1943, 56). When asked whether that was all, he replied, "That is enough."

In the world we live in, wherever someone can claim to own the land—or the sea, air, or stars—someone else has already set things up to let it be ownable. Wherever any of these is bought and sold, someone has made it tradable. How all this happens, and how far it might go, are questions with few obvious answers but big implications. What to call ownable, how easily exchanged it might become, and how much of it under anyone's personal claim is enough are questions of concern to all of us, wherever under the sun and the twinkling stars we happen to call our home.

Land, Money, and the Clock

This is a study of land and money and of how people think about these things in the interior of Africa. In it we go right to the innermost source of the White Nile, on the equator. The eastern side of the great lake that some have called Nam Lolwe, others Nyanza, and still others Victoria is a place without princes, but it is a place with probably as much human history as any on earth, and so one with the experience of many elders and ancestors. It is a region facing some of the same decisions about land, property, and finance as are being faced all over the globe. In some parts of the world where there is private property—for instance, in much of Islamic Arabia—mortgaging is forbidden, *haram*, by sacred law or shari'a as being a sin or sacrilege. In others—for instance, in most of western Europe and North America—both private land ownership and mortgaging have long and widely been deemed normal and natural. In yet other parts—for instance, in mainland China over the past half century or so—both private landowning and mortgaging have been forbidden by law. But then minds change. By a policy shift in China in 2007, private claiming of land was to be allowed by national law but its mortgaging was not.

People from all these parts of the world have arrived inside Africa, in waves; and they, and others, have lately been competing for influence there. But African people have their own ideas, no less wise or considered than any; and before history proceeds too much farther, it is perhaps time to devote some attention to these too.

Land is hard to move or conceal. Money, by contrast, is easy to move around, to hide, and to misplace. Across Africa, and in tropical settings around the world, a burning issue over the past century has been whether land may properly be bought and sold, or if not, exchanged in a more gradual, conditional, and subtle kind of transfer: pledged as security (or collateral) against a loan. Where there is a clock involved—an alarm clock—and the loan is given a deadline, it is called a mortgage. Numerous African governments, with advice, support, and some arm twisting from outside Africa, have been gearing up at the start of the millennium to title farmland as private property in the hands of individual or group owners to make it more marketable and able to be mortgaged.

The bellwether for individual titling programs has been Kenya. Its program for adjudicating and registering land, formally launched under British colonial rule in the mid-1950s and still continuing under the national government from the time of Independence in 1963 to the time of this writing, is not the first to have been tried in tropical Africa, but it has been the first of nationwide scope. As such it has been closely watched by government officials, financiers, and scholars in the cities and overseas—as well as, of course, by farming, herding, and trading people in the Kenyan countryside.

Titling farmland as individual property, as its planners and proponents envisaged it, would achieve many aims at once. It would provide new security of tenure, giving users incentive to conserve its fertility. It would enable farmers to borrow against a new form of collateral, stimulating investment. It would quell and prevent disputes by providing a clear public record of ownership, allow land to pass into the hands of the most able farmers, and improve husbandry through consolidation of holdings. In doing all this, it would help promote not only economic growth but also political stability. In short, it would be a kind of panacea.

But the program has been producing many unexpected results, some quite opposite to those intended. One after another, its reasons and rationalizations are starting to be reassessed. The rethinking calls for a deeper look into the implications of making a market out of land—cultural, political-economic, and ethical. Lending with land collateral, a central subject of contention, provides a focal point to cross-cultural misunderstandings about land, money, and the relation between them. Here I concentrate on the case of the Luo, a population of over three million living mainly in the basin of Nyanza or Lake Victoria, and mainly in western Kenya. Over the past five centuries or so, this part of the lake basin has become their ancestral homeland. Some of their ancestors fought and died for it, and now the living too face big questions about who—among the living, the dead, and the unborn—might claim ownership or belonging on the land and the lake. Perhaps too, before long, they and we all may need to make decisions about whether anyone may own the air. But here, for the pages in these covers, the question of land will be enough.

A Common Ground

Scholars in recent times have also shown a tendency to fence off topics, or fields, into separate academic disciplines. Legislators and administrators, for their part, have divided their subject matter into separate ministries, departments, or bureaus. Sometimes these bodies, like academic departments, have their own corridors or buildings. People born into a world with disciplines, and with government sections, can be forgiven the impression that these are somehow natural and enduring.[1] Where land and human attachments are concerned, the artificiality of these divisions—whether they be ultimately necessary or not—can lead us to many problems, and not infrequently to tragicomic outcomes.

Human spatial relations, whatever innate territorial proclivities may underlie them, can be made as complex as anyone might wish, and as much a science or an art, allowing room for many disciplines—and for approaches and feelings not so disciplined. These things might seem obvious, but land tenure has been the subject of so many easy answers and disastrous experiments in engineering, both physical and social, because one or another discipline or profession took over and one or another of these things was forgotten—as to make it worthwhile to spell some of this out.

Since it is hard to discuss land matters without reference to time and space, the topic is geographical and historical. The topic has a physical side, since it is about our relation to places and the planet that are our home, to the substances and flows of energy thereon, and the potential these offer for life itself; so it is chemical, biological, and ecological. Since land, water, and air are where our food comes from, where our fights are fought, and as often as not what these are fought over, it is nutritional and materially strategic. Involving spatial perception, dreaming, and feeling, including emotions about attachment, it is certainly psychological; and as such, just as certainly electrochemical.

It is also a social topic, as this last implies; and it thus falls in the contested zone between sciences and arts. As its study can compare humans to other species, it is ethological. But as human (like other animal) groups differ within the species in their thoughts and actions, and differ in discernible patterns, it is ethnological. These two facts, and the fact that the topic involves both innate tendencies and communicated learning among groups, networks, and categories as well as individuals, make it both anthropological and sociological. Pertaining as it does to power, authority, and influence, and to physical barriers to communication and governance, it is political. As secular and religious legislators, and sometimes other ad hoc or unnamed authorities, enact and seek to enforce laws and other regulations about rights, duties, and access, and not least about marital claims and inheritance, it is legal. Bearing as it does so heavily on how polities of all stripes and sizes get along, it is diplomatic, and strategic again in the social sense this time. Since spaces and places have or are construed to have value; since production, exchange, and consumption occur in places; and since these things can all be subject to supply and demand—our topic is no less economic.

Any discussion of resource use and ownership must of necessity include ontological and teleological dimensions—about, for instance, for whom or what it exists or is destined, or whether it can be improved and destroyed or only transformed, and whether the ecosystems encompassing life tend toward equilibrium or disequilibrium. This and the epistemological problems of how we might know or communicate about these things, and whether our translations can adequately represent our thoughts and feelings or not, are all considerations philosophic. As the topic relates not just to the living but also to the dead and immortal—to the placement of bodies and the watchfulness of spirits or divinity, which as some see it are the guardians of our highest ideals and ultimate understandings, and as others see it the outward personifications of our basest and most hidden urges—it can be spiritual and religious.

As landscapes can be pleasing or displeasing, and since their look helps determine their use, the topic is aesthetic. The many metaphors and connotations about fertility and barrenness drawn in perhaps every culture between land and the human body give the topic an importance that is literary and poetic too. Nor are these always just flights of fancy. We shall hear of land as mother, land as life, in political rhetoric with high stakes. And it is through grandmother stories, camp dramas, and broadcast fiction that humans learn about dangers. About unforgiving landlords and lenders, for instance.

Truly this topic is no discipline's territory, and the fences that divide it cannot not long endure without gateways through.

Attachment

Graves, in Luo country, are sacred places. People live right around them—the dead are, and have been for many decades, buried outside the doorways of homes. Many consider the ancestors present, active forces in their homes. These people are likely to consider these spots on the landscape to anchor their membership in families and in larger groups that have been called lineages, clans, and tribes: living, branching groups with illustrious pasts and high hopes for their futures.

But other people are trying to take away land and homes from those who live, farm, sacrifice, and pray there. When, as has often happened lately, land has been pledged as collateral on a mortgage loan, and payments fall behind a contractual schedule set by the bankers or government officials, those lenders, their court brokers, and the highest bidder at the auction feel entitled to take over the land—graves and all. Luo people call it raiding.

Not just individuals are involved. A mortgager threatened with eviction is likely to have women, children, and elder kin, dependent and provident, who never signed the contract and may never have known about it, or agreed with it if they did. He (since it has usually been a he) is also likely to have kin and friends, as well as perhaps perceived spirits, living all around: people likely to look upon those graves and the land around them as a sacred heritage belonging not just to the dead and the living, but also the unborn. (In some eyes, it is the dead who look out for the unborn.) Between elders and juniors, between men and women, and between insiders and outsiders, the mortgage is a focal point of tensions in which the living bear the nonliving, constantly or intermittently, in mind. The clashes of interest sometimes lead to violence.

Conflicts around land sales and mortgages signify deep differences of ideology, a kind of plate tectonics with moving, counter-pressing ideas underground. An equatorial African civilization established by immigrants from northeastern Africa mixing with others from the south was subjected to British rule for well over half a century, and shakily but sometimes brutally administered by a national government and foreign financiers for nearly a half-century after that. The misunderstandings and manipulations surrounding land and "property," involving the gradual state registration of private titles as well as the erratic influx of capital from sources in other continents, are not just economic and legal. They involve a number of others that are cultural, social, political, and so on. Sometimes happening by circumstance and defying description or discipline, the causes and effects of the decisions, trends, and undecided circumstances of "land tenure" may never be fully understood. But this volume tries to sketch, in a preliminary way, the conceptual geology involved: to suggest the faults and folds, the plates and rivers, of ideas that move sometimes almost imperceptibly slowly—not always seen, heard, or named—but sporadically erupt into witchcraft accusations or armed strife, and more important, perhaps, potentially threaten the homes and ways of life of a population of millions within Luo country and beyond.

This brief study treats the freehold-mortgage process as a long-term trend, but one fraught with tension and not a steady movement. The aims of the work are three. First is to trace the antecedents of some of the most influential ideas about private property, credit, and the links between them: the theories and debates that have shaped public policy in colonial and independent Kenya and elsewhere. Some of the roots are European and American, but many centuries old and traceable to other parts of the world. They are now, however, so deeply intertwined with some strands of African social thought as to be African too.

Second, I attempt to describe a Luo understanding of landholding and the way it has been changing. Theirs is a pattern gradually adapting over the past century or two as populations have encountered each other and been forced to settle down to fixed territories. Its more sudden, purported "reform" has been unfolding in practice over the past half-century in a farming area where I have lived. This is an area of rather high population density but unexceptional infrastructure, productivity, and potential: the sort of area that might afford some glimpse into the future of a continent with a burgeoning inland population heavily dependent on farming. The over three million Luo-speaking people of the Lake Victoria Basin—an area known to most of the world for little over a century—demonstrate characteristically East African patterns of settlement, kinship, and social organization, and prevailing philosophies about time, space, and identity well suited to these. Luo people live mainly by farming, as does most of Africa; but typically again, they are unable and unwilling to rely on it for their entire living. They are a people constantly adapting to, and contributing to, wider economic, political, legal, and religious traditions that they cannot fully control—in some ways no one does—but that they struggle to make sense of and master. Their ways of doing so reveal a rich and ingenious mix of homegrown, borrowed, and adapted ideas about humans, ancestors, and divinity, and about forces and principles not always easy to name or translate, but always bearing on matters like landholding and trust.

The third aim is to explain, in cultural as well as political-economic terms, why the grand design of the linked land and capital markets, and of the mortgage that is its quintessence, is turning out to misfit so dramatically this setting and others like it in equatorial and tropical Africa. The story is not without parallels or implications elsewhere, for it highlights, among other things, a clash of industrial and agricultural civilizations, and of their urban and rural participants. If the mistakes, misunderstandings, and manipulations to be described in these pages are taken seriously, I hope that they may contribute to making the designs of would-be reformers for the lands and settlements of other people less presumptuous, and to cautioning people anywhere about the likely longer-term consequences of promised opportunities that might on the surface seem quite tempting.

The framing of the story concerns cultural philosophies that I broadly call "ideologies of attachment." By these I mean more than just the "attachment" of land to loans, the way financiers speak of it when discussing issues of loan security or collateral. I mean also the ways of thinking that people feel connect them to land, and also to each other—including at times not just the living but also the dead. In turn, these ways of thinking tie into yet other ideologies. They connect to evolutionary ideas about movement between savagery and civilization—ideas that seem to keep getting debunked and reborn in altered terms. They connect to familiar political-economic ideologies of capitalism and communism, and to the conceptual terrain in between, so hotly contested on one continent and another over the past century. And they connect to other ideologies or "isms"—political, economic, religious, or a mix of these—known only in African tongues or as yet unnamed.

The Freehold-Mortgage Doctrine, from Global to Local

International financiers and development technicians have long held a theory about how to improve African farming and boost African economies. This is that small-scale farmers need seasonal credit to adopt new crops, inputs, and techniques; and that their access to credit depends on their possessing individual land titles. Piece by piece, the old theory and doctrine is this: (1) To raise agricultural productivity, farmers need more inputs and new technology. (2) Farmers are too poor to save or to afford the inputs and new technology themselves. (3) They therefore need loans from better-endowed people until they can afford to finance their own needs. (4) Loans require collateral as security; this will ensure their repayment. (5) The best collateral is land, because it is immovable. (6) Land ought therefore to be negotiable (that is, transferable) for monetary or other consideration. (7) The way to make land transfers easier, and to keep track of them, is to issue titles of land ownership (or else deeds of transactions), registered with the national government.

This theory is deeply embedded in West European and North American agricultural histories. Phrased in various ways, usually abbreviated, it is heard as orthodoxy in international agencies, read in standard textbooks, and repeated in the manner of a credo in policy speeches almost wherever common law and neoclassical (that is, "mainstream") agricultural economics are taught as disciplines. Frequently mixed with other arguments about the benefits of private property and land markets, the doctrine represents a kind of core logic in arguments for tenure reform as land titling.

At the World Bank, the largest international development funding agency, the aims of financial credit and land titling have been expressed together as follows in *Sub-Saharan Africa: From Crisis to Sustainable Growth*, among the central policy documents of the Bank for the region at the time of this research and writing; and these words echo others in countless other World Bank documents before and since: "Despite the enormous range of ecological zones across the continent, there is surprising commonality in the kinds of policies needed to stimulate growth in Africa's agricultural sector. . . . An enabling environment for agriculture means . . . promoting credit at commercially attractive interest rates through private homegrown financial institutions . . . gradually reforming systems of land tenure to enable titles to be registered (and in the interim codifying customary land rights), thereby increasing security and encouraging investment in land improvements" (World Bank 1989, 8).[2]

In Kenya the theory was a colonial import, applied to the former "scheduled areas" of European settler farmers with leases or titles from the first decades of the twentieth century. It was extended right into the great nationwide titling scheme of the 1950s, and the government of independent Kenya, with much foreign funding and advice, has kept it standing and continued to build upon it since Independence in 1963. In the 1950s, the last full decade of the colonial period, the theory was incorporated into government policy as Kenya began its great nationwide registration of land as private property. From the earliest days of the reform, promises of loans have been held out to farmers as an incentive for cooperating in the consolidation and registration of holdings (Lawrance 1966, 24). From within the nation, the Kenya Parliamentary Sessional Paper no. 10 of 1965, a keystone of the government's post-independence agricultural policy authored with external collaboration, reads: "The need to develop and invest requires credit and a credit economy rests heavily on a system of land titles and registration. The ownership of land must, therefore, be made more definite and explicit" (pp. 10–11)." In national planning documents, the contention has appeared again and again.[3]

In the Luo country within the lake basin, the district development plans have consistently reflected the idea. The South Nyanza District's 1989–93 plan listed as a priority, "To complete all adjudication sections [areas beginning the titling process] in the District . . . [and] to open up new adjudication sections in areas which have not been started. . . . Justification: Land owners will be able to secure loans from financial institutions using their title deeds" (p. 68).[4] Within that district, the Migori Division government land survey office carried this sole stenciled sign on its door, as I copied it down in December 1991: "The land owner uses his land certificate to acquire [a] loan

from loaning institutions to be used for intensifying production and export."
The same dream can be heard voiced in chiefs' and subchiefs' assemblies
(*baraza*).

So all the way from the largest international agencies to rural homesteads,
the plan is proffered, the expectation raised. Lawyers are continually being
trained in the orthodoxy. The freehold-mortgage credo — the belief that land
mortgages justify tenure reform — is everywhere. In Kenya, in other African
countries with pro-market official ideologies, and in the agencies supporting
these states — more of the people in power than not have long been believers.
It is conventional, received wisdom.

But is the freehold-mortgage credo really so logical, and so wise? After
asking where this pillar of international and national development policy
came from, and seeing what kinds of debates have surrounded it, we look at
it from the grass roots. To do so means both seeing how a people, in this case
the Luo of Nyanza, have adjusted to both land tenure reform and seasonal
credit schemes; and placing these in broader social and cultural context.
Titling and lending can occur together or quite independently of each other.
As one examines the process in which they occur together, the freehold-
mortgage credo, seemingly so logical on the surface, begins to look increasingly foreign and fantastical, and the complex of institutions built around it
increasingly futile. Although the individual steps may seem defensible on the
surface, several are flawed, and in combination they may turn out to be quite
misleading.

Kenya's Great Experiment

Kenya stands out among African countries in the amount of international attention and funding it received before its independence from Britain
in 1963, constantly and heavily for about the first two decades afterward,
and more intermittently and tentatively to the present day. Having fertile
and well-watered highlands, a strong history of cash crop production, and
a government with consistently pro-market policies, Kenya was perceived
for decades as a promising borrower and a place to develop African farming
for export.

Kenya led the continent in its bold program of titling farmland as private
property nationwide: a program advertised to farmers as a way of making
them eligible for credit. Rather in the same way western European statesmen
took it upon themselves in the mid-1880s to draw seemingly arbitrary lines

between what are now nations, and just as the new colonial governments divided up ethnic groups with district lines, the British-controlled government in late colonial Kenya took it upon itself finally to draw new lines between what its appointed officers considered to be family farms — and to try to give these units a whole new meaning. This was not the first program to title land in Africa as private property — others had tried it on small pieces of the continent since the turn of the century — but it has been the first to attempt it nationwide.

Launched in 1954 by a British-run Department of Agriculture and still continuing under Kenya's own government since Independence in 1963, the great land registration program, based on a European model, had by the century's end covered most of the higher-potential farmland in the country, and among these lands, most of the farmland in the Luo country. Most of the people living on these lands had never held individual, freely alienable land titles before. Instead they had relied on more complex patterns of landholding based on membership in kin groups and neighborhoods, on recognition of need and of labor investment, and other principles. Title to land could now, in theory at least, be bought and sold for cash.

Farm loans and individual land titling are two kinds of programs tightly intertwined in development planning at international, national, and local levels. The hinge between them is a foreign dream that has become an official state dream: the dream of a mortgage system, a way for farmers and others to use private land titles as collateral for loans as never before. Although the promise of credit is not the government's only reason for registering Kenya's farmland as private property, it is the justification most commonly mentioned among development planners, and it has been the government's main lure to encourage rural people to participate in the titling program.

This study takes a sober look at that promise. Reviewing the nature of settlement, landholding, and burial before and since the titling program began, the process of titling land as private property as it has unfolded, and the evident outcomes of programs to issue loans on land security, it assesses the roles of both land and foreign-financed credit in western Kenyan farming and farm life. The three million or more Luo of Nyanza Province earn their livings in many ways and in a wide variety of ecological subsystems. Like other rural East Africans, Luo have coped with, transmuted, and adapted foreigners' financial interventions in ways not just economic and political, but also cultural. Many of their experiences are paralleled in other parts of Africa south of the Sahara. The accumulated experience casts serious doubts about the validity of development strategies based on credit—which also means on debt—and on the mission of creating a mortgage system in privately titled land.

Many other African nations have begun to follow Kenya's lead in land tenure reform and in farm finance. With encouragement and assistance from the same international aid agencies, their governments have begun setting up their own nationwide land titling schemes and farm credit programs to tie into them. Financial planners and bureaucrats in some of these countries have long nurtured dreams of small-scale farmers borrowing and mortgaging their way to a better life, with more and more access to capital, and in ever closer contact with financial institutions operating in the name of development and participating in the task of nation building. Kenya was, up to the early 1980s, a model for it all.

But Kenya's luster began to tarnish by the beginning of the regime of President Daniel arap Moi, who succeeded Jomo Kenyatta in 1978. For the remainder of the century, most analysts agree, Kenya's economy fell into serious decline under a form of government some have called neo-patrimonialism, others autocracy, and yet others kleptocracy.[5] By the time Moi yielded power to elected successor Mwai Kibaki in early 2003, the country was widely perceived as not only one of the most corrupt, but also one of the poorest, in the world. A dramatic civil crisis in Kenya following the disputed presidential and parliamentary election of December 2007 also rendered it—at least for the start of the new year—one of the most politically unstable.

Whether as a result of a broader slide in Kenya's political economy, because of the land tenure reform's shortcomings, or both, even the staunchest supporters of individualist land tenure reform began to admit that things in Kenya were not coming out as they had hoped. The kinds of economic developers who so nurtured hopes for credit and a freehold-mortgage system in Kenya began to transfer their hopes and ambitions elsewhere. But the Kenyan story may help foretell what will happen there too.

. . . and Its Luo Participants

Western Kenya and the Luo country that crosses through it are areas of high population density, and in this way they afford a glimpse into the likely future of much of tropical Africa, demographically one of the world's fastest growing areas.

With numbers estimated at about 2.7 million in 1989 and now doubtless well over three million, the Luo-speaking population of western Kenya
covers an area of varied landscapes and land uses.[6] Rural locational population densities vary from under fifty to over five hundred per square kilometer, high by African standards. The emphasis of exploitation varies cor-
respondingly, from extensive grazing on the lower, drier flat lands around
the Lake Victoria shore at about 1,133 meters above sea level to carefully
intercropped farming on better watered and greener hillsides at about 1,500
meters as one rises into Luhya-speaking or Gusii-speaking districts adjacent
to the north and southeast, respectively.

Living in homesteads scattered across the countryside, rather than
in nucleated villages like the barricaded settlements found abandoned by
around the turn of the twentieth century, Luo and members of other groups
living among them till and weed with short-handled hoes—female hands do
most of the agricultural work—and, increasingly since the 1920s, animal-
drawn plows. They grow grains (maize, sorghum, and millet now being their
biggest staples) and root and tree crops, for food and cash; and they keep
cattle (much beloved, by elder men especially), sheep, goats, and fowls, some
of which sleep inside their homes. Just about everywhere, their farming depends on rain. The provincial capital, Kisumu, and smaller towns, some irrigated rice paddy projects, and several sugar factory plantations all constitute
patches of space managed very differently from the rest of the Luo countryside, making it hard to generalize about land use there. Fishing sustains a
lakeside or streamside few with cash, and rounds out the diet of most of the
others.

Other Kenyans like to stereotype Luo as great cattle keepers and fish
eaters, downplaying the mainly female farming that is the mainstay of Luo
diets. But steep population growth, measured from 1989 to 1999 at about
2.9 percent per year (one of the world's highest rates, having reached 3.4
percent earlier nationwide), is altering the reality further, forcing both more
intensive land use and, at the same time, a harder scramble for incomes off
the land. Rural-urban and rural-rural migration, and an infinity of cottage
industries, supplement incomes and diets importantly throughout the Luo
country. Land remains the main source of Luo livelihood, but variety is that
livelihood's essence.

Luo ways of organizing and thinking about family and kinship tie closely
into their ways of arranging their settlements. Luo are well known for patriliny (here taking the form of branching or "segmentary" patrilineages, in

anthropological jargon), virilocality (bride's residence with the groom's people during or after marriage), and cattle bridewealth (payments or transfers of property from groom or his kin to the bride's kin)—three patterns often associated with patriarchy, though they may or may not be indispensable to it. Women's reproductive, productive, and organizational powers, and the important roles of youth and children in caring for other children, are not always openly acknowledged in public but are always important in day-to-day life and in private thoughts. Seniority and sequence are vital principles of family, lineage, and clan life: doing things out of proper order, when it happens (as of course it does), brings frightening spiritual and metaphysical threats to family, lineage, and community that must be ritually addressed. The power, prestige, and authority of elders, though challenged by bold youth, by novel socioeconomic circumstances, and by a government jealous of power, are far from being things of the past. For the elders are nearest to ancestorhood, and deemed the ones in the best condition to communicate with those in that condition already. These latter are all around. Burial of the dead—male and female—within homesteads provides crucial fixed points on the landscape for the reckoning of personal, familial, and political identities and allegiances. Luo people make it clear that they look upon graves and the old homestead sites of their forebears as their anchors—in time, in space, and in culture and society. They do so in ways hard for outsiders to appreciate, and to a degree not lessening over time, but indeed, if anything, augmenting.

Toward their new contacts in the wider world, Luo people remain variously welcoming and defensive, but rarely apathetic. Christian churches have proliferated dramatically since the first church missions were established in the first years of the twentieth century. Taking advantage of church, state, and local self-help movements, Luo have taken to schooling and higher education like few other ethno-linguistic groups in Africa, becoming internationally known for scholarship and proficient English language. Politically, however, Luo have remained rather on the outs in Kenya most of the time since Independence. Despite sporadic, high-profile reconciliations of some of their leaders with the nation's first three presidents—the Gikuyu, Jomo Kenyatta; the Tugen Kalenjin, Daniel Toroitich arap Moi; and another Gikuyu, Mwai Kibaki—Luo have sided at least as often as not with opposition movements and parties. They have deemed themselves, and been deemed by others, a large but geographically marginal, economically disadvantaged, politically fragmented, and generally neglected minority in a lately troubled and at times autocratic state. So Luo variously look inward to what they consider to be their own rich traditions, outward to a world of education and worldly affairs beyond the nation's borders, and beyond to divinity and spirituality—as their three-way hope for improving or transcending their place in Kenya.

Luo are not an unusually enterprising people from a financial or commercial standpoint. In Kenya, Gusii and Gikuyu are on the whole more zealous and meticulous farmers, as the richer and better-watered soils of their home areas better warrant; and both these and Swahili are deemed more deft traders and more accomplished capital investors. And yet, one who digs into Luo culture finds a rich and elaborate understanding of money, markets, and the human relations that undergird them. If rural Luo, living far from the centers of wealth and power, have developed their own involved mechanisms of credit and debt, and their own sophisticated understanding of entrustment and obligation—an elaborate fiduciary culture, in short—then most other farming peoples south of the Sahara surely have too. Anyone arriving to implement a foreign-formulated program of land tenure or financial reform, here or elsewhere in equatorial Africa, ought to understand that he or she is not beginning with a tabula rasa.

Luoland toward the end of the twentieth century was a testing ground for theories about private property and credit. When I first visited the Luo in the early 1980s, the land titling program had been completed for decades in some parts of their country but scarcely begun in others. This slow, dispute-filled process still proceeds along the ground there; and one can watch the adjudication and registration of landholdings still going on while nearby observing the early outcome of the freehold-mortgage system the titling is meant to make possible. The dream, the hard adjustments, and the surprises of the outcome are all becoming clearer.

Luo country offers a wide diversity of human types, ranging from among Africa's most cosmopolitan to among its most provincial. Luo practically dominate East Africa's intellectual elite, but inaccessibility of information remains a big problem still in their homeland, as a Gikuyu man visiting from Nairobi once reminded me in calling Kadem, downhill from my Kanyamkago home, *mwisho dunia*, "the end of the earth," a phrase that drew a resigned laugh from the two Luo men with us. Straddling the Kenya-Tanzanian border, which for nearly two decades represented the line between capitalist and socialist government policies, Luo have pretty well seen it all. On either side of the line their public sentiments, not easily swayed by government dogma, run the full range from individualist to collectivist—and all mixtures. Luo ideology fits into no box.

The Luo cultural heritage as Nilotes, cousins of the Nuer, Dinka, Shilluk, and other well-known groups in southern Sudan (and others less well known in Uganda), lends itself to comparison involving classic themes in the anthropological literature, such as patriliny, polygyny, cattle bridewealth, and sacrifice. Their being now nearly surrounded by several Bantu-speaking groups with very similar material culture allows some insights into which facets of culture spring from environment and economy and which do not. Where ecological and economic life is concerned, looking over the more densely settled areas, where Nilotic-speaking Luo live side by side with Bantu-speaking Gusii and Luhya (to name only two of the largest groups), one is likely to be struck far more by the cultural commonalities than by the differences. Similarities in settlement patterns, farming and herding techniques, dress, and to an extent food customs are much in evidence—far more than ethno-linguistic maps with sharp dividing lines between "tribes" might suggest.

A central theme of this volume, and of the informal trilogy of which it is a part, is entrustment. People in the middle of Africa who borrow and lend, or partake more generally in entrustment and obligation, do so according to their own customs, those of others, or mixtures of the two. *The Nature of Entrustment,* the first volume published in the set, examines local borrowing and lending among Luo themselves, the "internal" entrustments of basically indigenous rooting. The central point is fairly simple. The deeper one looks into a rural economy, and into its social and cultural nature, the greater the role that borrowing and lending, and the trust and confidence on which they are built, appear to play in it. Rural people in Luoland, and elsewhere in tropical Africa, live in a credit economy already—they always have—and they have more debts already than outsiders tend to suppose when arriving with offers of credit. Some of their own local credits and debts carry deeper meanings for them than bank loans of cash, or cooperative loans of seed and fertilizer, ever have. For they are not just economic credits and debts, but entrustments and obligations tapping into the very heart (or liver, in the Luo conception) of their cultural being. This is a field rich in symbolism, though seldom recognized as such. It taps right into ethnicity, kinship, religion, and so on—the stuff of anthropology and humanistic study.

No African society is without loans and other entrustments. Some of these exchanges involve money, but most do not. They include delayed marriage payments, or school fee payments from elder to younger kin, reciprocated many years later or in indirect ways. Other entrustment may include ox and plow sharing, share contracts, and human and animal fostering that neither insiders nor outsiders might necessarily conceive of, or recognize, as loans.[7] A lesson from the Luo, and others around them, is that entrustment of a *reciprocal* nature (as in loans expected to be repaid to their lenders) does not necessarily take precedence over entrustment of a *serial* nature (that is, a favor expected to be passed on to someone else, and to keep moving). To see these fiduciary principles in action, and to learn what happens when they compete, there is no better place to look than the crossroads of money and land.

A word on the where, when, and how of the research on which this study is based. The project began in the late 1970s and has taken place intermittently since then in situ, in libraries and archives, and elsewhere. My work in Kenya has been carried out mainly in districts of Nyanza Province dominated by Luo people and some immigrants, with intervals in Nairobi and other parts of the country, at first from late 1980 to early 1983 (with a few weeks lost to illness). I revisited Kenya more briefly in 1987, 1988, and 1991, and have maintained contact with Luo and other Kenyans and East Africans abroad in the years between and ever since. After a brief settling-in period in a small town called Awendo, most of my time in western Kenya has been spent in Kanyamkago and Kagan (formerly North Nyokal) areas in southern Nyanza; for other periods I lived in Isukha (mainly a Luhya, not a Luo area) and briefly, Uyoma. These areas were becoming subdivided into smaller administrative locations, a process that has continued, but they remain popularly known by these names. Of these, Kanyamkago and Isukha had had their lands titled as private property by the time I first arrived; Kagan was just undergoing titling; and Uyoma remained untitled. I have lived mainly in or adjacent to farming homes, and been nourished mainly on local foods, when in Kenya, and worked in the Luo, Swahili, Sukha (variant of Luhya language spoken in Isukha), and English languages, often with the help of local assistants serving as interpreters to the varying extent needed as my skills improved. (The Swahili language I had studied before arriving in Africa; the Luo language I learned there more or less from scratch.) My spouse has accompanied me during periods when not away working in Nairobi or overseas.

The methods used in the research have been numerous, and they have involved people who have made up a mix of good friends (as some have become during the process) and more casual acquaintances. They include participant-observation; extended and repeated interviews with key inter-locutors; and surveys including general censuses (of up to 286 homesteads) as well as more focused genealogies and structured question sets, asked of both sexes and different ages. They have also included use of archives and official records, mapping and use of aerial photos and data from them; an essay contest; . . . and more passive absorption of local concerns, a method so often omitted in research proposals or field reports. Not all the kinds of data obtained over these many years have been able to be directly represented here, but all have contributed somehow to these pages. Numerous officials of different sorts, in government, businesses, and charitable organizations, and teachers in schools have been among those interviewed formally or infor-mally. Parts of my work have been done in cooperation with international aid agencies large and small, and other parts with economists and other specialist researchers and advisers who work around them, giving me access at times to the inner workings of some of their offices and lives. Some other parts have been done as part of Kenyan government-sponsored studies. I have been fortunate to have Luo, Kenyan, and other East African colleagues working around me in universities who have provided feedback (also solicited in-country) as my drafts have progressed.[8]

Once in 1991, a mature man from Kanyamkago and I were discussing what had been happening in the Luo country in land titling, and in mortgag-ing in particular. He expressed concern, as he had done before, about what he perceived as a growing threat of dispossession, and asked that I let it be known in my home country. I told him I had already done some publishing and given some talks about it, telling much of what I knew of what he and others around had taught me a decade before. He simply said, "Tell them again."

Luo are not the only people on whom a study like this one might focus. Indeed, in some economic and political respects, it is their ordinariness within their region—their rather marginalized but far from hopeless condition—that deserves attention. I draw occasional comparisons, not always explicit, between Kenyan Luo and their Bantu-speaking neighbors, on one hand, and Gambians of Fula and several other ethnic groups at the other end of the con-tinent who are also familiar to me: people with entirely different settlement patterns, economic histories, and religious mixtures, but with some striking similarities in their circumstances, their strategies of livelihood, their philosophies of human responsibility. Most Luo, in the present uncertain times, are seeking to make sense of a century of momentous challenge, struggling imaginatively to fit the pieces of their lives together, and working, waiting, praying for a better one. In this Luo seem pretty typical of tropical Africa.

Partitioning

The freehold-mortgage process is not, historically, a Luo or African idea, but a twentieth-century import into the continent's inland region. How it worked its way into the heart of Africa, and how it is received there, is the story to be told. The two topics of this volume are private land tenure and institutional financial credit. They tie together in the freehold-mortgage process: the land titling, the lending on collateral security, and the risk, for borrowers, of foreclosure, land takeover, and eviction in the event of failure to repay on terms agreeable to the lenders.

The story begins some centuries ago. Chapter 2 combines some history and some theory. First it describes some historical roots of private property, financial credit, and in particular the mortgage, in British common law tradition, suggesting how much flux and moral uncertainty had surrounded the practice for centuries before it was grafted onto inland equatorial Africa. North American variants, also influential in Africa, are briefly described too. Then I discuss two intertwined strands of theory—about property, credit, and the mortgage—in the history of European and American social philosophy. These are ancient, but for our purposes the eighteenth century serves as a convenient starting point for discussing some theories still in circulation. The chapter presents favorable views of private titling and institutional credit. Then it presents critical views of the same topics. Together, these "bookend" sections show that theories about finance and land tenure, mainstream or radical, have never strayed very far from fundamental human concerns about evolution: about savagery, civilization, and movement between. They also show that the jury on the freehold-mortgage process—in public programs and in private consciences—is still out. In later chapters I propose a simple rule of thumb for thinking about this momentous social process: that what some deem the lifeblood of an industrial economy can be the scourge of an agricultural one, and the bane of a farming people, particularly where their farming depends on unreliable rains and risky markets. But it takes an extended case study to see why and how.

How Luo and neighboring people in western Kenya have traditionally related to land is the subject of Chapters 3 to 5. Kinship and descent are critical parts of this understanding. Graves are the symbolic focal points of human attachments to place: the living and the dead, the social and the material, all connect here. Whereas it has commonly been assumed that African lineages and clans (like ethnic groups or "tribes") are primordial social forms that disappear with economic modernity or nationhood, I suggest on the contrary that they are better understood as adaptations to contemporary demographic, political, and economic conditions—and that they have become, in recent decades, more pronounced and more relevant than ever. Comparing some histories in the lake basin and farther afield shows patterns of lineage formation varying with population pressures over both time and space. These discussions show the great importance of sequencing of settlement, and of land lending, to the identities of Luo and of neighboring people in the basin.

Widening the view to national scale helps put these things into perspective. In Chapters 6 through 8 we observe the government's bold attempt to create private property in rural lands—a long, involved process filled with debates and uncertainties, and not immune to manipulation. Kenyan agricultural policy, parts of which are briefly sketched in Chapter 6, is traceable in its main lines to European and American theories of modernization. It has grown directly out of colonial policy, but since before Independence in 1963 it has also been heavily influenced by conceptual models, and vogues, in the large international agencies. A central tenet of Kenyan policy beliefs has been a faith that making land alienable, and tying finance to land in a system of mortgage collateral, should help enterprising farmers and the nation to prosper. So these chapters trace the process of land tenure reform, or what was so conceived, before and after Kenya's independence. We then look directly into the mortgage system and its consequences among Luo. The mortgage system remains an experiment in East Africa after several decades of determined effort by international and national development planners to make it work. It has not been working, and these chapters show why not. We see whom mortgaging touches and does not, and who tends to gain and lose. It becomes clear what some of these people's vulnerabilities are, what they do and cannot to protect themselves and each other from disastrous losses of land and home, and how some financiers and politicians participate in the process.

Land, sometimes called Kenya's obsession, has become a focal point of bloody struggles in which titling and (to a lesser extent so far) mortgaging have played a part. A final section of Chapter 8 describes the trend of "land clashes" or (as they have more recently been called) "ethnic cleansing" in a kind of inland archipelago of resettled areas. The contagious and self-consciously "tribalist" violence that flared up in the early 1990s and has continued sporadically into the new millennium has evoked memories of many earlier rural movements and incidents, and it sheds an interesting light on claims that state-guaranteed land titles constitute security of tenure. There is a ritual and symbolic dimension in these occurrences. There is a political one too, and questions of state sovereignty and leaders' responsibility have remained salient throughout.

A broad, nationwide attempt to take stock of a land tenure situation that has locally erupted into crisis, and to redraft policy about it, is the topic of Chapter 9. In it a frank outpouring of opinions, male and female, from town and country, has been sifted and sorted for inclusion in national policy initially meant to be part of a broad constitutional reform. Particular terms of discussion, symbolically emotive and politically explosive, disappear from successive drafts of the policy document. Here again, national independence and sovereignty have remained at issue.

The Kenyan story is not entirely unique. Parts of other African countries have undergone rural land titling experiments of their own, and some of these, experiments with rural mortgaging too. Problems like the ones western Kenyans have encountered in the freehold-mortgage process are likely to be found elsewhere in tropical Africa too. The concluding chapter returns to some of the most basic questions of about individualism—the concept on which the Kenyan land tenure experiment was ostensibly built—and its applicability to inland tropical African settings and others like them.

Property and Improperty

Humans rely more heavily on verbal language for their communication than other species do, and we seem to use more complicated language. In any study related to land matters, as I suggest throughout this study, it is well to attend closely to the terms used, and to what they connote. This study is about belonging (a warmer, homier-sounding word) and territoriality (a colder, nastier-sounding one)—which, when they both refer to inclusion and ex-, can in fact denote the same thing. It is about property (a nice-sounding thing, connoting propriety as it does) but also *im*property. This latter is an old and much underused word, which I shall define here as property with unfairness, unkindness, or moral dubiousness about it—as in the takings of extortion, theft, or plunder that become ownership over time. Framing is critical.

Translation matters no less. In African tongues we encounter some terms that you can translate easily enough to English—for instance, tiller (becomes *japur* in the Luo tongue). But others you cannot—for instance, the Luo *jadak* (which means neither guest nor tenant nor squatter, but something of all three). Or, difficult again, the French *terroir* (which can be used to mean territory, rootedness, or something like local essence or regional flavor). Nor might all our English terms translate neatly into African or even all other European tongues. Income, entitlement, ownership, for instance. Or rights.

Along other lines, differences may be found in our very spatial perception and the ways we communicate about it. This topic we might call dimensionality. Some people focus their deepest attention on fixed spots like graves, shrines, or waterholes. Some focus more on one-dimensional access routes, in the way of, say, transhumant herders (people whose livelihoods depend on going back and forth between dry and wet season grazing), or traders who go back and forth to link supply and demand—and may feel pretty well at home most anywhere along the way. Some frame their thoughts more in terms of flat surfaces, as farmers or mappers are more inclined to do. And some must try always to keep three dimensions in mind, as fliers, mineral prospectors, or ocean divers must. These modes of spatial awareness are not so much a matter of cognitive ability—since we humans can all think in all these ways when we must—as of enculturation, training and habit, and of communicational idiom. This opens room for misunderstanding and manipulation. But there will be occasion to discuss that.

CHAPTER 2

Sand and Gold

Some Property History and Theory

The magic of property turns sand into gold.
— ATTRIBUTED TO ARTHUR YOUNG

Nothing gold can stay.
— ROBERT FROST

The world did not spin into being, it is safe to surmise, with private land titles already here. If it had—and if the late eighteenth- and early nineteenth-century British agronomist and political economist Arthur Young is right—there would by now be little sand left.[1]

If private property in land is a human contrivance that only some times and places morally accept, the mortgage is a more recent and odder one, more scarcely accepted still. A mortgage, or pledge of security for a loan with a deadline, is a work of imagination, requiring as it does a land title (or something else deemed property), a loan and counter-loan (of money or something else, and of the security or collateral itself in the other direction), and a clock or calendar. It is inherently a gamble—for borrower or lender, and usually both. And it is one where one party may hold better knowledge, of ability or probability, than another.

This chapter offers a brief discussion of what private landholding, the mortgage, and their regulation looked like *before* the ideas were imported as colonial policy into Africa, in the British Isles from which they were transplanted—and briefly, in some North American settings through which some of those British traditions, models, and aspirations have indirectly reached Africa. Its second purpose is to examine some of the theories in the social studies that were brought to bear on that transplanting, and to try to capture something of the spirit in which an ambitious reform of tenure and fiduciary life has been attempted.

The history and theory in this chapter will appeal to some readers more than others. For the reader who finds the history too old or the theory too abstract, and would rather skip or skim, here are some essentials. Even in parts of the world where private property and credit have long been con-joined in the mortgage for centuries or millennia, there has been little lasting consensus about the latter's moral propriety, about how it ought to happen, or about who ought to be in charge of making or enforcing the rules. As for the theory, both optimistic and pessimistic visions about private property, credit, and the mortgage that links them keep being reborn. Often they are framed in very similar idioms, one inverting the other. As often as not, those idioms have some relation to theories about social evolution—about growth and maturation, or about savagery, civilization, and movement between. Even though such theories keep getting debunked, they keep reappearing. There is something about them, and the stories within them, that people of influence have found almost irresistible. But how well they fit the African interior's contexts is another matter. The reformer impulse has been vari-ously critical and charitable, but often, in retrospect, presumptuous either way. That's the gist.

A Notional Nexus

The intellectual antecedents of the freehold-mortgage process, whether dream or nightmare, are old and diverse; and its theoretical justifica-tions, right or wrong, are firmly entrenched in Euro-American social science, particularly of an evolutionist cast. Here two processes, neither necessarily irreversible, are at issue. One is the transformation of one or another kind of "customary" land rights and duties into a system of easily transferable individual landholdings under titles ostensibly protected by nation-states. The second is the deepening involvement of farming people in long-distance networks of financial credit and debt. To survey a few of the most influen-tial ideas on both processes—and much has been written on each—requires treating them at times separately and at times together. They intersect in what one might call the "freehold-mortgage nexus": the notion that land, if freely owned and transferable, can be used as collateral for a loan, and that creditors have the power or right, if the loan is not repaid on a schedule, to bring about the removal of people with debts from the land. This notional nexus provides the supposed justification for a legal-financial mechanism, and a political one too, with a substructure of cultural assumptions that need examination.

In both common law and civil law, the freehold-mortgage system that is at the heart of our analysis rests on a particular way of understanding property, and a particular way of conceptually linking time and space. A land mortgage implies not only that the land is bounded and alienable from the person, but also that time is in some sense linear, unrecoverable. Hence the etymology of mortgage as *mort gage*, a pledge "dead" forever, as distinguished from a *vif gage*, a living one.[2]

Some scholars and others try to understand these things, and their changes, in a Latinate idiom of "-izations." These tend toward vagueness. "Privatization," for instance, leaves doubt about whether private means individual or just nongovernmental. "Rationalization," a favorite of sociologist Max Weber and his school, can be taken to mean turning systematic or sensible—two different things often confused. The still vaguer "civilization," a stock term of late nineteenth- and early twentieth-century social theory, yielded by the 1950s and '60s to "modernization," and by the late twentieth and early twenty-first centuries to "globalization" as a buzzword and loose frame of thought and analysis. "Westernization" does not say where to locate the "west" (west of whom?) or whose agency is involved. None of these terms serves much analytical purpose. They all can easily mislead—as when one of them connotes another. Each also suggests a dubious teleology: assumptions about starting and ending points hard to know (or just wrong), or shaky assumptions about destiny.[3] So I do not use them much. But they do need mention, since more than a few would-be reformers and reformed, inside and outside the continent, have sought to justify their actions in precisely such terms.

The remainder of this chapter presents three things in order. First comes some history to outline briefly some of the early antecedents contributing to the tradition of mortgaging, in Britain and in the United States. Second, some of the theories that have been adduced in recent centuries to justify titling land, lending money, and tying the two together in the mortgage. Third, some "radical" critiques of these theories and processes. These last parts take us to extremes: evolutionist and anti-evolutionist, capitalist and communist, authoritarian and libertarian. The three parts offer some ways to frame all that follows—in time, space, and ideology—as we see how some British and Euro-American ideas, after being transported, adopted, and adapted, have played out in the middle of Africa.

The Grafting Stock

People like to experiment on other people's soil. That anyone ever supposed a small, rainy, crowded, and by the twentieth century largely industrial island in the North Sea should serve as a model for property in a tropical, drought-prone, agrarian, and pastoral inland region on the equator is curious in itself. That anyone might further have imagined that Britain's remarkably complex legal tradition of landholding and conveyancing, entangled as it was in centuries of feudal remnants, could be grafted straight over to where conditions and customs were so different, is perhaps more noteworthy still. But grafted it was—titles, mortgages, and all—in laws sometimes copied verbatim from English legal texts into African statute. To be sure, it was done with experience from other colonies, especially India, in mind. But their laws too, in the early to mid-twentieth century, had been largely copied from Britain's. Concentrating on pledging and mortgaging for the sake of brevity, let us now ask: what *was* that British legal tradition, and how traditional was it?

No one knows where or when mortgaging began, but this way of treating land and capital together is not new in the western European countries that formerly ruled Africa, or lands farther east. Some of the earliest known cuneiform writing from about 3000 B.C.E in Babylonia (that is, in irrigated southern Mesopotamia, currently part of Iraq) reveals records of loans and debts, and also of names attached to signs for fields. Well before 1000 B.C.E., palace-temple authorities (political and religious centers not always being clearly separated) who allocated fields and houses sometimes took these away, and sometimes made or freed slaves or other persons too—to recover borrowers' unpaid debts. They also enacted periodic "jubilee" proclamations of debt forgiveness, and remission of forfeited lands, as (or on) occasions of general celebration; probably calling such occasions a ruler's coveted privilege. By about 1400 to 1200 B.C.E., in the eastern Mediterranean kingdom of Ugarit, redemptions of land for silver shekels are recorded. But those who have applied terms like "mortgage" to such times are presuming a lot: whether or how land or house loan security was tied to any calendric schedules or deadlines, in the way of today's mortgages, is hard to know. Something clear enough, though, is that in Mesopotamian and other "near eastern" lands, rules and expectations about pledging or selling inherited lands often differed from those about other land, in such a way as to maintain the holdings of kin lines or kin groups.[4] Comparable distinctions, giving special recognition and protection to inherited land, remain common in many settings across Africa too to this day.

Moving west: The remains of about 150 engraved boundary stones (*horoi*) denoting use of land or house as security for debts have been found in Athens dating from 500 to 200 B.C.E. (Fine 1951), and testimony from authors including Aristotle attests to the common use of land or a house as security for loans in that city-state, though it is not always clear who benefited from the land during the term of a loan. Whether one could apply the term mortgage to Athenian loan security arrangements has been disputed. Some authorities, including Moses Finley (1952), have thought not; he has tended toward the opinion that the mortgage, as now known, began as a peculiarly Anglo-Saxon contrivance.

In any case, land pledging in Britain from before the Norman conquest in 1066, and land mortgaging in the eleventh century, were recorded in the Domesday Book, that famous record of land relations compiled just after that conquest.[5] Ranulf de Glanvil's *Tractatus de Legibus et Consuetudinibus Regni Angliae* (Treatise on the Laws and Customs of the English Kingdom) text of common law, written (perhaps by his nephew) around 1187, described various forms of "live" and "dead" pledging. The mortgage as known today seems to have become increasingly common from the sixteenth century.[6] By this time English land law was a chowder of Anglo, Roman, Norse, and Norman ingredients, at the least. So one who looked for the origins of mortgaging in Britain would need to search in many directions. This may help explain why its character has been so unstable, elusive, and anxious.

Adding to the instability were the two great waves of "enclosure" movements and the evictions of rural people from the lands they had occupied. One occurred between the fourteenth and sixteenth centuries, in the Tudor period, when landlords converted arable land to grazing, mainly for sheep farming to take advantage of rising wool prices. The other, taking somewhat different form, occurred in the parliamentary period of the eighteenth and early nineteenth centuries as the industrial revolution got under way; it was aimed more at setting up larger farms for new rotated and fertilized crops.

Many historians have concluded that enclosure in its different forms, and the dispossession and displacement implied, have together been a main force behind the formation of a British proletariat—for better, for worse, or both—and not just in Britain.[7] This is a process the mortgage too would seem to have abetted over the centuries.

An important thing to know about the history of the mortgage in Britain is that it has taken many forms, and that the privilege or duty of trying to regulate it has shifted again and again, at frequent intervals—between church, monarch, and parliament, between legislators, judges, and administrators, and between different authorities in each of these (for instance, between royal courts and Chancery [or equity] courts). Accordingly, the rules and expectations have changed too, radically and almost constantly, over the centuries. Even the most basic understandings—such as whether the mortgagor or mortgagee is allowed to use, occupy, or profit from the land during the interval of the loan; how long a loan might last; whether, how much, or for how long "interest" is allowed to accumulate; or whether distraint from a debtor leaves open any recourse of redemption afterward—have repeatedly shifted back and forth, never seeming to reach equilibrium for long.

The centuries have added layer upon layer of legal terms and devices into the picture, seldom expunging all that had come before. The result, for most of the past millennium, has been a legal world like Alice's down the rabbit hole. (Oliver Cromwell is said to have called English land law "an ungodly jumble.") Turn left, and you encounter escheat, mortmain, or maritagium. Turn right, and you face frankalmoign or novel seisin. Try to back up, and you run into "freehold" classed as "unfree tenure." This is a legal world always colorful, even fun if approached in a certain spirit, but dauntingly arcane and convoluted even to specialists.[8]

For most of the period since the Norman conquest, the mortgage has been known or classified by terms only obliquely or obscurely related to borrowing, lending, pledging, or mortgaging—often under one or another pretense that it was something it wasn't. Not always have sacred or secular authorities treated land as something separate from human statuses, relationships, or "estates," even after the ostensible legal abolition of feudal relationships and obligations. Nor has the picture been at all one of steady progress toward a free land market or toward unrestricted individual rights. Rather, it has been more like an unsteady zigzag in which individual and group claims of different sorts keep recombining and reasserting themselves. Loans have lengthened and shortened; debtors' prisons have come and gone; usury laws have been written and rewritten. A watershed, though, was the year 1925, when a spate of new laws amounted to a broad attempt to reform tenure and simplify conveyancing, simplifying and standardizing the picture partly by sweeping away some laws deemed obsolete.[9]

Strikingly often, the legal distinctions invoked to regulate and administer land pledging and mortgaging have been simple binary ones. But there are many. Here are just a few: folkright (popular law and custom)/privilege (royal law)—an ancient Anglo-Saxon distinction; free tenure (for example, tenure in chivalry, in socage, or spiritual tenure)/unfree tenure (villein tenure or copyhold); property/possession; realty/personalty; corporeal (possessory)/incorporeal (nonpossessory); citizens/aliens; infants/persons of age; movable (chattel)/immovable; tenure/estate. In our times, no distinction about land has been more often invoked—for better or worse, and often for worse—than the one between public and private.

All these dichotomies are devices for simplifying complex realities, and for gaining control over large numbers of people. Where they do this, they also, in one way or another, turn most real people and their situations into misfits. They tempt disbelief, resistance, or subversion. As often as not, therefore, the jurist's or administrator's reach for control involves invoking the authority of the dead through anachronistic material paraphernalia (gavels, pillars, powdered wigs), or semi-mystical, archaic language unintelligible to most people ("fee simple absolute . . . for the consideration aforesaid . . . from the date hereof without impeachment of waste subject to the provision for cesser hereinafter contained").[10] The tendency of jurists and administrators dealing with land to try to concoct or co-opt tradition, recruit the dead to their causes, and reach beyond the commonly known finds its own counterparts in tropical Africa, and it is readily adapted there. Equatorial African people are no less intimidated by authority, and no less easily mystified, than Britons or anyone else. But they also have their *own* ancestors to respect.

The mortgage has never held still for long, never been easy to pin down. The millennium-long history of flux and experimentation, of euphemism, arbitrary dividers, and opaque idiom, all amounts to evidence of moral uncertainty—on the part of the rulers, the ruled, or persons between. The mortgage per se was never given formal legal recognition even in Britain until the twentieth century, a sign that even where widely practiced, it has only slowly gained acceptance as a cultural construct or social institution.[11]

Trust a Mortgage: American Dreams and Nightmares

North American farm finance, which like Africa's has been profoundly influenced by British common law tradition, leads us too far from
our topic for more than a brief mention. It deserves that mention though,
not least because policy in the most influential international aid agencies has
been so heavily influenced by American financial and managerial input, for
better and for worse—and since the models its designers have often borne
in mind are ones from their home countries. A North American mortgaging model is one with pronounced upsides and downsides. Some of both
have been potentially transferable to African and other settings around the
world.

It is doubtless true at times, in America or anywhere else, that as Robert
Frost put it in his laconic Yankee way, "good fences make good neighbors."
And it is no less true, in America or anywhere else, that good loans can help
out in a crunch. But the glitter of the gold, where these things combine in
rural mortgages, may be delusory. American land law and agricultural economy have lately included some institutional safety nets that program planners have not always been able to replicate as they have tried to redesign African and other property systems and financial markets. And even in America,
as I shall now show, the nets have holes.

United States mortgaging has varied widely in sources of capital and
in form and duration, in part because of the size of the country and the
variety of its landscapes. Generally, before the 1930s, farm mortgages came
from private lenders and had durations between about three and five years.
Since that time, longer-term mortgages up to thirty years have become more
conventional; and from that time too, government and government-backed
lenders have become major players. From about 1968 into the start of the
twenty-first century, as the use of small computers became common, the
terms and conditions of mortgage proliferated into an enormous variety of
options that would be hard for any individual to know or comprehend in
their totality. Particular religious groups, moreover—for instance, Muslims
and Mormons—have their own strictures and ways of getting around them,
and some of these are opaque to financiers and lawyers who do not deal with
those parts of the population in particular.[12]

The rural United States provides ample evidence of the hazards of mortgaging to rural people in areas dependent on rain for farming—even where

they enjoy some of the world's most favored soils, technical extension services, and market infrastructure, and in some cases protected or government subsidized pricing too. Foreclosure and dispossession strike in episodes. Some strike particular sectors of the population, as racially or ethnically defined. One particularly dramatic episode came in the thirty years after the passage of the General Allotment Act (Dawes Severalty Act), which awarded individual land titles to American Indians (Native Americans) on many reservations in 1887. General poverty, illiteracy, and other problems related to racial discrimination forced many into mortgaging or selling off against their own longer-term interests (about two-thirds of their titled land was gone from their hands within thirty years).[13] For the broader rural population, the most dramatic episode to date has been that of the Great Depression of the 1930s (and especially of the "dust bowl" years from 1933 to 1935). But other waves have happened during recessions closer to our times.[14]

While the vivid imagery of Depression-era literature like John Steinbeck's on the hardship, displacement, and migration have tended to focus attention on the poorer and middle classes, mortgage foreclosure also strikes better-off farmers of the sorts who use combine harvesters and the like, and ranchers with large tracts. Discontent has been voiced in many ways. Popular protests by defenders of persons threatened by foreclosure have taken forms like the "penny auction," in which prospective buyers offering more serious sums have been scared away from bidding.[15] On other occasions, farmers and their supporters able to afford doing so have organized long-distance "tractorcades" to Washington and other centers for protest.

Even in relatively prosperous parts of the rural United States—as in the ones where Peggy Barlett interviewed in Dodge County, Georgia, or Kathryn Dudley in the pseudonymous Star County in Minnesota—the emotional pain and anguish, the often surprising neighborly (and vulture-like) opportunism, the family fragmentation, and the kinds of humiliation, ostracism, and social death surrounding loss of farm and home in the event of mortgage foreclosure have often been devastating,[16] particularly where homes have remained in families over multiple generations. While buybacks afterward in such cases are not uncommon, as Barlett observed in Georgia, many of those who have succeeded in moving back home have sometimes done so only precariously.

The bitterness of dispossessed rural Americans toward the mortgage has long been part of popular arts and lore, though frightening enough to remain often submerged. Take, for instance, the poem of Will Carleton, a poet lionized in his native Michigan, called "The Tramp's Story," first published in 1882.[17] The narrator he calls a prophet, for he knows both past and future.

> If experience has gold in it (as discerning folks agree),
> Then there's quite a little fortune stowed away somewhere in me

This is his narrative in brief. A prospering farmer with a loving, hardworking family, on eighty acres from his father, became tempted to buy more land. He bought another eighty, then another forty (and a covered carriage), with a mortgage, against his wife's objection, but with her cooperation in farm work once it was signed. Now the debts began to mount. He found the mortgage worked year round, building up interest even while the farm family slept—watching, ruling. . . .

> It nailed up every window—stood guard at every door—
> And happiness and sunshine made their home with us no more.
> Till with failing crops and sickness we got stalled upon the grade,
> And there came a dark day on us when the interest wasn't paid;
> And there came a sharp foreclosure, and I kind o' lost my hold,
> And grew weary and discouraged, and the farm was cheaply sold.
> The children left and scattered, when they hardly yet were grown;
> My wife she pined an' perished, an' I found myself alone.
> What she died of was a "mystery," an' the doctor never knew;
> But *I* knew she died of *mortgage*—just as well's I wanted to.
> If to trace a hidden sorrow were within the doctor's art,
> They'd ha' found a mortgage lying on that woman's broken heart.

The narrator recounts turning to drink for an easier "liquidation," which of course impoverishes him further. Still avoided by his children and by women, he finds himself homeless, penniless, and old, but wealthy in experience. He offers this final advice (in Carleton's own italics), "to take or not to take it—with no difference in the price":

> *Worm or beetle—drought or tempest—on a farmer's land may fall;*
> *But for first-class ruination, trust a mortgage 'gainst them all.*

It could have been written almost anywhere the mortgage finds families farming by rain. Here are the wealth that fuels optimism, the temptation and growing ambition, the temporary blindness to risk, the knowing vulnerability of kin, the temptation to divert a bit for a use unapproved, the unbudgeted twist of illness, the sting of loss, the spiral of intoxication for escape

. . . and the destitution, censure, and abandonment. On what continent might one not hear such a story—or, if one could but hear it, the woman's? Or the story of the child who has lost the farm to inherit?[18]

The strong emotional attachments to land and home, in North American contexts usually understood to be characterized by bilateral kinship and inheritance through both males and females, are almost as striking as those observed among men in "unilineal" societies of East Africa like those of the Luo, Luhya, and Gusii, where land inheritance has occurred usually through one sex only. But missing from the interview accounts like Barlett's and Dudley's, and from Carleton's ballad, are the constant references to the graves and bones of ancestors that one hears when land attachments are discussed in the lake basin and much of East Africa. It is different, that is, where the bodies are buried right outside the front door.

Mortgaging, foreclosure, and forced sale have contributed in a major way to a thinning out of the United States farm-owning population over the past century, even while the nation has grown in its numbers. Prospects of alternative urban employment have helped cushion the blows of dispossession and displacement for many land losers in the United States. Farm subsidies have saved many from foreclosure, and insurance, welfare, and very unusual bankruptcy laws have also reduced their hardships.[19] These official and unofficial safety nets have had few parallels for rural tropical African borrowers, who have had to rely more heavily on their kin and friends for charity in cases of dispossession. But there is no guarantee, as noted earlier, that these will be any better off or always willing to help. If the hazards of the mortgage for farmers depending on rain in America are great, in equatorial Africa they are certainly greater still.

The freehold-mortgage process, in all, has come to seem natural in Euro-American settings only since the industrial revolution. It is a way of thinking particularly suited to an industrial way of life, with its possibilities of steady factory production and fixed wages and salaries. It may be a tolerable compromise in farming systems with regular irrigation, constantly replenished soils, dense transport networks, and reliable prices and markets. But I shall suggest it is a scourge of dry-land agrarian farming, where not all these hold true—and a threat to African agrarian life.

First, though, some theory, for an idea of the spirit in which land titles, loans, and the mortgage have been offered and debated. We back up in time, looking first at some of the kinds of ideas generally considered mainstream or establishmentarian, where land is titled and mortgaging readily accepted. Then we look at some others deemed in one way or another more radical or critical.

Land, Evolution, and the "Social Contract"

That western European people's ideas about land tenure, and about finance too, have been wrapped up for centuries in their ideas about civilization, progress, and evolution—and indeed imbued with them—becomes clear enough if we look back to a few seventeenth- and eighteenth-century social contract theorists in Britain, and to others in France, Germany, and the United States who have shared certain of their ideas. The brief survey that follows touches on a succession of theorists now well known in Europe, in Africa, and around the world, to see what they said about private property, the mortgage, and their part in civilization.

Some of them have been treated together before as clusters. That is as it should be, since authors set the framing, the terms of debate, for others (for instance, on the "state of nature," "the social contract," or evolution by "natural selection") and schools of thought become recognizable through tracer terms like these. But the clusters or schools have not yet been well conjoined, or their authors compared between schools—at least not on matters of land and credit. The records do not always tell, alas, exactly what difference the authors made, severally or together, to European colonial land policies, credit, and mortgaging in Africa, but framings and tracer terms in the language of policy speeches and documents give us some good clues. And so pervasive has been the influence of these authors over all political and economic thought in the imperial centers and overseas, in their times as in our own, that we can be sure they have made more than a little. The most influential of them all, I shall suggest, have done it less by science than by storytelling: by making up plausible-enough-sounding yarns about the dimmest recesses of human prehistory, and by using their literary gifts to frame these in a language with which their readers would already be familiar.

A further word on these "dead white European men" and their politics. Some of them might seem easily dismissible by contemporary lights as politically "incorrect" if not laughably archaic. I hope to show, though, that there is usually something about each that prevents such easy dismissal. This is so for two reasons. One is that a theorist who seems orthodox in one way usually turns out unorthodox in another. This is in turn because orthodoxies don't usually travel through time and space in yoke with other orthodoxies. So we shall encounter, for instance, one who seems an economic conservative but also a political radical, another who is a sexist, racist, ethnocentric anti-imperialist, and a third who is an anti-slavery pro-colonialist. Gross categories like liberal and conservative, right and left, populist and elitist, or even realist and idealist change unrecognizably in their contents and implications. (So too will politically correct and incorrect, given ample time or space.) This fact may contain a lesson about how much trust we ought to place in such monikers today. There are also a few key figures (in particular, Jean-Jacques Rousseau and Lewis Henry Morgan) who have changed their minds about land matters in ways that proved momentous—and not all in the same direction. One who can suspend stereotyping, appreciate uncertainty, and tolerate some seeming contradiction will appreciate much better the personalities as well as the issues of the times and places concerned.

The other reason is that the questions these men were asking were so deeply rooted to basic mysteries about territory and belonging, and about the human place among animals (and for some, spirits, divinity, or nature) that few have firmer answers, let alone good generalizations, even now. And yet it is our purpose to find better, more nuanced, maybe more applicable answers. That will be the point of the equatorial African story to follow.

Most theorists who speak of a social contract can trace their intellectual genealogies in one way or another to Thomas Hobbes's *De Cive* in 1641 and its more famous, if more ponderous, revision he titled *Leviathan,* a decade later.[20] To Hobbes (a man living in unusually insecure times, partly in exile from his English home), protection of private property in land was part of the social compact or contract to which humans in a prehistoric, or a-historic, "state of nature" submitted themselves. He imagined them to have been originally solitary, innately hungry for power and property, and perpetually insecure (though not necessarily sinful). To improve their security, he supposed, they created and appointed a human sovereign (an individual or assembly) from among their own number to rule over them with awesome and overwhelming power and thus, with the aid of reason, to keep their own powerful, innate, and inevitable passions under control.

Hobbes seems scarcely to have considered the condition, common in tropical Africa in our times, in which rulers and their accomplices succumb to their *own* insecurities. He did not seem to expect they would give free reign to their own passions, turning against, dividing, or willingly or negligently impoverishing their own subjects. Hardly does he seem to have predicted the condition in which divided ethnic groups, kin groups, or chiefdoms, even under an elected government, continue competing and even struggling violently over control of that government, the state, and the state's wealth and privileges. And he might have been dismayed to see churchmen and aid agency officials vying with statesmen for sovereignty centuries hence—as we shall see them doing with land at issue.

To John Locke, writing about half a century later with clear influence from Hobbes, the origin of private property as part of a prehistoric social contract, and thus as something governments came to need to protect, was a mystery that needed explaining. Having been involved in keeping accounts by correspondence with colonial planters in the Americas and Caribbean, and having thus been exposed to many stories true and false about American savagery both brutal and noble, but being at the same time a Christian who believed God had given man land in common, Locke invented a story and a philosophy to make it all fit together. This he published in his famous *Second Treatise of Government* in 1690. Each man naturally owns his body, Locke reasoned, and thus his labor. When one invests one's labor in land, for instance by picking up an acorn or by tilling land, one's work creates a right in that land and its fruits, by extension of the right over the body. God's command to subdue the earth, and the need to do so by labor, thus gives personal claim, and value too, to the land worked. Natural spoilage of foods limits the accumulation of wealth; but the invention of money (in his time, silver or gold), as durable wealth, allows some men to accumulate more than others. That Locke described this much as having happened "out of the bounds of society and without compact" (p. 30) leaves some ambiguity about whether he thought economic inequality tolerable. Most commentators have inferred he was giving economic inequality his approval, but they have done so on scant evidence. What everyone can agree on is that Locke did, following Hobbes, deem the protection of property (whether justly unequal or not) to be a principal purpose, function, and justification of government. Locke differed from Hobbes in stating that humans unhappy with their government may justifiably change not only the incumbents of its offices but the form or "constitution" of that government itself (since in Locke's view, then more radical on this point, it is the people themselves, not their rulers, who are sovereign—a point to matter in our time). But both believed, in the end, in the solitary natural man, in personal property, in its protection by government, and in the concept of mutually agreed sovereignty.[21]

And so, across the channel, did Jean-Jacques Rousseau, our third social contract theorist of note—at least by late in his career, when his strong earlier skepticism about private property and national governments (more on that later) had tempered or eroded. That was when he quilled down *The Social Contract*, that partly enigmatic document that lies, like Locke's second treatise, at the foundation of so many national constitutions. If Locke cribbed heavily from Hobbes, so did Rousseau from both Hobbes and Locke—while twisting certain of their ideas inside out. While Rousseau's "natural man," who had and needed no property, was basically a loner, like Hobbes's or Locke's natural man, his was more benign when in chance social encounters.[22] And once humans had learned to farm, and thus to accumulate grain, governments were devised to protect private property as it accumulated in different amounts in the hands of different people. Once this process got under way, governments eventually had to be formed to defend their people's land and other property from *other* governments.

There were things none of these theorists—Hobbes, Locke, or Rousseau—knew or appreciated about inland equatorial Africa, in their times or our own. One was that the human body is not necessarily considered an individual's own property. (There were and still are slaving societies in Africa. Even where not, a young man's work is sometimes deemed properly under the control of his father or wife's father, or a young bride's under that of her husband or husband's mother.) A second is that the natural human is not always deemed a solitary man. (Both Hobbes and Locke tended to downplay the role of kinship, age sets, and such things.) A third is that currency inflation (at least in our times) can sometimes render money worthless even faster than grain in a granary might rot. But let us move on.

"A Passion Over All Other Passions": Evolutionist Approaches to Property and Its Exchange

The notion that property naturally evolves from communal to individual has been part of European and American social philosophies, and part of the reasons or rationalizations for laws, from Locke's time to our own. In Sir William Blackstone's standard *Commentary on the Laws of England*, published between 1765 and 1769, "The earth and all things therein were the general property of mankind from the immediate gift of the Creator. . . . By the law of nature and reason, he who first began to use it acquired therein a kind of transient property that lasted as long as he was using it, and no longer. . . . [But] when mankind increased in number, it became necessary to entertain conceptions of more permanent dominion, and to appropriate to individuals not the immediate use only, but the very substance of the thing to be used."[23] In this view, we humans were given everything in common but have gradually *crowded* ourselves into accepting private, permanent property. Blackstone's pen makes the process sound like civilization.

But in Africa—and anywhere else—we must be careful not to assume that property was "originally" communal or individual, and mindful that any account of such origins may be more valuable as story than as history.

From Blackstone's time and before, right down to our own, more than a few social philosophers have assumed a natural and inexorable human progression in *stages* from foraging (hunting, fishing, gathering), through herding, through farming, and finally to industry or beyond. Exemplary as a stadial theorist is moral philosopher Adam Smith, whose *Lectures on Juris-prudence* gives much space to such presumed progression, and whose broader opus has formed so much of the foundation of so much of economics, both classical and neoclassical, and in fact also of other traditions, like Marx's, more critical.[24] The mortgage, for Smith, makes its debut in the third stage, coming with a specialization of labor (of financiers, realtors, registrars, and lawyers, for instance). But these things are all an outgrowth of humans' "natural propensity to truck, barter, and exchange one thing for another," as he wrote in *The Wealth of Nations* (bk. 1, ch. 2): a phrase that continues to echo wherever anyone seeks to justify or promote market activity—like renting, selling, or mortgaging land for money.

Something Smith and other stadial theorists of economy may not have fully appreciated, though, is what we can see today so clearly in East Africa. This is that the *same people* can be—at different times in the day, year, or life cycle—foragers, herders, farmers, and industrialists: Luo people and their neighbors in the lake basin, for instance. And people who move from being industrialists to being farmers and herders, as some Luo have done and continue to do, are people who have specialized and de-specialized their labor, and integrated and de-integrated their finances with others', in ways not so easy to plot as an arrow moving in one direction, or even as a steady accretion of stages or layers. In one place, people quit foraging or herding as they take to farming, or farming as they take to manufacturing. In others they do not.

But stadial theories of livelihood, and of the evolution of property and finance, would continue appearing in the works of one philosopher after another, on both sides of the English channel and both sides of the Atlantic.[25] By the time evolution—that ancient idea with no sole author—had worked its way into biology as natural selection, through the efforts of Charles Darwin and Alfred Russel Wallace, Herbert Spencer had already begun elaborating his own elaborate, stadial understanding of evolution in all of life and the universe.[26] As the most eminent and famous philosopher of his time in the English-speaking world, this mainly self-schooled walking encyclopedia and single-minded proponent of evolutionism—he who provided his great admirer Darwin with the phrase "only the fittest survive"—exerted as much influence as any theorist in fashioning British understandings of not only science and economy but also colonial policy and what so many Britons deemed a civilizing mission.

There is irony in this, because Spencer was *not* at heart an imperialist, and indeed was a committed anti-imperialist—something often overlooked. But others exported his ideas anyway, applying them abroad in ways he never wished or expected. Where they concerned property and finance, those ideas were not only as evolutionist, but also about as libertarian and individualist, as anyone's in his day. That day, which lasted from 1829 to December 1903, spanned the Victorian era and the beginning of British exploration, settlement, and colonialism in Kenya and the Lake Victoria Basin.

Much could be said about Spencer's philosophy of evolution and the roles of property and finance in it, but let us boil it down to a few essentials. Spencer drew (and tested the limits of) many analogies between organisms and societies. Among them were those linking blood and commodities, including money, as vitally circulating things; hearts as commercial or financial centers; and governments as brains (Spencer 2008, 21–22). Economy and religion require little regulation. Spencer's alignment of related polarities (or continua), arranged Lévi-Strauss style, would look something like this:

    animal/human
    early/late
    low/high
    incapable of abstract thought/capable of abstract thought
    indefinite/definite
    unorganized/organized
    homogeneous/heterogeneous
    autonomous as parts/interdependent as parts
    less efficient/more efficient
    collectivist/individualist

Humans and animals have much in common, in Spencer's view. Humans are not the first to want property or act territorially. "The desire to appropriate, and to keep that which has been appropriated, lies deep, not in human nature only, but in animal nature: being, indeed, a condition to survival" (Spencer 1892–98, 7:554, sec. 541). So men "even in their lowest state" (he cited "Bushmen" in the Kalahari, along with North American "Chippaway-ans" [or Ojibwa, or Anishinabe—the same people] among his examples) hold "those ideas and emotions which initiate private ownership" even if they do a lot of borrowing, lending, and free taking (7:538, sec. 536). In Spencer's view, only necessity of movement, for hunting, fishing, herding, or other things, keeps humans from privatizing their property as they'd naturally like. But civilization sharpens ideas of property, and care and attention humans give it. Humans privatize small, easy movables first, then animals, captives, and homes, and land last—so that among "savages," only land remains common. After the transition from foraging, through herding, to farming, tradition and sacred forefathers still impede land's privatization.

Eventually, as in "primitive European societies," comes clan land tenure in common, reverting to public use after harvests. "With the passage from a nomadic to a settled state, ownership of land by the community becomes qualified by individual ownership; but only to the extent that that those who clear and cultivate portions of the surface have undisturbed enjoyment of its produce" (Spencer 1892–98, 7:555, sec. 541). What brings about the change at first is one thing only: force and the personal claims of a conqueror. Kings of Abyssinia, or conquerors wherever in the world anyone can conquer, stake their own claims. Then, if they wish, they begin to allocate land to their sub-ordinates (7:547, sec. 539)—the British monarchy to its soon-invited settlers in East Africa, for instance.

Barter yields to purchase and sale by money or quasi-money as societies move from military to industrial forms, Spencer thought. It happens first in cities and towns, where commerce is freest and safest. Restive, ambitious individuals start splitting away from families and clans and claiming their own lands. (From here, it is easy to see how pledging, mortgaging, and complex financial markets might arise.) As Spencer saw it, the whole process had proceeded farthest in Britain, the most civilized and powerful country on earth.

Ethnocentric, undeniably.[27] And it can all look a lot like one-way evolutionism. Many have held up Spencer as an exemplar of this simple-minded thinking. But Spencer didn't necessarily see things this way. With further industrialization, Spencer supposed, community claims might resurface above individual ones. And anyway, over the eons, all of history might reverse, private property sink back like slavery before it. Britain might sink back into the mud, and the universe complete a great cosmic loop.[28]

Not all in middle Africa, to this day, accept evolutionary theories like Spencer's tracing continuities between animals and humans. Certainly not all have cause to perceive the course of history to date as a glorious upward progress, as he did. Nor does Spencer's image of stages of evolution (foraging, herding, fishing, industry) fit the case any more neatly than Adam Smith's, much like it. War and force can destroy property rights (and duties) as well as create them, as we shall see. But Spencer's body-society analogies and his integrative vision of civilization's progress—with territoriality, property, and economy as central parts of it—still had close parallels in neo-evolutionary thinking at the turn of the twenty-first century.[29] Ideas like these are just too seductive not to keep reappearing.

Ideas like Spencer's lean heavily on notions of natural laws, and they are in turn easily translated into human laws and ideologies about them. Among the jurists most influential for an evolutionist outlook was Spencer's contemporary Henry Sumner Maine, a London lawyer and historian of Rome and the world. Maine's vision is pretty well summed up in his famous dictum: "The movement of the progressive societies has hitherto been a movement from status to contract" (Maine 1986, 163). By status he meant ties we're born with—kinship and clanship, for instance. By contract he meant the ties we forge for ourselves. Writing, secularization of law, the formation of political allegiances based on territory rather than descent, and the rise of individualism and free choice were all part of civilization's progress, evident to him from early Roman times to his own.

Land, as part of all this for Maine, becomes more freely tradable, with all its rights and duties. Maine lamented the fact that in a Hindu understanding in India, "a landholder . . . can sell or mortgage his rights, but he must first have the consent of the Village, and then the purchaser steps into his place and takes up all his obligations": a view "curiously different from that taken by jurisprudence in its maturest stage" (Maine 1986, 255–56, 250). It wasn't a free enough contract for him to call civilized: if they still allowed the stubborn "co-ownership" of kin and neighbors, or religion or ceremony with their "embarrassing formalities" to get in the way of their land deals, these people were still in "the infancy of law" (pp. 257, 267). Moving from status to individual contract—and an unfettered mortgage system—meant freeing up and *growing* up.

It is not hard to see why infantilizing words like these—a veritable charter for evolutionist modernizers up to our time—are resented in former colonies like India and Kenya, even if still repeated by legal theorists and sociologists in each. Mysterious to Maine was why anyone would ever have *wanted* not to dissolve the social bonds—between contemporaries, and between ancestors and descendants—that stood in the way of land sale and mortgage. Our equatorial African case will help answer that.

Maine's evolutionary status-to-contract theory was paralleled, in some ways, in the early work of that other lawyer, Lewis Henry Morgan, in Rochester, New York, and the United States, from the 1850s to 1880s. Morgan, equally influenced by Roman history (as well as his own pioneering study of Ho-de-no-sau-nee [or Iroquois] and other societies worldwide), used the Latin terms "societas" and "civitas" to mean, in essence, kin-based and territory-based polities. In the movement from one to the other, through the three stages of savagery, barbarism, and civilization, the idea of property arose slowly. "Its domination as a passion over all other passions marks the commencement of civilization" (Morgan 1964, 13). But Morgan remained far more respectful of kinship, religion, and ceremony than his fellow lawyer Maine did. And he gradually turned far more skeptical than Maine did of private property's magic—a turn with momentous worldwide implications to be suggested, once his book fell into particular hands.

In a German philosophical and sociological tradition too, where the ideas were being put forward to govern Tanganyika, land, money, and the modern link between them were providing new fascination. Immanuel Kant and Georg Hegel, much influenced by social contract theorists like Hobbes, Locke, and Rousseau, had paid much attention to state-overseen, legal contractualism between individuals, and protection of property, as basically good things. These they described, along with free will, in universal terms as "rights" (sing. *recht*), which in German carries overtones no less moral than legal.[30]

Now Georg Simmel, a close associate of Max Weber's, looked deeply into money as a potentially liberating but alienating invention for individuals. Money and credit were both based on trust, he found. But "in the case of credit, of trust in someone," wrote Simmel in about 1907, "there is an additional element which is hard to describe: it is most clearly embodied in religious faith. . . . Economic credit does contain an element of this supra-theoretical belief" (Simmel 1982, 177). The belief, he found, is farsighted and symbolic at the same time.

Simmel found individualization and centralization (in state authority, for instance) not at all contradictory (p. 183); the personality divides to attend to both. Like Spencer, Maine, Morgan, and so many Victorian evolutionists, Simmel still perceived "a correlation between primitive economy and [local] collectivism and, on the other hand, the mobilization of possessions and their individualization" (p. 353). Inheritance fetters individualization. Money frees it up (p. 354). Monetary contracts—including land sales and mortgages, one may suppose—are part of modern sophistication, for better or worse. Simmel was able to see modernity both ways.

So too in France, meanwhile, were Alexis de Tocqueville and later Emile Durkheim, two of the great founders of French political science, sociology, and anthropology. Tocqueville, an evolutionist of sorts, stayed twice in Algeria, in 1841 and 1846, at first as a prospective settler—episodes far less well known than his famous earlier visit to America. Whether it was what he saw in America, or what he saw in Africa, that formed his opinion, he made up his mind that mortgage credit was an answer to the problems of North African people—at least of the sedentary ones—and of others farming around them. Tocqueville favored French colonization of Algeria, but he lamented the cumbersome bureaucracy that French financial institutions had brought, and its crowding out of other institutions.

Let Algeria have loans on land mortgage, he said in his second parliamentary report after his 1846 visit, and let them have it quickly and efficiently. "There are two reasons that the farmer in Africa cannot borrow, for want of guarantees. The first is that since most of the lands were granted by the government in return for the fulfillment of several conditions, as long as the conditions are not fulfilled, the land can neither be sold nor serve as the basis for a mortgage." (Might these land attachments be a vestige of feudalism, exported from France where the revolution of 1789 had swept so much of it away?) He continued, "The second reason, and the main one, is that the mortgage system we imported to Africa, which is copied in part from our own, as well as the accompanying law of procedure, prevent lands from serving easily as security. . . . This system, however good or in any case bearable it may be in France, will paralyze agriculture, the chief industry, in Africa. . . . Generally speaking . . . the newer the society, the simpler and prompter the formalities of real estate sales should be" (Tocqueville 2001, 195–96). As progressive as these words were doubtless meant to sound, the words ring careless today, particularly in a Muslim country, where European-style mortgaging is at least ostensibly disapproved as sin (in Arabic, *haram*).[31]

Durkheim knew his Tocqueville and his social contract theorists. He also knew his German philosophers and his English evolutionists, especially Spencer (whom he copied more than a little in his grand schema of social evolution, but also sharply contradicted on the question of the primacy of the individual). Durkheim's keystone 1893 work, *The Division of Labor in Society* — taught for generations not just in France but in Britain and abroad — may be considered a kind of amalgam of their works on social evolution, with a newly combined emphasis on ritual, role specialization, and (the beginning and end of all good things, to Durkheim) social solidarity. Durkheim treats communal and individual property as typical of two types of society, which he unabashedly calls lower and higher. Basically, these are ones with unspecialized and specialized work roles, respectively. Lower societies, earlier societies based on kinship or clanship, have homogeneous, more or less self-sufficient parts, which he flatteringly likens to the parts of an earthworm that can all, if cut up, crawl off and survive on their own. Higher societies, later societies, are like more complex organisms, held together by the interdependence of their organs and basing their polities more on territory. So far, so much like Spencer, Maine, and Morgan.

But Durkheim went off on his own in insisting that contractual relations always entail noncontractual obligations too. They must always subject to moral control — for instance, the control of judges over the timing of the return of loans according to the relative urgency of borrowers' and lenders' needs (Durkheim 1964, 228). Durkheim was a great believer in laws of society, but his writing implies that a strictly imposed, legalistic regime of mortgage deadlines, for instance, is inadequately moral in itself: too unfair in the real world of accidents and contingencies. Social morality, the real basis for religion and economy, precedes, outlasts, and ultimately supersedes contracts. What matters is that people get along and society hold together.

Durkheim was convinced of society's general progress from "lower" to "higher" forms. By lower forms he meant kin groups and what he called "mechanical solidarity" (based on shared ritual and similar beliefs). By higher forms he meant territorially defined polities, professional associational ties, and "organic solidarity" (based on interdependent, specialized labor roles). Like Spencer, Maine, and Morgan, though, he might be surprised, in Africa since his time, to see kinship and clanship not only persisting but even deepening, and ethnic or "tribal" loyalties intensifying episodically, with the land attachments these all involve. But those are things we now can see.

In their own times, what these prominent thinkers all agreed on — in Britain, France, Germany, and the United States; in philosophy, sociology, political science, and anthropology; from the time of Hobbes in the sixteenth century to that of Durkheim in the early twentieth—was that human society was evolving away from an animal-like condition, by natural process or by agreement, and that kinship was yielding to other principles like contract or territorially defined polity. The rise of private property and money, and the mortgage connecting them, was part and parcel of civilization. Some, like Spencer, Maine, and the young Morgan, thought this all a good thing. Others, including the mature Morgan, and Simmel and Durkheim, were more tempered in their enthusiasm, being wary of the social divisiveness of this and other aspects of modernity, and not knowing where it all might end.

Most of these men also assumed (and some, for instance Hegel and Spencer, expressly stated) males to be better than females as abstract thinkers and long-range planners. They deemed this so whether because of differences in natural ability or inclination, or biased education—or just because of these authors' own "positioned" perceptions. That big decisions like what ought to be the law on land and loans, or whether to mortgage a farm or home, or whether to migrate away from it might rest in male hands would not have cost them much sleep.

The Colonial Philosophical Export

Key policy makers in Africa bought the evolutionary theory whole, with all its implications about the inferiority and immaturity of societies and the importance of males. These were the most inviting parts, perhaps, since they justified imperial expansion or paternalistic protection. Here is how Frederick J. D. Lugard (later Lord Lugard), a chief architect of British indirect rule in Nigeria and the crown's other African colonies, grandly put it in 1922:

> Speaking generally, it may, I think, be said that conceptions as to the tenure of land are subject to a steady evolution, side by side with the evolution of social progress, from the most primitive stages to the organization of the modern state. In the earliest stage land and its produce [are] shared by the community as a whole; later the produce is the property of the family or individuals by whose toil it is won, and the control of the land becomes vested in the head of the family. When the tribal stage is reached, the control passes to the chief, who allots unoccupied lands at will, but is not justified in dispossessing any person or family who is using the land. Later still when the pressure of population has given to

> the land an exchange value, the conception of proprietary rights emerges, and
> sale, mortgage, and lease of the land, apart from its user, [are] recognised. . . .
> These processes of natural evolution, leading up to individual ownership, may, I
> believe, be traced in every civilization known to history. (Lugard 1965, 280)

As ethnocentric and overgeneralized as it may seem, this idea linking individual property, the mortgage, and social progress has continued to appear
in national and international planning documents about Kenya and other
African countries in the late twentieth and early twenty-first centuries. So
have infantilizing implications about the unevolved, as seen so clearly in
Cambridge economist Alfred Marshall's words in 1923: "We now know that
primitive folk do not form large purposes in advance and pursue them on set
plans. . . . The notion of a definite measurement of give and take, whether
in regard to exchanges that were completed in a single transaction, or to the
return for past aid in the form of labour or goods (advanced on 'credit,' to use
a modern phrase) emerged but slowly" (Marshall 1929, 265).

By the 1950s and '60s, in western Europe, North America, and around
the world, the explicitly evolutionary idiom of "civilization" had receded
from both academic and policy discourse, but the idiom of "modernization"
had taken its place in all the social studies. Many of the most influential authors in the social studies used this or closely related terms. In economics,
this meant replacing barter with cash sale, the gift with sale or credit, subsistence with market exchange, and industrial "take off" (Walt Rostow). In political science, it meant abandoning tribalism for nationhood and citizenship.
In psychology, it meant movement from ascription to achievement (David
McClelland). In anthropology and sociology, it meant progress from folk society to urban (Robert Redfield), from particularism to universalism (Talcott
Parsons), and from large families to small. Literacy, secularism, and open-
ness of spirit were all part of it. Indeed, modernization meant so many different things that it cannot be considered a discrete idea, but more a Wittgen-
steinian "family resemblance" among theories with partial overlaps.[32] But
individualism was the nearest thing to a common theme, credit was increasingly deemed a way forward, and the free exchange of private property was
the prevailing ideology.[33]

These ideas would penetrate deep into Africa, if not convince it. In a
bookshop in Kisumu, Kenya, in the 1980s, a 1975 book by Eric Furness called
Money and Credit in Developing Africa said this on its first page: "What real
use are money and credit to mankind? . . . The short answer is that finance[,]
. . . the whole structure of financial institutions, can contribute greatly to the

standard of living of society. . . . by helping man to become more produc-tive." It continues. Subsistence economy dooms a people to poverty; spe-cialization and exchange mean wealth (p. 3). Mere barter, without money, means awkward or backward (p. 5). "[I cannot] do justice to the enormously important role which credit plays in facilitating economic growth and in promoting economic welfare" (p. 14). "There is much to do if an effective financial structure is to *evolve* in a relatively short period of time . . . dispel-ling ignorance . . . overcoming deep-rooted suspicion and of changing deep-rooted habits: to raise "effective demand for credit and saving facilities . . . co-ordinated closely with the development plans of government" (pp. 26–27, italics added).

Such optimism, such missionary zeal. A benighted people to enlighten, an economy to grow and watch over, a world to sew together, an evolution to speed up. Even classical economists like Adam Smith or David Ricardo had never placed this much faith in credit, whatever they thought of money, banks, or government.

Meanwhile, from the late 1960s on, biologists writing about population ecology too were chiming into policy debates about property. One of the best known is Garrett Hardin, famed for his phrase "tragedy of the commons." His brief original article was written as a comment on population growth; it argued that this growth has no technological solution, and that freedom to breed must therefore be restricted by mutual coercion. But it has been taken up by political economists of every stripe and used to frame debates about property for decades. In brief, the theory—leaning partly on Malthusian economics and partly on a book by a little-known mathematician named William Forster Lloyd published in 1833—is that rationally self-interested actors with open access to common resources will seek to exploit them to the maximum without regard to the resource exhaustion that will result. "Freedom in a common brings ruin to all" (Hardin 1968). The idea was not exactly new; one can trace it to ancient Athenians, among others.[34] And it was only vaguely grounded, in Hardin's original article ("Picture a pasture open to all. It is to be expected that each herdsman will try to keep as many cattle as possible on the commons."). But nowhere perhaps had it been expressed with more punch, and it has caught the imagination of many. The idea has commonly been adduced by tenure reformers and would-be reformers con-vinced that only individual or other private property can protect soils and waters. It has occasioned much heated debate, sometimes disguising capital-ist and socialist, or pro-enterprise and pro-government, subtexts. Some of its critics have raised, as qualifications, the potential workability of "managed commons"—imposing restrictions and limiting overuse by common consent—whether through group limitation, representative governance, evolving law, moral education (through shared ritual, legendry, or schooling), or other means.[35] The debates continue.

In the early twenty-first century, one of the most outspoken and popular voices in favor of titling land as private property, with the express purposes of making it usable as loan collateral, has been the Peruvian-born Hernando de Soto. He has set himself up, or been set up, as champion of the small entrepreneur, decrying the bureaucracy that prevents the latter from registering wealth as property (1989, 2000). In de Soto's vision, expressed (much like Hardin's) in stripped-down prose for accessibility and persuasion, bringing the world into one "social contract," through paper records accessible to all, and bringing "dead" capital to "life," is the key to uplifting the world's poor (2000). Unlike many who tout such lines, though, de Soto does not assume the poor too poor to save; on the contrary he finds them eager to do so.[36] A powerful wave of enthusiasm for small enterprise has carried de Soto's work to the attention of many contemporary policy makers—in governments, corporations, and aid agencies alike.

But some very different voices have found their way into print throughout the entire period covered in this brief survey of theories so far. To understand where they have come from, we must back up again in time, and start again with another line of questioning. If the magic of property turns sand to gold, who gets the gold? What might they do with it—and to whom?

The Ghost Walk: Voices of Some
Dead White European Male Radicals

"It is an enchanted, perverted, topsy-turvy world in which Monsieur le Capital and Madame la Terre do their ghost-walking as social characters and at the same time as mere things," wrote Karl Marx in *Capital*.[37]

A ghost walk. The ideas in the preceding pages about evolution, progress, and economy-building have never been without their critics, and even many theorists who thought they perceived societies to move generally toward private property, financial credit, and the mortgage have been frightened by moral or practical implications of such movement. The ideas of these and other critics help explain the caution and ambivalence of British (and other European) land policy in Africa until after the second world war—in Kenya,

Uganda, Tanganyika, and elsewhere—until the last decade of independence, when a wholesale reform by titling began in Kenya.

"Critical" philosophies about private property in land in European traditions may be found back at least as far back as Plato.[38] For our purposes it suffices to reach back to the mid-eighteenth century to find critical ideas that some would try to bring to bear on African land matters from that time on.[39]

We can begin with one already encountered. Jean-Jacques Rousseau, a peripatetic loner never much at ease in society despite its attentions, wrote sometime between 1753 and 1755 one of the most influential essays the world has known, the "Discourse sur l'origine et les fondements de l'inégalité parmi les hommes" (Discourse on the Origin and Foundation of Inequality Among Mankind). In it he pointed to the concept of private property, particularly in land, as the taproot of human woes. Wrote he, "The first man, who after enclosing a piece of ground, took it into his head to say, *this is mine*, and found people simple enough to believe him, was the real founder of civil society. How many crimes, how many wars, how many murders, how many misfortunes and horrors, would that man have saved the human species, who pulling up the stakes or filling up the ditches should have cried to his fellows: Beware of listening to this impostor; you are lost, if you forget that the fruits of the earth belong equally to us all, and the earth itself to nobody!" (Rousseau 1967a, 211–12). Rousseau later tempered his views on private property, and on the states that supported it, as seen earlier.[40] But his poetic early essay's punch has always continued to resound in French and European thought on land tenure, echoing in lines like the gradualist reformer Pierre Proudhon's aphorism, "La propriété, c'est le vol" (Property is theft—1849, 2). It also crossed the Channel and the Mediterranean.

Another critic we have met already too. Lewis Henry Morgan, that Rochester, New York–based lawyer, anthropologist, and classical historian, changed his mind too about land tenure, but not in the direction Rousseau had. After defending the rights of Iroquois and other native people to land titles and full citizenship (in his early ethnographic work published in 1851), Morgan came to think of private property as something like a new and dangerous weapon. In his *Ancient Society*, published in 1877 as railroad companies were laying tracks through the American West, and as some of the first European travelers were penetrating the Lake Victoria Basin, Morgan offered his more apocalyptic vision at the very end of his book. "Since the advent of civilization, the outgrowth of property has been so immense, its forms so diversified, its uses so expanding and its management so intelligent in the interests of its owners, that it has become, on the part of the people, an unmanageable power. The human mind stands bewildered in the presence of its own creation." Humans needed to climb back on top of it, to set limits to it, to achieve democracy, equality, and fraternity (the virtues of "the ancient gentes" or descent groups). "The dissolution of society bids fair to become the termination of a career in which property is the end and aim; because such a career contains the elements of self-destruction" (Morgan 1964, 467).

No one who has read Karl Marx or Friedrich Engels can miss the influence of these words of Morgan's on them; and indeed it was from Rousseau's and Morgan's work that both Marx and Engels derived their main inspirations on land, property, and the perils of its financing. Sterner than Morgan in criticizing individualism, Marx, in his broad and heavily theorized indictment of the "bourgeois order" in the first and third volumes of *Capital*, depicts credit, together with competition and the private ownership of the means of production, as a central part of what is wrong with capitalism.

Marx, like Adam Smith, Lewis Henry Morgan, and others before him, was a stages evolutionist.[41] As tribal and kin-based relations gave way to feudalism, feudalism yielded in turn to capitalism (to lead in turn to socialism, then true communism). "With capitalist production an altogether new force comes into play—the credit system. (Para.) In its beginnings, the credit system sneaks in as a modest helper of accumulation and draws by invisible threads the money resources scattered all over the surface of society into the hands of individual or associated capitalists. But soon it becomes a new and formidable weapon in the competitive struggle" (1906, Ch. 25, sec. 2, p. 687). Morgan's influence again. While conjuring such vividly personified imagery, Marx deplored the classical economists' tendency to speak of land and money as things with their own lives independent of real labor and social relations—that is, to fetishize them as commodities with exchange value free of any use value (Marx 1906, Ch. 1, sec. 4, pp. 81–96). "It is an enchanted, perverted, topsy-turvy world in which Monsieur le Capital and Madame la Terre do their ghost-walking as social characters and at the same time directly as mere things."[42]

The ghoulish liaison, Marx found, took little time to wreak its effects on a farming people. In *The Eighteenth Brumaire of Louis Bonaparte*, in 1852, Marx moralized on the combination of freehold tenure with financial capital for newly entitled small-scale farmers in Napoleonic France. Although land tenure reform had liberated and enriched that population at first, he found, the division of land into private smallholdings was two generations later "causing the ruin of the French peasant" as "the inevitable result: progressive deterioration of agriculture, progressive indebtedness of the agriculturalist." As he saw it, "In the course of the nineteenth century the feudal lords were replaced by urban usurers; the feudal obligation that went with the land was replaced by bourgeois capital" in mortgage finance and debt (Marx 1963, 126–27). He continued, now pulling out all the stops in his prose, "Small-holding property, in this enslavement by capital to which its development inevitably pushes forward, has transformed the mass of the French nation into troglodytes. . . . The bourgeois order . . . has become a vampire that sucks out [the smallholding's] blood and brains and throws it into the alchemistic cauldron of capital . . . [by] distraints, forced sales and compulsory auctions" (p. 127). Marx's use of the term "inevitably" serves as reminder of his evolutionary thinking, but also, if believed, implies that the freehold-mortgage mechanism will impoverish African (and American, Chilean, and Japanese) smallholders as well as French. The personification of land and capital, with sex and with vivid body imagery, opens up a psychological and literary dimension into which East African thought too offers some insights—a topic touched upon later.

Friedrich Engels carried on Marx's critique. His quasi-historical *Origin of the Family, Private Property, and the State* (orig. 1884) relied on Morgan's stadial schema as much as on Marx's in lamenting early civilization, the stage at which the "gens" (descent group) yielded formerly communal land to the individual as heritable private property, and at which the mortgage reared its head (Engels 1972, 225–26). "Never again has the power of money shown itself in such primitive brutality and violence as during these days of its youth." Early cash sales led straight to credit, interest, and usury. With the invention of money and commodities also came slavery and private property in land at the same time. "Scarcely had private property in land been introduced than the mortgage was already invented (see Athens). As hetaerism and prostitution dog the heels of monogamy, so from now onward the mortgage dogs the heels of private land ownership. You asked for full, free alienable ownership of the land and now you have got it—'*Tu l'as voulu* [You asked for it], Georges Dandin.'"[43] The next paragraph gives the big picture: "With trade expansion, money and usury, private property in land

and mortgages, the concentration and centralization of wealth in the hands of a small class rapidly advanced, accompanied by widespread impoverishment" (Engels 1972, 226).

At this unhappy stage of incipient capitalist civilization, wrote Engels, the "gentile constitution" or kin-based nature of society collapsed under class antagonisms and there arose in its ruins the state (Engels 1972, 228) — defined (following Rousseau) as "an organization for the protection of the possessing class against the non-possessing class" — and thence state borrowing and debt and a whole new set of problems (p. 230). For Engels, as for Marx, finance capital and the mortgage represented evil itself.

Ideas like Marx's and Engels's about credit and private property seldom found explicit expression in African colonial rule, or early scholarship on it. But they would appear to have influenced British policies designed to protect African people from usury by immigrant minorities. By the 1950s influential African politicians themselves, including the Luo Oginga Odinga in Kenya (or Julius Nyerere in Tanzania, or Kwame Nkrumah in Ghana) had used some aspects of Marxist property theory to evoke class consciousness — and in Odinga's case, to encourage Luo people to resist land titling — to serve, among other things, the cause of national independence. Colonial and independent national politicians and administrators in Africa also had gradualist reformers to turn to for inspiration. At the level of rumor and legend, Marx's and Engels's vampirism that included the "blood sucking" by bankers and other financiers under state protection anticipated countless popular stories about capitalist, imperialist, and neo-imperialist vampires, were-hyenas, and the like — that have circulated clear across Africa, Luo country included, up to our times.[44]

Progress, Poverty, and Compromising Reformism

While Engels was carrying Marx's torch and attacking private property and the mortgage in Europe so controversially, in America the egalitarian philosopher Henry George spelled out his own thinking in *Progress and Poverty*, first published in 1879, and gaining quieter influence. In brief, George found, in moving east from frontier San Francisco to New York to Dickensian London, that the older the cities got, the deeper the inequalities in wealth seemed to be. Poverty and progress were two sides of the same coin. The richest people were found right alongside the poorest. The problem he put down to "a great primary wrong — the appropriation, as the exclusive property of some men, of the land on which and from which we must all live. From this fundamental injustice flow all the injustices which distort and endanger modern development" (George 1938, 340). Much like Rousseau, George deemed this kind of progress only hollow, destructive progress. The solution George proposed, "single tax" on land as a solution, has never yet been tried out at a national level.[45] Whether land tenure is the problem and taxation the solution or not, George's writing certainly strikes a chord in the African or Latin American tropics, where the most astonishing wealth seems so often found in the midst of the direst poverty.

George's ideas on private property and land maldistribution reached readers on both sides of the Atlantic. They reached British and colonial power brokers partly through populist writers like the Irish-born London transplant George Bernard Shaw and the Fabian Society, a group or net-work of socialist-leaning but gradualist reformers that coalesced in the 1880s and remained influential into the 1940s. This last is noteworthy because of the activism of women, particularly Beatrice Webb (joining spouse Sidney Webb), almost from the society's outset. While their concerns were mainly urban and industrial, the Fabians' activism reached into the countryside too, and it reached overseas to Africa.[46]

Whereas Marxists favored abolishing private property altogether, Fabi-ans favored allowing leasehold. And that is the form that much rural prop-erty would take in British Africa. But the leases were typically long, as if to compromise again: Ninety-nine- and 999-year leases became common in Kenya for British and other immigrant settlers in the first decades of the twentieth century. Some of those leases are still in their youth today. Like private property, though, long leases will be seen to have come under fire, not least from newly outspoken African women wishing to free up land titles and leases from the firm clutch of their menfolk.

By about the time Fabianism was waning in Britain, around the time of the second world war, the Viennese-born Hungarian economic historian Karl Polanyi was offering up a new vision of the world's property and financial history. His was sharply critical of the observed order, like Marx and Engels, but less utopian or revolutionary in implication, more like the vision of the Fabians. In Polanyi's eyes, reciprocity and redistribution predated market exchange, and never until the nineteenth century were markets or economy seen as anything more than accessories to life in society or allowed to oper-ate free of social or governmental restriction. A market for land was a recent historical aberration, a "crude fiction" and part of a "satanic mill." Land, like labor or money, is not a true commodity made for sale, said his 1944 book, *The Great Transformation*, but something "tied up with the organizations of kinship, neighborhood, craft, and creed—with tribe and temple, village, gild, and church." To isolate it as a market "was perhaps the weirdest of all undertakings of our ancestors" (Polanyi 1957, 72–73, 178). Allowing land markets to escape control, and overextending credit in the name of a free market, had dragged down industrial society and contributed to the Great Depression—and might do more of the same. Polanyi's words might almost have been written about Kenyan settler farmers—many of whose farms, plantations, and ranches were ruined by mortgage foreclosure during the Great Depression—and about other, African farmers to be given land titles and loans later for them to try their own hand and take their own chances in the mortgage gamble and to see if they could keep from being chewed up in the market's "satanic mill." Polanyi's anthropological followers who worked on Africa did much to reintegrate the study of land tenure with those of kinship, religion, and so on, but not always in a way as politically pointed as Polanyi might have done.[47]

Sharper critiques of markets, financial imperialism, and land tenure relations would come into African studies from different angles in the 1960s and '70s. Influenced by a basically Marxian Latin Americanist school of "dependency" theorists like Paul Baran, others like Samir Amin and Walter Rodney imported into African studies a concern about the active, deliberate, and exploitative "underdevelopment of development"—of rural tropical commodity producers, by northern metropolitan financiers and industrialists, and by co-opted bourgeoisies and rural buyer ("comprador") elites reaching into the countryside in tropical countries. Colin Leys, a specialist on Kenya also inspired by Marx and Engels, was among those influenced to write on the corrosive, divisive, and dangerous effects of foreign finance there. Up to the 1970s, he wrote, "the general effect of credit was to accelerate the emergence of a small profit-oriented class of farmers capable of accumulating capital, and differentiate them progressively from those whose plots were destined either to be sold or to move gradually towards a predominantly food-providing function" (Leys 1975, 101).

Work like this was not lost on African scholars themselves, and among these rose some strong voices of concern and complaint along similar lines. Zimbabwean critical economist Dani Wadada Nabudere, after visiting Kenya in the 1980s, described the attempt of the World Bank Group and other international agencies to overpower and marginalize African governments and pave the way for commercial banking's penetration into the countryside. This was all part of "globalizing finance capital in its speculative aspect to encompass Third World peoples. . . . By removing the state from the economic sphere, the idea is to establish a *nexus* between the local comprador capitalists with their international 'counterparts' to milk the African countryside and that of the other Third World countries" (Nabudere 1989, 3; emphasis in original). The steep growth of African countries' debt (which he reported as rising from U.S. $13 billion in 1970 to $200 billion in 1986) was evidence of "the parasitic character of international finance capital which had brought about . . . *negative* development in African countries" and would end in the abolition of capitalism and the nation-state system (Nabudere 1989, 3, 136; emphasis in original).[48] Vampires for Marx and Engels, milkers and parasites for Nabudere. New language, new financiers, new victims . . . but a continuing process and flow?

Marxian and neo-Marxian critiques like these were not designed to warm the hearts of international financiers, and they gained little hearing in the aid agencies. But other, non-Marxist critics *did* gain official respect and influence through development and economics journals and in some cases through regular consultancy. In the late 1970s and early 1980s, economist J. D. Von Pischke and political scientist Robert Bates criticized the use of subsidized credit (money, seeds, fertilizers, and other farm inputs on loan) in Kenya, and other countries they compared with it, to reward supporters of regimes in power. Elites' devouring these inputs kept them scarce for most farmers, they found. Economists Dale Adams, Douglas Graham, and Richard Meyer and anthropologist Keith Hart came up with some of the same insights about state-subsidized finance across Africa.[49] Their critiques, adding to the critical political economy of "urban bias" championed by Michael Lipton, Paul Streeten, and others since the 1970s, added up to a wave of populist criticism not even the World Bank could ignore—particularly since much of it was pitched in neoclassical economic idiom and heavily backed up with figures.

Indeed, a few critics even lodged in the belly of the beast itself. Von Pischke carried on his heretical critical analyses of World Bank–sponsored and other credit activity in the 1990s as a World Bank officer. While he wrote much less about land tenure per se, work like his showed other Bank staffers hired soon afterward, including John Bruce and the Kenyan Shem Migot-Adholla, that there was room for internal criticism on land tenure policy too. Whether the Bank could so easily turn its policies on property and finance around, though, was another matter—and here we get ahead of ourselves.

More voices from the academy were still weighing in on land tenure and finance, changing minds official and unofficial, at the century's turn. Combining political science, anthropology, and several other disciplines, and building on a series of his earlier books, southeast Asianist James Scott mounted from Yale a broad critique of older and newer modes of national land and resource administration worldwide—a critique that might alternatively be described as populist, pacifist, anarchist, or all three together, but seldom just capitalist or socialist. Scott compared and analyzed older and newer attempts to render humans and human spaces more "legible" for purposes of exerting more state control over human bodies, minds, and lives—and over whatever might be deemed nature—for instrumental purposes like, say, taxation or military conscription, or just for some aesthetic sense of order. Tools and strategies within that project of simplifying, ordering, aggregating, and quantifying complex settlements and locally adapted lifeways included mapping, cadastral surveying, "villagization" (concentrating formerly scattered settlement, in the style of post-Independence Tanzania or Ethiopia) and the imposition of gridlike land layouts. (Other parts included standardized weights and measures; codified laws; creation and use of surnames; and documents like identity cards, certificates, and passports.) In a way, these diverse ways of exerting control seemed all of a piece: all part of the title of his book *Seeing Like a State* (Scott 1998). Ambitious, authoritarian projects of social engineering—ones Scott calls "high modernist"—risk failing or turning disastrous, in Scott's view, when they neglect, deny, or attempt to override what he calls by the classical Greek term mētis (knowledge derived from practical experience) with an unscientifically optimistic reliance on science and rationality—and particularly when they use force in a zealous quest for visual order.

A comprehensive history of eastern Africa would show many such state impositions in colonial and independent times. None have been more blatantly draconian than the doomed "villagization" programs tried in adjacent Tanzania and Ethiopia, but others have been found in Kenya. They include the drawing of district and provincial boundaries, the issuance of identity cards (Sw., sing. *kipande,* pl. *vipande*), and the registration of title deeds. They would also include the attachment of those title deeds to state or bank loans in mortgages. These are all, among other things, means of raising "legibility," regulating lives, and centralizing that control. And they all deny or sweep aside important local realities, meanings, and feelings—in

past, future, or perennially recurring time. It remains for us to see how they
have transpired and how they seem to be playing out.

This sketch history of theoretical approaches to land, finance, and the
mortgage link between them has presented some bold presumptions, and
some bold critiques of those presumptions and of the conditions into which
they lead. Of course, even some of the critiques involve presumptions of their
own. One of the most constantly recurring themes, in the writings of both
the proponents and the critics of a land market, is evolution.

As I have tried to suggest, evolution can mean many different things,
among them gradual change, willed progress, or a natural or human-made
culling of unfit specimens or ideas. It can mean an inexorable flow of history
with fixed origins and destinies, or an entirely mindless and directionless
process. It can refer to an individual, an ethnic group or race (a lately contested but maybe ineradicable concept), or a species, among others. It can
mean competition, cooperation, or both. Assigning just a single meaning to
evolution would be presumptuous in itself.

But that does not invalidate what seems a basic truth: that humans—or
at least the kinds who have proffered the best-known theories about nature and culture, about kinship and polity, or about society, economy, and
law—have remained obsessed with questions of savagery and sophistication.
Scholars, like others, seem to crave information and reassurance about where
humans place and rank with respect to each other, and to (other) animals—
if not also to spirits, divinity, or machines. Whether discussed in the late
nineteenth century as civilization, in the mid-twentieth as modernization, or
in the late twentieth to early twenty-first as globalization, the sociocultural
sort of evolution has kept surfacing. Whatever one might think of its moral
or religious implications, evolutionism—in science or in social and cultural
philosophy—is not about to go away.

That so many theorists about land and property have tried to map the
economic ideologies of capitalism and socialism, and the political ones of
authoritarianism and anarchism, onto biologically based ones about savagery and civilization should not be surprising. Humans will try mapping
just about any dichotomy or linear scale onto any other. We make conflations,
and draw metaphors and analogies, to tidy up a messy world, to fit some aesthetic template, or to make it easier not to think.

If biology, economy, and politics seem to furnish a basic toolkit for discussing land attachments and tenure policies, culture might seem to some just an add-on. But without attention to language and communication such as a social perspective provides, or to the symbolic, emotional, and aesthetic sides that a cultural, psychological, or literary turn might add, the kit will always be deficient. You might forget the graves or ancestors, for instance, and fail to understand the idiom when the fights break out.

The theories discussed in this chapter have been penned mainly by persons in positions of some security and privilege in their times, mostly European and North American men not too threatened by cold, heat, or hunger. But they had little protection against error. Nor, in the end, is there anything proprietary, or necessarily novel, about their ideas. Wherever they came from, these are all African ideas now too — no less than the persons who wrote them down, like all humans, seem to have sprung originally of African descent. Some of the most convinced evolutionists and creationists, communists and capitalists, authoritarians and anarchists will indeed be found among farmers, herders, traders, or persons with no simple occupational labels, in rural hamlets in the hills and savannah of the African tropics. But that does not mean that their ways of life all conform to their respective ideologies, or that their "foreign" ideologies have expunged their local ones. How well might these people, under all these influences, coexist? Just how easy are these grand ideologies to live out, and to impose on others? Finding out these things is the task of the rest of this work.

CHAPTER 3

Luo and Others

Migration, Settlement, Ethnicity

If there is one lesson which must be drawn, which applies to all, it is that all people come, in history's long run, out of a variety of ethnic backgrounds, intermingled. History brooks no claims of ethnic purity . . .
— CHRISTOPHER EHRET

Some speak of human cultures or societies as though genetic stock, language spoken, and material culture neatly coincided in each case. But sometimes they do not: a people distinct in one way may not be so in another.

People known as Luo live at one of the more important frontiers in Africa, at the edge between the language family called Nilotic that occupies much of east-northeast Africa, and the one most often called Bantu that takes up most of Africa's southern half.[1] Around the edges of the Luo country one can walk from one farmer's field to another's and hear an almost entirely different language, and maybe discern a different human physiognomy too. But in fact the Luo people as Nilotic speakers share much of their way of life with their Bantu-speaking and other neighbors, whether they look or sound alike or not. These people have been influencing each other's habits, and selectively intermarrying and interbreeding, for centuries.

The aims of this chapter are simple: to indicate roughly what is known and unknown about how Luo people got where they are and became who they are, and to give a general idea of their mode of livelihood, particularly in the more rural settings that make up most of their country. A few points are crucial. First, the people now known as Luo share much of their culture with others speaking different languages in the lake basin with whom their forebears jostled and competed for land in the past, or whom they have absorbed as Luo. They look with reverence upon early settlers of their own ethnic group, and mix with and tolerate some neighboring groups much more than others, while caring less about prehistoric settlers of unknown languages and identities. Second, the pattern of settlement around the eastern lake basin, where Luo live, has not always remained constant but has seen episodes of concentrated dwellings and periods of homestead spread-out. It has also seen, over the twentieth century, a dramatic growth of towns around new or burgeoning market places. The ecosystem sets limits on the balance of strategies required to survive in it, but human usage has altered the rest of the ecosystem in turn. Finally, and most importantly for our topic, the mode of living that Luo and their neighbors have evolved over centuries and millennia—in the lake basin and a much broader stretch of middle Africa—precludes any simple notion of individual or communal property in land as the characteristic local tradition. Instead, their custom has been one of seasonal oscillation between more tightly and more loosely restricted access.

Being and Becoming Luo:
Migrations, Encounters, Displacements

To ask how Luo people got where they are on the map is also to ask how other people there became Luo. The ancestors of present-day Luo have not lived forever in these people's present-day homeland around the eastern side of the lake basin, nor were they the first to arrive there. The best available evidence suggests they came in waves from the north-northwest, from a part of what is now southern Sudan—somewhere around where one now finds the Nuer and Dinka people, who like them still speak tongues that linguists class as Nilotic.[2] That area remains much more thinly settled than the eastern lake basin where Luo now live. Back in that Sudanese land of putative origin, Nuer, Dinka, and other groups continue to subsist in an area of broad plains laced with seasonal swamplands, practicing a mix of herding, farming, and fishing that shifts dramatically from one season to the next, and that keeps many of them moving between wet season villages and dry season cattle camps still more sparsely spread around.

Evidence is scarce on the whens and whys of the south-southwesterly migrations. It comes in several forms: linguistic (glottochronological), archaeological, and oral-historical. Analysis of DNA from human remains is likely to add more information. Nothing much can be added here to what is already in the published record, but a few things need mention.[3]

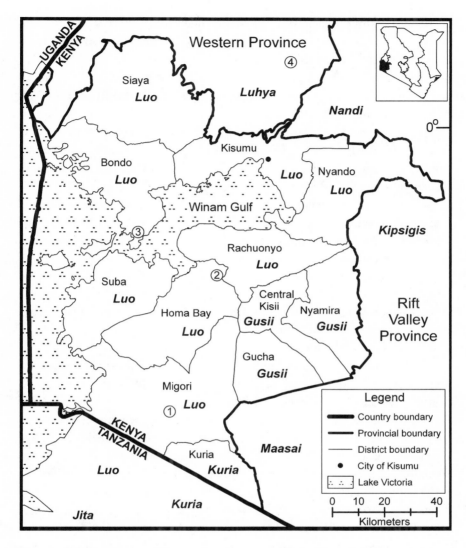

Nyanza Province, western Kenya, showing eastern Lake Victoria/Nyanza and predominant languages (in italics). Study sites: (1) Kanyamkago, main site; (2) Kagan; (3) Uyoma; (4) Isukha. Sources: adapted from CGIAR/IPC (2006) and World Bank (2006).

A number of peoples from southern Sudan to northern Tanzania consider themselves to belong to a macro-group variously spelled Luo, Lwo,
or Lwoo but all pronounced alike. They are the various groups who settled
down along the way in the great southward drift. All the languages they speak
are classed within the more encompassing group called Nilotic. It is only
those in present-day Kenya and northern Tanzania who use the ethnonym
Luo all by itself, rather than some other more specific one referring to some
smaller group when talking about who they are. For instance, in Uganda,
the Acholi, Langi, Labwor, or Padhola all sometimes add Luo as a second
ethnonym to refer to the more encompassing category.

It is the ones who deem their people's homeland the lake basin in western
Kenya and northern Tanzania, then, whom I refer to in this study simply as
Luo. Following convention, I shall reserve the spelling Lwoo (or Lwo) for the
members of the broader category that includes the Ugandan and Sudanese
groups. How any of these people came to be known as Luo is unknown. The
name may be a variant of the word used in the lake basin today for soil or
land, *lowo* (pronounced like the English word 'low')—as it appears in usages
like masters or sons of the land, or people from here—but this is only one of
several competing theories.

It is certain enough that not all the ancestors of the present-day Kenyan
and Tanzanian Luo—whatever they called themselves—migrated south
toward the lake basin at once, but that they came in trickles or waves over
several centuries. The earliest dispersals from a Sudanese point of origin may
have begun sometime between the seventh and eleventh centuries C.E. (Herring 1976, 89; see also Blount 1970). The ancestors of Luo seem always, since
then, to have been farmers, herders, and fishers, if in shifting proportions for
the livelihood. The migrants came by different routes, evidently following
rivers and streams, dividing and recombining, and stopping and starting for
periods along the way, some for generations. By one estimate from genealogies, published by B. A. Ogot in 1967, "The first Luo settlers arrived in
Nyanza about fifteen to sixteen generations ago, that is, between 1490 and
1600 A.D." (or C.E.) (p. 152). They and others came from the northwest, north,
and northeast.

The land they moved into as they spread south along the lake shore, or
parts of that land, had been occupied since an unknown time. Its earliest
denizens are known only by stone and bone remains. If linguistic evidence
is to be believed, later waves deemed to have spoken tongues of the Bantu
and "southern Cushite" families began arriving probably by about 400 C.E.;

some of their descendants are known today as Luhya and Gisu. They were joined, or maybe preceded, by yet others lately classed as "southern Nilotic-speaking pre-Kalenjin communities" from the Rift Valley to the east, and "Teso-Masaian" people from the north of the great lake. All the more populous groups in the area between 500 and 1800 are thought to have been producing, not just foraging, food (Ehret 1976, 2–5).

We know the migrants from whom Luo trace their descent pushed away some of the groups they encountered along the way; and that they absorbed others, including some of those they found in the lake basin when they reached there. Oral histories tend to focus on the battles more than the negotiations, peaceful accommodations, and opportunistic identity-switching that surely have been no less real as the ancestors of present-day Luo moved south, established a reputation as brave fighters and successful strategists, attracted women and youth from threatened or subjugated groups, and found their numbers swelling to the present size of millions.

By the time the Luo arrived in the great lake basin, that area was already a rich mix of ethnic and linguistic communities.[4] Some of the people absorbed—for instance, the people known as Suba—spoke languages lately classed as Bantu, a language family entirely different from the Nilotic family. (Suba, who live south of the Winam Gulf, now speak Luo.) Others speaking "Bantu" tongues closely related to Suba, including groups now known as Gusii (to the east of the present-day Luo country) and some of the peoples lumped as Luhya (to the north), appear to have been pushed up onto higher ground they now occupy, while yet others, now called Kuria (to the southeast), got pushed south to around today's Kenya-Tanzania border. Nandi and Kipsigis, both classed today among Kalenjin, were pushed northeast and east. These people all borrowed words from each other's tongues, and eventually from coastal Swahili (inland, a shared trade language) and English. Maasai, who speak a Nilotic tongue distantly related to Luo, were pushed east and southeast. Among all these peoples, it is Suba and a minority of southern Luhya who seem most recognizably to have blended themselves into Luo culture among Luo; in parts of southern Nyanza (including in Kanyamkago) they occupy richly blended communities.

Luo oral histories associate particular spots on the landscape, notably unusual rock outcroppings, with particular war heroes known to have dwelled or died near there—or in some versions, turned to stone. The place names serve as mnemonics, keeping history alive and reminding the young of their people's claimed place in the world as they grow up. It is what graves do too on a smaller scale. Places, times, names, and stories all partake of each other, and all contribute to a sense of belonging.

As the ancestors of present-day Luo expanded and moved from the flatter lands of the lake and river basins up toward the higher, hillier, cooler, and more heavily watered uplands—a trend evident by around the end of the eighteenth century C.E.—they adjusted their strategies of livelihood.[5] They have had to continue doing so, not only to adapt to different ecozones—taking advantage of what grows and how well—but also to cope with rising population, rising competition for land, and increasing difficulty of shifting fields and settlements.

They very likely came to rely less on animal keeping, and more on farming, while some evidently fished, as today, to supplement the diets of many. One reason for deemphasizing herding was that the more heavily wooded areas were, or were becoming, infested with tsetse fly and thus trypanosomiasis (sleeping sickness), dangerous to cattle as well as humans. Another was that competition for fertile upland volcanic soils increased steeply as those areas later got cleared of forest and brush. Colonial settlement and upland human clearance for tea and other cash-crop estates on both sides of the Rift Valley, the Pax Britannica, and the imposition of new government-enforced territories for named ethnic groups (sometimes only newly named) only intensified local pressures. Labor migration as well as farming gained importance. But it remains unknown how heavily the early Luo ancestors relied on herding in the places from which they migrated. They had a mixed farming-herding economy, perhaps with fishing too—but little more about it can be said for sure (Herring 1976, 80–81). Luo became, in their modes of livelihood, much more like Bantu-speaking neighbors, while some of these Bantu speakers learned the Luo tongue, adopted Luo initiation customs, and effectively became Luo. What all seem to agree on is that attachment to fixed sites, including graves and abandoned homesteads, has heightened over the past century or longer as Luo have become more sedentary and more crowded in their lake basin home (Ogot 1967, 38–39).

In the process of adapting to their environments, Luo and neighboring people have altered those environments. Cattle, sheep, and goats dramatically change foliation, and the grazing and browsing affect soil fertility, though the effects of "overgrazing" have sometimes been overstated, or blame for it misattributed, where territorial and property regimes have restricted movement. Sugar plantations have taken over several large tracts for monoculture in their nucleus estates, and in wider areas, both sugar and tobacco companies have brought a patchwork of small plantations onto family landholdings under contract farming arrangements. Flue-cured tobacco, grown in southern Nyanza since the 1970s, requires much wood to fuel the fires in the drying barns day and night, contributing to deforestation and thus also to soil erosion. Having been constrained to a limited territory heightens the need to grow cash crops, some including sugar very volatile in value, to make ends meet—and thus can force decisions that rural people themselves may know or suspect are not in the longer-term interest of their neighborhoods. It is little wonder that many have fixed their hopes for their children on migrating away for work.

Luo visited by Europeans and others in the late nineteenth century showed them old fortified settlements with walls of earth or stone, and sometimes trenches, around their perimeter.[6] Some were abandoned and others still in use. The walls were called *ohingini* (sing. *ohinga*), the abandoned settlements *gundni bur* (sing. *gunda bur*).[7] Administrator C. W. Hobley wrote, at the turn of the nineteenth century, of walled settlements of between ten and fifty "huts," that is houses (1902, 26); others have written of up to hundreds. In many sites in and around Luo country, the walls and trenches surrounding these disappeared settlements can be seen today, eroded and overgrown. A gunda bur in Kanyamkago, near where I lived in the early 1980s, was shrouded in mystery. No one, even among those living next to it, knew who had built it or lived in it before the earliest known ancestors of the neighborhood's current residents had arrived around the 1870s.

There is little evidence that the inhabitants of a typical such settlement were related or organized by lineage or clan. On the contrary, there is at least some oral evidence, from lakeside Gangu in western Siaya District, the site of "seven trench and wall settlements, probably two to four centuries old," that they were groups composed of people of diverse families or lineages who happened for one reason or another to have chosen to live together, before or after some intermarried: "alliances of unrelated individuals and alliances marked by affinal connections" (D. Cohen and Atieno Odhiambo 1989, 13).[8] Nor were the groups very stable: David Cohen's oral histories suggest that a series of "micro-conquests" changed the occupants of a fortified settlement often.

While some ethno-historians have suggested it was the Pax Britannica that let Luo spread out of these stockaded structures, others suggest that a spreading had been going on for as much as a century before the British arrived (D. Cohen and Atieno Odhiambo 1989, Ch. 1, esp. p. 10). The political

implications of the debate are great, but it remains unresolved. There may
never have been a time when all, or even most, Luo lived in gundni bur.

In any case, by the first decades of the twentieth century, most Luo lived
in smaller homesteads (*mier*, sing. *dala*), dispersed over the landscape; and by
early to mid-twentieth century, increasing numbers in towns or cities in the
lake basin and beyond. The thick, thorny euphorbia fences that surrounded
their homesteads, mostly circular like the bigger old stockades of the gundni
bur, were still conventional in mid-century. But by the last decades of the
century these fences were fading away too, sometimes replaced only by symbolic entry posts.[9] The walling or fencing of the perimeter, the multi-house
pattern, and the terms *ligala* and *gunda* (for new and old settlements, respectively), and *gweng'* (for a community or its land), are all continuities linking
the older and newer settlement patterns.

What is new in Luo country, over the past few decades, is the fencing of
fields outside the tight little homestead compounds, on newly titled lands,
and the exclusion of animals and occasional users from even seasonal access
to the fields of individuals or small families.

An Eclectic Agrarian Living

A word now on agriculture and other modes of livelihood.[10] Luo and
most of the other people in areas surrounding their country—including all
the most densely settled ethnic groups—have relied heavily on farming since
first contacted by Europeans. Luo have also herded cattle, sheep, and goats,
and kept chickens and other small animals, since earliest recorded history.
Always have at least a small minority also fished; and some Luo, especially in
hard times, have also continued to hunt and gather wild foods from the land.
It is easy to make mistakes about these things since Luo and others nearby,
notably Nandi to the northeast and Kipsigis to the east, take much pride in
what some consider a more pastoralist prehistory. But in fact little evidence
exists to show that there was ever a time any of these did not rely heavily
on agriculture. Maasai are the neighbors who have relied most heavily on
herding since before European occupation; but in fact agriculture and trade
with agriculturalists have been a larger part of their past and recent present
too than some Maasai or most of their journalistic admirers have wished to
suppose or admit.

In any case, Luo and all their neighbors have since the early twentieth
century supplemented their farming, herding, fishing and hunting with mi-

grant work undertaken mostly for cash. They go to cities, including Nairobi and Mombasa, to tea and coffee plantations, to mines when open (and sometimes after they close), and elsewhere in Kenya and a few places abroad. For most of this period men have done more of the migrating and living away from rural homes than women have; hence what has become now a long tradition of divided families partly dependent on cash remittances in one direction and sometimes food deliveries in the other.

As farming people, most Luo and most of their neighbors rely on dryland agriculture. Irrigation accounts for only a small fraction of their fields (mostly in a rice scheme around Ahero, a stretch of plains southeast of Kisumu); and the problems of malaria and schistosomiasis accompanying standing water discourage its further spread. Two relatively reliable rainy seasons in the higher-altitude zones, and one rainy season plus a hope of spotty rains in the lower zones, mean a big advantage for the upper-altitude farmers, some of whom benefit from richer, volcanic soils anyway. Traders use donkeys and motor vehicles when available to move food up and down between the altitude zones, and into town markets and rural selling points.

Luo and other western Kenyans grow grains as their staple foods: sorghum, millet, and increasingly over the past century, maize. All these, sometimes mixed, form the basis of *kuon* or (Sw.) *ugali*, the mass of boiled and stirred flour. Cassava, a drought-resistant crop which, like maize, originates in the Americas, which provides starchy bulk in its tubers and other nutrients in its leaves, has become increasingly important and also finds its way into kuon. But white maize has become the favorite, displacing some of the sorghum and much of the millet from Luo fields. Beans, other pulses, and kales and a wide variety of leafy vegetables (some indigenous, some exogenous) round out the daily diet, mostly in sauces for the kuon. Liquid, sweetened grain porridge makes a filling snack, as do sweet potatoes. Locally grown citrus and other tree fruits like mangoes and bananas, and occasional imported cookies and sweets, number among the treats popular with children. All the crops mentioned here are cash crops as well as food crops.

The crops Luo and others in western Kenya grow mainly or only for cash include, from highland to lowland, tea (most of Luo country does not reach up into the tea zone, though), coffee, sugarcane, tobacco, groundnuts, and cotton. Sisal is used for marking fields and making rope for home use or sale. Of all these, tea, coffee, and sugarcane are grown on factory plantations and on family or individual farms; tobacco, groundnuts, and cotton are farmed mainly on the family and individual holdings. Pineapples, flowers, and French beans are among the crops involved in an important recent movement for horticultural export.

The cattle, sheep, and goats that Luo and neighboring people keep are best understood as prestigious forms of saving, investment, and for their herders, company — and not just as sustenance. Meat from the larger animals is usually eaten only in times of special celebration (including marriage and funeral celebration, and honored visitations) and pact-making, and for those who can afford it, on visits into towns. Chickens too are saved for special occasions. A few grow caged quail and other birds, and lately, with international aid agency encouragement, caged rabbits.

No discussion of what is consumed in the Luo country and its surroundings should ignore alcoholic drink — traditional (grain beer, nutritious if inebriating), neo-traditional (strong, mostly home-distilled cane or grain alcohol), or factory-made (mostly beer from Kenyan cities). Customs of alcoholic consumption are a matter of stark differences within Luo country and surroundings. Quite a few individuals and families are strict teetotalers (as only some of their churches require), while others suffer seriously from alcoholism and related problems like men's squandering of family income derived from women's and children's work, or entering into fights or perhaps ill-considered land deals. "Light" social drinkers in between seem less common than in some countries.

Luo country, if so it may be called, has one quickly growing city, Kisumu (the lakeside capital of Nyanza Province), one shared with other ethnic groups from near and far. Kisumu's population numbered about 504,000, roughly a quarter of the capital Nairobi's, in the 1999 census (v. 2, pp. 1-116, 1-1). Many smaller towns have grown up around their open marketplaces in and around Nyanza since the early twentieth century. Much of the space in town-built structures is privately owned and rented. A railroad since about 1900 and a network of roads also mostly built shortly thereafter provide access in, out, and around Luo country. The roads, less densely networked than in Kisii or other highland areas of Kenya, remind Luo both of an early colonial history of forced labor and of a continuing infrastructural disadvantage vis-à-vis highlanders near and far. Lake Victoria, also called Nyanza or locally Nam Lolwe, has enjoyed steamer service between Kisumu, Kampala (Uganda), and Mwanza (Tanzania) at times but lately has been trafficked by smaller boats only, powered by sail, paddle, or motor. The lake fishing industry has seen dramatic downturn in recent decades, as a combined result of the spread of the exogenous Nile Perch and of water hyacinth around the shores. Luo miss their favorite fish, *ngege* (tilapia), and many other species they formerly enjoyed; and lakeside dwellers and traders miss the income. But some in recent decades have begun raising such fish in small dug ponds.

Luo, among Kenyans, have long showed a relatively strong interest in Christianity and churchgoing, and an aptitude for schooling first introduced in Luo country by church missions in the first years of the 1900s. The European- and American-based Christian churches that have spread all over Luo country in hegemonies arranged among themselves have been supplemented by ever-growing numbers of African independent churches and prophetic movements, many of which continue to claim Christian faith and allegiance. Islam has also gained a footing in parts of Nyanza, mainly around towns.

Luo have readily accepted the notion of a supreme creator; arguably it was there before any Muslims or Christians arrived, but this is hard to know. Many pray or invoke divinity often in a day. What is certain, though, is that neither the ubiquitous Christianity (or -ies) nor the so far more tenuously rooted Islam has expunged other aspects of indigenous East African faith or practice from the region: not the observance of or sacrifice to ancestors or their spirits, nor the common understanding that witches and witchcraft are about and active. While there more than a few who insist that their Christian or (for a smaller number) Islamic faith has ended the need for ancestral spirits, or that divine protection guards them against malevolent spiritual agency, I have yet met few in western Kenya (or almost anywhere in Africa south of the Sahara) who appear not to perceive, fear, or take measures to guard against witchcraft or sorcery. Divining, herbal healing, and magical action provide both some women and some men with valued sources of income: all the more important if they are elderly, physically weak or disabled, or abandoned by kin.

Luo in my acquaintance have been a peaceful people, but not always or everywhere have they managed to maintain the peace most of them cherish. Episodes of organized violence have taken several forms. A long history of cattle raiding (mostly conducted by young men in armed gangs) has colored their relations with several neighboring groups (Nandi, Kuria, Maasai in particular). A history of border skirmishes over land and leadership has tainted their relations with others. Before and during early colonial times these included southern Luhya, western Gusii, and others still living in areas adjacent to those where Luo predominate.

In more recent decades, and particularly around election times (and in one failed coup d'état in 1982), people of Luo and diverse other ethnic and linguistic identities have been involved in episodic armed skirmishes, massacres, and displacements. These have been organized by various parties with shifting casts of perpetrators and victims—not infrequently involving the same people as both. Most of these incidents have taken place in scattered rural resettlement areas of rich ethnic intermixture. In 2007–8, however, the nation tore itself up more deeply, in city and town as well as country. In one way or another, these episodes have involved not just Luo but also Gikuyu (with Meru and Embu who have identified closely with them), Kalenjin (including Nandi, Kipsigis, and other subgroups), Luhya (in numerous subgroups), and other, smaller groups. This time, within a month or so of the outbreak in the first days of January 2008, several hundred thousand people were thus displaced within Kenya, many to find their only shelter in large tented relief camps, while smaller numbers found refuge beyond the nation's borders.

An immediate effect of the rural and latterly also urban purges was the separation of much of Kenya—already a country of areas heavily dominated by particular ethnic groups claiming them as their homes—into still sharper divisions and more homogeneous ethnic territorial blocks. Another consequence, because or in spite of all this purging, was more suffering, anxiety, and uncertainty for many people about who belonged on what land: effects sure to endure, for some, over generations. These episodes of violence and dislocation are discussed more toward the end of the study, when the question arises whether land titling and claims of private property offer real security of tenure and position.

Overlapping Claims and Seasonal Oscillation

One set of potential misunderstandings needs to be dispelled before going any further. This has to do with the nature of African landholding as "originally" being about "public" or "private property"—or in other terms, about communal or individual rights. Just as interested outsiders have long been wont to assume that African landholding was "evolving" from kinship to territory, or in Maine's terms, from status to contract, many have also been quick to assume that it was evolving from public or communal to private or individual ownership. If anything like the latter supposition was ever true at all, it is true in no simple way. Landholding and access were probably never entirely communal *or* individual anywhere in eastern or equatorial Africa before, or even during, times of European contact. What the discussions have tended to neglect are two issues: overlap and seasonal oscillation.

One of the reasons why concepts like "ownership" mean so little in Luo country or much of rural East Africa is that persons representing different kinds or orders of group hold simultaneous claims, perhaps rights, in the same land. A field a woman claims the sole right to hoe, her husband claims the right to swap, and his father (if he has modern ideas) the sole right to reallocate to his second wife, who has had more children than the first. What Max Gluckman (1965) called a "bundle of rights" is not, in such a setting, merely about "rights" (for these do not guarantee real access). Nor is what he called a "hierarchy of estates" necessarily about hierarchy (since a young adult man and his mother, or an initial clearer and a later long-time tiller, may not agree which of them is senior with respect to a given field). But his basic point holds true, that usually more than one person, in rural Africa, can claim an interest in any given piece of land.

Land tenure in Luo country could never be correctly described simply as communal or individual "property." Before the state attempt to reform land tenure, land that an individual or small family could legitimately claim as their own during a growing season because they had tilled, planted, and weeded it, flipped over to larger units, *dhoudi* or *ogendni,* for any member to have freer access at the end of the growing season, when stubble provided valuable fodder for grazing. Fields were marked, quite commonly, with sisal or other markers, but seldom fenced off, except right within homestead enclosures themselves: most of the growing and grazing went on outside.

The ways Luo move their herds, and their children, around the broader landscape also reflect seasonal changes. The peaks and troughs in the cropping cycle, with its heavy demands at the times for clearing (for men), hoe tilling (for women and men) and, since the 1920s, ox plowing (for men and lately some women left on their own), bird scaring (for children), and weeding (mainly for women), all affect the number of hands available for herding. Families short of hands may farm their cattle out to trusted friends or bring in foster children from the homes of kin or neighbors.[11] Uplanders and lowlanders depend on each other seasonally for grazing ground (more open and abundant downhill) and crops (the "short rains" of October and November are usually adequate to produce a crop only uphill).

One of the subtler aspects of herding on unfenced lands is the quiet role animals play in the redistribution of plant energy and soil nutrients. By being led or allowed to range widely on crop stubble, fallow land, or forest's edge, but then returned at night to enclosures where manure can be collected, or tethered intermittently and strategically on fields needing fertilizing—cows, sheep, and goats help concentrate organic energy where humans need it most. In some circumstances, and in their tacit way, they also transfer it from the fields of the larger landholders to those of the smaller.

Seasonal movements of humans and animals, and seasonal shifts in land usage and tenure, are inimical to bureaucratic regulation and control. Luo yearnings for cultural and political autonomy grow partly from ecological necessity. And their visions of more autonomy find concrete expression in graves and other sacred sites—the places that connect the living and the dead.

This brief sketch of how Luo and their neighbors in the lake basin got where they are, and of how they live on their land, has suggested a series of movements and of adaptations to rising population density. It has also suggested a considerable degree of culture sharing, even among ethnic groups with histories of jostling and competing over land, and of moving into and over each other's territories.

Ancestors of present-day Luo arrived from a supposed starting point or points along the upper reaches of the Nile now in Sudan, to where most Luo people now live in western Kenya. Much remains unknown about the movement, but it is clear enough that it has displaced some people and incorporated others in the process. Some of these may have survived precisely by attaching themselves to Luo and eventually becoming Luo in one way or another. The fortified settlements have come and gone, but just who built them and lived in them, or for how long, still await better evidence. Since these fell into disuse, the general pattern of scattered homesteads has covered the landscape. What may have been a pattern of mixed herding, farming, and fishing has leaned increasingly on the farming part, and over the past century, on town trades and on migration to and from emergent cities and plantations outside western Kenya. Seasonal oscillation between family farming and more open grazing renders irrelevant any simple notions of public or private property in local traditions. And circular migration in and out of the lake basin, over seasons and lifetimes, has challenged any attempts to keep people in confined spaces, geographically or conceptually. Traditional people are modern people too. Divinity, ancestry, magic, and witchcraft—in older and newer understandings—are not detached from land, ecology, or economic affairs but very much a part of them.

There is a social and local political dimension in all this. We now turn to the aggregations by which people in the present-day Luo country in western Kenya have organized themselves and the principles by which they have regulated their land affairs. It is best to begin with the ways deemed their own.

1. Elders recount a historic southward Luo migration along the lake shore, absorbing earlier occupants and displacing others into surrounding highlands. All photographs by author.

2. Mythicized history associates unusual features of landscape, like this rock outcropping, with local heroes who died fighting for land, or with animal or other local spirits.

3. An abandoned *ohinga*, or defensive village stockade, in Kanyamkago. Its builders, occupants, and time of use remain unknown. Thatch and iron roofs of newer houses appear behind it.

4. A Luo style multi-house homestead (of a polygynous family) at turn of twenty-first century, near lake. Small structures are granaries. Sisal plants divide fields.

5. Polygamous families, like this one with some of its children, remain a minority. Kanyamkago.

6. Fallow field open for common grazing. Strip-divided layout on hill reflects lineage divisions. Kanyamkago.

7. Children's farm work deepens ties—and rights—to family land.

8. Even on men's fields, women outwork them in time spent. Men's mortgaging threatens women's and children's land interests.

9. Plowing by oxen (or donkey), in pairs or fours, expands arable fields, raising competition for land.

10. Building house, where bride will join groom's family homestead. Smallest structures are granaries. Kanyamkago.

11. Cash crop estates (here, highland tea) squeezed out many family farms in colonial era, and some rural people lacking good land keep returning as laborers.

12. Lake fishing canoes. Dwindling fish stocks raise pressure on land. Winam Gulf.

13. Upon *buru* mortuary rite, evoking historic skirmishing, mock war party returns with plants symbolizing plunder. Kanyamkago.

14. Widow grieving with husband's clothes, beside new grave and stones marking an older one. Some widows seek stronger rights over lands left to them. Kanyamkago.

15. Luo and other western Kenyans, Christian majority included, prefer burial at home. Note cross atop grave. Kanyamkago.

16. A man's cemented grave in a homestead anchors family claims to belong on land around.

17. Fencing formerly enclosed only immediate homesteads (like one visible in background). Here new fencing closes off lands beyond for first time. Herd-owning neighbors used to at least seasonal access may protest. Near Kisumu.

18. Islamic teaching, reaching inland from coast via cities (here, Nairobi), forbids loan interest, mortgaging, and some speculation.

19. Women on plain near Kisumu. Escarpment of Nandi hills in background long divided ethno-linguistic groups. Resettlement schemes test mixtures.

CHAPTER 4

An Earthly Anchorage

Graves and the Grounding of Belonging

Home is where the placenta is.
—LUO SAYING

M ost scholars who have speculated over the past century or so on the origins of human society have supposed that the earliest, most sparsely settled human societies were organized mainly on the basis of kinship and descent, and that only later, under denser population settlements, did there evolve forms of organization based instead on territorially defined polity. Many have inferred from this premise, as noted earlier, that societies with central political organization were generally more highly evolved or civilized than those without.

In Africa though, most societies combine the principles of kinship and territorial polity somehow in organizing loyalties and authority. Even among people long supposed to typify social organization on the basis of kinship and descent—for instance, Nuer in East Africa or Tallensi in West—one finds some indigenous political groupings based more on place of residence than on biological affiliation. Nor is it easy to find a "modern" state where one cannot find close kin living in clusters, identifying or associating more with each other than with strangers. Moreover, human creativity in fabricating kinship out of affinity and circumstantial co-residence—manipulating genealogies, inventing confraternities—is practically unlimited. Kinship reinvents itself everywhere. Dichotomies like "status/contract," "societas/civitas," or "gemeinschaft/gesellschaft" prove more useful as heuristic devices, as a kind of shorthand, than as analytical categories, let alone as discrete stages of human evolution.[1] Yet the nineteenth-century evolutionists have a point: in some times and places, kinship ties are a more salient form of community and political organization; in others, territorial ones.

What not everyone realizes even now is that some societies "progress" in a direction *opposite* the one that the evolutionists of the nineteenth and early twentieth centuries hypothesized. That is, a society where humans form their most useful and visible political allegiances on the basis of where they live can "evolve" into one where they do so more on the basis of whom they are most closely related to by kinship or descent.[2]

How so? Such transformations have much to do, I suggest, with changes in population densities and competition for resources. Often, in tropical Africa, where an agrarian society with abundant land and fairly free movement and recombination of kin groups finds its land becoming scarcer over a period of decades or longer, its people become more inclined to stay close to one sort of kin or another (for instance, patrilineal or matrilineal), and to subdivide the lands of their parents (or of one spouse's or another's parents) or stay close to them and other kin for security against others who may wish to encroach. In this way, kin groups deepen and broaden, becoming territorial groups too in their intentions if not also their actual settlement patterns.[3] Common descent becomes a more salient idiom of human allegiance. Society becomes *not less "clannish," but more.*

This is what seems to have happened over the past century or so among both Nilotic-speaking groups (notably the Luo) and neighboring Bantu-speaking ones (those now called Luhya and Gusii) in the eastern lake basin. It has happened despite, and in some ways partly because of, Christian (and Islamic) mission influence and colonial and postcolonial rule that often misunderstood, disparaged, or openly condemned kin-based loyalties. Partly it has happened because of the rural crowding that has arisen from territorial confinement of ethnic groups and races as recognized or constituted under colonial authority, and as enforced with identity cards and restriction of movement.[4] Once the official restrictions to movement have been lifted, the settlements have remained crowded. Innovations like the ox plow and new cash crops have also sharpened land competition. The hardening of clan and lineage groups for new competitive purposes has strongly influenced how farming people present their land claims to state authority—for instance, at law courts and in land auctions.[5]

There is another dimension to the change, at once material and symbolic. Ancestral *graves and their placement become more important.* The graves, homestead sites, and clearings of ancestors become place markers for those who can claim descent from them. Whereas in the past people did not build grave markers, using mobile shrines or none at all to commemorate ancestors, now they place cement slabs or build raised monuments atop graves. These, and other remains of ancestral settlement, have become sites as sacred as any: the very anchors of social identity for living persons and groups.

What some observers mistake, then, for primordial loyalties to kin and clan in tropical Africa can be better understood as rather recent historical developments, or refinements, in response to particular ecological, economic, and political conditions that foster competition. What to some seems primitive can be in fact quite modern. Kinship and descent are not new in equatorial East Africa, but some of their uses, extensions, and manifestations are. And the kinds of developments that nineteenth-century sociologists called modern—the bureaucratic, impersonal, anonymous—do not so easily replace them.

The most detailed information available until now on structure and process of Luo land tenure has come from ethnographers of the mid-twentieth century, mostly trained in a British anthropological tradition. Paul Mboya's and Edward Evans-Pritchard's early sketches of Luo "tribe and clan" organization were elaborated by Aidan Southall, Gordon Wilson, Michael Whisson, and others—in Wilson's case with the mandate of drawing up a manual of "customary law" for use in courts. Their accounts remain most useful, but they are not complete. Heavily influenced by the structural functionalism of Bronislaw Malinowski and A. R. Radcliffe-Brown, the training of some, even most, of these ethnographers predisposed them (in their earlier works at least) to look for logical consistencies and continuities in culture and society, and not to place heavy emphasis on material concerns or constraints, long-distance contacts, or changes over time. From their accounts, mostly written in the ethnographic present, it is easy to deduce a coherent picture of bounded, homogeneous societies or "tribes," each with interdependent customs and homeostatic adjustment mechanisms. Viewed in an era that allocates the emphasis differently—paying more attention to rival interests and positioning, national and global influences, cultural disjunctions and indeterminacies, and disequilibrium—the mid-twentieth century accounts, and the people in them, can look rather homogenous, hidebound, and static. Yet those mid-century accounts have much to tell about recurring process, and if their perspectives are rounded out with some earlier and later ones, including indigenous ones, they afford a picture of custom in adaptation. In trying to sketch the picture without judging what is observed, I try here to suggest that there has been a kind of order discernible in it: not a perfect, bounded, or timeless order, not always a self-regulating or harmonious system, but an ordered process nonetheless.

A Multi-Polity People: The Oganda, an Indigenous Form of Clan Federation

Historians and ethnographers agree that Luo-speaking people in Kenya lived without any central, generally recognized political regime at any known time before Europeans came. Arguably they didn't need one.

The largest indigenously recognized unit for political and military purposes was called an *oganda* (pl. *ogendni* or *ogendini*), a kind of federation of clans (*dhoudi,* sing. *dhoot*). Early ethnographers counted more than thirty of them, of which only about thirteen were deemed both Luo in origin and Luo speaking and the remainder had been assimilated or partly so, when Evans-Pritchard visited in 1936 (1965, 208). An oganda was "the largest unit within which all disputes were usually settled by mediation" (Whisson 1964, 23).[6] According to Ogot (1963, 252), Luo ogendni in late pre-European times varied in size from about 10,000 to 70,000 members.

Beyond this, some basic questions remain open. For instance, how formal or hereditary was the position of *ruoth* (pl. *ruodhi*) at its center, and how permanent or context-specific were the councils of elders, are subjects of continuing debate. It seems only a few ogendni, possibly including Alego or Gem north of the gulf, produced hereditary, truly chief-like ruodhi who rose to exert continuous power or influence over others. Within most ogendni, authority since earliest known times has remained more broadly diffused. A family or extended family homestead has typically enjoyed much autonomy. Within the "tribes" or clan federations, both political-military and ritual leaders and their councils of elders in ogendni have typically been weak in authority, with little coercive power in precolonial times as far as is known, and less or none in colonial and independent nation times, when these positions have all but disappeared. Among Luo and related groups, some leaders in the past seem to have claimed superhuman ancestry to bolster their prestige and authority (Herring, Cohen, and Ogot 1984, 129).

Some of these things are matters of degree. Luo in Kenya have looked up to centrally influential and popular political leaders—for instance, "Jaramogi" Oginga Odinga and his son Raila Odinga. They have also tried to breathe new life into a position called *Ker,* meaning something like a central, personified repository of custom and tradition. But never in memory have they had a central indigenous bureaucracy comparable to, say, the kingdom of Buganda across the lake. Not even have they gone in for anything like the colonially encouraged Wanga paramount chiefdom in Luhya country in the northern Nyanza region of Kenya, or the paramount chiefdoms of Ugandan Padhola or Acholi being resurrected, or in the latter case concocted from a memory of earlier competing chiefs, in the early twenty-first century.

Luo in Kenya, that is, have never entrusted their collective well-being to just a single bureaucratic structure or process, or to a single high official. Their authority and prestige today are more diffused—not just geographically, but also by type—between state, church, company, academy, and aid agency, as well as the subtler authority and prestige of clan and lineage heads and elders, of diviners, healers, and prophets. This gives them many persons and entities to pin their hopes on, but many also to hold responsible when things go wrong.

Some Euro-American commentators—for instance, Evans-Pritchard— seem to have wanted to play up the kinship and play down the territorial polities, as if to portray the people as more primitive. Some Luo commentators have reacted by playing up the hereditary offices in territorial polities and playing down the kinship as if to show, on the contrary, how civilized they were.[7] But the argument I propose in this chapter, that segmentary lineages are *not* less modern or civilized than territorial polities with centralized bureaucracy, may obviate such debate and leave more room for scholarly consensus.

Oral and written histories, by Luo and outsiders alike, feature many wars and skirmishes between Luo ogendni, often occasioned by cattle raids, animal damage to crops, deaths attributed to witchcraft from members of other ogendni, or vengeance for these. Contemporary funerary rituals sometimes stage mock invasions across oganda boundaries; formerly these may have sparked real conflict. But since wars stand out in memory more than peace does, available histories have, by compression, left a cumulative impression of constant fighting that may be misrepresentative. In any case, ogendni had buffer zones of no-man's-land (sing. *thim*, wilderness, or *lek*, grazing commons) between them, where none may till but any might hunt. Under the colonial umbrella and under rising population pressure in the twentieth century, most of these buffer zones shrank or disappeared altogether.[8]

Some have called the oganda the indigenous aggregation of most importance to Luo landholding, suggesting that in the past, being a member of one gave one an inalienable right to cultivate land somewhere in its territory. It seems, however, that such "rights" were put into practice only at more local levels.

British colonial government seized upon the oganda, as it understood it, as a natural unit of aggregation through which to govern and to collect taxes. It gave ogendni official recognition as "locations," and in the early 1900s it appointed chiefs to administer them, with powers and duties to conscript labor and collect taxes. Before long these chiefs had their white-washed compounds, flagpoles, and uniforms to remove any doubt about their importance, and elite mission education for their sons. The administrative and judicial duties and privileges of the chief remain too numerous to list. Adjudicating land and livestock disputes — with all the opportunities for personal profit this can involve — is one of the biggest. But disputes have usually passed through other mediators or adjudicants before they reach the chiefs or subchiefs. Such processes tie into broader processes of domestic and neighborhood life. A look into Luo kinship and descent will be necessary to see how people have related to land and each other within their neighborhoods. To do this, it is best to zoom from large scale to small and begin in a Luo home, the conscious root and model for the progressively larger units that together constitute the oganda.

Homestead Development Cycle: Belonging When Living

Homesteads have a development cycle, and so do the families that live in them — along, that is, with occasional sojourners and attached dependents may who join in. Observations from around Luo country show a fairly consistent pattern, the variations in practice arising mainly from crowding and migration.

Luo women traditionally, at least until lately, give birth inside their houses. The afterbirth, including the placenta and umbilical cord, is buried in the brush behind the house, thus becoming a key point of reference to last a Luo lifelong. "Home," it is sometimes said, "is where the placenta is buried" (D. Cohen and Atieno Odhiambo 1989, 25). But one need not really have been born in the house itself for the parental homestead to be an emotional anchor. (In fact many and maybe most today are born in clinics, from where the placenta is unlikely to make it home.) Luo when living away — for instance, in Nairobi — sometimes refer to the parental homestead back in the countryside as "home squared," as Barack Obama learned on his visit through Nairobi and Kisumu to his Luo father's natal home near Ndori (Obama 2004, 369, 374). It means the real home, the home of homes.

Typically after marriage and the birth of a first child, and in any case before that child is old enough to marry, a young couple asks permission of the home's patriarch or other senior kinsman to establish its own homestead, *goyo dala* (or *goyo ligala*), an act performed with several key ritual elements (an axe, a rooster, and fire) symbolically controlling and mediating the relationship between father and son, and expressing the idea of piercing the wilderness beyond the paternal homestead. By the time a couple establishes its own homestead, the in-married woman has usually been farming the land she will receive in her husband's name, under the supervision of his mother. While cultivated land ostensibly passes from father to son, it also passes in actual use from husband's mother to son's wife: this is the subtler, female flipside of patriliny. Formerly, it was expected, and it is still preferred, that the patriarch direct his son to set up his home outside and downhill from the homestead (*dala*). In recent decades, however, many have found no space to do this, and some have either built an appendage onto the euphorbia fence of the paternal homestead, or built wherever they could find a patch of unused ground. But it should not be uphill from the parental homestead, as this breaches a fundamental Luo understanding about seniority.[9]

Particular sons get particular sites to build their homesteads, depending on their genealogical order; and if they eventually marry more than one wife, these wives too take particular positions on the landscape, depending on their order of marriage (and not on age). Once again there is an ideal order in Luo minds. This is symbolically charged. Looking outward from the homestead gate, right is superior to left, center to periphery, and near to far. In theory, then, every male has a position on the ground that corresponds to a position in a genealogy. But once again, under conditions of uneven terrain, land scarcity, and migration, reality does not always fit the ideal cognitive map neatly. How well it does depends largely on the age of the settlement. In some newer-settled areas, the genealogical-spatial correspondences are strikingly clear, and a hillside can seem like a giant kinship diagram, even though inside a homestead one may find attached affines, land clients, fostered children, and maybe overnight guests.

Upon the death of a male deemed a homestead head, at least until recently, his widows have ordinarily been "inherited" by his brothers or gone to live with their married sons or other kin, and the homestead has sometimes fallen into disrepair. But sons, or some of them, have usually stayed on its land and established their homesteads there if land sufficed, the first son of the first wife assuming a position of leadership or influence among his brothers or half-brothers. In this, as in much of Luo life, sequencing is a paramount concern.

In the bed, the house, the homestead, and the lands around it, Luo people perceive an order that is social, spatial, and temporal. They consider both beds and houses to have female and male sides. Homesteads and the lands beyond have uphill and downhill (that is, senior and junior), and right and left sides.

Within a homestead, then, as well as outside, there is an order to who belongs where. The ideal models take concrete form with somewhat more consistency within the homestead than without, since house placements depend less on soil qualities than field placements do. A visitor entering a rural Luo homestead can usually tell which wives and other family members sleep in which houses, and which kitchens and granaries go with which wives.[10] One can speak of all this in the present tense—since it all continues in practice and as a template in Luo minds—but only with the caveat that there seem to have been more and more exceptions under crowded conditions. Traditionally for the first wife, *mikayi,* a house (*ot,* pl. *udi*) is built directly opposite the gate of the homestead enclosure, at the other side, the senior side (uphill if the homestead is on a slope). To its right, looking down toward the gate, goes the house of the second wife, *nyachira,* if and when one comes along. The house of a third wife, *rero,* is placed to the left of mikayi.[11] A pattern of alternation is thus set up, such that if the husband marries more wives, the odds and evens are situated on their respective sides. The forming of "sides" both channels and expresses the pattern of jealous rivalry Luo often expect of co-wives (*nyiego,* pl. *nyieke*).[12] Luo people use the same term for them and it.

Meanwhile, if there are sons who grow to young adulthood, their houses too are expected to be placed in a prescribed space-time sequence within the homestead, in the lower—that is, junior—half of the space. Again, it reflects both seniority and a pattern of alternation. A first son's house is placed inside the right side of the gate, a second's just opposite to it, inside the left, a third's beside the first's, a fourth's beside the second's, and so on. Of course, young men's migrations away and back sometimes scramble the order, but social pressures and mystical sanctions encourage conformity to it. Eventually they and their spouses can establish their own homesteads adjacent to the paternal ones, or away; and at this point personal choice is likely to play an important role.

Outside the homestead enclosure, or (where there is no more enclosure) beyond and before its houses, Luo people have favored a layout of fields that in some ways reflects placements of houses within. The following pattern, as described in Gordon Wilson's work from the 1950s, is still discernable in our times—not just in informants' sketches of their ideals, but also in the allocations of real lands where space has allowed following suit.[13] If there is more than one son in a monogamous homestead, the eldest takes land in front of or to the right of the entrance, and the second son takes land on the left. The third receives land to the right and center again, but farther from the father's homestead. The fourth son, if there is one, goes to the left but farther from the paternal homestead than the second. Further sons alternate right and left. While elder sons might thus receive larger shares than the younger ones, the youngest takes over the personal garden (*mondo*) kept by the father for his own use—as if as a consolation prize.

In a polygynous homestead, land is expected to be allocated in an analogous way: the land that would have gone to the first son, had there been only one wife, goes to the first wife's children, the land that would have gone to the second son goes to the second wife's children, and on it goes (Gordon Wilson 1968, 42). "Linked" wives (first with third, second with fourth . . .) end up on the same sides of the homestead, farming adjacent and sometimes shared plots. The most junior wife's youngest son, assumed otherwise to be the most vulnerable because of arriving so late on the scene, takes the *mondo*, the husband's personal plot. This can all still occur where enough land remains for it, but some shifting and adjusting can be necessary as new wives enter a homestead, and it is a husband's formal responsibility to see that any frictions get smoothed over.

The pattern, in its locally ideal form, suggests this series of linked correspondences:

junior/senior
downhill/uphill
left/right

Genealogical seniority took precedence over age as a criterion for determining shares of land to be allocated or inherited. Thus if a man's first wife had not borne a son until after the second wife had had one, the son of the first wife would still receive the first share. The principle applied at other levels of organization. A lineage leader who sought to exert authority or influence over a leader of a rival, structurally adjacent group might try to prove that the apical founder of his segment was the senior co-wife. In such cases, the placement of abandoned homesteads or current landholdings might be used as evidence.

. . . and When Dead

Just as Luo people assign themselves and each other to particular places in their beds, houses, and homesteads when living, they tend to bury each other's bodies in predictable places when dead.

An honorable death is marked by burial inside the homestead (*dala*); a dishonorable one (for instance, a suicide) or an anomalously timed one is marked by burial just outside, to the left of the gate.[14] Elders in the mid- and late twentieth century spoke of earlier times when Luo buried their dead beneath the earthen floors of houses, but by the 1980s, all or nearly all were buried outside. A man was, and is, conventionally buried outside the doorway of the house of his first wife, mikayi, to the right of it from the vantage of one looking out. That wife's body after she dies is buried to the left of it. Other wives are buried outside the doorways of their own houses. Formerly, bodies were placed on their sides within their graves so that they faced inward toward each other and toward the center of ground in front of the doorway (man with his right side up, with head toward house; woman with left side up, again with head toward house). The analogy

right:left :: male:female

is familiar from different societies in many parts of the world—whether it appeals or not—and can be interpreted as a comment on the putative social superiority of males (Needham 1973), just as the previous analogy can be taken as a comment on the social positions of elders over juniors. Recently, under foreign influence, it has become more conventional to place bodies on their backs rather than their sides; but when they are buried at home, as they usually are, they are still buried in the same places.

Some Christian missionaries from Europe and the Americas have tried hard to persuade Luo to use separate graveyards away from their homes. They know, as Luo know, that the presence of graves inside a home serves as a constant reminder of the dead, and a kind of anchorage for their spirits (*tipo*). Christian missionaries have sought to weaken what some call "ancestor worship" by doing away with the reminders. So far it has not worked. The only people likely to be buried in church or community graveyards are ones with no one to claim them as kin or to transport the bodies home.

Burial siting can be hotly political for Luo and other western Kenyans. The most celebrated case was that of the lawyer Silvanus Melea ("S.M.") Otieno, Luo born and raised, who died intestate at age fifty-five in Nairobi on 20 December 1986, having married a Gikuyu (Kikuyu) wife and lived for much of his career in Nairobi. His widow, Virginia Edith Wambui Otieno, sued for the right to have his body buried at their farm at Upper Matasia, Ngong, near Nairobi, but a group of kin representing his lineage and wider clan wanted it returned to his natal homeland. The "S.M." case seemed to sharpen and polarize interests along practically every axis: living versus dead, Luo versus Gikuyu, ethnic group versus nation, kin group versus individual, male versus female, agnates (kin through males) versus affines (kin through marriage), elders versus juniors, cosmopolites versus local-traditionalists, and maybe executive versus judiciary. Fierce controversy surrounded words like "home," "belonging," or "next of kin," calling into question some of the deepest assumptions of cultures and of laws.

The case froze in the courts, with constant debate, headlines, and letters to the editor outside. Finally, 154 days after the death, upon a decision by the High Court at Nairobi and an appeal to the Court of Appeal, the body was interred with a funeral in Otieno's natal home at Nyalgunga, Nyamila, in Siaya District within the Luo heartland. Because this internationally famous case has been examined in some depth elsewhere, it need not be discussed further here, except to note that it has not been the only case in western Kenya contested in these various ways.[15] Luhya and Gusii peoples, also noted for patriliny, have also been deeply divided by comparable if less widely publicized burial sagas.

Women's burials, while they attract less public attention, are no less fraught with tension and anxiety, since women too can be, as Nancy Schwartz puts it, "active dead or alive." Arguing against some other feminists that "Luo and Luyia [or Luhya] women in western Kenya have not just been 'passive' pawns of 'patriarchal' patrilineal, patrilocal, polygynous ideologies, 'mystified' through the 'cunning' manipulations of men," she notes that women wield their own kinds of power through those very ideologies. When living, they can manipulate kinship structures by moving, refusing to cook, or cursing, for instance. After death, they gain a power of spirit possession—a set of practices and beliefs that some feel the living maintain with reference to the dead, and others think the dead willfully manage. Spirits become vengeful when they have been given a "bad burial"—without proper fire, feasting, prayer, and grave placement. Women participate in the "reciprocity of enmity and aggression,"[16] finding ways to repay dishonor—if they choose.

Luo people have steadfastly continued to bury their dead at home, and many continue to speak of spirits as residing around the homesteads where their descendants live and remember them. The cementing and monumentalizing of graves in recent times underlines resistance to external influence (an ironic expression of it, since it was from foreigners that Luo appear to have acquired the habit of cementing graves in the first place). It also bespeaks the heightened importance of kinship and descent in the reckoning and defending of land claims under conditions of rural crowding and competition for land for tillage and grazing. Luo people, and especially men, have made graves into *tools of territoriality, and anchors of being.*

Luo in the countryside grow up, then, in a world where everyday life powerfully shapes their expectations about who belongs where, and when; and where placement corresponds in important ways to roles in social structure and process.

From a Luo Doorway

One who travels around the Luo country is likely to be asked often, by elders, "*In wuod [nyar] dhoot mane?*" literally, "You are a son [daughter] of which doorway (or clan)?" as a first identifying question. The expected answer refers to kinship, not just place of origin.

Luo and most neighboring people speak of a small family as the germ or prototype of a lineage and clan. While Luo lineages may have female eponyms, they are patrilineal in just about every way: in descent reckoning, marriage payments, virilocal postmarital residence, and most inheritance and succession. To be left without progeny (particularly male, at least if one is male oneself) is for a Luo the worst possible fate, far worse than just one's own death.

Three kinds of key images come constantly into play in verbal if not also visual representations of family and kinship. The first is the womb and birth from it. *Nyuolo,* to bring forth or give birth to, is the root of *anyuola,* a lineage, or people of one birth.[17] The second is the doorway, *dhoot* (pl. *dhoudi*), literally mouth of house (*dho* = mouth, *ot* = house), a term also used for lineage or, most often, clan. Luo wordplay often draws upon perceived resemblances between womb and house.[18] The third image is the branching plant: *keyo* (pl., *keshe*) is a species of tree whose branches ramify in a particularly clear and consistent way, and this term too is used for a kin group, in this case a lineage segment, usually of lower order.[19] The use of body, house, and tree metaphors for family growth and reproduction—familiar from so many other cultures around the world—stitches together what might be otherwise disparate domains into a more coherent view of the world and the human place in it.

Luo like to think of lineages and clans as living and growing indefinitely: "A lineage group of people, once formed, never dies, unless swept away by a flood or other natural catastrophe" (Ocholla-Ayayo 1976, 195–96). Life starts indoors. A family can sprout from the *jokamiyo*, the household or offspring of one woman (and incidentally her male husband or mate), grow into the *jokakwaro*, the offspring of one grandfather (and incidentally his wife or wives)—and keep on growing as women marry in and reproduce over the generations. Speaking as if a kin group extended like a folding telescope, Luo use some of the same terms for smaller patrilineages and larger lineages and clans. Since the usages vary somewhat from one locality to another—and also from one contextual usage to another—it is futile to try to construct any hard-and-fast rule about which terms correspond to levels of segmentation—say (in Meyer Fortes's graduated sequence) to minimal, minor, major, or maximal lineage.[20] The accounts of ethnographers of Luo often look precise but turn out, when compared, not to match up. These authorities tend to agree about which terms ought to be applied to bigger and smaller sorts of groups, but they do not agree where to draw the cutoff lines along the size scale. It can be hard to find two Luo (or even anthropologists of Luo) who assign the same ranges of generations, or sizes of living groups, to all the terms.[21]

The variation in itself underlines the point that terms for lineages or clans can slide up and down a scale of depth or size in Luo minds. Some, like *piny* or *gweng'*, are used most often to refer to settlements or occupied land areas rather than to the people in them, and their inhabitants need not all be related, whether by agnatic or affinal ties. Other terms, like *libamba*, typically refer to people in lineage segments other than one's own—that is, to rival factions. To this must be added the differences between colloquial and technical uses of terms.[22] In all, Luo kin group terminology is potentially confusing, but nicely versatile and flexible withal.

If it is hard to specify the sizes and depths of lineages and clans, it can be equally hard to pin down their leadership. Most who have commented on this speak of ogendni, clans, and lineages as having individual, usually male leaders (for example, *ruoth piny, jaduong' dhoot, wuon pacho*), and of these in turn as having their councils of elders (*buch piny, buch dhoot,* and so on) who served a variety of juro-political purposes. But the truth is that no one committed any serious study of these to paper before they were touched and altered under colonial influence.[23] Only hearsay and distant memories are available to rely upon. This is one more way women, by outliving men, can get some of their own back out from under patriarchy.

English terminology applied to Luo aggregations and settlements, as spread out on the landscape as they are, has been full of inconsistencies and malapropisms. "Village" has been used to mean anything from a *dala*, homestead of one or a few houses, to hundreds. "Chiefdom" and "tribe" have both been used to mean a clan—that is, a large unilineal kin group, or an oganda having a recognized space but no overall kinship unity. For purposes of bureaucratic administration, the English and Luo languages have a hard time connecting. And Luo people have enough anti-authoritarianism in them for some to like it just so.

Descent and Descent Groups: A Few Cautions

No part of the world is better known for lineages and clans than Africa, and the Nilotic region in particular. Since about the 1950s, though, the concepts of descent and lineage have been topics of lengthy, sometimes highly technical debates including some of anthropology's most noted polemicists.[24] There are several main issues of contention. Here let us set out just enough guidelines on these delicate matters to alert the reader to some areas of crossfire and to ensure him or her against some common pitfalls of inference.

Some anthropologists, for starters, feel discomfort with the notion that humans can be born and die within positions fixed by society (what Maine called "status" as opposed to "contract").[25] To find a time or place where life is lived this way, some feel, is to call a people primitive.[26] It harks back to evolutionist theories about early status ascription, and to functionalist ones about social action being mechanically governed by kinship and other social roles. Then African models have been tested, applied, and misapplied in other parts of the globe (New Guinea, for instance) where they usually fit less well.[27] And indeed, some of the models turn out not even to fit very well the African societies (Nuer, for instance) they ostensibly came from.[28]

One way or another, branching ("segmentary") lineages and something more nebulous that has been called the "descent theory" of human group formation have become closely identified with Africa south of the Sahara.[29] Without going too deeply here into a critical literature that has generated perhaps more heat than light, three caveats are worthwhile at the outset. First, as every student is told in introductory anthropology classes, patriliny is not the same as patriarchy, though they can and often do coincide—and they certainly do in the Luo case. The former is basically a principle of descent, the latter one of power or formal authority.

Second, there are different ways of "being patrilineal" (or matrilineal, or ambilineal, or bilateral). Group identification, postmarital residence, naming, and inheritance are four that do *not* always coincide.[30] That these happen to do so in the Luo case, as closely as anywhere, is one reason one can comfortably call Luo a patrilineal people. Residence on contiguous lands is a fifth criterion, and on this, Luo and their near neighbors are not unambiguously patrilineal (nor is anyone anywhere, as far as I know), since far from everyone lives adjacent to agnatic kin.

It helps, third (if the point isn't too arcane) to distinguish "descent," a principle one can liken to electricity transmitted serially between generations, from "cumulative filiation," a mere adding together of a series of discrete parent-child bonds without that kind of transitivity. Not everyone in the world points to descent from common ancestry as the basis of group formation, as Luo so often do. On this point, "classic" African models of descent, like vin de terroir, do not ship abroad well (to highland New Guinea, for instance)—or even over the border from Kenya into Ethiopia.[31]

Finally, in deciding whether any person X's being descended from person Y makes him or her a member of group Z, it is well to distinguish between *necessary* and *sufficient* conditions of recruitment or belonging. In not all parts of the world does descent from a given ancestor make one inescapably a member of a particular group, and in not all is it adequate to make one so.[32] At the risk of oversimplifying, among Luo and their near Bantu-speaking neighbors (the Gusii and southern Luhya groups), patrifiliation is both a necessary and sufficient condition of lineage or clan membership.[33] If you are the son's son's son (or daughter) of Ochieng' (or even a woman Achieng'), and there is a question of who is in and who is out of the lineage of Ochieng' (or Achieng') . . . then you're *in*, like it or not. If not related that way, you're *out*, again like it or not. It takes imagination and fancy footwork (semantically, historically, genealogically) to get into or out of a Luo lineage or clan as a full member.[34] There always remains some ambiguity in the position of married women, however, as these do not relinquish all ties to their natal families or lineages even after moving away.

With these caveats, then, Luo are, and have been for at least several generations, about as patrilineal a people as any reported in Africa or anywhere. It remains now to look at some of the kinds and scales of Luo descent groups, and to see what they have to do with land use and tenure.

Doorways and "Key Units" of Society

Not everyone in Luo country—or anywhere else in East Africa—shares all land freely for all purposes. In following descent groups up the ladder of scale from small household to large clan, it is tempting to assign particular kinds of "land rights" to particular levels of aggregation. Some have asserted, for instance, that it was the dhoot that held grazing land in common (McEntee 1960, 68), or that fishing rights to the lake and rivers could be divided at the levels of the dhoot or smaller lineage groupings (Bond in Kenya Land Commission [KLC] 1934b, 2286). Some have claimed that the libamba (in the meaning of a group, say four to seven generations deep, whose members shared sacrifice—a group of lower order than a large dhoot) was the largest descent group within which individuals could freely swap rights to plots or prevent others from bringing in land clients from outside, or see to it that a stepfather did not usurp the land rights of a widow and her children.[35] Some have said the *keyo* (lineage branch) three to five generations deep was the smallest unit to cohere in a pattern of settlement on extendable parallel strips, or to have an organized council of elders to settle internal disputes.

Of the jokakwaro too, many specific claims have been made. It is said that this was the largest group within which a sole survivor could inherit all the land (Gordon Wilson 1968, 49; cf. Ocholla-Ayayo 1976, 130, 132 n, 15). Each member of the jokakwaro had, according to one source, the right to cultivate land in each part; this was the unit in which Luo would let none starve unless all starved (Whisson 1964, 30, 45). It is perhaps for the latter reasons that

Wilson (1961, 49) calls the jokakwaro (at the smallest, the descendants of one grandfather) and its territory "the key units in Luo society." As if following the lead of Wilson and his informants, Kenya government land officers introduced their program of consolidation and registration to Luo, at least in its early decades, through what they could best identify as the jokakwaro unit. In this they showed more attention to men than to women, for whom the *jokamiyo*, or a woman and her progeny (often living under one roof), was perhaps more "key." Patriliny is surely one key to understanding Luo society, but it is not a skeleton key that opens every door.

This brings us back for a moment to the dala (pl. *mier*) or *pacho*, or homestead, that hive of activity, that nexus of symbolic meanings and sequential processes so rich as almost to defy description.[36] One who looks around the Luo landscape today will identify the homestead as the most clearly visible social aggregation, visible by its houses in a circle or two parallel lines, and perhaps its hedge or symbolic gate posts, and its marked, and commonly cemented, graves. One who is walking on a path, and is asked where he or she is going, is likely to answer, "adhi dala," I am going home; and dala can mean practically everything home can mean.

Luo often speak as though a homestead head (wuon dala) has unchallenged authority over the other members, having the power of the ancestors behind him and the authority to sacrifice to them. (Yet a widow who calls on ancestors may well call on those of her deceased husband.) A wuon dala is deemed the custodian of the group's cultivation rights, and he (or she) claims the authority to represent the group in its biggest dealings with outsiders. Internally, however, the group's land, like its cattle, is divided among the offspring or, if the family is polygynous, among its houses — that is, its wives. The wuon dala is expected to make these allocations, and he may exact labor from all household members for his fields. He is also expected to arbitrate disputes that arise between members of the homestead. But otherwise it is deemed improper for him to interfere unduly with their cultivation rights. Jokamiyo groups can thus live, day to day, largely independent of each other in land matters.

These things are not set in stone. I have suggested that attributing land rights and duties to particular levels of aggregation can be misleading, since smaller and larger groups seem to have asserted new claims when and where competition for land and its resources has risen. Hence, picking the wuon dala as the sole title holder introduces a kind of artificiality into the Luo way of landholding. As the tenure reform has played out, it has mainly been male "homestead heads," *weg mier*, who have received the titles to land, acting ostensibly on behalf of their homesteads and families, monogamous or polygamous, as wholes. Homestead heads act ostensibly on behalf of all members of their homesteads, but in practice they often do so without even consulting them. When they do this with a mortgage, they gamble the rights and claims of their families and dependents, in ways hard for these to know about or control. But we will come to that.

The word for doorway, dhoot, has, as we have seen, a figurative usage in referring to the clan, much bigger than any house or homestead. Now it is time to look at that unit or level of aggregation. It is the largest within an oganda; this last is a kind of federation of clans. Too large and genealogically deep to most allow members to remember all the links connecting them with their eponymous founders (for anthropologists this is the identifying feature of a clan), dhoudi were, and are today, patrilineal and exogamous, that is out-marrying, in theory and practice.[37]

By and large, dhoudi (as clans) are also patri-virilocal. Women move, that is, between dhoudi, and in doing so also frequently move between ogendni (which are *not* necessarily exogamous), upon marriage. These movements, and the visitations (including funerary ones) that ensue, have long been the main stitching binding Luo country together as a whole linguistically, cultur-ally, and socially — to the considerable extent it *has* held together.[38] Although many clans have female eponyms, this does not indicate matriliny, as descent from female founders is still ordinarily traced through males. The dominant clan of an oganda has sometimes lent its name to the oganda as a whole, and weaker ones have sometimes attached themselves to it by genealogical fic-tion.

Dhoudi, like ogendni, have kept uncultivated buffer lands between them in the past.[39] The clans of an oganda sometimes fought each other over land in precolonial times, we are told, but at this level the fighting was expected to involve sticks only, and not spears or arrows. Whereas homicides between ogendni did not require compensation payments, those between dhoudi of an oganda did.[40] Moreover, this killing was ritually dangerous.[41] The elders of a *buch dhoot*, or clan council, are said to have served as a kind of appeals court for disputes between smaller lineage segments in the early twentieth century, until this function was taken over by colonially appointed Native Courts, later called African Courts.[42]

But the clan never disappeared. It remains alive in daily discourse and the reckoning of individual and group identities. It is also the unit that has served as the basis for administrative "sublocations" in Kenya's government in Luo country, and of the land "registration sections" for the nation's titling program there. Even though the assistant chiefs who now head dhoudi are appointed by central authority, and endowed with statutory powers that no similar leader had in the Luo past (such as the power to arrest local beer brewers—part of a persistent campaign of the central government), the dhoot is still the dhoot.

Principles That Slide Up and Down

Relativity, fluidity, and flexibility are central themes that emerge from descriptions of Luo landholding up to late colonial times when the tenure reform was launched. Genealogical seniority and the relative size and strength of lineage segments determined who was considered the senior representative of clans and lineages; his age, wealth in wives, children, and cattle, and general character (intelligence, bravery, generosity) might also make a difference. The leadership of a clan or lineage could shift from one section to another upon a leader's death. British administration and missionary schooling tended to select chiefs and subchiefs on a hereditary basis, singling out individuals to train for the various responsibilities as they grew up, and giving them the important new credential of fluency in Swahili and English.[43] Because this made it harder for groups to change their leaders according to the relative size and strength of lineage segments within them, no longer was it politically so advantageous for competing groups to invite outsiders to come live on their land.

Just as Luo expect some jealous rivalry between co-wives, they expect it too of adjacent lineage segments. Friction is a good term for it, since it captures proximity and rivalry.[44] But it is expected to be contextual. Aidan Southall wrote this passage, reminiscent of Evans-Pritchard on Nuer: "The Luo regard every segmentary relationship as having its symbolic prototype within the compound polygynous family. The essential principle of lineage activity is the opposition of co-ordinate segments to one another, coupled with their unity within the same superordinate, itself in similar opposition to other co-ordinates and bound with them in the unity of a still higher superordinate" (1952, 6).[45]

Anyone who has a hard time grasping the concept of "structural relativity" need only to think of the following analogy. Two sports teams compete locally. But then they unite on the all-star team against another league division at a larger scale. And then these unite in turn with that division too as their league plays against another league (say, town, then state or province, then nation . . .). It is not just Luo and Nuer, but probably all humans, who can turn enmity to amity and back, relatively and contextually, this way. But Wilson, true to the tradition of Evans-Pritchard and Southall, called the *nyiego* concept — the jealousy of structural adjacents — "the most important in Luo law and custom."[46]

In Luo tradition, dispute settlement involved elders chosen as representatives of their respective clan or lineage segments, if at lower levels, or of their clans in interclan disputes within an oganda. Elders with knowledge and authority or influence over land cases were known as *jodong' gweng'* (sing. *jaduong' gweng'*, lit. big one of the settlement). Segmentary lineages formed a kind of ladder, we are often told, for appeals in land cases (*buch lowo*): disputants would begin in the smallest lineages in which both or all were members.

The appeals reported in land cases and other cases of dispute paralleled, or intersected with, appeals in prayer and sacrifice on behalf of families, lineages, and clans.[47] In serious cases involving witchcraft or accusations thereof, the higher levels of lineage or clan leaders are said to have been expected to become involved; and they alone held the privilege and power of prayer and sacrifice to the founding lineage or clan ancestors to restore broad harmony.

The Kenyan government administration has, since Independence in 1963, appointed locally prominent men, such as might have served as jodong' gweng', as unsalaried officials to head so-called ten-homestead (Sw. *miji kumi*) cells. But the size of the units under their ostensible supervision has not remained constant. By the early 1980s some grew much larger. The Kenya government has alternately given authority to lineage and clan elders and taken it away, vis-à-vis its courts.[48]

Much of the Luo clan and lineage subdivision, at least in recorded memory, has occurred in such a way that newly formed segments remained near each other.[49] Where Luo have had space, they have put into practice a characteristic form of settlement featuring extendable parallel strips of land. These show up clearly in aerial photos of the Luo countryside.[50]

Early twentieth-century sources tell how larger-order lineages commonly subdivided on the death of a leader, when tensions over inheritance or succession came to the fore. One of the subgroups, usually the smaller or weaker, might claim lands nearby to move onto, and a new buffer zone be established between the segments' lands. To commemorate this act, a conventional ritual involved cutting a dog or goat in half, dripping its blood on the boundaries, and smearing its contents (chyme) on the chests of the recipients.[51] The rite expressed symbolically the original unity of the groups, on the one hand, and their new separateness on the other.

In recent generations territorial expansion has been all but impossible in most parts of Luoland, discouraging lineage subdivision. So some lineages have grown deeper and larger without spreading or splitting, their members turning to litigation, rather than movement, to settle their grievances. Unsurprisingly, most land disputes in the twentieth century appear to have occurred between co-members of the same smaller-order lineage segments.[52]

Units or levels of aggregation smaller than the oganda were, from the best available evidence, constituted largely on the basis of patrilineal kinship as their dominant or ostensible principle in late precolonial and early colonial times. Most also agree, however, that for patriliny to work in practice—as a principle of settlement, group recruitment, or labor organization—*matrilateral and affinal ties are crucial too.* Some have suggested that anthropologists such as Evans-Pritchard, Southall, and Whisson have overdrawn their emphasis on patrilineal kinship as an organizing principle (D. Cohen and Atieno Odhiambo 1989, 13–15). As to this last issue, I suggest, both sides are right. The segmentary patrilineage pattern should not be projected too far back into the precolonial past, as some have done, but it has *become,* in recent generations, a set of principles second to none in importance to Luo.

No longer, however, can an anthropologist call lineages "the key units in Luo society" without a disclaimer. In some ways, female-centered households rival them—and so, now, do churches, particularly for married women, whose lineage status is more ambiguous than men's, their loyalties divided between natal and conjugal groups.

Women's Roles in Patriliny

Too strict an adherence to formal models of patrilineal descent—in which women are sometimes entirely erased from the diagrams—can mislead the analyst into supposing that women do not matter in Nilotic and East African land matters or related political economy. Nothing could be farther from the truth.[53]

There are several reasons why. Agnatic kinship itself is only an abstraction, since, as Evans-Pritchard once noted himself, men can only relate to their fathers or sons, and hence to paternal kin, through women's childbearing in the first place.[54] Patriliny is not just a men's abstraction and ideal construct, but a women's and children's one too; in western Kenya it is general, though it has its strong detractors, some of whom are women and girls.

Patrilineages, secondly, can have women as their founders—for this is just a matter of drawing arbitrary pyramids with arbitrary apices—and in the Luo country and surroundings, many lineages are indeed named after women at the pinnacles—for instance, the Jokatieno, the lineage (*jo*—people) of (*ka*—the place of) Atieno (name meaning 'female born at midnight').

Third, people grow up in houses. In the Luo country, it is women who are deemed the masters of houses (*weg ot*, sing. *wuon ot*), whereas men are more often deemed masters of multi-house homesteads (weg mier, sing. wuon dala)—except in the case of widows (and then often only temporarily). Whether one focuses on the homestead or house as the basic building block of society determines whether one ends up focusing on men or women as the heads. The picture is not, however, a cut-and-dried one, since the pointed spire pole (*osuri*) atop a house symbolizes a living male head of homestead and also another symbol of male dominion, the homestead rooster; and since the interiors of houses also have their own spaces designated for males and females. But the house and its doorway altogether are themselves strong, polyvalent symbols of femaleness and female domain.

Next, since women are the ones who actually do most of the farm work, the fields that ostensibly pass from father to son in a patrilineal system are more aptly seen as passing in reality from husband's mother to son's wife (that is, from mother-in-law to daughter-in-law). Apprentice farming, like apprentice cooking, forms an important part of Luo family life for a young bride, and it is to her husband's mother that she first reports. Where husbands are away in town or on the plantation, as they have been for decades in a sizeable minority of Luo homesteads, their absence makes their spouses, mothers, and daughters all the more important in daily home, farm, and herd management.

Even among Luo, who are in many ways among Africa's most patrilineal people, matrilateral and affinal ties, which perforce involve women, are likely to determine who entrusts land to whom—and with it, who settles, herds, and farms near whom—during or after the process of marriage. Luo expect ideally that young women will join their husbands in the latter's compounds as part of marriage: a pattern of virilocality and (since young men are supposed to stay put in their paternal homes) patri-virilocality. But it doesn't always work out this way. It frequently happens that a young man who cannot get along with his natal kin, or who cannot find adequate land in or around his paternal homestead, moves to the area of his wife's homestead instead—a de facto uxorilocality—receiving an allotment of farmland from her parents or other members of her natal lineage, or from a neighbor. Since land clients are sometimes known to graft themselves onto the lineages of their hosts by fictions and renaming, patrilines sometimes jump their wires.[55]

By the late twentieth century, Luo marriage with bridewealth appeared to be yielding to increasingly frequent unions without: more and more couples seemed to be cohabiting, and even reproducing, without the transfer of marriage dues.[56] In these cases, the natal relatives of the woman might claim her children as their own—for instance, in the event of a separation or a young cohabiting woman's premature death. In the latter case they could, and sometimes did, contest the male partner's and his natal kin's putative right to determine where she would be buried. If, on the other hand, a woman outlived her husband and refused to be taken over by one of his agnatic kinsmen—another pattern seen increasingly at the turn of the millennium, in the era of HIV/AIDS—she might try to claim his erstwhile lands as her own, at least for her lifetime.[57] At the time of writing, however, the trends of cohabiting without marriage dues and of flouting customs of widow takeover appeared unclear and likely in flux.

A region famed for patriliny, and no less for patriarchy, makes much of its branching lineages. Its home and farm layout, and its lately cemented male grave sites right outside front entryways, are all of a piece with lineage and clan structure and process. They structure family and social life as constant reminders of place in a process and on the land. The sexual and reproductive symbolism of male roof spires and roosters, and female houses and doorways that become lineages and clans, is unmistakable. Real females are born into one lineage but move to another's home upon marriage—or lately, often, upon *not* marrying. Formal models of patriliny may deny women's importance, in the eyes of insiders or outsiders, but abstract models make women and girls no less important to the real business of farming and herding, or indeed to the continuance of a patrilineal idiom of discourse and understanding. Women not only outnumber men but also tend to outlive them, in East Africa as elsewhere. Death and widowhood bring out tensions and misunderstandings, not just between locals but also between them and those from afar, usually men, who set themselves up to regulate or administer them.

That colonial officials in Kenya and East Africa tried to seize on the model of the branching and re-branching lineage as a potential tool for governance may be related to their images of kinship and tribe as primitive forms of social organization. This primordialist notion of the atavistic Africa is not hard to discredit as "invented tradition."[58] And yet the traditions were not made up out of whole cloth. If lineages hadn't been there since the dawn of time, they were certainly coming into being—not out of administrative mandate so much as out of demographic pressure and, for farming people, political and legal expediency. Ancient traditions or not, lineages and clans have come to make good tools for pressing land claims, whether in gradual field encroachments, in court, or in armed strife.[59] But that last topic must wait.

CHAPTER 5

Birthright and Its Borrowing
Inheritance and Land Clientage Under Pressure

It may be that whenever or wherever land gets involved, any family matter is
bound to become more complex, less reasonable, more desperate.
—PETER TAYLOR, *A SUMMONS TO MEMPHIS*

If humans have roots like trees, they are roots that sometimes
tangle and compete with other humans' roots. But a human's
roots, unlike a tree's, can depend on continued connections to other humans
in a particular place. Not just humans, not just their territories, but human
territoriality itself may alter as people move and mix.

Who claims to belong where in equatorial Africa, we know by now, depends on who can trace relationship to whom. We have seen that in the Luo
country, ancestral graves are, or have become, a crucial part of that reckoning.
Not anyone may be buried anywhere, and contests over the disposition of
bodies can become as intense as competition over land.

Strengthened Attachment and Partible Inheritance

Until recent generations, some say, Luo did not look upon particular
pieces of land, or ancestral traces on them, with great reverence, but treated
these in a rather matter-of-fact and utilitarian way.[1] They neither tied down
their cattle, we are told, nor conducted many of their rituals in special groves
or other fixed spots. No one lacked land who needed it, but no one felt inextricable from it.

If this was ever true, it has all changed. To begin with, more than a
few Luo seem now convinced that their people are permanently based in
the Nyanza or lake basin. Their settlement there is justified by the myth of

Mumbo, a giant serpent who led them up the Nile, and who, by appearing from time to time in the gulf, confirms to them that their home is the proper one (Whisson 1962a, 6). As they moved south from Sudan, oral history and geography suggest, they increasingly used the prefix *ka* (the land of, place of) in connecting groups of people to specific places (Ogot 1967, 12; Ocholla-Ayayo 1976, 17). A Luo arguing against some land alienations before the Kenya Land Commission in 1932 claimed, "The land is our mother" (KLC 1934, 2166). Land tenure issues played a major part in Luos' participation in the drive toward independence, through their leaders like Oginga Odinga and Tom Mboya. Michael Whisson generalized, at about the time of Independence, that Luo had elevated claims to land "almost into the realms of Luo religion" (1962a, 6; see also Ocholla-Ayayo 1976, 169; Odinga 1967, 5). Were he to write the same today, in view of the "ethnic cleansing" campaigns that have been about land as much as anything, he would probably drop the "almost." Lately Luo and other western Kenyans, in making sacred things of graves and ancestral homes, and political rallying points of dead bodies, have reflected the increasing importance of agriculture as against herding in their livelihood, and they have sharpened and highlighted a patrilineal principle in economic life—one much disputed in an era of feminist reform. Land matters for the Luo have constituted the hottest political issues of the past century.

Dense human settlement encourages a heavier reliance on farming than herding, and if, as some Luo suppose, their forebears once depended more on herding than farming for their food, there is no doubt which way the wind blows today. For Luo and even for many of their famous herding neighbors to the southeast, the Maasai, and for other people well known for cattle raiding, *la vache cherchée* is now *la terre*.[2] Formerly, Luo disputes over land seem to have been mainly about grazing land and damage to crops done by animals; in recent generations they have been mainly about plot boundaries and inheritance, and since the start of land titling, about farmland sales.

If graves, ancestral homestead sites, and cleared fields make the focal points for land claims, it is because Luo deem land one of the things subject to inheritance and succession. Nothing inherent in soil, rocks, or water makes it so, but human culture and history do. To speak of inheritance, however, is to use a term that only half-fits Luo realities, since much sharing and passing between generations occurs between the living. It also gives an inflated idea of proprietary claims, and of the separability of people and things. People do not just own or inherit land, in an East African way of seeing things; they also belong to it. Belonging to land is part and parcel of belonging to other people—in groups, networks, or open categories. I suspect that *keni,* a Luo term for inheritance, may be a cognate of *kendo,* to marry, and *keny,* bridewealth, the common idea being interpersonal linkage.

The technicalities of Luo intergenerational land transfers, including transmission *inter vivos,* have been extensively described by Gordon Wilson (1961, 35–60 and passim), on the basis of research that he, Luo jurist Shadrack Malo, and Wilson's other informants conducted in the early 1950s. No study so detailed on the topic has been carried out in the nearly half century since that effort to codify Luo "customary law." Much has remained recognizably constant in Luo ideals, if not also practice, concerning land tenure since Wilson's and Malo's time—such things do not change quickly. The use of the manual in courts has doubtless influenced custom in turn, though it has not, as some have claimed, frozen tradition by itself.[3] Here I note only the basics to expose what seem to be underlying assumptions and premises of Luo land inheritance and devolution, adding a few queries and a note or two on historical changes in Luo practice, and some idea of how these fit into a broader picture.[4]

Luo people in rural areas anticipate inheritance before a man's death by letting each son's wife or wives cultivate their own gardens on the land to which they deem the man the principal claimant and rightholder. Each wife is deemed a custodian for the rights of her young sons. Although these sons can be allocated plots at a young age, they do not ordinarily assume full responsibility for their own lands until after they begin their marriages. Sex, age, and stage of the life course, then, govern rights and duties with respect to land as much as anything does. When G. A. S. Northcote, an early district commissioner in South Nyanza, claimed in 1907 that Nilotic Kavirondo (Luo) "females can own no property, being themselves but chattels" (1907, 61), he oversimplified matters, but certainly women's land rights have long been more limited and conditional than men's. Upon a man's death, his senior son, not his widow, is expected to adjudicate any claims unsettled.

Although Luo divide land, and livestock too, in passing it between generations, they bring clear priorities to bear. If a man has "legitimate" sons (that is, those from marriages with bridewealth paid or being paid), all his land rights are expected to pass to them upon his death, even where a widow-heir or another has to hold them temporarily in trust for them. Only if a man leaves no sons can his land pass to his brothers. Full brothers take precedence over half brothers, and among half brothers, priority goes to those whose mother was "linked" to the dead man's mother by a pattern of alternation (first with third, second with fourth, etc.). If there are no half brothers, the rights pass to the dead man's closest agnatic kinsman. Daughters do not figure anywhere in this formal order, since they are expected to have access to land in the homes of their husbands upon marriage. A lot to assume.

Land, Lineage, and Marriage: Fairness Versus Equality

It is clear by now that Luo expect land inheritance to depend on lineage membership. This, in turn, depends on bridewealth payments, since it is bridewealth that makes one the (L.) *pater* (social father) of a child, as distinguished from a *genitor* (biological father). A son born before his mother's bridewealth is paid, called a *kimirwa* or *nyathi ma kimirwa* (basically, illegitimately born child), was not, in the manual Wilson compiled, entitled to inherit his father's land but only his mother's personal gardens — not ordinarily enough to live on. If a man provided the bridewealth for the marriage of an adopted son, however, then the latter, who by virtue of this payment became legitimized as a son, could receive a full share of inheritance from the father (Wilson 1961, 54–55; Ocholla-Ayayo 1976, 131). In the former case the son was not deemed a member of the lineage; in the latter he was.[5]

Similarly, if a woman was inherited by a non-agnate after her husband's death, she lost her connection with the dead man's lineage and with it the right to cultivate any of his former lands. Even if the new husband was an agnate of the dead man, the new husband and his other wives or children (if any) received no permanent rights to the dead man's land as long as any of the dead man's legitimate sons or descendants lived.

Like a number of other East African peoples, Luo have, in the past, practiced woman-woman marriage on occasion: when a man has died leaving a barren wife and no sons, she could marry a woman, who could bear children by the dead man's agnatic relatives. Sons thus obtained could inherit a dead man's land rights.

Underlying all of this is an assumption of patriliny. And "vertical" kinship, that is, ties by filiation or direct descent, seems in all the rule-expectations to take precedence over collateral kinship. In theory (as reflected in the Wilson manual and other texts), this rule could not be bent to accommodate cases of differential needs. A widow-heir and his original offspring could thus not jump the claims of a dead man's offspring even if the former were many and the latter few (Whisson 1964, 35). In practice, however, some of this claim-jumping has occurred through gradual encroachments, through the bribing of elders or court officials, or through courtroom uncertainties about "prescriptive rights."

To the extent, too, that patrilineal inheritance depends on bridewealth, and bridewealth depends on living animals, patriliny is vulnerable to drought, disease, and plain poverty. Marriages get postponed in famines, but some children continue being born. Patriliny is just a working model, to which not everyone, or everyone's actions, will ever fit.

Societies deemed egalitarian in one way can also be, in another way, deeply hierarchical. But does inequality imply unfairness? Luo custom may help us understand the difference.

Land rights devolved or inherited between generations have, in the past, been considered inalienable—that is, tough to take away. Once a wife begins to cultivate a plot allotted her by her husband or his mother or father, and once the husband has built a homestead on it, not even the husband's father was considered to have it in his right to take the land away, except in cases of a junior family member's extreme antisocial behavior leading to ostracism or expulsion. If a man dies having made explicit his will, his decisions do not lose force—at least in Luo ideals. Indeed, they gain.

Written sources disagree on whether landholdings of sons are expected to be divided equally or not—partly because not all distinguish between land and cattle in discussing "property."[6] In my observation, though, senior wives and senior sons more often than not end up with larger shares of land on the whole than junior ones.

Here it may be helpful to distinguish between *fairness* and *equality*. While most Luo patriarchs aspire, I think, to keep peace among their co-wives and among their respective offspring, equality is not always the easiest way of doing this. Senior co-wives *expect* bigger shares of land, as of cattle and other movable things; they look upon junior wives as beings whom they, through their efforts in home and farm management, have helped procure for their husbands and themselves.[7] A fair decision takes expectations into account, as a strict arithmetic equalization does not. Equal shares may not amount to equal satisfactions. And then, the passage of time changes things. Where a junior co-wife out-reproduces her senior one, her offspring are unlikely to remain content with shares that were smaller to begin with and continue to shrink. Also, if pressure of intensified farming and shortened fallows damages the more crowded land, shares that started out equal become unequal in *quality*.

Since equality can differ so much from fairness, and is so evanescent over time, it becomes easy to see why land comes so often under dispute and why men and their families so often find it expedient to move away from their agnatic kin. It is also easy to see why land lending and entrustment (as to jo-dak) are so important—and hence, why, after the passage of a generation or two, disputes arise over who got there first and whether the latecomers were invited temporarily or permanently. Migrations to towns, to plantations, or abroad help solve some of the problems but complicate others, since migration of one son (say) but not of another can make equal shares seem unfair.

Seldom, anyway, are land disputes just about land. What Michael Whisson wrote of Luo in 1964 remains no less true today, that a case thoroughly examined "usually reveals a mass of social tensions, witchcraft accusations, affinal relationships, alliance against common enemies in the past, all of which are brought into the conflict either as issues or evidence" (p. 87). Witchcraft, and accusations about it, have *not* gone away, in Luoland or in most of tropical Africa. Like lineages and ancestral graves, witchcraft has its own ways of being modern.

In Luo country, no less than in Tennessee, what novelist Peter Taylor wrote also holds true: the involvement of land can make any family affair more complicated and fraught. It remains to be asked, in later chapters, whether money, a market, and the mortgage make it any less so, or only more.

Belongers and Strangers: *Weg Lowo, Jodak,* and the Hierarchy of Egalitarians

"The land is our mother," say some Luo; but it is a mother they sometimes agree to borrow and lend.[8] Upon solicitation or invitation and by acceptance, they entrust to others the rights and duties, and allow them some of the fruits and the feelings, of using and residing on it. But they do so carefully, not just freely or randomly. Borrowing or lending land as an individual or group means taking on an important set of roles and relationships. While more than a few commentators have called Luo society "egalitarian" because of what they perceived as its "acephaly" and an ethic that favors sharing of food and other things, there is a sense in which Luo are profoundly hierarchical. This sense has to do with land and belonging.[9] In this respect, Luo people seem much like others in every continent: whether having arrived first puts you on the top or on the bottom, it is likely to place you in some sort of formal or informal hierarchy.

In and around Luo country, one is a first-class citizen if one belongs where one is by virtue of being a Luo first arriver or a descendant of one who was. (It also helps to be a senior male.) If one can demonstrate that one's patrilineal ancestors cleared a place of wild brush for first settlement, or cleared it of members of Maasai, Nandi, or other ethnic groups deemed enemies—one enjoys the status of *wuon piny* (pl. *weg piny*), master (lit. also father) of the land, or *japiny*, man of (this) country. One may also be called *wuon lowo* (pl. *weg lowo*), master of the land or soil, or *jalowo*, person of the land. Terminology varies somewhat, but the basic idea is the same.[10] A wuon lowo is a belonger.

If, in contrast, one is known to have arrived there by one's or one's fore-bear's begging or borrowing land, one is known as a *jadak* (pl. *jodak*). Perhaps best translated as "land client," but referring to much more than land, the term has no adequate English equivalent. Literally meaning one who dwells or stays, it connotes something more like "squatter," with much the same indignity implied. One does not call another "jadak" to his or her face, but at most turns to politer euphemisms like *jawelo* or (ja)*wendo*, visitor—honorific yet still a little alienating.

The distinction between wuon lowo and jadak is fundamental in Luo so-cial and political life, and a proper study of all its meanings and ramifications might fill a book in itself. The relationship does not typically depend on any written or even oral contract, and the invitation to use or reside on land is usually made for an indefinite period. But that does not make the tie or the status differential any less real. No Virginia "first family" scion, no Daughter of the American Revolution, feels more that smug sense of quiet entitlement or privilege than a Luo wuon lowo does at home—or risks more resentment either. The western Kenyan variant is not a class difference per se; it is a subtler, more situation-specific sort of distinction and contest of superiority that are at issue. The wuon lowo/jadak relationship is a matter loosely akin to that between nobles and commoners in some other parts of the world, or to that of ranked castes in others—but such analogies can easily mislead, not least because the public recognition in any particular case may not be as wide, and because the sets of reciprocal entitlements and obligations are likely to differ. The Luo relationship is, anyway, one more social and symbolic than economic, and hard withal for anyone to ignore.

These things can change over time. Insofar as Luo traditions can be discerned from ethnographic descriptions that may have helped create or cement these in the first place, persons asked to host land clients seldom refused them in times past, when land was more abundant, but used grants of land and place to attract followers.[11] Things have tightened, but not eliminated, the position of the jadak. All over Luo country, and over the densely settled parts of the wider region, there are people who divide themselves in their various tongues into natives and strangers, hosts and guests, belongers and — well, others who want to belong. It applies in Luhya, Gusii, and Kuria countries adjacent to Luo country; in central Kenya in Gikuyu country; and among other densely settled groups thereabouts.[12]

Many people deemed by their neighbors to be jodak either do not freely admit their status as such, or contest it. In our Kanyamkago subsample of 107 farmers, mainly Luo speaking, who were interviewed about landholding, only 2 percent, when asked how their domestic groups had acquired the main land they were using, said they had borrowed or been entrusted it. But among the 10 percent who said they had inherited it, the 24 percent who said they had received it by gift, and the 24 percent who said they had cleared vacant land, there were many whose domestic groups, on further conversation or cross-checking, turned out to have borrowed their lands at least initially as jodak.[13]

Jodak have not traditionally been allowed to build permanent (cement) houses or plant trees, let alone bury their dead on the land they occupy; for doing any of these implies a claim to permanency and does much to justify it. Unlikely to be given much voice or central position in big celebrations or other public meetings, a jadak is subject to stricter codes of good behavior than a wuon lowo, under penalty of ostracism and expulsion by a meeting of elders of the host lineage or clan. A jadak might also be asked to perform undesirable farm tasks like slaughtering a cow or removing a dead donkey.[14] Or a jadak might be given an assignment like "purifying" an unattractive widow by sexual intercourse to ready her for "inheritance" by one of the dead man's brothers or clansmen. Or more striking still to the outsider, he might be requested or compelled to have sex with the corpse of a woman who died with an unconsummated marriage before she could be buried. This last is deemed a necessary if unpleasant emergency measure, in many Luo minds, for some male (it matters less who) to be somehow induced to carry out, as a matter of maintaining the proper sequence of life in families and conforming to a more general order of existence.

A jadak's subordinate, tenuous position among weg lowo is symbolized by the common understanding that no jadak is to put up a roof spire (osuri) on his house, that sharpened stick pointing skyward that carries phallic and other evocations. A structure of metaphors suggests itself:

lending/borrowing
strength/weakness
permanency/transience
seniority/juniority
masculinity/(?)femininity or sexual neutrality

The greater point here is that positions on the land are tightly tied up not only with social position broadly understood but also with some of the most intimate, emotionally charged dimensions of personhood and pride. Whether the particular alignment of the practices and implications suits all tastes in an era of feminist activism and consciousness raising, and one of sporadic violence over resettled land, is another matter—and someone who chooses may make a great point of this too.[15]

The position of jodak is neither absolute, however, nor necessarily permanent. Weg lowo have customarily discouraged or forbidden jodak to invite others from outside onto the land as their own jodak, and some box them in by placing them between the weg lowo's own sons' or other kinsmen's fields on the land to make sure they don't. But some jodak *are* tempted to invite others along and do it anyway, just as they are tempted to bury their dead or plant trees where residing. Luo oral history, and bits of the written, are full of cases where jodak who eased in on amicable terms gradually came to outnumber and even sometimes crowd off the land their erstwhile hosts, a bit like the cuckoo who takes over another bird's nest to breed.[16] This common knowledge might discourage anyone from ever inviting any new jodak to live near one, were it not that jodak also provide potential mates and marriage partners (as *oche*, affines—these statuses often merge), often at a reduced rate of bridewealth or marriage dues in view of their humbler status. And that they can be expected to rally for support in neighborly disputes or fights, or in court trials, that might arise about other things. These are tests of loyalty—and of numbers.

Short of inviting in a crowd of followers to anchor a claim, must a jadak remain a jadak forever? This question of permanency and time limitations for jodak has given rise to heated debates and reversals of law and policy. The code of Luo customary law compiled by Gordon Wilson, with the help

of committees of local elders, completed in 1954 and published in 1961, pronounced itself firmly on the side of Chief Jonathan Okwiri, that "in the Luo
custom the tenants (*Jodak*) are tenants forever, even if they were good tenants and helping the owner of the land, and that does not allow them to natu-
ralize as clansmen."[17] The law code lamented British colonial administrators'
attempts to "introduce" the notion of "prescriptive rights"—that is, claims
that solidify over time into ownership. The issue might have seemed settled:
a jadak was a jadak for good.

But no. In 1968, five years after Independence, the National Assembly
debated and passed the Limitation of Action Act, limiting to twelve years the
period for starting legal action on old claims, including lawsuits over land.
The national ruling had unintended consequences. As Amos Odenyo has described, within five more years, the courts were clogged with new land cases
as weg lowo scrambled to claim land back and jodak pressed to formalize
their claims (Odenyo 1973, 776–77). All this occurred as the Swynnerton
Plan for individualizing tenure rolled out from central to western Kenya,
dividing Luo opinion about titling and individual ownership altogether. That
is a story to come, and it will get more explosive still.

But one can already say that the flexibility in traditional Luo patterns of
land allocation is hard to capture in statutory law, and that the question of
whether land borrowers and clients may establish more permanent claims
over time is hard to settle with bureaucratic decisions. On this fundamental
issue of human territoriality, in East Africa or anywhere else, law—however
necessary it might be—will never be any substitute for kindness and tolerant
accommodation between newcomers and old.

Multi-Plot Landholding, for
Ecological and Social Reasons

If people cling to places, not everyone clings to, or perhaps belongs
in, just one. Western Kenyans, like many other East Africans, have long
deemed it wise to diversify their sources of livelihood, within and beyond
farming.[18] Part of their strategy is to diversify the fields they farm as individuals or families; another is to make sure they plant diverse crops with
different requirements in terms of soil types, timing of peak labor seasons,
and so on. Planting on several separated plots within walking distance, with
different slopes, different sand, clay, and loam mixtures, and different shad-
ing and drainage makes much sense if the aim is to guarantee some sort of

harvest where drought and flood are twin risks. If the cotton in the valley fails, the maize or millet toward the hilltop may yet succeed, or vice versa. Thus Whisson, just after Independence, when most homesteads had two to four separated plots, noted "many illustrations of differential disaster over the past two years" (1964, 99–100).[19] Where moving clouds dump their rain in torrents, and hail falls in bruising barrages, often over sharply limited areas, as they do in western Kenya—it is not hard to see the sense in spreading bets.[20] There are other reasons, too, why farming people in the lake basin spread out their holdings. It helps add a variety of foods in the diet. Some observe that a patchwork of varied crops makes it harder for army worms and other "pest" populations that specialize in a plant species to move from field to field.

Then there are social reasons. Life in a Luo homestead can be socially intense, and some like a temporary respite from kin and affines. Others, contrarily, find the act of lending a relative or friend a small piece of land a friendly act that cements a tie, perhaps in a leveling way. Luo patriarch Oginga Odinga, always conscious of wealth differences, wrote, in his reminiscences of growing up, "the very dispersal of plots worked by one family was deliberate and a form of equality" (1967, 14). A subtler reason, or function perhaps, is that moving one's cultivation around from one bit of land to another, and letting others cultivate fields one has left fallow, proliferates claims in that land, and in doing so, makes it socially harder for any individual to exchange it away to a stranger.

Finally, political-economic reasons. Some appreciate the fact that having scattered holdings makes it hard for others, including government officials, to keep track of just how much land they have, and what they have planted on it. This has been a matter of much importance where official purveyors of "agricultural credit" have tried, by using crop buyers with monopsonies, to collect repayments in kind, and through extension agents, to monitor how much farmers have planted.[21]

Agronomists and economists trained in European or North American traditions have typically seen these things differently from farmers. They use the term "fragmentation" for the pattern of landholding they encounter in western Kenya, as though a proper landholding must be a unified farm. Agriculture Department and Ministry officials have expended much effort—particularly since the nationwide tenure "reform" began in the 1950s—in trying to persuade Luo and other western Kenyans to exchange their "fragmented" plots for consolidated ones. They have commonly cited efficiency of mechanization as a main reason. But agriculture on hills, such as where many Luo and western Kenyans live—and under population pressure they have had to farm increasingly steep ones in recent decades—is hard to mechanize anyway. Agricultural officials know this. A major underlying motive for many, clearly, has been to make it easier to extend their surveillance and control.[22]

To be sure, the advantages of dispersed landholdings apply only up to a point. Disadvantages include time spent walking between fields; the difficulty of scaring birds, rodents, or monkeys away from them all; and the increased likelihood of boundary disagreements with neighbors (since there are more boundaries with more neighbors).

But western Kenyan farmers have continued to feel these concerns outweighed by the risk-spreading and attention-avoiding advantages of diversifying, and one occasionally finds a farmer with more than a dozen small parcels, sometimes on loan, around and about a neighborhood.[23] Most have steadfastly resisted consolidation of holdings, even where allowing the government to title their land as private individual property. Not all parts of a multi-plot holding carry the same symbolic meanings for them, of course, that their homesteads (*mier*) and their forebears' abandoned homesteads (*gundni*) do. Lately, when western Kenyans have sold off land, they have tended to hold onto their homestead plots—the most sacred—until last.

Demography and Dynamism

If there may be something innate about territoriality, in the sense of welcoming others near or fending them off, there is nothing much innate about the kinds of political aggregations people form to defend whatever they deem their turf.[24] Nor does any of this necessarily correspond with races or ethno-linguistic groups. The striking similarities in land use and tenure systems evident to one who criss-crosses the borders between Nilotic and Bantu speakers in western Kenya attests to this. Among "Nilotic" Luo or "Bantu" Gusii to the southeast and Luhya to the north, one finds patriliny, partible inheritance, virilocal postmarital residence, and a pattern of cultivating family lands in extendable, parallel strips. In all, we find branching (that is, "segmentary") patrilineages to be the predominant pattern. And in all, we find sharp distinctions being drawn throughout rural neighborhoods between early comers and latecomers, analogous to those between Luo weg lowo and jodak. All these things were well-established traditions by around the start of colonial rule at the beginning of the twentieth century, to judge by what we can learn from the colonial anthropologists who began studying these societies in the early to mid-twentieth century. They were all part of what colonial administrators found they had to rule over and through. These societies had, by then, very densely settled populations, by African standards. By the 1962 census, on the eve of Independence, most of their home areas were recorded already to have densities well over 100 people per square kilometer (or 259 per square mile), with more local densities up to 500 per square kilometer (1,295 per square mile) or more—when Africa's overall average was only around twenty. Nowadays they all average far higher. Nyanza Province's average density in the 1999 census was 350 per square kilometer (the nation averaged forty-nine), and in some of the Gusii-speaking districts in Nyanza and Luhya-speaking districts in adjacent Western Province, densities rose to over 700 per square kilometer (vol. I, p. xxxiii), some of the highest of all parts of Africa deemed rural (some have even begun calling these areas of tightly settled farm-homes "rural cities"). Striking, in the Luo country and all these other adjacent, densely settled areas, is the attention paid to graves and abandoned homestead sites as markers of family or lineage belonging.

By contrast, around the northern and southern sides of the lake, where rural densities were and for the most part still are much lower, appeared quite a different pattern. Political organization in most of these areas, in late precolonial and early colonial times, was based more on hierarchies of hereditary political offices, over territorially defined populations. Here one found kingdoms (among Nyoro and pre-urban Ganda, for instance, to the north) or chiefdoms (among Sukuma, Nyamwezi, and other groups to the south), with local headmen as junior administrators. These had strong authority of command, and jural codes enforced over wide areas. In these areas it was only the kings, chiefs, and headmen who traditionally claimed the status of original settlers; and all others—that is, nearly the entire public—were deemed temporary dwellers on their lands. And indeed, they often enough were; as land was abundant enough for people to move around more freely than they could where densities were higher or competition more intense. People ordinarily cultivated their lands as square-ish or more irregularly shaped patches, rather than as long, thin, rectilinear strips arranged according to relative kinship positions, as found around the eastern side of the lake. Over large areas of these sorts—for instance, in Sukuma and Nyamwezi countries—burial was not customary until around early mission and colonial times; hence graves were not used as those crucial markers of attachment and belonging that they were becoming in the denser-settled areas. It was easier to move away from the ancestors if you knew you could easily get land somewhere else, where the chief and/or headman was only too happy to have you there to boost his numbers, contribute labor to public projects, add to his tributes of honey, beer, or ivory, and help scare away the wild animals. Rural populations in these areas, as measured by district in a 1957 census, still averaged only between about five and twenty-five per square kilometer (thirteen to sixty-five per square mile).

It is the density of settlement and the competition for land, more than a people's ethnic origins, that influence their way of allocating land, arranging themselves on it, and forming political aggregations.[25] As evidence, one can point to times and places in which rising populations led to increasing restriction of land to agnatic kin (that is, kin related through males), and lineage and clan organization sharpened as something actually visible on the ground. This was true for Luo, Gusii, southern Luhya, and others over much of the eastern side of the lake over the late nineteenth century (as far as one can know of it) and early twentieth; just as it happened to Kiga, another society with prominent lineage organization across the lake in Uganda. Or Nyakyusa, a people living in volcanic mountains in southern Tanzania. Among Suba, who migrated from the Ganda and Soga areas of southern Uganda to the Kenya-Tanzania border area where their densities rose, hierarchical political offices disappeared in a process of rising density and competition for land.[26] By contrast, in some other areas, where epidemics or war caused *de*population, something like this happened in reverse. Nyoro in Uganda, for instance, were remembered to have had tightly localized lineages until a wave of epidemic and related misfortunes brought about a period of demographic thinning in the late nineteenth century, and their lineages dispersed over the newly freer lands (Beattie 1957, 323–34).

The presence of localized lineages does not necessarily prevent a hierarchical chiefdom or kingdom from developing, or vice versa. There are many mixed cases in Africa, some of them on the western and southwestern side of the lake, including in Rwanda and Burundi. The main point is that it is wrong to think of lineages as just an archaic leftover and chiefdoms, kingdoms, and states as necessarily more modern. Up to a point, rural crowding encourages men to stay home and subdivide parental land holdings—and to do so repeatedly over generations—and this is how localized lineages form, with or without any overarching political structure or regime. Beyond that point, as in recent times in Gusii or southern Luhya countries, where farms become too small to support the families living on them, most young men need to migrate to find paid work or new land to farm far away, and the correspondence between places on the land and places in a genealogy loosens up again.

One can expect more parts of rural Africa to undergo processes like these if populations continue rising, as seems likely. In these ways recent history in the eastern lake basin, with its unusually high densities, probably offers a reasonable glimpse at the future of many other parts of the continent.

A unilineal kinship system contains a double edge. It can, for those who know it well, serve as a useful tool (more useful than a bilateral, or cognatic, one like a Yankee or "Eskimo" system) for mobilizing large groups. Basically, in a unilineal system, either you are a descendant of a given ancestor or you are not. Those who know who descends from whom—or who agrees on it—can use the principle to recruit labor to clear a path or build a bridge, to amass a gallery of supporters and witnesses for a court trial, or to garner votes for a parliamentary election campaign.

But for those who do not know it well, or cannot manipulate the nuances of language involved, the same system can be an administrative nightmare. The sliding and overlapping nature of kin groups and their terminology confounded early British administrators (and in Tanganyika too, no doubt, German ones) at the turn of the twentieth century who sought to identify indigenous "chiefs" through whom they could govern. Just about every elder they spoke to could claim to be chief of someone or something . . . and did.

Later, as agricultural officers and others sought spokespersons for indigenous views on proposed land tenure "reform," they had trouble identifying representatives of lineages and clans, and as often as not ended up taking the words of their interpreters or expatriate missionaries as local truth. After Kenya's sweeping tenure reform was begun in the 1950s, demarcators and adjudicators had a hard time setting limits on who would legitimately claim an interest in a particular holding by virtue of kin group membership.

For a century and more then, in Luo country and western Kenya, those who have sought to identify clear-cut landholding groups with fixed offices and leaders have kept finding the ground shifting from under them. The same principle that can serve so well to mobilize a fighting force or work team is double-edged. It can also serve to pry a country loose from its colonial masters, or keep it at arm's length from a central government or an international aid agency.

Drift Toward a Market?

Traditionally, Luo and their ethnographers like to say, Luo people did not sell, rent, or mortgage land. Many would like to leave it at that. To take it further is to distinguish rule from practice, or norm from contravention. On rules and norms, most would agree, to the extent that Luo had rules and explicit conventions about landholding, it was not, until well into the twentieth century, considered acceptable to transfer land, temporarily or permanently, for money or anything like it. And many have said, too, that before that it just did not happen.[27]

But there is evidence that some of this did happen at some times and places during, if not before, early European times, and well before the official land titling movement swept Kenya. One piece of evidence is that there were people trying to prohibit it. In Kanyamkago, I was often told in the early 1980s, the last *jabilo,* who died very old during the rinderpest epidemic in about 1890–92 (Butterman 1979, 100), had laid a curse on anyone in his oganda (or perhaps just his clan) who might sell land to an outsider; and at least some people still feared it might be effective. Likewise Elspeth Huxley reported at the end of the colonial period (1960, 101) that a dying Luo man might lay on his heirs an oath that bound them to his land forever, an oath that would destroy any one of them who sold it to an unrelated person. Whether it was only old men who cared to keep land untouched by commerce is harder to tell. Certainly senior men had, and continue to have, much at stake in keeping lineages intact, but present-day evidence suggests that women and youth have long been keenly concerned with keeping individuals—read individual men—from selling, renting, or mortgaging the land out from under them.

There are a hundred ways for sale, rental, and other market-like transactions of land to enter a country or society—even at the source of the Nile. Despite the widespread image of Luo as socialistic traditionalists, there is no evidence that Luo did not devise their own ways of transferring land for money. Certainly, swapping and longer-term entrustment of land are customs as old as any in Luoland. Those who did not share with needy kin risked not only malicious rumor and possibly accusation of witchcraft but also ghostly vengeance after the latters' death.[28] "The cardinal principle of Luo land ownership," wrote cultural conservative Oginga Odinga at about the time of Kenya's Independence, "is that land was transferable for use in the community" (1967, 14).[29] It is not a long stretch from local lending or swapping to renting or pledging, or to transfers involving strangers.

Another way is by seepage. By the early colonial years, the early 1900s, Luo who went to live among some other peoples—for instance, the Luhya to the north—found that they could obtain land there by rental. They did so to the consternation of Luo kin and neighbors back home, who were, however, powerless to stop them.[30] Renting and selling are reported to have before long caught on back home, in areas adjacent to Luhya country, or in the crowded Nyabondo Plateau (DeWilde 1967, 130–31). Missionaries, government officials, and Indian and other immigrants entered Luo country with cash for land—for instance, for the golf course next to Kisumu, which local herder-farmers continued to use as grazing—and often it was only through intervention by chiefs that individual Luo could be kept from selling the rights or claims that belonged at least partly to their lineages or clans.[31] Throughout the colonial period, Luo-staffed tribunals continued to insist that land pledges were redeemable, but it seems that their treatment of actual cases became less and less consistent under new economic and demographic pressures.[32]

Surely the introduction of the ox plow in the 1920s was part of what led Luo and neighboring people to experiment with new or forbidden forms of land transfer. Those with and without plows entered share contracts of different sorts, as they do today, ostensibly (at least) for mutual benefit.[33] Cash crops like cotton and sugarcane, and the introduction of new markets for food crops like sorghum and maize, doubtless played their part too by raising land values and by enriching some farming people far more than others. No society today is "pure" of market or market-like transactions, and I suspect the economies of most have been more impure, and for longer, than commonly acknowledged.

Ever Evolving

Current challenges to patriarchy, bridewealth, and "widow inheritance" are, in Luo country as elsewhere, also challenges to received rules of about land tenure, succession, and inheritance. It will not be surprising, though, if many of those most rebellious in youth eventually make their peace with an older order and even become its stauncher defenders. This pattern in the life course is an old order itself in Luoland, as most everywhere.

The involvement of Luo people in urban migration and landholding brings into play a wide set of expectations and presumptions not discussed here, more closely tied to statutory law because of easier access to legal authorities and because of rich ethnic intermixture in towns and cities.

At present, the devastating effect of the HIV/AIDS epidemic is leaving many elder kin and younger kin of disappearing young and middle-aged adults with land rights and claims beyond what they would otherwise have expected. Questions of custodianship for the land rights of the very young, and of generation-skipping in inheritance, can only become more salient, and perhaps rules about these will sharpen further. But the overall effect of the epidemic on evolving landholding tradition is still hard to tell.

In the formation of human attachments to land in Luoland and western Kenya, as outlined in this and the foregoing chapter, several kinds of principles stand out. Luo use birth order, marriage order, patriliny, affinity, generation, and the distinction between land hosts and land clients as key ways to classify people and assess their belonging. They also use friendship, which may or may not overlap with kinship and residency. *Whom* one belongs to has been, until now, part and parcel of *what* one belongs to. Ideologies of attachment are social and material in the same breath. Where you belong is who you are—at least until money, the mortgage, and the state enter the picture.

Most Luo who take over rural land from living forebears now do so before the latter die, and under their direction. Luo favor lineal over lateral inheritance—that is, sons inherit before brothers. And inheritance is partible: up to now, all sons have been expected to receive portions of a father's land, no matter how small the holdings may shrink in successive generations.

The patrilineal descent groups that Luo recognize can be understood as a continuum from the jokamiyo (or elementary family, a mother and her children) to the largest-scale clan, and the continuity is marked by the application of the same terms, like anyuola, dhoot, and keyo, from smaller to larger scale. Luo use birth, house, and branching—the concepts behind these three—as recurring metaphors in indigenous idiom as well as in ethnographic representation. Their Bantu-speaking near neighbors, the Logoli (Maragoli) and Gusii (Kisii), do likewise in their own tongues, and form comparable sorts of kinship-based land settlements, regardless of origins.

While Luo could, at least when first contacted by Europeans, be called a politically decentralized ethnolinguistic group, it is not quite accurate to call them (or their neighbors) "acephalous," since nominally at least, kin groups and political groups at various levels had individuals they turned to for leadership, and councils of elders, some with specialized roles in "medicine" (as magic, divination, or chemistry) for war-making, peace-making, or other purposes. But in a sense their decentralization was extreme: the stool, spear, and shield of a senior man in each dala were, as much as anything in Luoland, symbols of *sovereignty;* and while no longer found in every Luo dala, they remain respected as such today. So does the still nearly ubiquitous roof spire stick.

Luo understand time, space, and social position to be intimately bound up with each other. The placements of houses, fields, and graves all reflect this understanding. Like the placement of houses within the homestead, the pattern of extendable parallel strips outside—typical of Luo country in the twentieth century—both displays the position of individuals and groups in a structure and process, and reminds them of it constantly as they grow up. Luo tend to live among agnates (that is, patrilineal kin), but this is only a tendency, not an absolute rule. Where they run out of land, they move where not structurally programmed to move. There, they frequently begin the process of lineage formation on the ground again, cloning their lineages and clans in new ground.

Different levels, or orders, of lineage and clan have long corresponded to different kinds of claims over land. Luo sometimes speak of these things in precise terms: one level for water or iron collection, one for thatching, one for field swapping, and so on. But which purposes corresponded with which levels of grouping appear always to have varied enough to render futile any attempt to codify enduring formal rules about it for Luo country, the lake basin, or any wider region of East Africa.

Terms like public or private property, or individual or communal, ill fit Luo landholding in its historical or even current variants. Instead, a pattern of seasonal oscillation obtained, as it does over much of tropical Africa.

Likewise, terms like "status" and "contract," whatever their heuristic value, have serious limits. Initially they may help sort out lineage systems from chiefdom systems. But tenure system and process like that of Luo involve both principles at almost every turn. Status and contract are both involved in the quasi-contractual federation of clans that form an oganda. They both show up in the agreement of marriage by which a woman enters a new patriline without leaving her own. And they are both there in the agreement of land clientage that determines whether future generations of offspring will be born weg lowo or jodak.

Branching kin groups, what anthropologists have called "segmentary lineages," are *not* just a residue from an early form of human society. They are, among other things, tools constantly fashioned and sharpened, and deepened for particular purposes where large groups are desired. They are one way of reckoning time, space, and social distance, but not the only way Luo and African people know.

Women are far from irrelevant in land matters, or mere pawns, or duped stooges. Participating fully in the action and idiom of lineage life, they are reproductive nodes and lineage founders. They are not just currency exchanged against cattle, but the very producers whose hoes and weeding hands have made the kinship and tenure systems work as they have. They are cross-webbing, traveling teachers, conduits for migration, spiritual overseers, and more. They use and manipulate patriliny, virilocality, bridewealth, and polygyny, just as men do—whether they politically or philosophically agree with the principles or not.

Men and women carry over kinship principles into other walks of life. It is not just families, lineages, and clans that grow, divide and subdivide, and die like branches of a tree in Luo country, fissioning and fusing according to threats and opportunities from outside. Urban ethnic associations and Christian churches there do it too.[34] And these, in turn, constitute new indigenous ways of mobilizing support in court battles and elections that bear directly back upon land tenure. Ethnic associations fight and mobilize cash for bodies to be returned home, church pastors bless the homes and grave sites, and the lineage process continues in its modern way.

Patriliny, partible inheritance, and the importance of graves all play into an understanding of land attachments that is not simply egalitarian in nature but instead, in some ways, profoundly hierarchical. Firstcomers are assumed superior to latecomers, just as elders are assumed superior to juniors, and wife-givers to wife-takers. Those who have invited others onto their lands, as jodak, land clients, have at least until lately assumed prestige, influence, and a range of privileges, if not always firm rights or powers, over them. Those jodak who have managed to out-reproduce their hosts or graft themselves onto their lineages and clans have gained a kind of equality, or better, but seldom without some resistance from their erstwhile hosts.

The land titling program to which we next turn threatens to upset this deep-rooted system of prestige and privilege, for better or worse. If success-ful, it may amount to a revolution of a sort. But like so many revolutions, it may end up opening the door for another kind of inequality no less great than the one it swept away. Then if not all goes well, inequality may turn into unfairness, a different and more dangerous thing.

If African landholding must be spoken of in evolutionary terms, it helps to remember that evolution does not always mean moving upward or down-ward. It need not mean "progressing" from status to contract, from kinship to territory, from lineages and clans to chiefdoms or states. Nor need it mean moving from savage to civilized. What is needed instead is something like an evolutionism turned sideways, where changes over time and space can be traced without such normative judgment and condescension.

CHAPTER 6

The Thin End

Land and Credit in the Colonial Period

This is far too big an issue to be dealt with in a hurry. Nevertheless . . .
—R. HAUER, OFFICE OF CHIEF SECRETARY IN NAIROBI IN 1948, TO
PROVINCIAL COMMISSIONERS

No attempt to individualize or privatize landholding in Africa has been more sweeping than Kenya's, and no country's experience provides a more promising place to try to find out what can go right and wrong in the process, or how the experience can feel. This chapter is an attempt to offer a glimpse into the formation of that process, which proceeded from central Kenya outward and from the highlands down, and to suggest what part the people to be affected—including the geographically and socially more marginal people, and others speaking for them—played or did not play in it. Since the potential of making land usable in mortgaging was, and remains, the government's main promise held out to farming people as an incentive for them to submit to the nationwide program, it is worth asking whether this link between land and credit has represented a realistic hope, a chancy dream, or something more like a teasing bait or rationalization—and how it all looked at the front end. For other people in other times and places will want to know the same, and there as here, there will be more than a little at stake.

Kenya's has not been the first attempt ever to title land as individual or private property in Africa south of the Sahara; it has only been the first attempt to do so nationwide. As early as 1847, the year of Liberia's independence, that country had seen three attempts to set up land adjudication programs and cadastres in its settler areas. These doubtless seemed particularly important to administrators there in view of the diverse backgrounds from which incoming transatlantic migrants were coming, and the probable lack of general consensus among them about what might constitute appropriate or customary rules or procedures. Under the Glen Grey Act of 1894, in the Union of South Africa, titling was extended over parts of the Transkei; local titling programs were also under way in the Cape and elsewhere by about the turn of the century—before apartheid became official national policy.

Over most of the rest of tropical Africa, titling programs would wait until the late nineteenth-century scramble to get going, and most then occurred only in tightly circumscribed, widely separated areas. After the Belgians tried to register land in Congo in 1886, Germans in Togo began to register plots with a *grundbuch*, ground or land book, in 1888. (The French introduced a Torrens system of titling on Madagascar in 1897.) The best-known case of early titling south of the Sahara was the British-introduced *mailo* system in the mainly Ganda-speaking part of southern Uganda in 1900—the name coming from mile-square plots allotted to chiefs and other prominent persons whom colonial authorities wished to use for recruiting local labor, among other things. While none of these schemes can be described in detail here, what was already known about them in the 1950s, in African research centers, in London, and elsewhere, gave little hope for optimism that they would prove very popular or run smoothly or equitably.[1]

As farmers in the "native reserves" or "trust" lands held no private land titles until after the Swynnerton Plan of 1954 and the nationwide land registration that its approval officially launched, they were spared until then both the advantages and the hazards of this sort of private property and of the land mortgage system to come with it.

The idea of titling, trading, and mortgaging land would not be wholly new in Kenya, but there had never been anything like unanimity of opinion among government, settlers, and missionaries about its propriety. Many British and British-trained bankers in African colonies and protectorates favored the idea as a way of extending their lending arms with what they expected would be more safety against default.[2] Not only had British, French, and Belgian colonial authorities tried titling land in parts of several other African countries, but the idea had also been debated in the 1932 Kenyan Land Commission in the districts of Nyanza Province and elsewhere in the colony. When officials ventured out from Nairobi into the Luo part of western Kenya to test out their opinions, gather opinions, or prepare the way for plans they wished to implement, what did they hear?

"A Register in Our Hearts": Early Luo
Sentiment Against the Idea of Land Titling

In Nyanza, Luo and other local spokesmen, and missionaries of long
standing among them, had roundly and consistently denounced the ideas of
registering and mortgaging land. These ideas were dangerous, they said, and
contrary to Luo traditions. As these people's pleas and warnings are found in
sources obscure enough to risk being forgotten, but as they form a backdrop
for all that was to follow and might deservedly continue to echo through the
history of this part of East Africa, it is worth including some of these voices
here in their own words.

A few Luo quotations from the 1932 hearings, taken from the Kenya Archives, suggest the public sentiment at the time and the range of interrelated
concerns. It was, unfortunately, mainly male voices that got recorded—whoever may have been present or allowed to speak in the meetings, no one
seems to have made any attempt at gender balance in the transcripts—but
what voices there are in the record show pretty strong consistency in their
message. Opio Chocho told the Kenya Land Commission, "Individual land
tenure will bring trouble into the country. We should like to have a covenant
that our country will not be upset."[3] Ogada, ex-chief of Sakwa, uttered these
phrases, combining plea and lamentation: "We never sold this land. We see
the Government is always changing its orders, our oath is to cut a dog in
half. Government is much stronger than us. I, a chief of old, walk on my feet;
Europeans go about in motors. We must suck the breasts of the Commission.
. . . We came here over this land Register and cutting the land into title bits.
I oppose a Register."[4] Echoing Ogada's sentiments about transfer, a representative of the Native Catholic Union of Kavirondo (later Nyanza) entered
these words: "We do not know the sold lands and the lands that are not sold.
This is strange to us" (KLC 1934, 2147).

A memorandum filed by the chairman of the Native Chamber of Commerce commented on both pragmatics and social philosophy: "We submit
that the old system of holding the land in Communal ownership for the
whole tribe and subtribes is suitable to us as the African natives have not
sufficiently advanced to grasp the more complexed model of individual title
which is very expensive and the after results are ruinous to the natives. The
initial costs of such individual grants of title is so costly and out of proportion
to the capacity of average natives nothing to say about the subsequent costs of
transfer entailing heavy legal and stamp and registration fees. As already the
land is limited in size for tribes and subtribes and without a proper safeguard

the wealthier tribes may subsequently legally dispossess poorer tribes and subtribes and individuals."[5] He added that any departure from "holding land in a communal way . . . would result into detribalization and breaking up the social fabrik [sic] of the natives and economical ruin. . . . The natives would cease to think of the tribe as a whole and . . . selfishness would be developed in the Native's character."

Some did, however, want a boundary of a different sort. They wanted a major boundary drawn around the "Reserves" to protect them from European and "Asian" encroachments. Daniel Oviti, a Luo local native councilman, said, "Should the tenure be between clans or individuals? Location boundaries act to us as a register. In them there is a register in our hearts, we know where our separate boundaries are. As for the boundaries between the Reserve and settlers we want something so well marked, a blind man can see it."[6] Chief Ogada of the Luo location of North Gem couched a similar barb in diplomacy: "The reason we don't want registered titles to our land is we go in for fragmentation of cultivation and our cattle graze far and wide. Government is our father and if Government sees right to set a boundary let it be a boundary between black and white."[7]

Notably, no Luo in the hearings was reported to ask for titles in order to be able to borrow against them. Of the ten Luo of South Kavirondo who spoke before the Kenya Land Commission (Marinde, 20 September 1932), five objected to alien immigrants and possible dispossessions, three spoke out against titling, and none spoke in favor of it. One Luo named Apio commented, "We object to the register as we may have to buy new ones [landholdings]."[8]

Christian missionaries at the hearings chimed in on the side of these Luo speakers. Said Monsignor G. Brandsma, prefect apostolic of Kavirondo (later Nyanza), "The greatest danger of all would be that a man would be allowed to sell his own land, probably only to a man of his own tribe, with the result that it would create a low and a high class native. . . . Perhaps in another fifty years. At present it would be the greatest calamity."[9]

Summing up the hearings of the Kenya Land Commission in his province, the Nyanza provincial commissioner H. R. Montgomery generalized that "at all Barazas [public meetings] Natives made a point that they did not want Registration of their land."[10] What could be clearer?

What the Luo spokesmen were defending was the complex system of landholding outlined in the preceding two chapters. Based on membership in kin groups and wider communities, and on labor, it was intricately tied into many strands of Luo culture, including patriliny, virilocality, burial of the dead at their own homes, relations with the ancestral spirits, and, through them, divinity. It involved a system of long-term land exchanges by which Luo sought to reduce imbalances in family resource endowments and, if they were land patrons, to establish a social hierarchy in their neighborhoods. Birthright, marriage, clearing, encroachment, clientage, and swaps and other voluntary transfers were the ways to get land, and childbearing, active farming, and good citizenship were the ways to keep it. These were the sacredly anchored principles of landholding in the middle and later colonial decades, when the issue of titling and mortgages arose. If land were titled as privately alienable property, access rights acquired through work, kinship, and local citizenship stood to be challenged by rights acquired through capital alone.

"Customary" Loan Security: Anything but Land

Is anything like collateral found in local lending practice? Most kinds of loans involve no deposits of property or paper as security, and land mortgaging is a novelty of the past few decades, as both insiders' and outsiders' voices attest. As the knowledgeable and celebrated Anglican archdeacon W. E. Owen informed the Kenya Land Commission in Central Kavirondo District (later Central Nyanza, then Kisumu and Siaya Districts) in 1932, "To mortgage land would be against native custom here."[11] In South Kavirondo District (later South Nyanza and Kisii Districts), meanwhile, C. E. V. Buxton, the district commissioner, reported much the same: "I should have thought it was quite impossible for man to sell a piece of land or part with it in satisfaction of a debt."[12] The same was reported in 1949 for Luhya speakers of North Nyanza District (now Kakamega District), though it seems some rare instances of borrowing against land security had already been observed there in interethnic lending—where cultural rules are challenged first.[13]

But if land mortgages would violate Luo "native custom," the basic idea of collateral is not new or unfamiliar to the Luo. E. P. Oranga, an African working as an assistant agricultural officer (a rare post for an African) in Central Nyanza District in 1949, did a small investigation of local practice and opinion. His findings—some of the first recorded on the topic by a Nyanza local—are worth quoting; they would prove prescient.[14] He wrote,

> (a) *Land.* I have discussed the problem of using land as security with some of the L.N.C. [Local Native Council] members, progressive farmers and some members of several group farms and ultimate decisions in all cases have been

negative and so the question of setting land aside as security is unanimously rejected. According to the Luo tradition the system of setting aside a piece of land as security has never been practiced. (b) *Livestock.* The question of using livestock as a means of security was discussed by various interested bodies in the community and was found to be more preferable than any other means available at present. It is somewhat linked with old native tradition. According to Luo custom domestic animals are used as security whenever one gets a loan. [This is an exaggeration.] (c) *Plants.* Eucalyptus and fruit trees can be used as security. There are many people with several acreages of trees which are worth a great [deal of] money, which can serve the purpose of security. (d) *Non-living Properties. Buildings and Machinery.* There are now many Africans who have permanent buildings either for trade or for living which can be used as means of security and in fact they have practiced the way of using them as security. *Machinery* (Posho [maize flour] mills—Lorries). There are now a number of Africans who have taken big loans from Indian Money Lenders, who have used their lorries or Posho Mills as means of security and the method has worked well in some cases. So it will not be difficult for anyone who wants [a] loan and can use them as security. (e) *Sponsors.* This is a very common practice in the African community. In many cases where there has been no direct security there had been sponsors, these had been trustworthy and wealthy people, and in most cases the system worked well.

Oranga continued to describe the remembered practice of using humans (usually daughters) as security in marriage pledges—something he deemed to have ended, or at least said he did.[15]

The message here too was loud and clear. Luo people considered most anything *except* land to be acceptable to put up as security for credit. Land was too precious, too symbolically charged, and too fundamental to lineage and continued life to be gambled away. The proscription against pledging land was even more deeply rooted than the one against pledging humans. To pledge land was to arrogate, as an individual, rights that pertained in part to other members of a family and lineage. Later we see what has happened in recent decades as alien lenders have begun to demand land against loans, and why they have been mistaken not to heed early warnings like these.

But how many key decision makers in Nairobi would listen? Some of the speakers quoted above tied their fears and pleas into concerns to prevent settler encroachments into their land, and to preserve regional, ethnic, and racial autonomy—the sort of cause few people in government centers typically like to hear championed. Some voiced their sentiments in rather poetic, hyperbolic, or elliptical oratory unlikely to be fully appreciated by policy makers accustomed to more prosaic genres and likely to be more impressed

by numbers than by words. At least one referred to a local practice unlikely
to evoke sympathy from British ears (the traditional oathing or truce-making
practice of cutting a dog in half). Some of the speakers took the liberty to
be prophetic, rather than leaving the business of planning and prediction
to central authorities. The speakers were speaking as elders. That is who
got to speak in public baraza meetings in western Kenya—the elderly, the
wealthy, the reproductively prolific (these often coincided). They were exer-
cising their experience and sensibilities about the *longue durée*. But to do so
threatens, at least implicitly, the presumptions of paternalistic government.
This may be why some Luo spokespersons seem to have deliberately infan-
tilized themselves and their people to get through ("sucking the breasts of
the Commission," "Government is our father"), whether out of sarcasm or
just desperation. Paternalism was a coveted privilege.

Colonial Paternalism and the "One Important Safeguard"

Until the 1950s, colonial policy from London, as officials saw it, was
to prevent "Africans" from finding ways to pledge or mortgage land.[16] The
reason, as Sir Malcolm Darling boldly explained it for the Colonial Economic
Advisory Committee in 1945, was paternalistic. Darling had written extensively and influentially on perennially indebted peasants in Punjab, India.
He sought now to compare what he had known there to matters in Africa, a
continent still newer to Britain's colonial experience.

> If Asia is backward, Africa is primitive. . . . There is the same improvidence and
> want of thrift, the same ignorance of the proper use of money, the same care-
> lessness about repayment, the same tendency to borrow, not as need dictates but
> as opportunity offers. . . . In facing the modern world and its perils, the Afri-
> can peasant has one important safeguard: ordinarily he cannot sell the land he
> cultivates, and he can only pledge it as allowed by custom. The peasant in both
> Asia and Africa is so prone to misuse his credit that he must be either protected
> against himself or educated in the use of money. Education is the only lasting
> remedy, but it takes time. Meanwhile, the best way of protecting him is to see
> that his right of alienation remains restricted. . . . The peasant requires to be pro-
> tected against both himself and the money-lender. . . . It would seem necessary
> to limit his credit by not allowing him to dispose of his land as he pleases.[17]

Untangling the condescension and the (now) alarming imperialist attitudes from the genuine concern for the welfare of Africans in those words
takes a fine comb, but both are clearly present. In retrospect, it seems that

colonial administrators, once set up as such, would be damned if they allowed negotiable land titles and mortgaging, and damned if they didn't. They would be either condemning Africans to exploitation by insiders and outsiders or withholding "progress" from them. For the moment, they chose to withhold this sort of progress.

But in Kenya the ball was already rolling. The first institutions in Kenya to lend to farmers on security of land served "white" settler farmers.[18] The Equitable Mortgages Ordinance of 30 November 1909 ensured that nothing in the Transfer of Property Act of 1882, of India, as applied to Kenya, prevented mortgaging titles to immovable property (*Laws of Kenya*, Cap. 291). The Crown Lands Ordinance, which came into effect on 1 June 1915, replaced Europeans' land licenses with 999-year transferable leases, which settlers could use as collateral for bank loans.[19] The Central Agricultural Advances Board, created under legislation passed in May 1930, lent from public funds on the security of land, crops, or livestock. The Land and Agricultural Bank, established in 1931 for long-term lending on first mortgage of land, lent £32,300 in its first year and some £834,000 in the first seven years of its existence.[20] Foreign-based banks and these colonial government institutions helped many settler farmers set up, but heavy indebtedness to these institutions, combined with the vagaries of climate and of crop prices, ultimately drove many off their land during the Great Depression and other economic slumps before Independence.[21]

Lending to "African" farmers in Kenya on land security began on a small scale in 1945. At that time the Land Bank, as it was then known, began to extend its normal facilities for European settlers to Africans in settlement schemes, the only ones who could pledge land. In its first ten years, the Bank lent a total of less than £6,000 to fewer than seventy African farmers colony-wide (Yudelman 1964, 158). But soon the question about spreading access would come up. Something big would make it come up.

Mau Mau in the Distance, and the Directive to Move Money

As the 1940s drew to a close, a newly active underground resistance movement in Central and Rift Valley Provinces started shaking the foundations of colonial Africa. As yet unnamed, it would later be given the name Mau Mau. In it, loose networks of young and middle-aged Gikuyu (Kikuyu) men around their forties were emerging as freedom fighters, demanding, with violence mainly against other, loyalist Gikuyu, the return of alienated lands, and pressing for independence from, and expulsion of, Europeans. The rich and voluminous literature on Mau Mau and the related struggle over independence leaves little need for a blow-by-blow treatment here, but it must be noted how crucial a role the "emergency" played in galvanizing the British government in Kenya into its drastic attempt at land tenure reform.[22]

Even the state of emergency that was declared hardly suggests the puzzlement and panic settlers were experiencing: the fear of the oathing and reported blood-drinking rituals of bonding, and the shock at some publicized attacks on a few dozen settler homes and farms—only a tiny proportion of the violence, it would turn out, but a part that most quickly and surely made world headlines.[23] To many settlers, Mau Mau seemed like a movement of crazed savages, or at least of young male rebels hard at work imitating crazed savagery—and one aimed directly at them. In fact, this was not a wholly new form of movement in Kenya, and it was one whose hideouts, meetings, and oathing rituals were not, at least in hindsight, incomprehensible. The western lake basin area had seen Mumbo, a nativist revitalization movement focused on a western Kenyan prophet and a giant serpent by the same name, come and go in earlier decades of the century. Mumboites had held to a fervent aim and wish—expressed by the prophet Onyango Dunde, straight from the serpent's mouth—to see the country cleansed of all European influence.[24] But Mau Mau was the first major, violent, cultlike freedom movement to seem to threaten both the heartland of settler farming in the Rift Valley and the capital city's affluent settler suburbs. Now farm loans, the high-value cash crops hitherto prohibited for Africans, and the rise of a stable rural middle class were beginning to seem like good ideas to the administration.

And there would be money to be disposed of. The maize cess (a tax) imposed in 1942 had proved lucrative for the Local Native Councils, and moreover, war bonds purchased by these councils were maturing. In October 1947 the councils colony-wide found themselves with a surplus balance of between £250,000 and £300,000.[25] In Nyanza Province, North Kavirondo had £133,276, Central Kavirondo held £16,856, and South Kavirondo £36,797 (Kitching 1980, 194). A September 1948 letter from the chief secretary's office in Nairobi to the provincial commissioners of Central and Nyanza Provinces suggested a growing sense of urgency, as the author, signed as R. Hauer, seems to have written despite himself: "We are doing all we can to find some practical means of making loans to African farmers based on some adequate form of security. . . . This is far too big an issue to be dealt with in a hurry. Nevertheless the Chief Secretary and myself are very anxious that we should get going on this pilot scheme as quickly as possible and though I am far from asking you to 'throw the money about' I would like to suggest that you try to make loans to really suitable farmers, as soon as possible."[26]

From this point on, government money was to chase farming people as much as these chased money. But it would always chase particular farmers only, for particular reasons, and always with conditions. Some of these last could be stringent: whether the borrower had to be an individual rather than a group; what crop(s) or kind(s) of animal a farmer or rancher would use the loan for; what seeds and chemicals would be used; how much land would be involved; and how, when, and through whom the farmer would repay—as well as what sort of collateral or guarantees would be involved. If money were to be "thrown about," it would be thrown with careful aim, and usually with some sort of string attached.

Of the first four districts approved for loans—Kiambu, Fort Hall, Nyeri, and North Nyanza—all but one, the last, were Gikuyu, suggesting the importance of the political concern. And all had highlands suitable for coffee or tea. To follow were the Luo district of Central Nyanza, the mainly Luo and Gusii district of South Nyanza, and the Kipsigis district of Kericho, all less politically volatile at the time than the Gikuyu ones.[27] The formal approvals from the secretariat in Nairobi from July 1948 allowed £500 to each district commissioner for loans of £50 (Shs. 1,000) each to farmers, expected to be repaid in annual installments over five years from the crops financed.[28] Farmers would have to keep at least one quarter of their fields under grass fallow to borrow: one of many conservation rules to be imposed over the next decade, which ended up fueling Mau Mau in central Kenya and the movement for independence. Interest of up to 4.5 percent (a subsidized rate, also being the Land Bank rate for Europeans) would be charged, as the North Nyanza district commissioner rather presumptuously put it, "in order to get the African out of the 'everything for nothing' way of thinking."[29]

The potential loan channels were several, and district administrators picked and chose case by case. The channel the administration leaned on most often was the Local Native Councils (renamed African District Councils in 1950) and their Agricultural Betterment Funds (from taxing maize). Others included the Land Bank, which had lent to "Europeans" since 1931, and the African Land Utilization and Settlement Authority, a body with such a difficult set of tasks it had to be periodically renamed.[30] The one the administration leaned on most in the country's periphery was the councils.

It would take more than three years for Luo farmers to receive enough loans to be counted on two hands from the councils and their fund. Among the administration's priorities, the troubled Gikuyu in Central Province and Gusii in Nyanza came first, with their especially fertile and well-watered volcanic highlands. But a lending tradition for the nation was taking shape.

Moving Toward Mortgaging: The Prototype Plan

For the African "reserves" of Kenya as a whole, the land mortgage question reared its head in 1948 at a meeting of the provincial commissioners (PCs) in Nairobi. By this time, stirrings of political discontent in central Kenya were starting to be keenly felt—the movement developing into Mau Mau.

Meanwhile, the new postwar funding was becoming available for development programs there and around the colony. Primarily concerned with those they deemed "progressive farmers" among the Gikuyu, the PCs issued several recommendations, summarized by Desmond O'Hagan, the Native Courts officer in the secretariat in Nairobi. He wrote, "It is obviously desirable that it should be made possible to give individual Africans who had well-run holdings a better title to their land."[31] Listed were the reasons that titles would prevent contrary claims and disputes, prevent fragmentation and subdivision of holdings, and allow that "agricultural credit might be obtained with the land as security" on government loans with the permission of the provincial commissioner concerned. At some points, O'Hagan capitalized the words "Agricultural Credit," as though something sacred.[32]

A year later, colonial authorities took their next, and last, sounding of opinions colony-wide. The Briton-filled, seven-member Committee on Agricultural Credit for Africans, chaired by J. H. Ingham, collected memoranda from district commissioners, agricultural officers, cooperative registrars, and selected others. It was the opinions of officials that seem to have mattered most, and central highlanders after them: the committee's report to the governor contained seventeen memoranda by Europeans as compared with only four by Kenyans of African descent (two Gikuyu [Kikuyu], one Luhya, and one coastal Swahili, all already government employees themselves).[33] The picture was rather like Saul Steinberg's famous drawing of the New Yorker's view of the world, with Manhattan's West Side, the Hudson, and Jersey filling all but a thin strip on the horizon for the barely visible California and China.

As though to color in the cognitive map of the colony, the report used Gikuyu terms (*mbari*, patrilineage; *muhoi*, land client; and several others) in reference to *all* ethnic groups of the "Native Land Units" of Kenya as a whole.[34] Missionaries, a set who had been heard in the Kenya Land Commission but had since spoken out often against government policy, were not represented this time. Most importantly, but typically enough for the time, no female's words were included.

From this skewed sample of opinions, the report reached several clear conclusions. African farmers in Kenya used very little credit (except in Coast Province), and moneylenders (elsewhere "pernicious") and indebtedness were as yet insignificant but always a danger. But "Progressive" farmers wanted and needed more credit, and they weren't deemed progressed enough to know how to use it themselves: "There can be no doubt that the productivity of the African farming areas could be greatly increased by the application of capital under skilled guidance where it is most needed to secure good farming practice."[35]

Loans through cooperative societies should be the answer, the report determined. The Land Bank (under the Member for Agriculture and Natural Resources), not the Local Native Councils (which were in "African" hands), should handle the money, but the councils should help screen applicants. District loan committees should pick the borrowers on the basis of personal acquaintance and character. Loans should be made "only for genuinely agricultural purposes," including herding (Ingham et al. 1950, 5). "In those areas where clear individual title to land exists, land should obviously be demanded as first security. . . . Elsewhere, stock and chattels should be pledged" (p. 8). Government loan funds should be increased, the report said, from £3,000 annually to £60,000 (pp. 1, 8).

The land mortgage issue came into sharper focus in the first appendix paper by H. E. Lambert, D. O'Hagan, and E. J. Leslie—a paper some of whose wording would reappear five years later in the Swynnerton Plan, making the latter assistant director of agriculture lastingly famous.[36] It recommended that "special titles" be issued to some proven "good farmers" (but not to all farmers), in view of the following "desiderata" quoted from its first paragraph (p. 11): "(a) To secure the greatest possible degree of beneficial occupation of the land. (b) To prevent fragmentation and subdivision.

(c) To provide security to encourage Africans to invest capital on the development of their land by removing the fear that the land may be taken away from a right-holder by some court action. (d) To provide security on which some form of long-term agricultural credit may be based." The committee recommended that titles be heritable, and, if a holder had bought the land, saleable or transferable by gift—as with perceived "customary" rights.[37] Overlapping rights of lineage mates would be recorded right in the land register. Foreclosure on a land mortgage would mean taking over not the ownership of the land, but only usufructuary rights until a loan was paid up (p. 15). Disturbed on the one hand by the fragmentation of holdings they saw happening, and on the other hand by the specter of land concentration in the hands of a few, the authors recommended "that there should be an upper and a lower limit to the size of the holdings" to be titled (p. 13).

As it happened, land titling as implemented later under the Swynnerton Plan would neglect the qualifiers and mollifiers. Private property would be more cut and dried—at least on paper. The government would execute *blanket titling* on all farmland, *not* just titling for a few selected farmers. The government would try unsuccessfully, under the Swynnerton Plan and land control boards, to impose minimum size limits to ensure "economic" holdings. But it has never imposed a maximum. (The emphasis would always be on economic growth, never on distribution.) The overlapping rights of lineage mates would *not* be recorded on individual title deeds. Titled land would become mortgageable and saleable *no matter how acquired*. It would be mortgageable *not* just for "long-term" but for "medium-term" or even "short-term" loans. And foreclosure would mean *absolute loss* of ownership with all its rights.

Kenyan land law, in short, would strongly embrace individualism and the market principle—and it would leave the safety nets behind.

Luo still deemed the plan inappropriate. In mid-1951, South Nyanza District commissioner P. Low showed the African District Council a provincial commissioner's circular in Swahili raising the possibility of future land titling. The new feedback from the council—the nearest thing to the voice of the country—resembled the old:

> Their reactions were, I am afraid, entirely negative. They realized that the introduction of a system of land titles would be the thin end of the wedge which would eventually break up the existing system of land tenure under customary law and also break down the existing system of inheritance under native law.
> . . . The Africans in the District would strongly oppose any move to introduce

a system that made commerce in land a possibility. . . . They were all directed against the system and not for it. . . . In the event of a title holder taking a loan on the security of his land, and defaulting on the repayment, the sympathy of members was not with the title holder, but with his wife and children. The wife would be shambaless [without field to farm] and the children would lose their inheritance.[38]

But the pleas went unheeded; the colonial administration was not to be stopped. And when the mallet hit the wedge, the clang would repercuss.

"We Must Go All Out": The Swynnerton Plan as a Blueprint for Private Property and Land Mortgages

By December 1953, when Kenya's assistant director of agriculture, Roger J. M. Swynnerton, submitted his now-famous "Plan to Intensify the Development of African Agriculture in Kenya," the titling of land as individual property, with goals including the setting up of a mortgage system for the nation's farmers, was already becoming entrenched in Kenya's agricultural policy.[39] This plan made it official.

The Swynnerton Plan—as it became universally known—was a hydra-headed proposal, but it had two main thrusts.[40] One was to lift restrictions on Africans' growing high-value cash crops colony-wide (they were already being grown in parts of the highlands), and indeed to encourage them to do so as "white" settler farmers had long done. The other, and the more central to our topic, was to set into place a system for registering all farmland in the "African lands" as private, individual property on a European freehold model. Each of these bold proposals represented a radical about-face for Kenya.

To put the land titling initiative into perspective, this was the first such nationwide attempt in Africa (though a number of much smaller such schemes had been tried unsuccessfully elsewhere on the continent).

Behind the scheme was an evolutionist notion of social progress, a "modernization" theory with counterparts in all the social sciences at the time. Swynnerton summed up the thinking as clearly as could be, in four sentences that keep ringing in colonial African histories (1955, 10): "In the past Government policy has been to maintain the tribal system of tenure so that all the people have had bits of land and to prevent the African from borrowing money against the security of his land. The result is that there is no agricultural indebtedness by Africans to the other races. In future, if these recommendations are accepted, former Government policy will be reversed and able, energetic or rich Africans will be able to acquire more land and bad or poor farmers less, creating a landed and a landless class. This is a normal step in the evolution of a country."

Shocking words, today. What they neglected was that Kenya did not—and would not—have the industries to absorb all those newly land-poor or landless people. Nor, the report also failed to foretell, would other parts of the world be eager to absorb many of these African people as migrants. No one where it mattered seems to have been thinking ahead that far.

The urgency and the dramatic, wholesale shift in policy had much to do with the political agendum behind the plan. By 1953 the violence of the Mau Mau movement had shaken up central Kenya for over a year. The administration sought to stabilize Gikuyu country by placating repatriated Gikuyu and by promoting and coopting a rural middle class. "In the long run the greatest gain from the participation of the African community in running its own agricultural industries will be a politically contented and stable community" (Swynnerton 1955, 8). Titling, credit, and "progressive" farming were considered inextricable. "Special attention can and must be given . . . to provid[ing] the farmer with . . . sources of agricultural credit big enough to meet the requirements of very large numbers of very small farmers. . . . Once registered, farmers will be able to buy and sell land, amongst other Africans only, and to mortgage titles to land against loans from Government or other approved agency" (p. 9). Stop at nothing, the authors said: "We must go all out for the primary objective, to give security of tenure and an occupational license" (pp. 10–11).

Lend more and more, the report instructed. Double the size of allowable loans to African farmers and set up a new "Loan (or Land) Bank" as a vehicle for millions of pounds to deliver to them once titling gets under way.[41] "If Africans are to develop their lands to their full potential they will require much greater access to finance and if they achieve titles to their land in economic units, much greater facilities should be made available to them for borrowing against the security of their land" (Swynnerton 1955, 55). That representatives from large parts of the country, like Luoland, had long spoken out against the ideas of individual land titling and mortgaging did not particularly matter.

The expressed notion of "economic units" is worth note. The Swynnerton Plan lamented, as colonial officials were wont to do, the successive subdivision and fragmentation of fields in partible inheritance. The cure would be imposed top-down: "By suitable reforms to the system of land tenure and inheritance, these fragments can be amalgamated" (p. 9), and minimum holding sizes imposed. The model in mind, presumably, was primogeniture in the British pattern. Neglected were these crucial facts: that fragmented holdings over varied terrain cut agricultural risks, and that they help absorb labor and smooth out its seasonal peaks and troughs.[42] But the government would soon learn how hard it is to "reform" inheritance.

The proposals were not without curious irony. In Kenya in the late 1950s, the administration's plans to register land included a complex provision to keep private moneylenders from gaining access to defaulters' lands, and especially to prevent their taking over the lands without canceling the debts.[43] At the same time, interestingly, the government was setting up its own credit schemes for African farmers on the principle of land mortgage and with a possibility of permanent alienation. The issue, then, was not just whether pledging or mortgaging would occur, but just as important, who would control it.[44]

For all its seventy-five pages of detail, the Swynnerton Plan did not substantially discuss any ways of helping farmers' own *saving*. It merely assumed farmers would reinvest their new cash crop earnings in farming, and that lending institutions would build up their finances to help with more loans (p. 55). Once private property in land was established, the key to everything was *credit* — or, seen another way, *debt*.[45]

In hindsight, the hubris and optimism of the Swynnerton Plan are striking indeed. While the evolutionist and modernizationist presumptions may seem outdated, these ideas come and go, and they are certainly not gone for good, in Nairobi, London, Washington, or anywhere else. As an exercise in social engineering, the Swynnerton Plan stands out as one of the world's more vivid blueprints and one of its bolder package deals. Anyone who stood in its way could be accused of antediluvian racism in that it favored allowing Africans at last to grow high-value cash crops, and this may be one reason why it gained such total acceptance within not just the colonial government but the independent one as well. For who could conscionably object to this part of the plan?

It was the second half of it — the titling, the buying and selling, the mortgaging, and through these the "creation of a landed and a landless class" — that would come to look more ominous, and by the turn of the twenty-first century more fraught and frightening, whether they be "a natural step in the evolution of a country" or not. Luo elders and certain sympathetic missionaries interviewed by government officials certainly foresaw dangers in all this clearly enough. Central planners with experience in India saw it too. Even the authors of the prototype plan, the Ingham Committee report just a few years ahead of the Swynnerton Plan, saw it as well and exercised enough prudence and compassion to build in safeguards against potential land loss and impoverishment.

But safeguards like the ones they put in, defending the interests of people in marginal positions by definition and having no powerful persons with vested interests behind them, sometimes get stripped away when planning gets rushed and when push comes to shove. For those in charge in Nairobi, hearing the rumblings of an independence movement growing, an emergency was an emergency. Central Kenya, not peripheral areas like the Luo country in Nyanza, was what mattered to them. But they seem not to have felt they had time for distinctions like this. It was all or nothing. The Swynnerton Plan went forward as a plan imposed from Nairobi, with political stabilization as a hidden agendum, and economic growth and social evolution as the twin explicit rationales.

A half-century later, as we shall see, the cautious Ingham report was all but forgotten, while the bold and more uncaring Swynnerton Plan was nationally and internationally famous, still basically in place as national policy, and wrongly imagined by many to have been the start of the whole titling and credit project, when it in fact was only reworked for eventual passage into policy and law.

The most wide-ranging and ambitious plans of nation states and their international sponsors are often born in response to the worst of perceived crises. And commonly, for better or worse, the policies and institutions formed long outlast the crises. Their overseers then have to seek new justifications, in a way turning the planning process backward. Since centralized development planning just about anywhere is a process often born of crisis, the chances for a history like this one to repeat itself, with its strong ideological thrust and optimism, and its eventual streamlining and hardening of goals serving some people's interests to the likely detriment of others', and seeming to gain its own momentum as it goes, are worth taking seriously.[46]

In this story so far, what had been a long history of uncertainty and debate in policy circles and a resolute resistance in some of the provinces suddenly—within a very few years—developed into a teleological vision, solidified into an ideological orthodoxy, and emerged in practice as a full-scale program for the transformation of a country. That plan would remain in place for many decades, and up to the time of this writing. How effective this particular plan would turn out to be, and just how true its predictions, is the topic of the next two chapters.

CHAPTER 7

The Ghost Market

Land Titling and Mortgaging
After Independence

There can be no freedom or beauty about a home life that depends on borrowing
and debt.
—HENRIK IBSEN, *A DOLL'S HOUSE* (1879), ACT I

Every radish I ever pulled up seemed to have a mortgage attached to it.
—ED WYNN (1886–1966), EXPLAINING WHY HE SOLD HIS FARM

R ural people in many parts of the world whose communities have
allowed their national governments to register their land as private property have done so largely in the hope of obtaining farm loans on
the security of their land titles. The romance of the ghostwalk is a seductive
fancy for Monsieur le Capital and Madame la Terre. Whether that scene
be an enchanted, topsy-turvy world as Marx deemed it, or a straightfor-
ward place of pragmatism and "natural steps to evolution," as the authors of
the Swynnerton Plan theorized no less grandly, the temptation is palpable
enough to farmer or financier. And once the titles and banks are there, capitalist and communist alike can sense it.

The hope has been an important part of the popular lore surrounding
the tenure reform in Kenya, as the Lawrance Mission on Land Consolidation and Registration in Kenya noted in 1966: "Propaganda has . . . perhaps
unwisely, been concentrated on the opportunities that registration affords
for the grant of credit. In a report from one district a responsible official is
quoted as saying 'registration is important so that every farmer can get a
title deed and can thereafter get a loan to develop his shamba [field].' We
fear that misleading propaganda of this kind has been commonplace. . . .

During our tour of the country we were told with monotonous regularity that the people wanted land registration so that they could go to the banks to obtain loans with which to develop their holdings" (Lawrance 1966, 24, 126). Where lands are still being registered now, government land officers continue to dangle the carrot of credit before farmers. We see in this chapter and the next how that promise has worked out in reality.

The Land Tenure "Reform"

The process of titling rural land has proved slow and difficult for all concerned, and its outcome different in many ways from what its designers and implementers have envisaged. As other writers and I have described it elsewhere, only its barest essentials need be noted here.[1]

When the colonial government began adjudicating land for private titles in the late 1950s, landholding was already showing some discernible changes. Sales and other transfers once forbidden or unknown were noted more and more frequently, particularly in the crowded highlands of what became the western Kisii and southern Kakamega districts; but those who wanted land to be freely alienable were also encountering some popular resistance, symbolic as well as practical.[2] New technology like ox plows, new cash crops like coffee, steepening population growth, travel and ethnic intermixture, and other factors had given rise to new competition over land. They were making the definition of land rights and duties ever more important. To most colonial agricultural planners, all this looked increasingly like pressure, and justification, to title land as individual holdings.

Enabling a mortgage system was, and still is, only one of many ostensible aims of the effort to reform landholding, though it is probably the one most often cited. Others, it may be recalled, were expressed in the Swynnerton Plan and other planning documents. They included giving farmers personal incentives and protection for investing labor and capital in their land, encouraging them to conserve soil as their own, preventing and quelling disputes and litigation by providing a clear public record of ownership, allowing enterprising farmers to acquire bigger holdings more easily, promoting "modern" herd management and controlling epizootics through easier fencing and controlled pasturing, speeding general social and economic "evolution," and (especially in the Mau Mau era) promoting political stability. The Kenyan titling plan, in short, arose as a panacea. Was there any hope it would prove any more helpful than most other imported panaceas?

Accepted as government policy in 1954–55 and passed into law in 1959, the program met widely varied popular responses across the country. Luo at first resisted the titling program more stiffly than did other major ethnic groups. Luo perceived Kikuyu land alienations from afar with suspicion that the colonial government and settlers might threaten their lands too. More important, as seen earlier, they deemed "freehold" tenure and a mortgage system unnecessary for their needs and expected these would tear the social fabric. Colonially empowered chiefs, already rather resented, were deemed likely to grab lineage land, or land of other lineages, for their own if the reform came. The planned consolidation of fragmented landholdings also struck many Luo as unnatural, since (among other reasons) it would heighten farming risks by cutting the ecological diversity of plots, and therefore the variety of possible cultigens, contributing to any given farmer's or homestead's livelihood. Seizing on and reflecting popular sentiment, leading Luo politicians, including Tom Mboya and Oginga Odinga, spoke out against the tenure reform as a foreign ideological incursion. Resistance stiffened, and it was not until after 1958, when South Nyanza district commissioner P. McEntee switched from a zealous, propagandistic approach to a different, self-help tack, that significant numbers of Luo began to get interested. Not until after Independence in 1963 did any holdings in the Luo country finally get titled.[3]

By the early 1980s, when I first lived in the Luo country, popular sentiment about the reform was much more mixed, and more resigned. Elder men with large herds of cattle seemed usually to be against it, junior men without them appeared as often to be for it, and women seemed more complexly divided in opinion. But in view of the government's strong determination to carry the reform through nationwide, most everyone by then seemed to consider the change inevitable.

The Kenyan titling program has broadly proceeded, as noted, from the rainy and fertile highlands down. The Gikuyu country and Gusii country, with their important cash crops, were thus among the early titled areas; lakeside areas of Nyanza Province, agronomically more marginal to government interests, were still in process but nearing completion of titling at the time of writing. The mechanics of the program divide, at the simplest, into these parts: demarcation and surveying of boundaries, adjudication of claims, consolidation of fragmented holdings (in some areas), and registration of titles with issuance of title deeds to individual owners. By popular demand, many Luo localities have gone without, or with only minimal, consolidation as part of the process. Locational committees, with representatives from sub-locations (and less formal *miji kumi* [Sw.] or originally "ten-homestead" units within these), meet in hearings supervised by government lands officers, and sometimes others, at the adjudication stage. Committee members in my experience have been almost exclusively male. Not coincidentally, so too have been the recipients of the titles, and of the loans that have followed them. And so have been the divisional land control boards that are supposed to protect women and dependents from dispossession after titling. But let us not jump ahead.

Land titling has raised tensions, at least temporarily, in several ways:

1. *Between men and women.* Few women have received titles to land under the new system. In my Kanyamkago research site, only 7 percent (17 of 246) of titled land parcels had women as joint or exclusive owners in the registry as of September 1982. The twenty-one women concerned represented only 7 percent of a total of 286 joint or exclusive owners. Only nine, or about 4 percent, of the parcels had women listed as exclusive owners. These women numbered eleven, or again about 4 percent, of all listed owners. All this parallels findings elsewhere.[4]

Being denied land titles means losing some access to institutional loans—for what they are worth. While women theoretically can use their husbands' titles to borrow, this happens only rarely if at all in western Kenya. Instead, men's mortgaging jeopardizes women's and children's access to the land, and women and children usually have little control over how the loans are used. As long as land can be mortgaged, and as long as men hold the lion's share of land titles, mortgaging will jeopardize the well-being of the lionesses and cubs.

To be sure, however, some widows with access to government channels can gain in titling by obtaining legal rights they can use against leviratic husbands and the latter's clansmen, who may otherwise more easily take over claims to their and the dead husbands' landholdings.[5]

2. *Between elders and juniors.* Elder men tend to have more cattle than younger men and more control over family herds. They thus have much stronger interests in seeing that commons grazing not be restricted. They also have interest in seeing that access routes between grazing grounds (for instance, between dry-season and wet-season grazing, where separated) not be impeded by private land claims and fencing along the way. Young men, in contrast, are more interested in possibilities of labor emigration and therefore want land titles to help secure their claims while away. They are also

more often optimistic about progress through land-secured credit. Where titling has not occurred, its prospect seems for these reasons to polarize the generations.

3. *Between autochthons and immigrants.* In any land titling initiative, land borrowers and long-term land clients (jodak) stand to gain permanent, heritable rights at the expense of their hosts (weg lowo), if they can get titles to the land on which they live or work. As individual tenure became national policy in Kenya in the 1950s, and the question of titling arose for Luo and others in and around the lake basin in the 1960s and beyond, the big question arose: Would existing borrowers be given their own titles, or would the titles go to the lenders?

Jodak thought they had a chance. In Kanyamkago, in the 1960s, jodak (in most places, a majority) pressed locally for land registration when weg lowo were still against, to the latter's great displeasure. Old quarrels about jadak tree planting or house building reopened. Immigrant Maragoli Luhya, Bantu speakers only partly assimilated into local society, got the most heat. Some worried jodak began inviting their own jodak onto the land from outside, thus collecting potential supporters and sometimes cash payments in the bargain. Further displeased, weg lowo tried many means to get rid of jodak, including witchcraft. Some Maragoli and others deemed jodak did move away, but most stayed.[6]

Cases were decided on their own merits. The issue that became central was how long the jodak had been on the land. No hard-and-fast rule about when a jadak becomes immune to eviction had ever been popularly accepted in Kanyamkago or the rest of Luoland. Some whose families had immigrated to Kanyamkago as early is 1918 were still considered jodak, and potentially subject to eviction, in the 1960s and 1970s. But friendship and personal rivalries mattered too, and in particular cases, some who were weg lowo themselves sided with jodak against the latter's hosts. The government's land adjudication committees (which included local members of both wuon lowo and jadak groups as well as officials from outside) also asked weg lowo where their jodak might go if evicted. It seems most had no satisfactory answer.

The jodak prevailed. When registration was locally completed in 1973, most Kanyamkago jodak still remained on the lands they had borrowed. The same happened elsewhere in Luoland. Some who had arrived just a year or two before were made to compensate their hosts in cash or did so on their own; others just received small landholdings. In one way and another, jodak became titled owners.

But this did not extinguish all interests of the old weg lowo in the land.[7] Some farmers felt, after registration, that any former jadak who wished to sell the previously borrowed land should return a piece of it to the original wuon lowo.[8] Nor did the jadak stigma just disappear. Grace Omamba, whose husband's family had immigrated from Nyakach Location a generation earlier, lamented in 1981 that even though she or her husband could award part of their titled land to a schoolteacher as their jadak if they chose, Kanyamkago autochthons still deemed her husband a jadak himself. She felt his land title had changed his standing economically, but not socially.

In brief, land adjudicators and registrars in western Kenya have tended to allow jodak full ownership rights (and more than a few of these have thus become larger landowners than their old hosts). In this way these have gained, and their old hosts lost not just land to farm and call home but also potential loan collateral, for whatever that may be worth.

To the list of tensions above one might add others between labor outmigrants and their kin remaining at home. Men who had gone to cities or plantations to work before the land registration, leaving brothers in charge of their shares of paternal homesteads, commonly found upon returning that the brothers' shares had somehow expanded during their absence. In Kanyamkago some such cases turned violent.[9]

Some of the "category conflicts" that land titling intensifies may be only temporary parts of the titling process, others seemingly permanent effects.[10] Boundary disputes seem to become more common as a rural community nears the time of registration but less so after titling.[11] Disputes over whole plots, by contrast, do not appear to farmers any less frequent after titling.[12] They may become more so as sales and mortgages become more widespread issues of family contestation and as locally novel legal concepts come into play in an alternate system of dispute resolution.

The Land Market and Its Ostensible Control

The registration was expected to stimulate a land market. It is hard to measure its effects in this regard since sales were not recorded beforehand, but evidence from interviews suggests that land sales became much more common in western Kenyan localities as the reform approached, as though it were seen more as a commodity than before. More farmers began selling off idler parts of their holdings. In the most densely settled areas of Nyanza and Western Provinces, the land market remained relatively sluggish.[13] Probably the best explanation is that rural men refused to part with land that marked their social identities as members of lineages—land that, for many who lived away, also meant future places to retire with relatives around to care for them.[14]

Most land buying and selling, in my experience, have remained local. As before titling, rural-rural migrants such as Maragoli moving to southern Nyanza have tended to stay with host relatives where they intend to settle, initially doing so as land clients like Luo jodak, then sometimes borrowed or bought other land once established there. Either the land market has not really opened up for long-distance purchasing by buyers from other parts of the country interested in coming to farm, or these have remained uninterested.[15]

While initially expected to increase security of tenure,[16] titling can ironically *reduce* it. It does so not only by introducing new temptations to gamble with mortgages, but also by vesting family rights and interests in individual hands in a way that renders them hard for other members to control. Not only kin of titleholders but also titleholders themselves are at new risk as it becomes easier for one member to hypothecate land others always considered held in trust.

The government's Land Control Boards are officially supposed to regulate transfers to safeguard poorer farmers and especially their "dependents" from ill-considered land alienations. Formally empowered by the Land Control Act of 1967, they are usually made up of elder men representing locations or sublocations and meet periodically at divisional headquarters under the supervision of divisional officers. These boards have not provided much of a safety net, as my observations of the Migori Division Land Control Board and a broader literature make clear.[17] Part of the problem is the political pressure larger buyers can bring to bear on the boards and their members. Another is in the wording of the Ministry of Lands and Settlement Handbook of 1969, interpreting the Land Control Act for the boards and still in use at the time of research. It gives clear priority to economic growth rather than equity: "First of all, a Land Control Board shall consider what effect the grant or refusal of an application is to have on the economic development of the land. . . . A highly successful and progressive farmer may find 500 acres insufficient for his farming potential. This proviso depends entirely upon the capabilities of the man seeking to acquire more land" (pp. 7–8). Note the emphasis on the (male) *individual* as the crucial farming unit. The great majority of applications to the Migori board for approval of sale were passed;

this board and others seem really to serve as rubber-stamp bodies. Applications for loan collateral charges (that is, mortgages) were usually approved automatically.[18] Thus, although land-secured credit is hard for smallholders to obtain, there is little official bureaucracy to safeguard farmers from risking a permanent loss of land once they have access to such credit. The land control boards are structurally incapable of doing their jobs effectively. Their goals are contradictory and they are subject to easy manipulation by anyone with vested interests and local power.

Titling is opening the door for a concentration of holdings into fewer hands. This was part of the explicit idea in the Swynnerton Plan, as noted earlier, but most observers since that time have deemed it a bad idea. There is still much room for debate about whether and how fast it might be happening, but there are some preliminary indications that it is indeed occurring.[19] Concealed in such an apparent trend are local counter-movements of *de*concentration, in which unused parts of larger holdings are sold off to smaller buyers. A net concentration of holdings may affect not only the rural population but also temporary city and town dwellers dependent on their families' rural farms for subsistence in periods of joblessness or upon their eventual retirement. Poorer farmers' losing land is likely not only to speed up movement to the cities but also to make life harder for those already there.

The ratchet effect of poverty, as observed in many rural East African settings, is such that a concentration of landholdings, once begun, can probably perpetuate and maybe even quicken itself.[20] This can happen in several ways, some subtle. Among other things, larger landholders can fallow their holdings more easily than smaller ones, they can more comfortably devote substantial hectarage to high-value cash crops without jeopardizing subsistence, they can secure cheap services and obligations from land clients, and they may speculate in grains—all of which may help enable them to buy up lands from less well-off neighbors in bad seasons. A pledge or mortgage system may contribute to any vicious circle of poverty or ratchet of class division that arises with broader processes of land concentration. It can do so by linking financial transactions with land transactions and by adding deadlines that can favor lenders (and potential land buyers) and disfavor borrowers in a risky agronomic and economic climate. But all of this presumes the mortgage system actually works—which is to presume that the land titling system (as well as the financial system) works in the first place. And that would be a lot to say.

The Divergence of Official and Unofficial Land Markets

While land sales and other comparable exchanges may have become somewhat more common since titling, few buyers or sellers have informed the government about them as planners of the reform expected. Only eleven (4 percent) of 246 registered land parcels in the valley sampled in Kanyamkago had been listed as sold, in whole or part, by September 1982, seven years after the registration was completed. Interviews revealed that substantially more than these had been sold in fact.[21] Only seven (3 percent) of the 246 parcels had been listed as subdivided or transferred in succession; all but two of these enterings were just preparatory to sales of portions outside the families. Again, many more had been subdivided or passed in succession in fact. Then there were all the other temporary and permanent exchanges that went on unreported: loans, swaps, jadak land clientage, share contracting, and so on. Because many holders initially titled were elders, the official register has been turning quickly into *a land register of dead people*.

There are simple reasons, and also some subtle ones, why farmers refuse or neglect to keep state authorities abreast of their land transfers. Doing so costs them time and money.[22] It can take several days' travel to the district headquarters, and it may require bribes. The officers and clerks are of mixed ethnic groups. The paperwork mystifies the unlettered, and some farmers fear being tricked. Land buyers continue normally to rely on local witnesses rather than on officials to support their land claims. Sellers, for their part, know that they may have much to lose in reporting their sales and relinquishing their title deeds, for there is always a possibility of confusion later (or perhaps of redemption by refunding payment—common practice in generations past), allowing them to keep the land after all. Just as important as any of this, however, is farmers' general feeling that the national government simply does not serve their interests.

To land registrars and members of land control boards, the farmers' refusal to register land transactions and successions has been a nightmare. They cannot keep up. Many farmers too, as individuals, are unhappy with the current practices of land transfers they see around them. But a net effect of the refusals to register transfers has been to keep land matters largely in the hands of the elders.[23]

In keeping the government at bay this way, the Luo are by no means unique. As early as 1950, the Ingham Committee report on credit had stated, on the basis of early land registration schemes on the coast, "Experience has shown that there is a very serious danger . . . for the land Register to be ignored and for transfers to be carried out without any notification, very much to the disadvantage of the transferee who may be completely ignorant of a register. . . . Unbelievable chaos and hardships have occurred in the Lamu district as a result of such happenings" (Ingham et al. 1950, 15). So the story is not new. It is just a question of whether one reads it as a story of "unbelievable chaos and hardships" or one of healthy semi-autonomy for rural communities.

Indeed, it seems that most everywhere governments have attempted individual rural land titling in Kenya and elsewhere south of the Sahara, researchers have likewise noted official registers' quick obsolescing as local land transfers of whatever sorts continued unreported.[24] A lesson the land tenure planners in Kenya's and other governments have been learning and relearning in these titling schemes is that *the imposition of a "modern" system of titling and conveyancing does not expunge the systems there already.* Instead it adds an overlay, an alternate system of devices and recourses. Having more choices now, between older and newer ways of staking or maintaining claims, opens new doors for some adept farmers and other rural (and urban) operators to take advantage of others. Some of these devices and recourses involve mortgages.

Double Dealing with Land Mortgages

Rights in mortgaged land are particularly easily to manipulate and make confusing, because they are divided and usually therefore in some way ambiguous. Of the many ways in which disputes are arising over mortgages, two are especially common in my data. One is that farmers borrow land titles from relatives or neighbors to use as security for loans and later find themselves unwilling or unable to make the repayments. The other is that farmers who have pledged their land titles as security for loans are sometimes tempted into selling their land to strangers without informing them or their witnesses of the charges on the land. Doing so leaves them free to default on loans if they wish.

The following case, from Kanyamkago, shows how both these things can happen together. Ocholla Ogweng' of South Nyanza sought a loan from Barclay's Bank in Homa Bay in 1979. Having no land title of his own to put up as collateral, he approached his wife's father, Ogwok Nyayal, to ask for help in obtaining one. Ogwok Nyayal went in turn to his own sister's husband,

Alloyce Ohero, and, paying him K.Sh. 400 (then about U.S. $53), persuaded him to let his (Ohero's) title deed to a thirteen-hectare plot be put up as collateral for the loan for Ocholla Ogweng'. The latter applied with this, and the bank issued him a loan of K.Sh. 30,000 ($4,000). Meanwhile, however, Alloyce Ohero sold parts of the land to two strangers, and these moved onto the land. Ohero did not tell Ocholla Ogweng' about these sales, or the buyers about the mortgage; nor (as with so many sales) did anyone register the sales with the government's district land office. Alloyce Ohero, the owner of the title, died in 1981. Ocholla Ogweng', the borrower, did not manage to repay his loan. The bank foreclosed and turned the case over to a court broker to auction off the land. One day surveyors showed up, much to the surprise of Alloyce Ohero's two sons, who had never been told of the mortgage and were expecting to inherit the unsold part of the land. By the end of 1982, it appeared that all the land, including the parts sold, was to be auctioned. The two buyers, in danger of being thrown off the land then, were angry at Alloyce Ohero's sons, holding them responsible for the actions of their dead father. Ohero's sons, in turn, were angry at their mother's brother, Ogwok Nyayal: they claimed that he had arranged the mortgage in the knowledge that Alloyce Ohero was to blame for the unhappy situation, but he being dead, no one was sure with whom to seek redress.

This case involved perhaps a rather unusual degree of duplicity or negligence on Alloyce Ohero's part, and carelessness on the part of some of the others, but its main elements are now familiar in the titled parts of the Luo countryside. Other cases of double deals have led to violence between neighbors as the parties playing by different rules have found out about each other.

Land titling has been accompanied by a proliferation of other double deals involving sales but not mortgages. Sellers change their minds and try to cancel sales — for instance, where buyers pay too slowly (and high inflation rates encourage a buyer to stall) or try to pay in goods of questionable worth, like used radios. Some sellers try to raise the prices initially agreed upon or reduce the hectarage, often because better bids come along before the price is paid. Others try to cancel sales when buyers do not move onto the land bought and cultivate it. They suggest, in doing so, that they still deem land rights dependent on good use, and perhaps that they wish to associate buyers with land clients (jodak). Some sell their land to several buyers in separate deals unbeknownst to each other, using different elders as witnesses. Others sell their land expecting that their divisional land control board will rule the sales void (to protect the sellers' dependents) once they, the sellers, have collected the money.

Individuals who gain personal title to what was once family land take on a kind of trust they can easily betray. Selling or mortgaging it for purely personal gain is indeed considered a betrayal, and this is the kind of dealing that Luo continue to say can produce *gueth makech*—roughly translated as "bitter blessings" or dangerous rewards—of which *pesa makech*, bitter money, is one type. One exposes oneself and one's descendants to retribution, if not by divinity then by the spirits of ancestors, particularly those of persons buried on the land, and also by the persons who have lost out, once they have died and become spirits themselves.

Luo farmers in my experience generally see both pros and cons in the tenure reform, and most who have been through the process are less troubled by the registration itself than with the later use of titles in mortgages that most deem dangerous to them and harmful to their communities. Since land tenure revolves largely around ancestral graves and involves the dead and unborn as well as the living, the dangers perceived in the new mortgage practice are not just practical but spiritual at the same time.

Even farming people who do not, for religious reasons having to do with Christianity or Islam, want to believe in local ancestral spirits still continue commonly to bury their dead in and around their homesteads, and to reckon their social identities in relation to the graves and abandoned homesteads of their forebears. These customs and understandings are so deeply embedded in Luo life, it seems, as to defy abolition by doctrine alone. And some who do not wish to entertain their people's more traditional-seeming ideas about spirits are none the less troubled in one way or another by mortgaging, not least because others around them continue—and will probably continue for a long time—to identify land and place with kinship and ancestry in a multi-dimensional understanding of belonging.

CHAPTER 8

Nothing More Serious

Mortgaging and Struggles over Ancestral Land

You can go to bed as an autochthon and wake up to find that you have become
an *allogène* [alien].
—AN ANONYMOUS CAMEROONIAN, ON PERSONS DEEMED NATIVES AND
STRANGERS

If human attachment to land is not by its very nature a matter of
life and death, it can certainly be made to be. "There is nothing
more serious in Luoland than someone snatching your land. . . . Land is life,"
said Aluoch Ondiek of Kanyamkago. Juni Asiyo, a young woman from Karachuonyo and Nairobi, once added this wry remark when explaining such Luo
feelings about land and about ancestors: "If you want to make an enemy for
life, mess with a dead Luo."

But neither Aluoch Ondiek nor Juni Asiyo was talking about just the
dead or about just Luo. This chapter is about encounters between people —
Luo and others — who lay claims to land and positions on it that others associate with their deceased forebears, and about some of the unhappiness that
can arise from the strong feelings involved. The mortgaging of homes and
farmland is, as should be getting clear enough by now, an issue fraught with
problems in western Kenya and elsewhere in tropical Africa. The invasions
and bloodshed over ancestral land are another. These need not always be the
same topic, but again they can be made to be, and in Kenya and Africa they
sometimes have been.

Of all the cultural misunderstandings surrounding finance in rural
Africa, perhaps none is more fundamental, or more instructive about both
borrowers and lenders, than the misunderstandings behind attempts to use
land as loan collateral in places where personal and family identities revolve

around lineage settlements and burial sites.[1] For it is here that we see, among other things, the stark contrast between people who assume that finance and economy are divorceable from social identities and histories, and others who assume that they are not.

Public lending in Kenya for farming on collateral security has been the task of a long series of organizations. Their frequent reshuffling and renaming reflect the enormous difficulty of their task as well as the changing needs to respond to resettlement initiatives—and there can be little harder than this—that were initially part of decolonization. The main overseeing board for resettlement for "Africans," opened in 1945 as the African Settlement Board, had been renamed six times by Independence: to the African Settlement and Land Utilization Board in 1946, the African Land Utilization and Settlement Board in 1947, the African Land Development Board (ALDEV) in 1953, the Land Development Board (Non-Scheduled Areas) in 1957, the Board of Agriculture (Non-Scheduled Areas) in 1960, and the Central Agricultural Board in 1963.[2] This last change, as Independence approached, represented the combining of administrative bodies for "white" farmers (in mostly highland and Rift Valley areas that had been called the "Scheduled Areas") and nonwhite or "African" farmers (in the "Non-Scheduled Areas," formerly called the "Native Reserves").

The lending authority from the early 1930s was the Land and Agricultural Bank of Kenya, generally known as the Land Bank. It served mainly "European" settler farmers until after the second world war, when as seen earlier, new money became available for various official bodies to start lending to "Africans"—and until the Mau Mau movement of the late 1940s and '50s helped scare the administration into launching a wholesale program of titling and lending.

In 1969, a successor body, the Agricultural Finance Corporation (AFC), was chartered by an act of parliament as a statutory board—that is, a quasi-autonomous, state-owned body or "parastatal"—under the then minister of agriculture and livestock.[3] Initially formed to promote land resettlement, the AFC assumed the wider functions of the Land Bank. Its activities came to include more diverse lending for seasonal and other crops, for machinery, for animals, and for other things. From then on the AFC, several commercial banking companies, and a number of small financial institutions have together composed Kenya's field of organizations issuing loans against titles to rural land on the basis of the mortgage. By the 1990s nearly all government farm credit secured with land titles in Kenya was issued by the AFC. Let us look first at the AFC and how its mortgage lending worked—and still does at the time of this writing.

Government Lending on the Land Mortgage

As the government's main lender on land collateral, the AFC lent for crops and livestock for both domestic consumption and export, with a heavy emphasis on export crops and European-interbred dairy and beef cattle. From its beginning the AFC lent to large- and small-scale farmers, but mainly large—for long, medium, and short terms, at interest rates usually a few percentage points below those of commercial banks and below official and unofficial rates of inflation (that is, at negative real interest).[4] Generating negligible if any profit, and paying lower salaries than private banks or other corporations, the AFC, like other public organizations, has had a hard time retaining highly qualified staff.

Borrowing from the AFC has never been easy for most farmers. Even though the AFC had branch offices in cities and towns across the country, the time and expense of what can be multiple trips for loan applications, as well as for subsequent dealings, can be difficult for farmers; the distances and transport costs have also discouraged AFC visits to borrowers' farms. As of the 1980s and early 1990s, at least, most AFC loan decisions, and especially those for bigger loans, were made in Nairobi, and the branch officers who must help prepare the applications and administer the loans were not present at the loan committee meetings. Branch officers complained that centralized decision-making lowered their morale. It also put heavy emphasis on high-level contacts and on criteria like landholding size and attachable salaries, and it deemphasized farmer character and local reputation. In all, communications between borrowers and lenders were few.[5]

The main land-secured loan schemes administered under the AFC for small farmers in the post-Independence decades were the series of four World Bank–funded Smallholder Agricultural Credit Projects (known in Nairobi as "Credit I, II, III, and IV"), from 1967 to 1989. For more than two decades the AFC expanded its lending manifold, from hundreds to many thousands of loans. From 1967 to 1989 the AFC expanded its lending from 546 loans totaling K.Sh. 17.9 million approved in 1964 to 15,037 loans totaling K.Sh. 1.24 billion (U.S. $76 million) approved in 1986—and it advertised a loan portfolio of K.Sh. 3.3 billion ($118 million) in 1991, including land-secured schemes and others.[6] By 1991, however, "parastatals" like the AFC had gone out of fashion in international development circles, particularly in Washington, D.C. World Bank support for the AFC and other parastatals had cooled, and tightened financial controls by this and other agencies, and some internal reforms, had begun to shrink AFC lending back down.

Who Borrows

Historically, lending under the AFC and its predecessors had been strongly biased toward larger farmers and toward the districts of highest agricultural potential. These districts were, as noted earlier, the first to receive the land titles. During the presidency of Jomo Kenyatta, a Gikuyu (Kikuyu), which lasted up to 1978, loans went mainly to the Gikuyu-dominated Central Province, though by whose actual direction is not entirely clear. Luo received far fewer than their proportion of the population would justify. The pattern, already well established by the time of Independence, was merely continued in the first two World Bank programs.

A few numbers will illustrate. While Central Province received 349 smallholder farm loans under the African Land Development Board (ALDEV) from 1948 to 1959, Nyanza Province, with a comparable population, received only 21 (Vasthoff 1968, Table 2). The First Smallholder Agricultural Credit Project (1967–73) under the AFC, costing about U.S. $6 million and assisting mainly projects for European-interbred cattle, provided more than thirty loans per thousand registered holdings in each of Kiambu, Nyeri, and Kirinyaga Districts (all Kikuyu districts of the Central Province), while providing only twenty-one loans per thousand registered holdings in Kisumu District and only three per thousand in each of Siaya and South Nyanza Districts (the last three being then the Luo-speaking districts). The three Luo districts together received only 208 (2 percent) of 10,000 farm loans issued under the project, though they accounted for well over a tenth of the country's population.[7] A similar pattern also obtained in the Second Smallholder Agricultural Credit Project (1973–76), which cost about U.S. $18 million (or about K.Sh. 142 million). No less than 58 percent of the country's 13,552 livestock and crop loans went to the Central Province, 26 percent to Kiambu District alone.[8] Patronage, pork-barrel politics—call it what you will, the pattern is familiar enough on any continent.

A change of regime altered the geographic pattern but not the principle beneath. After the death of President Kenyatta in 1978, the Central Province's and Gikuyu people's hold on AFC loans weakened. (This was a period of rapid expansion in World Bank–financed lending to small- and medium-scale farmers in Kenya, with somewhere between 44,000 and 50,000 new AFC loans in the third and fourth World Bank projects, accounting for some U.S.$75 million of credit.)[9] By the end of this period the share allocated to Rift Valley Province, the home province of President Daniel arap Moi, had risen markedly. In fiscal year 1989–90 Nyanza Province, with about 17 percent of the country's population and 2 percent of its land, received less than 2 percent of the funds in new AFC loans from all projects, by shilling amount; whereas Rift Valley Province, with some 21 percent of the country's population and 29 percent of its land, received 64 percent in that year.[10] Again a political explanation would seem self-evident, though by whose actual decision the regional allocations were made is harder to know than it might seem. As much as officers in the World Bank grumbled about patronage and threatened shutoffs for what they deemed corruption, certainly they did not prevent the funneling of their money to local interests.

The great majority of AFC borrowers by the early 1990s had been men, rather than the women who do most of the farm work in Kenya. That well over 90 percent of the land titles had been issued to men in the first place skewed the land-secured borrowing in itself.[11] Women did, however, share the risks of dispossession in the event of men's defaulting on their loans. Attempts to reach women's groups, lately a popular approach in development circles, were still in their infancy in the AFC in the early 1990s.

The AFC policy of rotating officers around the country had put a limit to the extent to which kin ties could be invoked in loan allocation. But bribes and kickbacks to loan officers or branch managers, as borrowers have told of them, seemed often to serve as a surrogate for kinship or friendship. Some who recounted having paid bribes had gone into debt elsewhere to finance them before starting. Others who said they had paid kickbacks off the top of their loans had still been charged the full principal and interest when these fell due. In effect, then, these people had to pay interest above that warranted by official rates.[12] Some farmers spoke of such hidden surcharges as a natural part of the price of getting a loan.

That AFC loans had helped the borrowers in the aggregate remained unproven. There were no reliable data, official or unofficial, on the social class of borrowers, beyond simple tallies of their official landholding sizes and the amounts they borrowed and repaid.[13] The most thorough study of the AFC to date found it "plagued with operating inefficiencies and financial mismanagement and [having] a weak administrative framework" (Paulson

1984, 109), an impression confirmed by other observers.[14] The task of monitoring farmers' use of borrowed resources had proved nearly impossible for the AFC, and whether it should be attempted at all is debatable.[15]

Evidence from South Nyanza District in the early 1990s (and the newer districts into which it has subdivided) showed that the institution's credit had made no big positive difference to this predominantly Luo district. The district's population had surpassed 800,000 by the 1979 national census, and the more fertile lands had already been titled for a decade or more by 1982. But, by June of that year, only 217 farmers had received credit from the series of Smallholder Agricultural Credit Projects. Fewer than 335 had borrowed from the office under all its land-secured loan schemes (source: AFC). By the end of 1990 some 3,970 had borrowed from the then two branches of the AFC in the district under all the institution's schemes: this is still less than 0.5 percent of the district's population (sources: AFC, World Bank). It was a slow start, given that about half the district was titled and that its higher-potential lands had been so for one to two decades.[16]

The AFC was an institution with high public visibility and political sensitivity, being closely followed by the newspapers. It was also, as suggested earlier, an important tool of political patronage, subject to manipulation of many kinds. Cabinet ministers and assistant ministers, parliamentarians, party officials, and other notables all had dealings of one kind or another with the AFC. About one-fourth of the AFC's farm loan recipients in the five sample areas of Jo Ann Paulson's study were government officials, including members of Parliament; she arrived at very similar figures for recipients of commercial bank loans.[17]

AFC lending officers knew that "political" loans are not usually recoverable — they called influential borrowers the "untouchables." Sometimes commanded by public presidential order to repay the AFC, cabinet ministers and other high government officials and contestants for office scrambled to look as though they were doing so, but, as a Kenyan news magazine put it, "the list of AFC defaulters resembles a roll call of Kenya's political leaders."[18] And in reality, by the early 1990s, repayment rates reported by the AFC continued to fall.

Whether politically connected or not, AFC borrowers nationwide tended to be wealthy. Borrowers were required to offer as security assets worth at least 150 percent of the loan amount, by the agency's rule; some branch officers used 200 percent as a rule of thumb. As of 1983, about 70 percent of AFC loan funds had been advanced in "large-scale" loans — that is, loans of over 20,000 shs. (sources: AFC, World Bank). The large loans, and some of the smaller ones too, had gone to large landholders. A 10 percent sample of loans issued by five AFC offices in Kenya, from 1976 to 1982, revealed that the borrowers' farms averaged eighty-nine acres, or thirty-six hectares.[19] Even those who borrowed less than K.Sh. 20,000 held an average of thirty-eight acres, or 15.4 hectares (Paulson 1984, 111). Later, under pressure from the World Bank, other international agencies, and the government, the AFC increased the proportion of its lending to farmers with less than eight hectares. In Kenya's densely settled central and western areas, however, where most of the country's farming population lives, eight hectares could still put a farmer among an elite.

Borrowers as well as lenders could be deemed responsible for the allocation of loans, since only people who think they have a chance are likely to approach the lenders in the first place.[20] But as farmers usually know eventually who among their neighbors has borrowed and who not, and as any offer of credit draws applicants, it is safe enough to say that the suppliers have a history of actively favoring larger landholders.

Borrowing, Repaying, and Misunderstandings About Interest

The AFC's borrowers in southern Nyanza, in my experience, had usually taken as much money or inputs on loan as the lending officers allowed.[21] AFC loans had usually been, as my interviews have made clear, the biggest or only ones most had ever received from any formal institution.[22] That the amounts issued in starter loans were broadly comparable at any time was noteworthy, in view of farmers' widely variant abilities to use and repay loans. The farmers who visited the AFC office seemed almost invariably to press for the maximum. But wants, needs, and repayment capacities are not necessarily the same.

Rural Luo borrowers of the AFC, like those who borrowed elsewhere, seldom seemed to know or understand interest charges in the same way as their lenders. Even where the borrowers accept the idea of "interest," one not directly translatable into DhoLuo, many continued to think of it as something that ought not to continue accruing over time. That is, *some never supposed it would or should be charged according to a "rate."* Some thought it was, or should be, set as static *ratio* — that is, a fixed proportion of principal, not one rising over time. Farmers sometimes said that the AFC branch lending officers, like others in the banks, cooperatives, and elsewhere, had not clearly spelled out to them terms of their loan agreements at the time of applying or borrowing. As even the lending officers acknowledged in interviews, they had had little incentive to explain the institution's policy clearly at the time. Their job, as they saw it, was to get the papers processed on the loans Nairobi approved. True, farmers could find the terms written in their loan agreements if they had the English proficiency to handle the legal English, but few borrowers seemed ever to have read these through. While most had heard at least from other farmers that they would be expected to repay more than they had received, many said they never asked and were never told at what rate interest would accrue, or from what starting date (the AFC in fact began charging it immediately). Most had not had the kind of schooling that would prepare them for the arithmetic—this was true even for many of the elite borrowers—and others had had it too long ago to matter. Still others who might have handled the math were sanguine or optimistic that they could use their loans profitably.[23]

Both farmers and AFC officers agreed that *borrowing farmers had expressed very little concern about interest at the time of borrowing:* they seldom asked about repayment schedules or calculated them out with the lending officers. Their questions were different. As both they and the lenders reported, they had wanted mainly to know whether they could take their loans in cash and in lump sums. Some borrowers supposed retrospectively that even if much higher interest rates (say, 100 percent per annum) had been charged, they would still have borrowed—they would just have gotten into quicker and deeper trouble with the lenders. Observations like these would, as noted earlier, be easy to misconstrue. They should *not* be construed as implying mental incapacity on farmers' part, but rather as reflecting the differences of schooling, and of cultural orientation concerning money and official bureaus, in which neither side was clearly right or wrong. And also serious needs or desires for cash, for any or many purposes—for borrowers themselves or for kith or kin.

Because the AFC did not write off "bad" debts, default rates were always hard to calculate. But Paulson calculated that by 1983, for all AFC schemes, only about 32 percent of the loans with installments due had been repaid (1984, 130). A later report indicated that by the end of the 1990–91 fiscal year, between 18 percent and 25 percent of all funds that had been lent from or through the AFC in the previous four years and been claimed as due had been repaid (source: AFC). Such figures must of course be taken with caution.

Available evidence in the 1980s and early '90s suggested that larger borrowers (that is, larger landholders) tended to have repaid no bigger proportions of their loans, and indeed *smaller* ones, than smaller borrowers. The issue seems to be not so much whether farmers could afford to repay as whether they could afford *not* to repay. Indeed, according to Jo Ann Paulson, "Clients with higher non-farm income have higher average arrears and a greater tendency to have been in arrears over six months. The evidence on repayment performance suggests that the key to the repayment problem is in the *willingness* to repay."[24] Reports from AFC officers also suggested that elder and illiterate farmers repaid more reliably than younger and literate ones, perhaps because the latter had more confidence of being able to manipulate the system or were more likely to pin their main ambitions off the farm anyway. Women were reported to repay more reliably than men, probably for some similar reasons—though the loans the institution had issued to women had been few.

Farmers are not just farmers, and farm loans to them are not just farm loans. Just as in Will Carleton's American ballad the narrator used part of his mortgage loan for a covered carriage (not a farm wagon), so too in western Kenya do farmers divert parts of their loans for other ends of their own. Borrowers divert much, and probably most, of their AFC agricultural credit to non-farming purposes like trade, housing, school fees, and consumption, and not least to the marriage payments and funeral contributions and travels that are so important in western Kenyan life. Among these, it would be hard to sort out the productive from unproductive uses, since some are productive indirectly or obliquely. Marriage payments, funeral contributions, and school fees are the uses rural people speak about as the most honorable, though many have lately considered second or further marriages an expensive luxury for men. Schooling has until lately been looked upon, rightly or wrongly, as a good long-term bet not just for the student but the parent or other benefactor as well. Taxi purchases are thought to be about the safest investment and the most lucrative over the medium term; they are popularly deemed wiser than most rain-fed farming pursuits. Rental properties in and around towns are another popular investment for those with the means to get in the door.

The case of Julius Omolo of Kanyamkago, established from interviews with him, his family, and his neighbors as well as from the AFC records, is an example of how loans are used and repaid. In the late 1970s, with the encouragement of a senior politician of his district, he borrowed K.Sh. 9,000 (about U.S. $1,125) from the AFC. He did so against the advice of his own two wives and neighboring elder brother, who all feared the risks. He handed over his title deed to seven hectares (just over seventeen acres) and agreed to plant four acres of sugar cane and buy six oxen. His second son needed secondary school fees, however, and after planting three acres of cane, buying another piece of land from a neighbor, and buying two oxen, Julius Omolo resold the oxen and his other animals to pay the school fees. He also used part of the money for bridewealth for his second wife. The cane field overgrew with weeds for shortage of available labor, but the son eventually made it through Form IV in school. Omolo had thought when he took the loan (or so he later recalled believing) that interest would not begin accruing for three years—enough time for a cane harvest and ratoon—but it began immediately. For eight years after the loan the AFC sent letters periodically, as the records showed, but Julius Omolo feared answering. About 1981 the AFC began sending vehicles to his farm. By this time Omolo had borrowed three more cattle from neighbors. When these owners learned that he was being dunned for repayments and might be in danger of having the animals and other "chattels" on his farm seized, they immediately took their animals back. In 1984 the mortgage was foreclosed. The auction date was delayed until 1986, but by then it had become clear that the politician who had introduced him was no longer protecting him from the worst. At the last minute, however, Omolo persuaded his first son, salaried in town, to clear the accumulated debt for him and recover the land title deed. Once through with school, the second son too found paid work as a clerk in a nearby town, and his salary was adequate to make occasional contributions to the parental homestead like iron sheets for his mother's (the senior wife's) house. The second wife gave birth to a son, who Omolo knew would be eventually be able to help him tend the reconstituted cattle herd even when other sons were at school or living away. So the outcome of the story for this borrower and his family was not unhappy, but partly because Julius Omolo and his kin made good use of the funds they "diverted" to purposes somewhat different from those initially approved. (Whether Omolo and his family would have done as well in the end by simply investing in the sugarcane and oxen, as instructed, is unclear.) Omolo reflected in 1992 that the episode had been so frightening and divisive that he would never consider borrowing against his land title again.

The case was fairly typical for the Luo country in several ways: the differences of opinion between the borrower and his kin about whether he ought to borrow, the use of the loan for more and different purposes than the one specified, the poor communications between borrower and lender and the surprise about mounting interest charges, the failure to repay and the foreclosure, and the family crisis. The case was also typical in that not only its real uses but also the sources of its repayment were mainly nonagricultural. One who understood Omolo's family situation in the round would not accuse him of having been shortsighted or unable to plan ahead. He was planning in more ways and over a different span of future time than his creditors or the international financiers behind them were likely to know or care about.

"Diversion" of funds from agreed to unauthorized purposes had caused much consternation to AFC lenders and other agricultural financiers whose jobs, office corridors, and programs are set up around the idea of an agricultural "sector." Different indeed were farmers' views. From their perspective, these diversions could be sensible responses to the risks of farming and to interest rate differentials between "agricultural" and "nonagricultural" loans. And, certainly, some of the purposes to which rural people had diverted their borrowed resources were economically productive in one way or another.

It was clear, by the 1980s and '90s, that the AFC had never been able to control or accurately monitor the uses to which rural people put their loans. Spot visits to farms were infrequent, the transport expensive. Given the scattered nature of many landholdings, the delicate differences in soils that only farmers are likely to perceive, and the resentment that sector-"targeted" lending can incur, it may be futile for official lenders to try to control loan use.

Whether the land mortgage makes much difference to loan repayment is debatable. Paulson's study compared "secured" (usually land mortgage) loans and "unsecured" loans within the AFC portfolio. Her discriminant analysis of 381 loans from 1977 to 1981, of which 72 percent were secured with the borrowers' property, found that "the accounts that are secured with the land titles of the clients have lower arrears but this relationship is not statistically significant. . . . The discriminant analysis does not show a strong relationship between secured lending and repayment."[25]

The World Bank's and USAID's rechanneling of funding away from the AFC and other state-controlled institutions in the early 1990s, as part of a broad movement away from parastatals and the "public sector" as a whole, began to threaten this heavily dependent institution. (The international donor and lender agencies' broader moratorium on new aid projects to Kenya from November 1991 to 1993 of course threatened it further.) The AFC continues to the time of this writing. If it were to go under, however, another institution might well be implanted in its place, for the periodic recreation of such institutions, with public fanfare, is a recurring pattern in East African countries as elsewhere.

The record of the AFC by the end of the twentieth century showed little hope that the institution would provide loans to a major part of the small-farm population in western Kenya or in the country as a whole. As the main arm of the government's land-secured lending, it had not covered the countryside. But since credit could only mean debt, it is perhaps just as well.

Bankers with Cold Feet:
Commercial Finance in the Countryside

The most important remaining sources of land-secured farm loans in Kenya in the late twentieth century were the commercial banks; normally these lent only against some form of collateral (or with an institutional guarantee). The first of them in Kenya was the British-run National Bank of India (later of Grindlay's), which opened in Mombasa in 1896. Like the government's Agricultural Finance Corporation discussed above, the banks began lending significantly to persons deemed "African" farmers only when these had begun to receive land titles after the 1950s.[26] Of twenty-four open in 1990, the most active in the countryside were the three largest, the multinational Barclay's and Standard Banks, and the state-controlled Kenya Commercial Bank. These institutions had handled nearly all bank loans to medium- and small-scale farmers. As of 1990, these three had about 137 of the nation's 205 full lending branches.[27]

The bankers considered their main business in rural areas to be deposit taking, and they took far more in deposits than they lent. Many of them, British trained, tended to be financially rather conservative. The independent Kenyan government had consistently pressed them to expand lending for small farmers, but they were reluctant to do so because of perceived default risks and administration costs of tending large numbers of small loans.[28] As the national *Development Plan* for 1989–93 noted (p. 124), the commercial banks had failed to meet the Central Bank's requirement of lending 17 percent of deposits to farmers.[29] Interestingly, the government's attempts to strong-arm commercial banks to lend in rural areas since Independence contrasted sharply with the early colonial government's policy of trying to *protect* African farmers from banks and individual moneylenders.

Lending rules, in any case, had inhibited smallholder participation. Borrowers were required to have savings records, and forms had to be filled out in English. Just as in the case of the AFC, farmers have often told me that prospective borrowers expected to have to pay bribes, kickbacks, or other sweeteners to the lending officers or bank managers unless they were related or somehow strategically useful to them. A variant was that some found they were talked into signing loan agreements but made to leave the precise terms unspecified for the bank officers to "discuss" and complete later themselves without the borrowers present. In the Luo-speaking areas I have studied in Nyanza Province, however, farmers who were asked what sources of credit were open to them almost never mentioned commercial banks. This was a finding also obtained in previous surveys.[30]

While commercial bank loans are hard for most farmers to obtain, they are no less useful a tool for lenders with political aspirations than government credit is. The case of a western Kenyan bank manager I shall call Simon Mirambo Duya, during the years of the Moi presidency, shows how financial credit and political patronage can intermingle and reinforce each other in the public mind if not also in private practice. Duya's case is noted here not as a statement of facts (since some of these are obscure or debatable) but rather as an observation on popular perceptions. Having worked in a Nairobi branch for more than a decade, Simon Mirambo Duya was installed in one of western Kenya's larger towns, where he became a branch bank officer. Within a year or two observers began to comment that he had befriended a high official of the Office of the President and to voice suspicions that he might be nurturing political ambitions of his own. Meanwhile the bank had multiplied its mortgage lending to the constituency where his home was situated — something most everyone perceived on his or her own (and something a privileged few could observe, if they wished, in public mortgage records). Interestingly, though, his own clansmen, inhabiting a clearly recognized part of the constituency, did not seem to be well represented among the borrowers. While some may have explained this hole as the result of selflessness, others suspected he was allocating the loans to persons just distant enough from himself to be doubtful supporters, to win them over. Still others voiced the opinion that he was afraid of later being in a position of having to collect from his own clansmen. In any case, some neighbors of borrowers remarked how easily these seemed to have received their loans and how unusually little scrutiny the bank seemed to have given to the feasibility of their ostensible farming or business enterprises. Within about two years, Duya was generally recognized as a potential challenger for the national elected office of a long-term incumbent from near his home in the general elections coming up, and he soon began campaigning openly in that constituency. Locals noted, some not without envy, that personal businesses of his own, including a fleet of pick-up vans, were blossoming, and that he now rode about in several luxurious new cars and had erected more than one large new house in town and country. Before the election, but soon after his perceived patron was suddenly transferred out of his Nairobi job, Duya found himself abruptly transferred out of western Kenya and sent on compulsory leave from the bank (just a coincidence, some wondered?). Observers noted that the flow of new loans into the constituency seemed at least temporarily to be drying up—it seemed almost no one even bothered to apply now—but that Duya himself had not been stopped. He used his leave, they observed, to campaign vigorously around his home at fundraisers, funerals, and "hotels," and at meetings of women's groups, some of which seemed to have sprung up under his advice as a dispenser of bank loans.[31] Within a few months it was beginning to seem as if he might well unseat his rival for elected office. Opinions were divided on the propriety of his resource management, but no one denied that he had proved an exceptionally able strategist or that control over bank credit had been among the main tools of his advancement. What some wondered next was whether he would still be in a position (or of a mind) to protect his old borrowers when their loans fell overdue and the bank began to foreclose on their mortgages. For few doubted that this was to come.

Whatever the factual particulars, the case partakes of a familiar lore in western Kenya, in which the public expects wealth and power to be mutually exchangeable. Politicians are expected to win voters and key supporters with loans and reward them with protection from collectors, and lenders are expected to use their positions to seek power. Whether the loans come from public or private coffers may not matter, and there is little in any such dealings that a careful player cannot justify somehow as "development" or public spirit. (And of course some loans *are* genuinely useful for their ostensible purposes too.) That family and lineage land has entered the stakes seems easy for many individual borrowers to forget—though not necessarily for their kin.

Even once a loan is obtained, a commercial bank's repayment schedule can make it hard to repay. The banks have tended to insist upon regular monthly repayments, beginning immediately after the loan is made. (They do so even for loans issued only in installments—something that surprises many borrowers.) These schedules do not accommodate conveniently the delayed, lumpy, and virtually unpredictable returns of rain-fed agriculture.

Those who had borrowed from commercial banks by the 1980s and early '90s tended to have been, like AFC borrowers, among the wealthier farmers of their areas before borrowing.[32] Most had also had wage incomes or other steady off-farm incomes at the time. A 1978 study found that 70 percent of the people in five Kenyan provinces who had borrowed from Kenya Commercial Bank (ostensibly) for farming received income from wage employment, while the first Integrated Rural Survey showed that only about 9.7 percent of all the "household heads" in the same provinces had income from wage employment.[33] And in the districts I visited, the borrowers from commercial banks had been few.[34]

Hollow Promises, Heavy Threats: Foreclosure and a Monkey's Head

How common was credit with land mortgages? By September 1982, more than seven years since land registration in the sampled sublocation of Kanyamkago had been completed, 25 of the 896 registered parcels in the sublocation—just under 3 percent—had been mortgaged for loans from the AFC, commercial banks, or any other source.[35]

By the end of 1991, during one of my revisits to South Nyanza and sixteen years after the land registration, the AFC had issued twenty-one loans to nineteen farmers of the same sublocation against their land titles, while commercial banks had together issued loans to fifty farmers there against land titles, and other non-bank financial institutions had issued four. As the sublocation by then contained 1,242 titled land parcels, about 6 percent of land parcels had been mortgaged to all lenders combined between 1975 and 1991.[36] Of this 6 percent, almost none had been mortgaged more than once. Fifty-eight percent of the mortgaged land titles remained unredeemed, a finding consistent with the low repayment rates generally experienced by the AFC and other institutions in farm lending.

All the borrowers were male. This was no big surprise, since well over 90 percent of the land title deeds were in men's hands. Language and literacy problems too made women far less likely to apply for institutional loans than men. Men were usually bolder in applying, assuming better chances. The credit was available, and appropriately scaled, to only a small and wealthy male elite.[37]

Even where land titles are required, having one did not by itself entitle a farmer to obtain a loan. It was only a prerequisite. What Okoth-Ogendo noted in the 1970s remained as true as ever in the 1990s: "In order to receive a loan, what appears to count is the social status of the applicant and his liquidity in the monetary system," such as might come from salaries, savings, investment in rental properties, and so forth (1976, 175). It had been a flaw in development planning for Kenya to assume that registering land would make institutional credit widely accessible to small-scale farmers. The promise of credit had long been held out to farmers as a carrot to induce them to register their lands, but so far it had been an illusory one. And so it remains.

How have Luo and other neighboring farmers responded to the scarce opportunities of land-secured credit?[38] Most are well aware that a land title mortgage entails a possibility of permanent loss. Court brokers advertise these events weekly in the national newspapers, and word spreads by mouth. Land confiscation is a most frightening prospect for Luo farmers. Understandably, most are reluctant to apply for land-tied loans: many of them, particularly elders, say that they would never consider it. The small numbers of land-secured loans are thus not wholly due to inadequate supplies.

Efforts of lenders and court brokers to foreclose on land mortgages have been fraught with difficulties. District administrators and farmers tell of auction boycotts in which relatives and neighbors of loan defaulters showed up with machetes and throwing clubs to threaten any likely buyers. Often, police security at land auctions has been tight. But this does not solve all the problems. Dispossessed farmers have sometimes simply waited and settled their scores afterward, violently, in their home neighborhoods. Or they have found other ways. In our Kanyamkago neighborhood one buyer of auctioned land was widely reported to have awakened one morning and stepped out of his door to confront a monkey's head impaled on a stake. He was rumored to have abandoned the land in short order. Whether the tale was true or apocryphal, its repetition along with others like it got the message across to others of what would be thought of their trying to obtain land the way he had.

It has become clear to officials of the Agricultural Finance Corporation and other lending bodies that land auctions in western Kenya are potentially explosive. By the early 1990s so much disruption and sporadic violence had surrounded land auctions in the Gusii (or Kisii) highlands that land-mortgage lending had all but stopped there, and the Luo country was not far behind.[39] Both AFC and commercial bank branch managers in these areas acknowledged they considered land title deeds practically worthless in themselves as loan collateral. They had become only a prerequisite.

The acute sensitivity of Luo and other western Kenyans about land confiscations must be understood in terms of kinship and politics. Among the Luo and numerous other peoples with lineages represented in settlement on the ground, farmers identify a place on the ground with any ancestors buried there, and with a place in the social order. *Graves and abandoned ancestral homesteads are critical* and not to be divorced from farm economy in Luo minds. Land is considered a permanent family asset, essential to lineage survival, and never to be let go of lightly.[40] Past and future as well as present come into conscious play, as Aluoch Ondiek of Kanyamkago told me, again, in an interview: "There is nothing more serious in Luoland than someone snatching your land. Even snatching cows, not so bad. . . . Land is life . . . it feeds the unborn, it feeds the living."

For Luo, as for other Kenyan peoples among whom rural crowding and a lineage system concentrate many kin together as neighbors, mortgaging the land is *mortgaging the ancestors* and gambling against kinship and the social fabric itself. The attachment of a man to his land, particularly ancestral land, is conceived of as something greater than his attachment to his word, his signature, or (as on the "signature" blanks of many loan agreement forms) his thumbprint. Even if there are no ancestors on it, and less personal history and emotion invested in it, living and as-yet unborn kin, and neighbors around, still hold their interests in it. In a common Luo view, then, any confiscation of land by an unrelated authority is fundamentally unfair. Luo speak of such seizure with the verb *peyo,* to raid or plunder. It is something close to an act of war.

Local resistance to land confiscation is heightened by political sensitivities common to all farming peoples of Kenya. It is within memory of many adults that an uninvited set of about four thousand European settlers retained exclusive control over about 20 percent (Smith 1976, 114; Leys 1975, 29) of Kenya's usable land—and a well-chosen 20 percent it was. It was within their lifetimes that the Mau Mau uprising of the Gikuyu highlands, a movement with land rights at its core, kept Kenya in a state of emergency for four years (1952–55) and accounted for some 14,000 African deaths.[41] In Kenyan minds, land alienation and bloodshed are closely tied.

Though seemingly every Luo has heard of land auctions, there is much room for misunderstandings in the lending and foreclosing procedures of the financial institutions, public or private. Most obvious is the problem of language. Local lending officers, rotated from one district to another, may or may not know the Luo tongue. If not, borrowers must know Swahili or English, or use an interpreter. In 1992, as in 1982, the standard final written notice that defaulting Luo farmers received from the AFC, before their land was auctioned, read as follows (it was written in English, with no translations):

> Dear Sir/Madam,
>   In view of the infringement of the covenants contained in and/or implied in the Loan Agreement executed by you in favor of this Corporation by non-repayment of installments, I hereby demand from you full repayment of your loan and interest, such repayment to be made at this branch before [date]. In the event of your failing to repay your loan and interest by the above date, steps will be taken to realize the security held by this Corporation in accordance with the Agricultural Finance Corporation Act.
>   You are thus given until [date] to make arrangements to transfer your mortgage to another bank or financial institution or to find another purchaser for your property.

Hardly the way to communicate with a peasant farmer who may have had no schooling.

Further problems arose from cost-covering measures of the lenders.[42] It was AFC policy, as noted, to lend only up to two-thirds of the market value of the property used as collateral. But in cases of land auctions, tied holdings were sold in their entirety, any balance being returned to the farmers in cash. Such conversions of land to cash put family wealth into individual (usually male) hands, in a particularly volatile form.

But often there was no balance. Farmers were compelled to pay expenses for farm inspections when in arrears: costly visits usually involving four-wheel-drive vehicles. They were charged all other costs incurred in foreclosure, including advertising and auctioneers' fees. These charges often came as a surprise, either because the conditions were inadequately explained at the outset or because of the time elapsed since the initial agreement was made. In any case, the charges were out of the farmers' control. In the pressured time of a land auction they were unwelcome, to say the least.

When they saw their land about to go, most farmers tried any means to pay up. At this point they tended to turn to rich relatives, to clan or locational welfare groups (if any), or to churches. But kin or neighbors were not always willing to help. The mere act of going to the government to apply for an individual farm development loan and risking a family holding can be enough to alienate kin or neighbors in a society with some economically egalitarian ideals. Luo have a proverb for cases like this: *ong'er kodwaro ip mabor, to oyudo,* "the monkey who wants a long tail gets it" (that is, he tried to get ahead of us; now he can live with the consequences). An AFC officer who had worked in Nyanza and Central Provinces generalized that Luo are much less willing than Gikuyu to help kin in cases of land distraint—perhaps a hypothesis for future research.

Sometimes a relative intervenes on behalf of a borrower, but alas, such gallants may turn out to be acting in self-interest. Philip Odede of Kanyam-kago borrowed K.Sh. 14,000 from the AFC against a land title. Partly because he borrowed elsewhere too, he repaid only K.Sh. 3,000 of the 23,000 of principal and interest due by the time the AFC began foreclosure. A neighbor and clansman, Joseph Onyango, heard of the upcoming auction and invited Okumu Apiyo, a third clansman in Kano who was seeking new land, to inspect the plot. Okumu Apiyo knew that if he acquired the land through an auction, he would be unable to remove his clansman Philip Odede from it. So he agreed to help him repay the AFC the balance due to clear the loan, and the AFC returned the title deed to Philip Odede; and in return, Philip Odede gave Okumu Apiyo half the plot. Okumu Apiyo entrusted his new share of the land to Joseph Onyango, still living near the land, to look after it temporarily, and the latter's wife began planting and harvesting on it. Soon Joseph Onyango began calling the land his own, saying that he had bought it at the auction that the neighbors had seen advertised. By January 1992 the three men and their families were all claiming land where only one had been before. Even though a land register and title deeds were initially expected to resolve disputes like this, they seldom do, for as evidence of local belonging, the presence of ancestral graves and witnesses' reports of land use and transactions can carry more weight than possession of a paper title.

Land losses through mortgages can split families. Gambling away an inherited holding is a most serious offense to a family and extended kin group, as the case of wealthy Caleb Mumbo of Kanyamkago shows. His son had borrowed from the Kenya Commercial Bank against Caleb Mumbo's title deed to finance a shop that failed, and the bank had had the family's land auctioned off—complete with ancestral graves. The buyer, from a more crowded northerly part of Luo country, had moved in and for the time was letting Caleb and his family remain in their own home. But Caleb Mumbo's daughter was so angry she refused even to give the father water. This went on until the buyer had found life so difficult that he moved back to his crowded old home. In cases like this, Luo neighbors sometimes suspect witchcraft to have been used against the buyer who abandons the land. Others expect the buyer's crops to fail (as they began to do in this case) because the land was *makech,* bitter or tainted with evil, for him since it had come from an unwilling loser. In such cases the spirits of the ancestors buried on the land are expected to be able to act not just against the family members guilty of gambling away the land but also against the non-kin who have tried to move onto it. In Juni Asiyo's words, "If you want to make an enemy for life, mess with a dead Luo."

Foreclosures and the process of land seizure have been problematic for all concerned. Farmers threatened with losing their land have usually succeeded in repaying enough at least to postpone land auctions. Where they have not, the lenders have sometimes canceled the auctions anyway for fear of violence or political repercussions.[43] So touchy are questions of land auctions that on occasion they have been suspended nationwide.[44]

The impracticality of foreclosing on land mortgages was well known to at least some government officials as early as the mid-1960s (Lawrance 1966, 126, 130–31; see also Leys 1975, 71–72). The individualization-for-credit argument, so deeply embedded in government policy, rests solely on the supposition that lenders desire to have a threat to wield before they will lend. But since the threat is so often an idle one in practice, this structure of perceptions and second-guesses on the part of policy-makers and lenders would seem to be built on quicksand. Early in the history of an area's exposure to mortgaging, it may be true that farmers with little formal education or access to legal counsel will be confused about their rights and their chances in land distraint cases. Eventually, though, one can expect popular lore to fashion its own expectations and probably also warnings about what hazards and hardships are involved — for debtors and their dependents, for repurchasers, or for others involved — in cases where land is seized, auctioned, and reoccupied.[45]

By the early 1990s, only a small minority of AFC and bank borrowers, among the Luo and other people intersettled in their country, appeared to have benefited from their loans in the ways agreed upon and repaid them without problems for themselves or their kin. Some who had tried the loans said they would never consider doing so again. The land-secured loans issued had been so few, and the problems in their use and administration so great, that *the promise of a mortgage system could scarcely be said to justify the hard adjustments involved in titling all Luo farmland as private property. Culturally or politically, it just has not fit.*

A system of alienable titles and mortgages is to some a dream, to others a nightmare, and it seems to stir up deeply rooted feelings wherever tried. The Luo case shows how different the meanings of land can be to farmers and to financiers. To one it can be an occupation or a retirement plan, an expression of family and lineage (for a man), a challenge from a mother-in-law (for a woman), a link with the ancestors, and a place to sacrifice to spirits or divinity in a crisis—in short, a place in life. To the other, it is a collateral asset or a percentage: at the most immediate, a title deed pinned to a form with a signature or inky thumbprint, in a stack of faded folders.

Rich local meanings of land, however challenged, are not to be expunged by a bureau or a market. They keep surfacing as issues in Kenyan politics. Indicative was that internationally famous 1987 case of the lawyer S. M. Otieno. After his death in Nairobi, we recall, there ensued a lengthy court battle that captured the headlines for six months, about whether his body should be transported to the Luo country for burial among clansmen as a Luo, as important clansmen there demanded—or, according to the wishes of his Gikuyu-born widow Wambui Otieno, kept for burial near Nairobi as a Kenyan instead.[46] In the end, by court ruling, the body was moved back to the Luo country and a riot was averted. The case illustrated, among other things, the continuing relevance of "customary" links between kinship, ancestry, and landholding in the Luo country.

More dramatic still have been bloody clashes between members of different ethnic groups in heavily intersettled lands—sparked, according to some reports, by double deals with new land titles, among other causes—which riveted Kenyan attention in late 1991 and early 1992, and which have continued sporadically up to the time of writing. The wave of local clashes spread into many parts of Nyanza, Western, and Rift Valley Provinces, involving Kalenjin, Luhya, Kikuyu speakers, and others in unabashedly, indeed proudly, ethnic or "tribal" violence and mass evictions. They attested, again, to the continuing roles of genealogy and ethnicity in land rights: issues that stir up passions of many kinds, and that ramify well beyond financial or economic matters. Land, as one Nairobi newspaper repeated a popular phrase, remains

Kenya's obsession; but the real concern is the attachment between particular land and particular people. We look into some of these skirmishes, and their deeper underlying concerns about identity, in the following few pages.

Blood, Soil, and Sovereignty: Violence in Waves

One of the common arguments used to justify land titling, as we have seen, is that it will render insecure tenure secure. I have suggested that titles that tempt their owners into selling or mortgaging land as individuals, in contravention of older norms and expectations of family and community, can make that land's possession, and its occupants' positions on it, not more secure but less. But one need not sell or mortgage land oneself, or do anything unwise, to lose it, and to lose a place on it. One can also lose land and home by brute force. Does titling land really offer any protection against forceful seizure and eviction by political leaders or intimidation by neighbors? How secure does titling really make possession and ownership when someone wants its owner out?

A series of violent episodes that have arisen on resettled lands in western Kenya offers a chance to see just how little protection a land title offers its holder when push comes to shove, when formerly cordial and peaceful neighbors turn into enemies, and when politicians take sides. It also offers a chance to see some of the limits not just of "secure tenure" but also of peace keeping, of state sovereignty, and of sovereignty itself as a concept.

The dramatic and unhappy series of events that have become variously known as the "ethnic clashes" or, more often, as "land clashes," have taken place as occasional flare-ups since the early 1990s. They have occurred mostly outside Nyanza Province, and some outside the wider lake basin, but they have at times involved Luo and other people from that province and the basin—mainly as victims but also at times as perpetrators. It all makes a story too complex to be told in full here, nor is it necessarily over for good. But a few points bearing on land tenure, credit, and belonging need to be made, and the reader wishing a fuller recounting of the gruesome details or the party politics in the background can find more detail and analysis elsewhere.[47]

The story is best understood not in terms of isolated incidents but as long waves of successive outbreaks that have jumped as if by some quick, infectious virus or by spark from one resettled area to another in events prompted in part by imitation. The actions have had distinctive and striking character, but they have not been the first episodes of the sort that western Kenya or the nation as a whole had seen, nor was their timing purely fortuitous. Far from it, either way. The tangle of circumstances that have led to bloodshed, fear, and forced migration are historical and geographic. They are political and economic. And they are psychological and sociological no less.

Ethnicity is not the only way to understand these events, but there have probably been few involved for whom it was not a salient principle of division—anyone could see and hear deliberate division. Some if not most of the particular ethnic groups involved were ones that had had violent encounters before over land, cattle, and other animals at issue. Among western Kenyan groups, Nandi and others lately classed as Kalenjins had skirmished with Luo and with Luhya neighbors. Maasai had skirmished with Gusii and Luo—all long before titling and some indeed before the start of colonial times about a century earlier. Gikuyu from central Kenya had fought for their land not only against Maasai and other near neighbors in the hills and savannah, but also, in mid-century, against colonial occupants and (much more importantly, as it worked out) against each other over loyalties to those, in Mau Mau. Kenya had known ethnic struggles over land, in plenty—not least because of colonial land takeovers, and because of confinements of ethnic groups into demarcated territories with identity cards and other devices.

The fighting that began in the early 1990s sprang not just from tribal or national issues. It sprang from international ones, too, and must be understood in the wider context of policy pressures and contagious suggestion. The end of the Cold War (for the time, at least), marked by the fall of the Berlin Wall, had brought about a shrinkage of aid funds and promises—from important bilateral agencies including the United States Agency for International Development and multilateral ones including the World Bank—that had been used to entice Kenyan and other African rulers out of the Soviet orbit. But international pressure on the Kenya government, in the grip of the Kenya African National Union (KANU) party since Independence and, since 1978, of its increasingly corrupt and dictatorial president Daniel arap Moi, to open itself to multiparty elections was felt strongly.

Resettlement Zones: An Inland Archipelago

The debate about political parties tied tightly into debates and anxieties about *majimbo,* or federalism—a movement for the greater autonomy of regions (read ethnic blocs) within the nation, more along the lines of

Nigeria's policy. In Kenya, detractors of majimbo feared it might mean that people who were members of local ethnic majorities or pluralities, in the Rift Valley and elsewhere, could more easily squeeze out or just evict members of local minorities, less constrained by national supervision or interference. Arguably, KANU officials in the early 1990s fomented or turned a blind eye to ethnic violence in tightly intersettled areas as a way of scaring the nation into thinking that a multiparty system would lead to nationwide chaos.

The resettled areas concerned had their own longer histories and wider involvements. Many were located largely in the cracks between districts (and also between ethnic groups) in western and central Kenya, mainly in Western and Rift Valley Provinces (a few of the smaller ones were located close to the southern coast). Many of them were in areas that had been cleared or thinned of their inhabitants by European and other foreign settlers under the colonial umbrella in the first decades of the twentieth century in the formation of the large farms and ranches of the "white highlands" and later repurchased by the government for redistribution to "African" farmers.

Most of these latter transfers had occurred between 1961 and 1975 as part of the centrally planned Million Acre Resettlement Scheme, whose planning and launching preceded Independence in 1963.[48] Resettlers came not just from the populations that had been evicted from those very lands — a crucial point in the violence to come — but from whatever land-short or land-hungry families and communities around Kenya could get approved. This included literate, well-connected members of elites, not least those who shared Gikuyu birth, language, and heritage with President Jomo Kenyatta and his kin. It also included members of land-buying companies they formed, and others from around Kenya to whom these in turn sold or leased their holdings.

Allotments at the outset were relatively generous, by the standards of the crowded former "reserves" from which many were moving: a seven-acre minimum in higher-density schemes, and more than sixteen hectares on lower-density schemes. These minimums were lowered in time, to a hectare or less for some recipients. Still, for Luo, Gusii, Luhya, or Gikuyu, land allotments could be several times the local averages back in the former homes. For former Mau Mau prisoners (mainly Gikuyu) or landless laborers, for whom the program was in large part ostensibly designed, the allotments could represent a new start. The lands were attractive: most, it will be recalled, were or had been fertile and well enough watered to have attracted European settlers in the first place. Loan agreements stipulated that plots must be fenced around their perimeters, among other requirements. So although land was being transferred back from Europeans to African farmers, it was clear enough whose model of farming the program designers preferred.

Resettlers moved onto their new lands with the help of government-issued loans of ten to thirty years' duration, carrying annual interest rates of 6.5 and 7.5 percent and hypothecation of title. The payment of those loans became problematic for more than a few, whether because of need or refusal to pay.[49] In its first years, though, the process was otherwise pretty peaceful. When the former deputy director of resettlement wrote in 1979 that after the resettlement of 66,000 families on 1,325 former European farms there had "been no bloodshed" (Abrams 1979, 5, 69), few might have predicted the recurring bloodbaths between Kenyans over the next three decades in those selfsame resettlement areas. They would have had to listen harder, for instance, to what the deputy director remembered having heard in Baringo years before: the Tugen Kalenjin "school children singing for the return of their old grazing areas" (p. 39).

Resettlers came with different intents. Luo, Luhya, and other resettlers from western Kenya most commonly kept ties to homes and lands where they had come from; Gikuyu and others from central Kenya more often were persons who had lost their lands in the Mau Mau emergency or before and started new homes and farms they seem to have meant to become their main and permanent homes and farms.[50] But the resettlement areas where the fighting occurred were, by the 1980s and '90s, mostly areas of rich ethnic mixture and locally shared and blended culture. That is an important part of the context. But a point also crucial for this study of landholding is that many of the people involved had land titles or leases that were supposed to give them security of tenure.

The times and places where the fighting broke out were ones beset with uncertainties about jurisdiction over land disputes. The Limitations Act, passed in 1978, had brought one shift in rules, as seen in an earlier chapter, and courts were clogged with land cases resulting partly from that change. The National Assembly's passing of the Magistrates Jurisdiction (Amendment) Act in 1981, with presidential approval and executive initiative, took some local authority for settling land disputes away from the courts, putting more of it in the hands of district officers and local elders. (These were not subject to the new twelve-year limitations rule on old grievances, as the courts were.) In titled as well as untitled areas, district officers (ranking just below district commissioners, at the level of divisions) could now compose and dissolve hearing committees. In resettlement areas, this change brought to the fore the issue of *whose* elders—which ethnic groups'—would be represented on hearing committees, under executive protection. In rural areas where lawyers are few, and where many residents are only part-time residents, information about changed rules and policies spreads around unevenly, creating room for misunderstandings and aggravating disagreement.

Spark and Spread

Who started the actual fighting on 29 October 1991, at Meteitei (or Miteitei) Farm in Tinderet, Nandi District, matters little for our purposes and may never be known. Various accounts of the story differ so much that one might think they were describing different incidents. Meteitei was a resettled 900-acre farm where Rift Valley, Nyanza, and Western Provinces come together. There Gikuyu, Gusii, Kipsigis, Nandi, and Luhya lived intermixed. It was a farm where dispute about a decade old was simmering, about a land-buying company's having oversold its shares; far more occupants had moved onto the land than they had expected at the time they signed on.[51] The "tinder" in Tinderet could hardly have been more apt; all it took was an incident of stolen cows and one shooting to set many houses ablaze at Meteitei and lead to several deaths.

Within a few days, when provincial commissioners' paramilitary forces arrived, eight major settlement schemes were experiencing fighting, including the area of the Chemelil and Muhoroni sugar estates on the Nandi-Kisumu borderland and land along the Kisumu-Kericho road. President Moi's decision on 10 December to open Kenya to multiparty elections did not quell the fighting; it only intensified, because or in spite of the change. By March and April 1992, several more districts—West Pokot, Bungoma, and Uasin Gishu—were seeing fighting in resettled areas. By September, less than a year after the Meteitei incident, a parliamentary committee, leveling accusations against other members of parliament, estimated that 779 had been killed and 600 wounded, and as many as 56,000 families rendered homeless (Kenya 1992, 75). Land titles did nothing to stop all this.

The ethnic alignments, as the fighting spread, were not accidental or random. Gikuyu, in addition to being more committed as permanent transplants than some others, had long been at the center of Kenya's economic and political scene, and because of this and because they resented having been edged aside during the Moi years (he being a Tugen Kalenjin, it will be recalled), they posed as an ethnic group the biggest threat to Kalenjin political superiority in Kenya during that period. (Mwai Kibaki, who was eventually to unseat him in 2002, was Gikuyu by background.) Gikuyu became the most common targets of hostility from Kalenjin, Maasai, Samburu, and others. Kalenjin, Maasai, and Samburu were ones who in most of the resettled areas could trace ancestry to the lands in question as former home lands or farms—even if, as was often the case in areas formerly only thinly settled, they could point only to grazing land visited occasionally. Kalenjin, especially Nandi, targeted Luo and Luhya as well as Gikuyu.[52] More often than anyone else, if any such distinctions can be drawn at all, Kalenjin people of one ethnic subgroup or another were among the parties at the center of the clashes in the 1990s, most often as the ones staking claims of "original" occupancy—rightly or wrongly. They were quite possibly the ones who had been most resentful of the presence of others whom colonial and later independent authorities had invited back—in-movers who had arrived in such numbers as now to outnumber them and who seemed to threaten, if things bounced that way in the elections, to throw them off again.

But all these animosities and hostilities were requited in some measure before the violence had lasted long, and it would be an oversimplification just to call Kalenjin or any other one ethnic grouping, large or small, the main instigators. It was an era of *general* insecurity in the richly resettled areas—an era in which neighbors who had formerly gotten along cordially, letting their children play together with those of members of other groups and speakers of other tongues, suddenly fell out, reverted to ethnic name-calling, and organized militias as tribes, often literally overnight.[53] This is a crucial point: it was *not* just about "ancient tribal animosities," since for many these had long been in abeyance or overcome.[54] Land titles were not bringing peace, for there had already been peace—and they were not preventing fighting or evictions either.

Nor was the fighting really just about crowding by itself. The ethnically more homogeneous areas from which many of these settlers had come—in Logoli Luhya country of Maragoli, in the Gusii country, in upland and parts of lakeside Luo country in western Kenya, and in quite a lot of Gikuyu, Meru, and Embu country in central Kenya—remained far more densely settled, *and* more peaceful, than the resettled zones where the fighting took place.[55]

Ethnic intermixture was undeniably part of the formula for disaster in these particular episodes, but it was a richer mix of causes and motives, some of them psychological, that was at play. People get more upset, it often seems, about places or possessions taken away than they get pleased by ones gained; such are the asymmetries of human emotional response. People who considered their ancestors to have been evicted from land, and who saw others gaining by what they could often construe as connections or favoritism, were not about to forget it. In a time of economic downturn and pre-election political insecurity, in a part of the world that had over decades and a century become accustomed to winner-take-all politics, they *chose* not to forget it. And they were not about to be scared off by anyone else's land titles.

The ones who chose to act, or were egged into it, did it in distinctive ways. Young men in gangs, made up of friends or relatives, dressed up in uniforms made of tee shirts, often black or red, and school shorts. (The latter are ordinarily too demeaning for post-adolescents to want to wear, but now quickly transformed into an affordable combat uniform, frighteningly anomalous on virile bodies). And, on occasion, they wore clay face paint. Some of them spread around leaflets with warnings to members of other ethnic groups — *titled landowners included* — to clear out, and signed them with ethnic identifiers like (in at least one case) "Nandi Warriors." They armed themselves largely with very local and traditional-seeming weaponry like spears, machetes (*panga* knives), throwing clubs (*rungu*), and bows and arrows.[56] (Some of these men eventually turned to firearms, including automatic ones, in places heavily touched by cross-border trade and cattle raiding.) Also, fire itself became a weapon of choice.

It was all of a pattern, and a pattern seen before in boundary skirmishes in the late precolonial and early colonial period, in the Mumbo movement, and in the mid-twentieth century Mau Mau. These were angry, excitable young men, some self-mobilizing but many cheered and abetted from near and far. They now included educated and frustrated school leavers and even university graduates — deliberately *savaging it up*.[57] Tribalism was a tool of terrorism. What can a land title on paper ever do against forces like these?

Protestant and Catholic churchmen spoke up increasingly as the conflicts spread. They accused the president, Kalenjin parliamentarians, and KANU of what they said was actively fomenting the violence and committing human rights violations; and some issued veiled threats of spiritual reprisal. In a sense, all this represented a questioning of, and a challenge to, state and KANU sovereignty.

The timing of these and other concomitant challenges to party rule and national sovereignty must be understood in a wider regional context. Among Kenya's immediate neighbors, Sudan, just over the northern border, had experienced bloody and complex civil war in its south over most of the period since its independence in 1956. Tanzania, to the south, had in 1978–79 rebuffed a Ugandan invasion. To the east and northeast, in Africa's horn, the Somali state had just collapsed in 1991, and Ethiopia was just in the process of losing Eritrea to a secession movement. It was no longer to be assumed that Kenya as such would avoid a full-scale civil war or secession of its own and survive as a solid color on the map. It was no longer to be assumed, any more than it was in Thomas Hobbes's time, that state would enduringly prevail over church.

None of the mounting internal or external pressure daunted Moi or KANU, though. He and it were reelected with a reported 36 percent of the total vote, over a fragmented and disorganized field of opponents on 29 December 1992, in Kenya's first multiparty election in twenty-six years. And in 1993 the fighting continued to spread to new districts, including Nakuru and Narok. It spread into forests and on occasion even into the town of Kisumu. In resettled rural areas, sometimes thousands fled their homes at a time.

The words of at least a few were recorded not long afterward. A Luo woman survivor explained how a cooperatively owned Owiri farm, in Songor, Nandi District, was attacked and its houses burned in the night in late 1991. "I woke up, and I could hear the Kalenjins shouting in the dark, 'Luos, you must move.'" On the other side, here are the words of a Nandi Kalenjin survivor of a raid at Chepsweta, Kisumu District, in 1993: "I came out of my house at around 11:00 P.M. and saw burning houses and heard people screaming in Luo. . . . They were shouting, 'Let's kill this old man'" (Africa Watch 1993, 83, 24). By the time the Africa Watch three-person delegation finished its tour of seven districts, its report's author, Binaifer Nowrojee, could conclude, "The violence has resulted in the deaths of over 1,500 people and the displacement of over 300,000. The majority of the victims are non-Kalenjin." As the roundness of these numbers suggests, reliable figures are scarce or impossible to find.[58] In the shared opinion of this watchdog agency and some others, though, the president's conciliatory words and attempts to quell the fighting with paramilitary forces were too little, too late.

In the troubled resettled areas, society's torn fabric has not mended quickly. Once scared off the land they occupied, or once having lost it by forced sales at depressed prices or by mortgages foreclosed, most forced out-migrants have never returned.[59] Their land is gone. *The titles did not protect it,* and the titles lost have not come back.

The Rift Retorn, the Nation Swallowed Up

There is one more episode of turbulence to tell, one bearing on land and belonging in town as well as country. Upon the presidential and parliamentary election at the end of 2007, and into early 2008, a human volcano erupted—or re-erupted—in Kenya with the most destructive force seen since the time of the Mau Mau movement before Independence. It was a volcano many Kenyans and foreigners had expected for several decades might blow any time, but one that took special circumstances to set it off. The following brief description, drafted during the first six weeks of the action as this work was heading into press, cannot do more than give a flavor of the happenings still unrolling quickly. The country was teetering unpredictably on a knife edge between peace and civil war. The story was making front-page headlines worldwide, and diplomats were flying in and out of Kenya—from the United Nations, and from countries and churches in Africa and overseas—looking to help key Kenyans find solutions or persuade them what to do. The one they found was a trial compromise.

Just some basics then. By many economists' reckonings, the country had since the late 1990s begun an economic upturn, whether because of its leadership (Mwai Kibaki, president since 2002, being a respected economist himself), rises in export commodity prices, or other factors. There had been many government promises about cleanup of corruption since the end of the Daniel arap Moi regime, which had become world famous for it; and Moi had indeed honored democratic process by allowing himself to be voted out of office in Kibaki's favor. Although poverty and corruption remained big concerns for Kenyans, public expectations had been rising, as they had been before at least one previous incident. This time though, the violence happened after an election, not before, and it was directly triggered by the election's own outcome. The new violence and purges affected the inland archipelago of resettlement zones of western and central Kenya, just as in the incidents described above. But this time the blaze ignited in numerous towns and cities too, including the capital, Nairobi—and along transport routes across much of the country. Taking on more surface traits reminiscent of the most dramatic state collapses in the region (Somalia in 1991, or Rwanda in 1994), this crisis imparted more the feeling of national meltdown, causing Kenyans and foreigners alike to rethink their most basic impressions of what Kenya, East Africa, and their civilization were about.

The two main contenders and their parties in the 2007 election were incumbent president Mwai Kibaki (Party of National Unity—PNU), a Gikuyu; and Raila Odinga (Orange Democratic Movement—ODM), a Luo, son of the former vice president Oginga Odinga. This last, it will be recalled, had been chosen but then soon dismissed and marginalized by the nation's first president, the Gikuyu Jomo Kenyatta, just after Independence, and Kenyans had watched the son, another wealthy businessman-turned-politician, rise for years as if to take up where his father had left off. Now, in pre-election opinion polls, Odinga and the ODM (colloquially shortened to *Chungwa*, orange in Swahili) were favored to win. Ethnic alliances and fault lines had shifted somewhat between election years. This time, in the election and the violence that shortly ensued, Luo, Kalenjin, and Maasai (all "orange"), groups with their main home areas in and west of the Rift Valley, found themselves basically allied against Gikuyu, Meru, and Embu, the groups with their main home areas in central Kenya, and Kamba, whose homeland stretched from there east toward the coast. This latter set of ethnic groups comprised the main backers of the Kibaki regime. (If Luhya leaned more toward ODM and Gusii more toward the PNU and the Kibaki regime, as some reported, their positions were less clear.)

There was every reason to suppose that Kibaki, if bested in the election, would follow Moi's footsteps and hand over to Odinga. In parliamentary seats won, Odinga and the opposition outscored the president's party by roughly three to one (about one hundred to thirty-five), with more than half of Kibaki's cabinet being voted out of office in the process. (Gikuyu incumbents who were defeated included even the widely admired Nobel laureate and former assistant minister Wangari Maathai, among other prominent names.) Most reports during the counting seemed to have Odinga narrowly winning. So when on Sunday, 30 December, after several days of vote counting, delays, and a counting freeze, the Electoral Commission of Kenya (a government-appointed body) announced that by a narrow margin Mwai Kibaki had been reelected, and he was sworn into office within minutes, many Kenyans and foreigners alike were astonished. Angry crowds complaining of counting delays had already taken to the streets in Nairobi, Kisumu, and elsewhere.

It must be left to jurists, political scientists, or historians to sort out the many complaints about vote-rigging and fraud that were made during and after the election. They included stories about polling stations that were closed before their queues had voted or were barred from election monitors; local tallies above 100 percent of eligible voters; unexplained delays in vote-counting for key districts; and the like. They also included counteraccusations of rabble rousing. All this, and the incipient violence, were widely publicized in the national and international press in those last days of December and first days of January. Diplomats for the United Kingdom, the European Community, and then (rescinding an early congratulation) the United States and other bodies soon voiced skepticism about the election's result, variously refusing to congratulate or even to name Mwai Kibaki.

Town as well as country ignited with violence this time—in some places, but not everywhere, with heavy, armed response by military, paramilitary, and police forces. The towns and cities had reporters, amateur photographers, and movie makers right at hand to record stunningly vivid scenes of crowd and police violence and soldier brutality against unarmed civilians, and Web-loggers to help broadcast them around the world. Rural settings sometimes made the news, though only when something particularly dramatic occurred like the burning of a church or school packed with trapped people, by angry mobs, or the appearance of government helicopters firing over crowds.

For the first month and a half, up to mid–February, the disturbances continued in sporadic outbreaks in different places, adding up to a steady stream of splashy news. Some gatherings of protest were unarmed, but others were armed in various ways—sometimes in the same crowd. The weaponry most frequently depicted in news films included bullets, tear gas, rocks and rock-throwing slings, long *panga* knives (machetes), bows and arrows (including poisoned arrows), and improvised weaponry like table legs, iron bars—and fire fueled with gasoline, rubber tires, and the clothes and bodies of its victims. Once again, vigilantes mixed new techniques with old. But an underlying theme repeated. Once again, to the dismay of all who cherished the image of Kenya as a modern nation of skyscrapers, business suits, and constitutional democracy—and a tropical African exception—some of the gangs and street throngs were deliberately, and ostentatiously, savaging it up.

Once having begun in the form of political party demonstrations, the violence continued in other forms. It soon took on more the character of vengeance killings pitched along ethnic, class, or other lines, or just the seemingly almost spontaneous acts of angry, excited, or frightened crowds. A quickly expanding "slum" or shanty community like Kibera, which after several decades of rapid growth had reached a population approaching a million by 2007–8, had depended on informal networks of nongovernmental and church organizations as well as on family ties and friendships to hold together its members of disparate ethnic groups. It had relied on these to keep peace between landlords and tenants, between merchants and the broader public on whose presence and custom these depended. Now this webbing was stretched and torn. Named street gangs (for instance, Mungiki, a Gikuyu gang, and Taliban, a Luo gang), already becoming well established in the peri-urban areas, flew into action, as did ad hoc mobs and smaller groups of vigilantes. Homes and shops were left burned and ransacked (many in rows of others untouched), if the owners or their families escaped at all. Suddenly, neighborhoods, their associations, and the local economy had holes in them. Nairobi (at first in its burgeoning slums), Kisumu, Eldoret, Nakuru, Naivasha . . . city after city, town after town broke into crowd and gang violence, partly cleared out, and found itself with holes in it.

Meanwhile, members of Kalenjin and other allied groups in the Rift Valley pressed forward the covertly organized movement they had promoted in the two decades preceding, taking advantage of the nation's paroxysms to attack Gikuyus in particular whose families had resettled there among them. Truckloads of refugees with mattresses and whatever other belongings they could carry headed across the countryside for "repatriation" to "home" areas—if they could make it through the roadblocks of men with pangas asking for identity cards, and the body parts strewn about representing people with the wrong names or languages to respond with. Luo and other people similarly moved out of other parts of the country where they felt threatened by Gikuyu or their allies. Government trucks helped with the human transport. In more than a few places, vigilantes and looters held up traffic with impromptu roadblocks, some of them butchering hapless travelers who responded in the wrong languages. Others in other places broke up train tracks, while at the port of Mombasa, the docks filled up with unloaded containers and cargo ships backed up at sea. In one way or another, the country seemed to be grinding to a halt.

By the end of the first six weeks of fighting and destruction, in mid-February 2008, the counts by agencies like the United Nations and the Red Cross, reported by international news agencies (for instance, Associated Press, Reuters, BBC, *New York Times*), had risen to over 1,000 deaths (some publications stated 1,500 or more)—with well over a quarter million (some publications stated 600,000 or more) displaced from their homes. Displacement itself was likely, of course, to lead to much sickness and death in its own indirect ways—not least through the drinking of contaminated water—and thus to swell but also obfuscate the death toll. Just as in earlier eruptions of violence, no single authority's count—certainly not the government's, whose numbers were usually among the lowest estimates—seemed particularly worthy of trust, and most numbers were rounded to several digits. More accurate, perhaps, just to say a lot of people suffered.

By the time the violence and vengeance started seeming routine, journalists began looking to historians, anthropologists, and other scholars for other angles to explore beyond the election results, vote counting, and party proclamations, and beyond the shock and horror of mob scenes. Other longer-term reasons and subtler motives began to break through to public awareness at home and abroad. News stories touched more upon the history of the resettlement areas and ethnic skirmishes in Kenya, and about their rootedness in the problems of access to land, and the ideology of majimbo with its subtext of ethnic purging and separateness, which seemed to be turning into a de facto reality in Kenya. The troubles were about tribes, undoubtedly, but not about tribalism alone.

The troubles remained very much about sex and gender too, and this too was clear enough in the news coverage. The demonstrators visible in the film footage of angry crowds and gangs were mostly males who appeared to be in their teens, twenties, or thirties—many doubtless unmarried. Many behaved, in crowded streets, in ways probably few would have done if alone or under calmer circumstances. In some settings less public, the reported problems often included gang rape, sometimes with expressed interethnic hostility involved, and with much risk of infection, for victims if not also perpetrators, in a time of HIV epidemic occurring anyway. As all this suggests, the fault lines also concerned age and stage of the life course. Young men with uncertain job prospects lacked the means to marriage and local respectability. Their remaining "youth" into middle age could provide them with flexible options but also demeaned them in a society with a long gerontocratic tradition. Kenya's oligarchy and its main challengers in the 2007 election and its immediate aftermath were mostly men over fifty or sixty years of age—Mwai Kibaki being seventy-two and Raila Odinga sixty-one.

Ever behind the purging and pillaging were poverty and class resentment. Much of the violence was accompanied by looting, by solitary individuals or gangs—from shops, homes, and other buildings. But other violence involved burning and other simple destruction. Some was carried out by unarmed youth, but other looting and destruction were performed, as in previous episodes, by government soldiers, police, and paramilitaries. Many Gikuyu and other victims attacked in towns were shopkeepers, landlords, or other business proprietors—just the kinds of people most likely to have incurred simmering local resentment by their mere conspicuousness or commercial success. Some were titled owners of the property, others renters, still others unapproved tenants. The inequality of ownership and access to land and buildings is always among the factors determining class ascription and antagonism.

The violence was also about political disempowerment, something again tied into class. To some opposition supporters, the president and regime represented a class unreachable. One man in the Nairobi slum Kibera who identified as a gang leader, and who bore a common Luo name, was interviewed on film by journalist Paul Mason (BBC "Newsnight," accessed online on 1 February 2008). He spoke of sending a message about the "stolen" election, in a *stone* to throw: "This is the simplest . . . a phone call to the world" and its leaders to influence the regime to cede power. The leaders of both the regime and the opposition were widely accused elsewhere of having for years recruited ethnic cleansers—people who might mobilize street gangs and country lynch mobs. Right or wrong, such perceptions did open the door for foreign attempts at diplomatic intervention—from South Africa, Ghana, Britain, and elsewhere. But not all these were equally received. During a visit to Nairobi by United States Secretary of State Condoleezza Rice on 18 February (a time when former United Nations Secretary General Kofi Annan was in his third week of his own visit to reconcile the factions), Martha Karua, the minister of justice and constitutional affairs, commented, "We will not bow down to dictation" (*New York Times*, 19 February 2008, A11).

In any case, on 28 February, while Annan was still present as a mediator, the Kibaki and Odinga negotiating parties struck a provisional deal for a coalition government. Kenyans at home and overseas expressed much relief, even euphoria, upon the breakthrough. The process of coming to agreement on the terms of the deal took long enough that tensions mounted again, and deadly rioting recommenced in several cities, including Nairobi and Kisumu, by the time the precise terms were announced on Sunday, 13 April.

This was the deal in a nutshell. Kibaki remained president. The vice presidency went to Kalonzo Musyoka (who by election time had become a Kibaki supporter). But a new post of prime minister was created, and Odinga was appointed to it as agreed. Two deputy prime ministers were appointed,

one from Kibaki's PNU and one from Odinga's ODM. The cabinet was en-
larged to an unprecedented size of forty-two ministers and fifty-two assistant
ministers (together, nearly half the parliament). Some key positions in it, including finance, internal security, defense, and foreign affairs, went to members of Kibaki's PNU party; but land, agriculture, local government, and
national planning were among the posts that went to members of Odinga's
ODM party. A rough numerical parity in number between PNU at seventeen ministries and ODM at twenty (with a smaller third party, Musyoka's
ODM-Kenya, at three) meant, not incidentally, substantial division of posts
between Gikuyu and central Kenyans hitherto rallied behind Kibaki, and
Luo and other western Kenyan and ethnic groups currently behind Odinga.
Women got to head seven ministries, the most yet, though still only a sixth
and not the ones most coveted or closely watched. Included among four
new ministries created was one for northern Kenya and other arid lands–the
lower density areas most dependent on animal herding and thus on rural
mobility.

With one government again, Kenya could again call itself a nation. Its
road ahead was not without bumps. Some Odinga supporters grumbled that
he and his negotiating team had conceded too many of the most powerful
positions, and human rights activists and others complained that the government was becoming too bloated with high-paid and privileged officials
at the rest of the country's expense. Nor was all the violence over. On the
same weekend when the new deal and cabinet were announced, something
else happened as if to underline the country's bloody recent history and its
fragile condition. Virginia Nyaiko, wife of Maina Njenga, a jailed alleged
leader of the Mungiki gang, was found beheaded. Further deadly riots flared
right up in cities, along with more gang roadblocks and tire burnings, and
a train derailing, in towns and countryside. All this resurgent siege activity
made the new coalition government's promises of constitutional reform and
of a new national land policy seem a rather distant dream. But it didn't make
land shortage and maldistribution any less important as underlying causes
of violence in the first place.

Not just autocracy or democracy but the wider issue of sovereignty was
now at issue as clearly as ever before. Whether the street crowds, the current government regime, a bigger foreign country, or the world was to be in
charge in Kenya was anyone's call. But one category not likely to be in charge
any time soon was the quarter of a million or more—an unknown fraction of
the displaced—who had lost their land and homes and were set off in tented

relief camps, or kept under watch in churches, police stations, and prisons also turned into camps, for indefinite duration.

If some activists in high offices and in the streets were playing up tribal rivalries, other people demonstrating or remaining behind closed doors were terrified of their sudden resurgence as the issue of the day. Certainly the discourse of Kenyans interviewed by journalists, and of those in direct contact with me in the weeks while fighting was going on, was full of ethnonyms (that is, names of "tribes") as well as political parties. It was also full of mentions of land, attachment, and ancestral homes—all about belonging. But such connections had their limits. Some people who moved or were moved to what were deemed ancestral homelands had never actually lived there and had lost whatever contacts they might have had there. One longish newspaper article laid these things out especially vividly. "Luos have gone back to Luo land, Kikuyus to Kikuyu land, Kambas to Kamba land and Kisiis to Kisii land. Even some of the packed slums in the capital, Nairobi, have split along ethnic lines," wrote *New York Times* reporter Jeffrey Gettleman in "Signs in Kenya of a Land Redrawn by Ethnicity" (February 15, 2008, A1). But some of these people felt not just destitute but effectively rootless when they arrived. "We came here with nothing, like cabbages thrown in the back of a truck," said one William Ojiambo to Gettleman about his movement from Nakuru to Luo country after a gang of attackers from another ethnic group burned all he owned. In another case in the same article, a seventy-year-old woman named Sarah Wangoi, interviewed in Othaya, Central Province, recounted having spent her life in the Rift Valley, but she "was chased off her farm in January by a mob that called her a foreigner. She now sleeps on the cold floor of a stranger's house, seeking refuge in an area of Kenya where her ethnic group, the Kikuyu, is strong. It is, supposedly, her homeland. 'I am safe now,' said Ms. Wangoi, though the mob still chases her in her dreams." When asked what had happened to her neighbors, she said, "They were like sliced meat" (p. A10). Such a choice: being sliced up or becoming a stranger in old age.

The movement of the violence into the cities revealed something else important about claims to belonging. Most of the denizens of the new urban neighborhoods like Kibera were first- or at most second-generation migrants from the countryside. It is not customary to bury bodies around homes in these city settlements. So the interethnic violence cannot be said to hinge entirely on attachment to parental or ancestral graves or homestead sites, as it might otherwise be supposed in much of the countryside. Under circumstances of poverty, political anxiety, and dashed hopes, people can get plenty jealous about local belonging—even where they lack family "roots," tangible markers of identity in the landscape, and thick kin networks. And when humans gang up to hunt humans, in town or city just as in resettled farmland, a title to land or a claim to property makes an awfully thin shield for whoever becomes the quarry.

Just Call It Trouble

Just what to call the kinds of fighting and intimidation experienced in the resettlement zones will always be debatable. The violence can be called land clashes, ethnic clashes, or the party politics of redistricting carried on outside the voting booth and beyond the drafting table. It could be called anarchic chaos, as in the Somali state meltdown of 1991 that may have served as an example. Or, as in the case of the Rwandan bloodbath of 1994—possibly incited in part by the Kenyan example across the lake over three years—the bloodshed could be called crime, war, or a kind of purging or purification rite. It could simply be called terrorism, or (put in a juro-political idiom) violation of human rights, or even genocide. But each of these terms carries connotations that can easily mislead, and none roundly expresses the character of the events or the longer-term processes of which they are a part. Sometimes children born after such times are given commemorative names, chosen from a language that in inland settings feels foreign or neutral—like the Swahili "Tabu," which simply means trouble.

Interethnic competition has also proceeded in quieter, more genteel ways around and about the country. By decisions about where to open new Agricultural Finance Company branch offices, for instance. Or about loan approvals and mortgage foreclosures. But the gentility can be seen through, as it is, for instance, when Luo people speak of distraint after foreclosure as *peyo*, raiding—assimilating it semantically to the kind of hostility experienced in the purges or programs in the zones of resettlement schemes.

Where an area has shifted back and forth in ethnic composition, where members have come to have different, competing claims to primacy, and where for whatever reason it is hard to divide the resources equally or fairly, there may still be ways to keep peace. One is to find ways to overcome ethnicity itself as a divider—something never easy to do, unless ironically by emphasizing other, cross-cutting divisions (for instance, age or favorite inter-ethnic sport team). Another is to find at least symbolic ways of peaceably acknowledging each other's presence and dignity, and maybe at times even conceding prior occupancy. This is done in many different ways—for instance, by building monuments or museums, allowing representation in parades, placing flags or banners side by side, adjusting the content or sequencing of speeches, or paying tangible tributes. What forms of dignity and recognition are acceptable vary enormously by culture and context. But exclusion and denial of symbolic recognition are dangerous—as dangerous as poverty from land loss itself.

Something else might seem obvious, and easy to say in hindsight, but it must be said anyway. The entire recurring episode of the deadly and disruptive "land clashes" in the late twentieth and early twenty-first centuries might not have been so likely had European and other settlers not grabbed so much land and evicted so many of its occupants a hundred years earlier. Some of what they did may be excused by the culture and mythology of their times—the talk of civilizing the savage, the beliefs about being born to govern, the metaphors about overseeing the children. Some of these messages, encoded into so much imperial lore, seemed so convincing they convinced even some of those confined or dispossessed. Some of the evictions might also be partially excusable by settler feelings of vulnerability that led to a siege mentality or a desire to purge the country of elements deemed dangerous, and all the more dangerous perhaps because some of the latter's indignation about land loss and subservience was at some level so righteous. So steeply outnumbered, so conspicuous by their skins and hair, settlers could conquer and rule (and, the way some saw it, survive in Africa) only by dividing—both the people and the land—and divide and evict they did.

The later task of repurchasing and redistributing land in the intervening years, from around the time of Kenya's independence, was no doubt a large step in the right direction to rectify those now undeniable wrongs. And the late colonial and early independent governments were probably in as good a position as anyone to bring the change about on a wide scale. But these acts by themselves cannot guarantee peace or local harmony that can endure times of economic hardship and political uncertainty—even with "secure" titles. Once anyone is forced off land, and another has moved onto it and had a chance to start feeling rooted there too—whether by planting trees, building houses, or burying the umbilicals of their newly born or the bones of their dead—no one is likely to be able to restore the status quo ante without hardship and strife. And this last can keep rearing up for generations, with weaponry both old and new. There is nothing more serious.

The Luo titling and mortgaging story is far from unique in Kenya. Neighboring and intermingling Bantu-speaking groups in western Kenya, the Luhya and Gusii peoples, also have segmentary (branching) lineages that are reflected in settlement layouts, and among them too, the proximity of kin around the holdings of loan defaulters makes it hard or impossible for lenders to effect foreclosure under a mortgage system. Fertile and well-watered upland soils, high population densities, subdivided family holdings, territorially concentrated lineages, and burial of the dead at home all seem to come together as a package in these areas, and it is a package that militates against lenders hoping to be able to yank individual holdings away from loan defaulters.

Nor is Kenya unusual in the difficulties its land titling program has encountered. Strong gender and class biases in title assignment are familiar across the continent where registration has been tried. Though Kenya's was the first nationwide registration scheme in Africa south of the Sahara, it has followed the course of many previous and concurrent programs in that farmers have (often quite sensibly) refused to keep the government up to date with land transfers and inheritances, and in that *land registers have thus quickly obsolesced*. In rethinking land titling, what is needed is *not* to romanticize the past but to acknowledge enduring and constantly renewed cultural tendencies and the importance of contextual fit.

The freehold-mortgage system of credit, as the last chapter and this one have shown, misfits the western Kenyan context and is unlikely ever to succeed there—at least not for borrowers. Then what about loans *without* land mortgages? Might they serve the needs of Luo and other Kenyan farmers any better? A forthcoming third volume of this informal trilogy, on credit between cultures, picks up the threads from the earlier description of colonial experience, following several programs without land collateral, and comparing (while also complicating) the types of programs commonly classed as public, private, and self-help as they are examined more deeply in their workings on the ground. The story so far seems to suggest strongly that lending programs will continue, and will keep reappearing as others grind to their close, but offers only slim hope for their success. Further experience will show collateral to be only one of many stumbling blocks—cultural as well as political and economic—in linking the economic life of inland tropical Africa country with capital borrowed from outside.

Land titles that are likely to tempt individuals to sell or mortgage their land do not make land more secure. Indeed, they can make it less. Nor, as the "land clashes" have shown, do titles protect their holders from hostile neighbors, or from hostile or negligent politicians. Far from it. Titling is among other things an entrustment in the sovereignty and loyalty of the titling body, and when that sovereignty and that loyalty fall into question, titles and titling as a property regime do too.

Wherever forced evictions and resettlement have occurred—in equatorial Africa or anywhere else—people will need to rise above whatever part of their responses to each other might be traceable to the baser instincts of defensive territoriality, and to that reflexive terror of even partial loss that seems to be such a common part of our human makeup. These proclivities of response were adapted in earlier times when the world had more space, when it was easier to move away and around, when slower communication might give tempers more time to cool, and when genocidal weaponry was less easily available. They are no longer so adaptive today, and there is little to keep what might once have been adaptive from turning maladaptive. Xenophobia and the reflex of retribution also get taught and learned, encouraged in the young, and triggered as lethal violence even by remote example. Learning instead to accommodate, and forcing ourselves to get along with others, regardless of how early or late they came, will certainly take conscious and concerted effort. But it is not impossible, and it may be the only way to continue to survive at all.

CHAPTER 9

Bigger than Law

Land and Constitutionalism

They are landless when they are born and landless when they are buried. . . .
What went wrong?
—ORIE ROGO MANDULI, ON KENYAN WOMEN

The question of land is beyond law. . . . All these reigns I have counted here, all
these five, everything they did was legal.
—KITAMBE MWALIMU DIGORE, ON HOW DIGO ON THE COAST LOST THEIR
LAND UNDER PORTUGUESE, ARABS, BRITISH, AND KENYANS OF TWO REGIMES

There is change and there is change. Violence of the sort that
beset western Kenyans in the foregoing chapter is piecemeal
and sporadic, flaring up here and there in places of ethnic intersettling, and
in anxious times like the run-up to elections. There it was carried out by excitable young men in gangs, playing savage, evidently egged on by particular
politicians in the shadows (and maybe some women closer by), in insecure
positions, as some law enforcers turned a blind eye. But there is another way
of attempting change, a way more peaceful, sweeping, and methodical—or
anyway more official.

In the next few pages we see an entire nation searching its soul about
land, humans, and the connections between them—and testing how far its
principles and aspirations about such things can be set into official language.
Although the "land clashes" and attempts at ethnic genocide around Kenya's
periphery were still fresh enough in memory, the action described here took
place in and around the capital city, and mainly in words. Some of the words
attempted to express distinctively African concerns—for instance, those of
colonial legacy, farmer-herder friction, clan body burial, or widow inheritance—in legal phrases borrowed from overseas and stretched to their limits.

Kenya's government had by now long fallen from grace in the world's eye, but the ambitiousness of constitutional reform in question, and the intellectual renown of some of its authors, once again set Kenya up as a bellwether for tropical Africa. Can a populist agrarian reform in a multilingual African country be led by urban male lawyers speaking in English? And if so, what role can be played by rural women, who do most of East Africa's farming and do most of their speaking in other tongues? And how participatory, fair, and thorough might such a process be?

By early 2003, after the change of regime from the government of Daniel arap Moi to that of Mwai Kibaki as president, Kenyans and others overseas in contact with them were doing much rethinking about land tenure—about its nature, evolution, design, and effects—as part of a broader process of reimagining the constitution and government of their troubled but currently mostly peaceful nation. A three-year commission of enquiry into the land laws of Kenya, headed by former attorney general Charles Njonjo, had just completed its work. It concluded there was serious need for an overhaul of land law, and of a new national land policy for the nation as a whole (Njonjo 2002). That seemed (for the time being) to mean an overhaul of the constitution.

Toward a New Policy:
Convening for Constitutional Reform

This is not the place for a detailed blow-by-blow account of the meetings that took place in the early 2000s for discussing constitutional reform. But here are some basics, followed by a few quotations to convey a bit of the range and flavor of the dialogue. Because the debates provide a rare chance to hear the voices of rural people and women in a central arena of power and policy making, it is worth devoting those views some space here, and some verbatim rendition.

The Kenyan debates about private property and land titles were occurring while rethinking was going on in the World Bank about the wisdom of the standard policy of promoting the titling of rural African land in individual names (Bruce and Migot-Adholla 1993; cf. Deininger 2003). By 2003 at least one Bank publication on the Internet had specifically admitted that the Kenyan experiment had been unsuccessful, and it appeared as though the Bank might reverse its pro-individualization policy for the continent in general. A damning report by Human Rights Watch that year exposed the in-equities of Kenyan law and custom concerning women's land rights, linking dispossession (in inheritance and widow inheritance, for instance), poverty, and HIV/AIDS, among other hard conditions (Walsh 2003). Within Kenya, meanwhile, since officials under the Moi government had been keeping close watch over land matters, and allocating themselves more than a few sizeable plots, land distribution issues had become closely tied up with party politics and constitutional reform issues about the limits of executive power, and opposition parties all struggled against Moi's KANU for involvement in the process of negotiation.[1] By the end of May 2003, a kind of dam had burst, and public and private grievances and misgivings of all sorts about land were coming out into view and under debate—on the Internet, in the press, and in several critical public forums.

The most noteworthy forum was the hearings and debates on the re-form of the constitution that came to a climax between 2003 and 2004 after about a seven-year buildup and some difficult negotiations between members of the ruling and opposition parties and other bodies about who would be represented and by whom. The Constitution of Kenya Review Commis-sion (CKRC), consisting at first of some thirty commissioners who had been appointed by President Moi, first held preliminary hearings with local as-semblies on tours around the country in the second half of 2001. The com-mission then held the first plenary meeting of the National Constitutional Conference on 27–29 May 2003, at Bomas of Kenya (ordinarily a natural folkloric showcase and tourist attraction). The commission convened to hear and debate a bill for a draft constitution, including a chapter called "Land and Property Rights" (Ch. 11, later Ch. 7, "Land and Property").[2] About six hundred registered delegates, representing many parts of Kenya and many groups and categories of persons, attended to present the commission their experiences, opinions, and requests. In this and later meetings, in Septem-ber 2003 (Bomas II) and January and February 2004 (Bomas III), technical working groups would focus more on the details of the wording of the consti-tution itself and its included bill of rights. Certainly the formal and informal hearings of the Njonjo Commission and the broader Constitutional Review Commission were the most wide-ranging in Kenya since the Kenya Land Commission in the 1930s.[3]

The convention can be construed, in a way, as a ritual of rebellion and of renewal, in the vein of Max Gluckman's famous anthropological studies of

Zulu and Lozi, or Victor Turner's of Ndembu, in southern Africa.[4] Airing complaints against the colonial and "independent" governments was certainly somehow therapeutic for the nation, giving vent and a focal point to deep and widely shared emotions. It could certainly be construed as a purging, a purification of sorts, as well as a rite of passage—with emphasis on (re)aggregation or reincorporation—marking both the new century (by at least the most widely accepted calendar) and the change of regime from Moi's to Kibaki's.[5] But whether the proceedings would amount, in Gluckman's terms, to a contained and controlled rite of "rebellion," of the sort that only bolsters the existing order in the end, or to an uncontained "revolution," of the sort that actually changes it, was not yet known.

In these pages on the hearings, and on the written document based in part upon them, I remain as close as possible to the actual words used, in order to see the process of sifting, sorting, and silent denial by which power-wielders of different stripes, official and unofficial, together decide, and negotiate, what kinds of ideas are appropriate for turning into policy and law—and what kinds are not. About race, sex, and class, for instance. And about culture, religion, and spirituality—including concepts of nature and of rights. Something to become evident is a multisided process of sanitization, of secularization, and in a way of emotional cooling—in the gradual move from speeches to official policy document on the way to becoming law and perhaps a revised constitution. Certain key terms and concepts get chalked for chiseling into stone, while others get banished from the lexicon. Still others, on especially vexed issues of ethnicity, political economy, and morality, come and go, making it clearer by their intermittency what the dilemmas are.

Law in the Crucible: The Hearing Process

Who would participate, and how long the process would take, had been hot issues for some years, and much negotiation took place as bodies of delegates were invited and uninvited to represent a nation of some thirty million souls. The commission that formed was appointed by President Moi and the National Assembly, and headed for the time by law professor Yash Pal Ghai. It included opposition parties, faith groups, and others. By the time Moi and KANU were replaced by Mwai Kibaki and his recently unified National Rainbow Coalition (NARC) in the general election of 27 December 2002, the commission's members had toured the country, collecting facts and opinions, and were drafting a new constitution. The plenary meetings of the CKRC took place at Bomas of Kenya, in the outskirts of Nairobi. There as in the countryside, men did most of the chairing but allowed women to speak as delegates of organizations and interest categories. These included professions, political parties, civic and religious organizations, and voting constituencies, but not ethnic groups ("tribes"), classes (too much to the point), or age grades like youth or elders.

The keynote discussant and commissioner, Yale-trained law professor H. W. O. Okoth-Ogendo, from Nyanza, set the agenda and outlined possible needs for reform, setting a critical tone from the outset. Referring to a century of "conquest and plunder," colonial legacies, legal expropriation of "ownerless" lands, and dislocations in Africa, he called land in Africa "the last colonial question, which must be resolved before Africa can be truly independent" (Report of CKRC Proceedings, pp. 8–9 [hereafter "Report"]). He recounted Kenya's history of treaties, of official pronouncements about "ownerless" land, and of legal expropriations and removals, lamenting that "now . . . land belongs to the State and not to the people" or to communities, which needed recognition as "juridical persons" in a system simplified so that at least "the best lawyer" will not be "lost in it" (pp. 8–9). "The land question has never really been resolved" (p. 9). The second commissioner to speak, Mohamed Swazuri, agreed with much of this and added, "We were also told of increasing privatization of land, individualization of tenure because of the theory that individuals . . . once given titles to land can develop, because they can get loans and so on and so forth. Evidence from all over Africa ha[s] shown that theory does not work as envisaged" (p. 10).[6] These opening speakers opened a political space for criticism, perhaps emboldening others to speak their minds.

And they did, about a remarkable range of issues. To name just a few: sacred graves and battle sites, bribery in the issuance of land titles, limits needed for holding sizes and duration of leases, compensation for old and recent evictions, disposal of radioactive waste, bulldozing of shanties, neglect or dispossession of women in patrilineal inheritance, land losses by widows and orphans of HIV/AIDS, the centralization or overcentralization of land administration, and international policy pressures.[7] Despite the parliamentary-style formality followed in the vein of *Robert's Rules of Order* ("honorable delegates," "point of information," and so on), the issues and opinions came forth with often striking frankness.[8] Since their time was short, many speakers combined issues, rather than just sticking to the interests of the groups or categories they had been sent to represent. It was as if the public had conspired to show the nation's leaders just how broad, complex, and emotive a matter "land tenure" is—and thus how hard to legislate.

A few brief extracts suggest feelings, from varied perspectives, about the system of property combining titling and mortgaging. For the category of "Professionals," Delegate 483, Saleh Faad Yahya, reflected a perspective reminiscent of World Bank and international financiers' standard values and reasoning. He said, "The land market is almost collapsed because of dual titles. The courts have colluded with landlords and therefore the banks can't recover their money and so on and so forth. We must find ways of reviving land markets because it is through the land markets that the whole financial market in this country works" (Report, p. 17). The drift of his remarks contrasts strikingly with those of Mohamed Swazuri, above: a reminder that the land mortgaging issue might still be debated for some time—but one no less negative about its felt outcome.

"The Bottom at the Top": Women Speak Their Minds

Not until several more men delegates had spoken was the first woman given the floor. Mary Wambui Kanyi, Delegate 467, from "the NGOs" (nongovernmental organizations), noted that few poor Kenyans or women were even aware of the nation's laws on land. She spoke for devolving land administration to "the local levels" (Report, p. 24), capping holding sizes, and limiting leases so that they not last for ninety-nine years, as had become a national legal norm, but instead be reviewed every thirty years, which she reckoned to mean once every generation. She called for a "truth commission" to redress past land-related crimes and injustices, including dispossession for development or mining interests, and argued for systematizing the compensation for people evicted from ancestral lands (p. 25). The issue she saved for last was "the gender aspect" of land access and ownership: she spoke against dispossession of women in inheritance, and in favor of not just access but ownership for women as well as men.

Tabitha Seii, Delegate 499, again from the category of "women," argued for limits on the search for restitutions. She started by identifying land as "the one and only cause of conflict [in] many communities and between tribes," and then, citing long and complex histories of Highland Nilotes (evidently those groups lately called Kalenjin)—whom she identified as her own people—on their migrations from the river Nile, said there must be limits to how far back one can go to right injustices. In the Rift Valley, "If we go

back to all these places, we know the Maasais were there. How far back can
we go? . . . Let us just come to the more recent issues on land"—the land
grabs of politicians, "the present colonialists among us today." She questioned individual titling: "How individual is a land which has been acquired
recently, and by virtue of a title deed the person now calls it his own land?
Are we going to reflect that and say it is because you have a title deed, which
you may have gotten because you were able to bribe somebody, or you were
able to influence somebody to get that title deed?" (Report, p. 32). She continued, lamenting land dispossessions (by the government and Fluorspar,
in the Kerio Valley) that had rendered a local population landless squatting
rock-crushers on their ancestral lands—all, she claimed, for an individual
owner, and without compensation or infrastructural benefits to the dispossessed.

And she commented on mortgaged land and its bearing on families:

> When land is mortgaged and a bank comes and sells the land, we need to have a
> clearhead[ed] policy regarding what mortgages can be done and by who within
> the family. We have people who have been dispossessed; who have been made
> squatters because they did not understand the law, and that brings me to talk
> a bit about education. When we make a law, and the people do not understand
> what the law means, in connection with what they possess, they become losers as
> a result of ignorance and thus today we have people who have been thrown out
> of their homes, bulldozers coming in to push them out and they do not under-
> stand why. Personally I am a victim of this, when one morning a surveyor came
> and demarcated our land and we were told, "you don't have a title deed and this
> land is going to a particular school" and we did not know how to get that back;
> to this day, we do not have that land. (Report, p. 32).

Certainly these things needed to be said, even if a clear policy could
hardly remedy all this, let alone prevent its happening again.

Orie Rogo Manduli, Delegate 594, representing FORD (Forum for the
Restoration of Democracy) People as one of two women among the spokespersons for more than forty "Political Parties" ("how marginalized we are"),
spoke up for landless women and others: "They are landless when they are
born and they are landless when they are buried." Asking for time to speak,
"for all these millions of women," she begged the chairperson, "maybe we
will never talk again in the next two hundred years."

> A girl is born to a man and woman and she is a daughter and she has no land and
> no claim to any, in . . . most African Societies here. This girl has no land till one
> day she gets married and then she goes and squats on her husband's land and

works and toils on this land. Now, should this man die before her, she becomes immediately landless again, because the land is then entitled to her son who actually even threatens to evict her from this land. A son who does not even respect her, because she has no land to pass on, she is only squatting on the land of the father, and her own son who she give birth has the audacity to tell her that. A son who can easily disinherit her if he marries too many women and the land is not enough, he just tells the mother go back to where she came from, "because this land my father left for me." Now this mother who is being told to go does not have a place. Her father does not recognize her as a land owner where she came from; the minute she is married, she is a stranger in the home she was born in [to fathers, brothers, brothers' wives]. . . . She is always in between and she is always at the mercy of men . . . birth to death. This woman does not know where she will be buried, because eventually she is going to be buried on the land of some man . . . and for us Africans burial grounds are very sacred. At death you could find five, ten men, scrambling over this woman's body for various reasons, or rejecting her body for various reasons. (Report, pp. 34–35)

Amid what was recorded then as an "uproar from the Honourable Dele-gates," she again noted women's marginalization. Land, she said, is resource and livelihood, "a basis of everything in Kenya . . . the basis of everything that is Kenyan." "How come the women do not form part of the Kenyan people? What went wrong?" (p. 35). She was silenced by the session chair-man Norman Nyaga, in a back-and-forth exchange of pleading and refusal, before she finished her speech. But by this time, in their very responses, the Honorable Delegates would seem to have made her point for her.[9]

Women from both ends of the country and the middle joined in. Some, like Sophia Abdi, Delegate 470, a self-identified Somali Kenyan, broached title deeds and credit: "The use of Title Deeds as security to obtain loans from financial institutions should be stopped. My reasons are that, there are people who are in good positions politically . . . and they did not even step in some places yet they got Title Deeds and acquired loans using those Title Deeds. . . . Women also do not have Title Deeds, they are marginalized, they cannot acquire loans. Therefore, we need other options so that we can also acquire loans" (Report, p. 42).

Lorna Timanoi Tetu, District Delegate from Narok, lamented Maasai land losses through "technical fraud" and "tricks that were linked to soft loans," among other things (Report, p. 43). Arguing for decentralized land registration, she favored protection of "communally- and group-owned land" such as that of "pastoralists, hunters and gatherers," respecting rights in land hitherto mislabeled "vacant," compensating its erstwhile losers, and

BIGGER THAN LAW   209

granting communities around game parks, tourist centers, and water catch-
ment areas "at least 55%" of the total value of benefits from them. Calling
for "a moratorium on [sales of?] land" for twenty years, "so that our children
can grow and know the value of land," she lamented that "most of our men
sell our land at bars. They do not even know the value of that land" (p. 44).

From what is mainly Luo country, a Homa Bay schoolteacher spoke on
behalf of widows and persons with disabilities. "Firstly, the women have not
been given a voice even to talk about land. If you talk about land, you are
going to earn a wife beating exercise" (followed by "Laughter and Noise
from the Honourable Delegates"). Next, she said that "widows should not
be denied the land after the death of their husbands and that the disabled
people should not be disinherited" (Report, p. 47). After discussing varied
definitions of land (including subterranean minerals, water, and in other contexts the nation itself) and land's viability (as depending on environmental
conditions and use), she challenged the concept of a centralized land commission. "I am now saying it in black and white that there should be a regional representation in the Land Commission and it should be a regional
one beginning from the village by the way and going up to the top because
if a hole is dug, the centre space is just space and the bottom is important at
the top. So, we really need that it should begin from the village and that there
is a third representation of women and a third of women with disability and
other categories" (followed by "Clapping from the Honourable Delegates")
(p. 48). She drew further applause by proposing replacing the words "landless people" with "displaced landless," "because people used to have land but
they were displaced." Ruth Oniang'o, Delegate 221, a nominated member
of Parliament for the Kenyan African National Union (the recently ousted
ruling party), noted that land "does not exist by itself" but requires water,
plants, and animals to make an ecosystem, and that merely to say "we own
this land" or "I want my land back" neglects ecological responsibility that
accompanies ownership (p. 42). The same speaker lamented the frequency
of HIV/AIDS widows and orphans who lose their land, and called for provisions for a will to ensure adequate inheritance or custody.

So now children made their appearance—at least by proxy. A rhetorical
flourish was lent to the occasion by Grace Ogot, a celebrated Luo novelist,
former MP, and former assistant minister. In the case of a man, she asked,
who registers his title in the name of the first wife, and the second, third,
and fourth wives inherit naught, "Can the constitution take care of the second, third an[d] fourth wife? . . . In the beginning in all communities it was

assumed that when you are a girl child eventually you will get married. . . .
You can walk for three, four years to a Land Office before getting a title deed
until your husband dies and then you as a woman will never get that title
deed and then the stronger brothers-in-law will snatch all of it from your
family. Madam Chairperson, can the current Constitution also protect a girl
child?" (Report, p. 80).

Anne Okoth, representing "Professional Bodies," suggested setting time
limits on absentee landlords, and redesignating people hitherto called squatters in their own land. Insisting that a national land commission should have
women as at least one-third of its membership, but that commissions be set
up at other "levels" as well, she said, "If you go to the villages and ask any
woman in the village whose farm this is, they will tell you the boundaries
better than the men who are there. We should therefore have women at all
levels of those commissions" (Report, p. 54).

Men too, interestingly enough, criticized men's detachment and irre-
sponsibility about land. Sylvanus Onyambu Ogari, a "District Delegate,"
argued for joint titles to "ancestral land" held by husbands and wives, saying,
"Men have that tendency of selling land when the woman is not aware. The
man becomes very bitter one day and you find that he has just sold a piece of
land and he is enjoying it somewhere in the bar" (followed by "Clapping by
Honourable Delegates") (Report, pp. 54–55).[10]

"The Tribe of Kenyans"

On the whole, in the debate, most of the complaints voiced concerned inequalities and inequities; far fewer concerned inefficiencies. Among
the most often recurring themes in the debates was a need for strengthened
claims or ownership by women, including registration of family land in more
than a husband's name (and many men, as well as women, voiced agreement on this). Women, more consistently than men, spoke for regional land
commissions to be added to national ones—and several seemed to hold the
assumption that such devolution of authority would give women themselves
greater say in land matters. Other frequently mentioned concerns, some already mentioned, included a need for a ceiling on landholdings (one man
from Maasai country proposed taxing holdings over 100 acres); the need to
reduce the standard periods of land leases (most speakers deemed thirty to
thirty-three years better than ninety-nine); controls on absentee landlordism
and on landholding by foreigners; a need for restitution for lands recently

confiscated by government for developers, or by acts of violence; and a need to recognize group grazing land in pastoralist areas. On terminology, probably the word most strongly objected to was "squatter," used in reference to displaced persons.

During most of the debate, the names of ethno-linguistic groups or "tribes" (Kikuyu, Luo, and so on) were used freely. A few speakers, however, objected. One of them was Mungatana Danson Buya, representing Orma, Pokomo, Luo, and others in the Garsen Constituency, which had been lately racked by interethnic violence. Buya himself was of ambiguous ethnic identity; he said he had a Taita mother and Pokomo father. "I want to tell you," he told the conference, "that if you do not reflect the interest of *the tribe of Kenyans*, we shall come back to Bomas of Kenya, I shall lead that delegation here and we shall change the constitution again. . . . Don't talk about tribes because this is not our Kenya for now. Let us talk about the constitution in fifty years." Accordingly, he appealed to the commission to drop the concept of "Community Land"—a euphemism for tribal territories. "As far as Kenyans are concerned when you talk about Community Land, if you come to the Maasai area they withhold, it will only be available to the Maasai. If you go to Kiambu they will hold it, it will only be available to the Kikuyu who are living there. The same to Turkana, and this is how Kenyans are going to interpret community land. . . . Let us talk about County Councils and things that are recognized, we can create as many as we want but let us not talk about Community Land because then we are Balkanizing Kenya" (Report, p. 111, emphasis added).

"Beyond Law. Bigger than Law."

As if to close the conference by returning to where it began, but to add something else, Kitambi Mwalimu Digore, from Kwale District on the southern coast, traced the history of his district as a series of occupations. Starting "hundreds and hundreds of years ago," he said, came the Portuguese, but they were only the first.

> The Portuguese took the land, allocated it the way they wanted and whatever they did at that time, was legal according to them. Since they were reigning. The Arabs [under the Sultanate of Zanzibar] took our land and gave it to whoever they wanted and it was legal at that time according to them. The British took our land, they re-distributed it to whoever they wanted and that was legal according to them that time. Kenyatta took our land, he even took a very big chunk of Taita

Taveta District, two thirds of the District and that was legal according to him. It was legal because he was the head of state and we had a legal system, so it was legal. . . . We all know what happened during the Moi era. All the Beach Land. . . . We [Digo people] have been marginalized. . . . Now, I want to pose a question, before this Honourable Conference, this term we call legal, this term we call lawful, what is legal and what is lawful? To me I think [the] question of the land is beyond law. It is bigger than law. The question of land is one of politics. . . . All these reigns that I have counted here, all these five, everything they did was legal. (Report, p. 114)

How telling the finish. The difference between land law, and land tenure in lived experience, could hardly have been clearer. Nor, in my view, could the need for supplementing the concept of property with one like "improperty" — or for recognizing the forms and shades in between.

Labor Pains, and a New Policy Half Born

After the first plenary meetings just described, with their striking outpouring of grievances and concerns, the process did not go smoothly. Two more plenary sessions ensued, amid acrimonious political debate, delays, and changes in the cast of characters on both the commission and the Parliamentary Select Committee that served as liaison between it and the rest of Parliament. On the Ides of March 2004, the National Constitutional Conference, representing the commission's efforts, adopted a new Draft Constitution. But it was never to make it through Parliament (the National Assembly). Amid accusations of stalling and corruption variously directed at the Kibaki government, the Select Committee, and the commission, several Kenyan cities, including Kisumu on 7 July 2004, saw mass rallies repressed by police and paramilitary forces (in this case with deaths and hundreds of casualties). The broad constitutional reform, which would among many other things have limited the powers of the presidency, ended up on ice.

But the movement for a national land policy — to be implemented from outside the Office of the President — continued forward. By March 2007, two key players were the Ministry of Lands (still under the Office of the President) and the Kenya Land Alliance (KLA), a Nakuru-based umbrella organization of nongovernmental organizations and individuals funded by British and Danish bilateral aid sources, among others.[11] Together these issued in that month the Draft National Land Policy (hereafter, DNLP) from a Nairobi-based body, the National Land Policy Secretariat.

This is an unusual and most significant document, in that it represents a negotiated agreement, or at least a provisional one, between state officials and nongovernmental and nonprofit actors, between lawyers and academicians, and between all of these and the broader sector of the public they had consulted in the local preliminary and the centralized plenary hearings—with international players in the background behind Kenyan activist and charitable groups. It represents the sum total of what was certainly the most thoroughgoing review of land policy in Kenya since Independence.

Below are just a few of its key features as it appeared in March 2007.[12]

Colonialism and the legacy of a dualistic land policy (large farms for export, small for subsistence) were blamed as the taproots of the nation's evils (DNLP 2.2.2 and 2.2.3). "Historical injustices" as old as 1895, when Kenya came under British protectorate, would be righted by "redistribution, restitution, and resettlement" (3.6.1, 3.6.2, esp. para. 177) or "restitution, reparation and compensation" (3.6.2, para. 177). What any new land losers would have to say about such offers—human fear of loss and dislike of displacement being as strong as they are—remained to be seen.[13] Otherwise, the draft included verbiage likely to appeal to a range of political ideologies—pro-market, populist, and otherwise.[14]

The draft policy proposed a Land Act establishing a new sovereign owner, a new structure of administration and land law courts, and a new classification of lands. A new National Land Commission (NLC) would administer and manage land not for the government, but for "the people of Kenya collectively as a nation, as communities and as individuals," all of these last three holding "radical title"—that is, ultimate ownership (3.2.1, para. 43). A land reform unit would be set up (4.2, 4.3). Both individual and communal rights would be protected by registration, and to that end all the land in Kenya would be divided into "Public Land" (no longer "Government Land"), "Community Land" (no longer "Trust Land"), and "Private Land" (same as before) (3.3.1). Something really new here, for a Kenyan document, was that the government would recognize a "community," including "a clan or ethnic community" (or other kinds), as eligible to own land (in "radical title" or ultimate ownership) and manage its use as they saw fit (3.3.1.2, paras. 62–63).[15]

Land titling would continue. While the draft acknowledged that individual titling in Kenya had done great harm to customary rights, no proposal was finally made in it to abandon the nationwide titling program. As for allowable sizes of land holdings, the draft policy proposed only lower limits (unspecified), and restrictions on further subdivision (3.4.2.2). Notably, unlike a previous draft, it mentioned *no upper limits to holding sizes.*

When it came to land transfer—selling, mortgaging, and leasing—the authors of the draft policy walked a fine and wavering line between private and public interests, between local and foreign ones, and also between the status quo and any dream world. All these forms of exchange, it seemed, would still be allowed—but none without changes, cautions, or restrictions.

On sale and mortgage: The voices that had been heard in the plenary meetings condemning or questioning land mortgaging altogether were nowhere reflected in the draft plan as it emerged later. *Mortgaging and distraint would go forward,* evidently with legal protection. *But* an important caution was heeded. The draft specified the government would "put in place mechanisms to curb selling and mortgaging of family land without the involvement of the spouses" and family members (3.6.10.4) and require "written and informed consent" of all "secondary right holders" for land disposals, which might mean the same (3.3.3.1, para. 76).[16] This was what the land control boards had been set up to safeguard (and generally failed to do, at least up until the 1990s, as noted earlier). The newly worded provision would be an interesting one to see carried out, since so many of Kenya's women and children cannot write—and who was to do the informing, or what kind, was left unsaid. But the intent here was surely a laudable one.

Land rental would be allowed, as before, and encouraged (3.3.3, para. 73; 3.5.7, para. 163), but leases shortened to a maximum of ninety-nine years (no more 999-year leases as formerly issued to European immigrant settlers and still in force) (3.3.3.3, para. 78). *Some people would have to lose,* that is, what they had thought they possessed as the next best thing to permanent property. (Fireworks to follow.)

Other provisions were no less radical. On women's rights, the draft policy specified the *government would end discrimination by gender* and "outlaw regulations, customs and practices that discriminate against women in relation to land," including those of inheritance (3.6.10.3). Yes, that's right: the government would "ensure that men and women are entitled to equal rights to land" before, during, and after marriage or upon widowhood (3.6.10.4, para. 225). If taken seriously, in rural Kenya or almost anywhere in Africa, these last provisions would be revolutionary indeed, for better or worse—challenging widespread and deeply rooted customs.

Land taxes would be extended to raise revenue and discourage land hoarding (3.5.8). This too, if it reached most of the countryside, would be something new. Taxing land might help mitigate the concentration of holdings into fewer hands, if applied to large as well as small holders—but that is a big if.

Finally, a section about "vulnerable groups" covered redistribution, resettlement, and protection of land rights for persons including, but not limited to, "subsistence farmers, pastoralists, hunters and gatherers, agricultural laborers, unskilled and low-skilled workers, unemployed youth, persons with disabilities, persons living with HIV and AIDS, orphans, slum and street dwellers, and the aged" (3.6.5).[17] To these, other sections specifically added women before marriage, widows, widowers, divorcees, children, and (elsewhere) internally displaced persons and disaster victims.

No longer could it be said, if this draft was any indication, that policy in Kenya was only about the vested interests of powerful and well-off adult men. Call it moral responsibility or political correctness, the kinds of people lately called "subalterns" in the social studies were pretty well covered—or at least now, in linguistic terms, "marked."

But all was not over yet. The draft land policy was not without critics, a number of whom used the Internet to voice their concerns. Among the most sharply pointed were those of Michael Norton-Griffiths, a European-descended insider in Kenyan land management affairs, and a little-known associated body calling itself the Kenya Landowners Federation (KLF). This group pointed to foreign NGO co-financing of the draft (an infringement of sovereignty, it claimed), co-optation by particular ethnic groups (KLF 2007), and populist electioneering.[18] It warned that the draft policy, if approved as law, would "radically, seismically, and terminally change all our existing land legislation and much of the existing land rights contained therein, the very foundation of Kenyan society" (KLF 2007, 1). Reduction of freehold to leasehold, and shortening of leasehold, would be tantamount to "theft by the government." The draft would create "an all powerful presidential lands 'super ministry' that will have unparalleled power." The group warned of tribalist divisiveness, new taxation, "radical new squatter's rights," and chaos as all land titles would become open to challenge in "an unbridled assault on . . . all landowner's constitutional rights" (p. 2).

Credit too would dwindle, the critique continued, because of "banks being reluctant or unable to use property as security due to the increased rights of any other interested party claiming an interest in a property" and "the reduction in long term mortgages as they will be difficult to provide to properties with leases of 35 years or less to run" (p. 3). Indeed, the credit pullback was already happening, it said, merely as a result of the circulation of the Draft National Land Policy. The screed gloomily warned of chaotic transactions, floods of new litigation, overexploitation of holdings at risk, capital flight (as foreigners would pull out their land interests), an over-burdened exchequer, a land grab by government agents of "underused" or "idle" land (that old issue, again), and a possibility of increased interethnic violence as old grievances would get reopened (pp. 3–4).

Clearly there was plenty still to debate, for anyone who wished, even though the draft already represented so many hearings, debates, and compromises. Such is the politics of land.

Constants and Vacillations

Having seen something of the national effort at legal reform, the document as it was hammered out, and some criticisms of it, we now stand back a bit to look at the process of hearings and redrafting, and at what it says about the deeper concerns of land, belonging, and tenure. We do this by seeing what topics stayed in, stayed out, or came in and went out as the document moved from discussion to finished draft.

1. To start with the *constants*. The speeches and written drafts always remained critical of the effects of colonialism and dualist policy, and in places of every draft, also of individualized tenure. Personal identities as national origins continued to be mentioned. Settlers and settler economies were mentioned right to the end, as were Kenyans (though reference to particular nations of origin, like "British" and Britishers were ironed out of the drafts, perhaps as over-specific). The topic of socioeconomic classes also made it under the wire. "Rulers," "elites," and "the poor," for instance, were mentioned in writing in successive drafts, as well as in oral testimony. All sorts of other social markers—sorters, that is—made it into the text and consistently stayed in, as discussed: sex (more delicately referred to as gender), age, mode of livelihood (farming, pastoralism), uprootedness ("internal displacement" or refugee status), and health status with regard to both disease and physical handicap. And the first of these was to be made official in another way. The principle of women's representation in decision-making bodies was consistently (and repeatedly in each draft) noted as a desideratum—that is, as a good and necessary thing.

2. Then there were some *negative constants*. There were certain topics that, by their absence in the written documents (despite their frequent men-

tion in the earlier hearings) come to light as taboo. One had to do with race, as skin color or other physiognomy. No written mention of "white highlands" or of "blacks" or "people of color" was left in the document as it became more formal and official. "Arab" was left out, and explicit mention of Islamic faith and practice minimized too, even when special issues of the coast were described and addressed. Names of particular ethno-linguistic groups or "communities" (Gikuyu, Luo, Maasai, Swahili, and so on), which speakers from all walks of society had used freely and often in oral testimony, were by the end practically all left out of, or expunged from, the draft constitution and draft land policy. (Only in one instance did any still appear: as an illustration of an untranslatable term, for land clients such as Luo jodak.) All too incendiary, no doubt. Too close to the bone emotionally, and to the episodes recounted in Chapter 8.

The erasure of references to particular ethnic communities (or "tribes") in the government policy documents contrasts with their continued appearance in nongovernmental ones on land—both Kenyan and especially international nongovernmental ones.[19] (This all stands to reason. If foreign and international NGOs get in trouble with state officials for fomenting "tribalism" or broadcasting an image of "backwardness," they can just leave the country, publicize repression, or appeal to authorities like the UN.) Beneath all this, of course, smolder the buried old issues of "race" and evolutionism— easily accused, denied, or inverted, but always volcanic.

Some basic administrative issues, too, were left unopened throughout. One had to do with how territorially delimited district bodies would relate to "community" (ethnic and clan- or kin-based) groupings they cut across— and which, when push came to shove, would take official precedence. It seemed to be too big or too new a question. It was also one likely to lead to big questions, even crises, about how to define membership in the first place— since ethnic groups, unlike districts, nation-states, or other territorial units, have fuzzy boundaries.[20]

3. Finally, some *vacillations.* A number of specific proposals addressed, and categories of persons, kept changing, even in the few short years between 2002 and 2007. Some of them looked and felt like conventional "public policy" issues. First, upper limits to holdings. The question here is whether any official bureau would have the authority to impose any ceilings.[21] Second, claims to "natural" objects and substances found on the land. These include not just the most tradeable, transportable ones like precious metals, but also ones vital daily, like firewood for cooking and grasses for thatching.[22] Third,

encroachment. A fraught issue is movement from denser farming areas into more sparsely settled herding ones, for instance, and the inter-ethnic conflicts associated (for instance, between Gusii and Maasai in Trans Mara).[23] Fourth, compensation of persons involuntarily removed from their lands. How this might work is always difficult to decide, and rarely satisfactory to persons forcibly moved.[24]

Other ons-and-offs involved issues that reach right into the tightest circles of family and "private" life. One is the nature of marriage. Whether marriage is defined as necessarily heterosexual (and monogamous) becomes more vitally important than ever where rights are to be deemed co-owned by spouses. Phrasing narrowing the definition this way was inserted, but then removed—and at an interesting moment in history.[25]

Another issue that came and went was female land inheritance: the "right" of women to inherit on terms equal to men, or in equal acreage. This everyone knew would radically alter long-standing practice and would also run up against Islamic shari'a, holy law. In the hearing and writings, women's rights to land and to inheritance were vehemently defended throughout. But not rights to inherit equal shares; that part wavered.

Finally, the issue of the rights of the dead—and the rights *to* the dead. One clause that came and went stated that "the inherent dignity of every person . . . extends to their remains after burial" (6.4.4.2b in the draft constitution adopted by the convention but later shelved)—a reminder of the burial location issues like those of S. M. Otieno that had for months at a time split the country in two.[26]

Ancestors and divinity, not infrequently invoked or adduced in the discussions around the country and in the capital (and in the case of Christian and Muslim faiths, at least, explicitly represented in the policy hearings) got gradually filtered out of the policy papers heading toward parliament, just as they had been filtered out in the past from other policy papers and constitutions drafted by economists and lawyers. So did shrines and holy places. Gone from view were the homestead graves. Now any spirits or deities would need to speak or act for themselves—from the graves, churches, mosques, or wherever else they might be thought to dwell or move—through whoever perceived them or felt influenced by them. Hardly forgotten by Kenyan and African minds, and often enough adduced in oral discussions where land played a part, they seemed yet to have little explicit place in official Kenyan policy on the printed page.

These last several issues—the issues consistently avoided and the ones that vacillate—are all "deep" in more than one way. They are deeply rooted in history, tightly connected to other kinds of custom, and closely associated with emotions whose sources are poorly understood. These are wellsprings of political volatility. As such, they show us just where activists—including future policy makers and legislators—should tread most cautiously. This is the advantage of following the drafting process over time. The verbiage that shifts the most erratically points right to the questions most vexed.

Populism and Statism

In ideology, the Draft National Land Policy, as it rested in late 2007, represented a striking mix of populism and centralist statism, with acquiescence too to some forms and elements of capitalism. In championing the rights and interests of women including widows, children including orphans, "informal" land client "strangers," "informal" urban settlers, herders, foragers, disabled persons, and others classed as marginal or vulnerable, it represented a turnaround for Kenyan land policy no less dramatic than the pro-market Swynnerton Plan had been half a century before. As such, it reflected much sensitivity to the voices of the rural, the poor, and the underprivileged.

But there was the authoritarian side too. In proposing a centralized land bureau for making and implementing future policy nationwide, and leaving it or its ostensible agents the right to confiscate and reallocate lands deemed "idle" or "underproductive," the new draft policy seemed to leave a door open not only to state dirigism, but also to further land-grabbing and other abuse by government officials and persons well connected to them. The expressed prospect of land taxation, which might extend nationwide, pointed also toward centralizing power and wealth (though not just this, as local land taxes also remained a possibility).[27]

That a rather revolutionary populist document can also be a charter for authoritarianism, and for gain by new elites, is an irony indeed, but it is not a new lesson in human history.[28]

For a document both so populist and so statist, the draft constitution and land policy contained elements strikingly capitalist—especially in their later iterations. In this it bore likeness to countless other planning documents in Kenya since before Independence, the Ingham report and Swynnerton Plan included. Pro-market language about vibrant trading, incentives, ease of transactions, enforceability of contracts, and productive efficiency (left undefined) was sprinkled here and there throughout, sometimes seeming to clash jarringly with clauses about "redistribution, "sharing of benefits," "participation," and "sustainability" like pieces of a patchwork crazy quilt.

The eventual decision to keep up the titling, the turn against capping the size of holdings, and the counter-traditional profession that not everyone could own land left open the way, despite expressed aims of equity, for classes of landed and landless to polarize to the extreme. The continued allowing of not just land selling and renting but also mortgaging left open a door for a more subtle, more gradual concentration of holdings in the hands of banks and other financial institutions, and of any individuals or companies who would then buy foreclosed property from them and each other. For kin groups, ethnic groups, and the nation, it remained a gamble. But now there was at least attention, if not yet a wide safety net, for whoever might fall out as dispossessed.

Whether the Draft National Land Policy was destined to pass through Parliament into law (alone or within a rewritten constitution still under discussion) was still unknown at the time these pages went to press. In a sense, though, that matters less than the fact that it existed to begin with and the way it was arrived at. For even if it did not succeed, it still stood to represent what a hard-fought, pushed-and-pulled compromise between ideologies can look like. A symbol of a brittle nationhood and of a kind of secular faith in rights, it stood as one model to be emulated and adapted by other countries' governments. At least, that is, for ones that had embarked on a pro-market program of individual titling and found its results were not living up to hopes.

The hearings for a constitutional reform, and after it stalled out, for the drafting of a new land policy, were a diagnostic opportunity and a hopeful renewal, failings and foibles withal. In them much was covered, and some unaccustomed voices made public. Conquests, titling, resettlement, restitutions, and variations for different modes of livelihood were all explored. Whether landholding sizes should be capped, whether mortgaging should be allowed to be done by individuals, whether matrimonial land should be registered in an individual's or a couple's or family's name, whether elders' courts ought to be empowered, whether compensation for land lost by displaced persons should be issued in cash or in substitute plots elsewhere . . . the topics aired about land were remarkably comprehensive. Even if the end results of some of the provisions—for instance, on land taxation—seemed hard to predict, the conferences had given vent to sentiments seldom aired from a prominent podium and, at least temporarily, redirected the spotlight of government attention toward women, youth, herders, foragers, disabled persons, and others hitherto so often bypassed in official proceedings.

The back and forth, on and off of the drafting over successive meetings serves as a reminder that constitutions and laws are documents with some arbitrariness in them, and some guesswork and gambles as well as vested interests. How they look and feel in later ages depends on the precise moment when they were submitted for passage, and this in turn, in a document about many issues, might not be governed by any single issue among them. To think that a single legal code carved into stone can suffice for all times is probably no more realistic than to suppose one can suffice for all places (and in Kenya, as in Africa, the differences between places are deep). In the tug-of-war between centralization and decentralization, between general and special interests, and between special interests and *other* special interests, documents change form and flavor from draft to draft. Successive authors reinterpret and misread each other's interests as they pass along their drafts. Science and ethics merge and diverge. Minds hardheaded on Monday morning turn tenderhearted or vanish on Friday afternoon. Points get forgotten and recalled. Wrinkles get ironed in while others get ironed out. So constitutions need amending and laws overriding, right from the start.

Legislators and jurists are human—hardly more or less fallible, or self-interested either, than the rest of us. Law is an expedience cobbled together out of fragmentary information, uneven communication, compromised interests—always faute de mieux. Never will there be a perfect code. Not, at least, about land and belonging. A more cynical view might be that a law code ostensibly aimed at eliminating special privileges and leveling classes and categories would level the playing field for more centralized, even autocratic governance by putting more land issues under Nairobi's control.

If the constitutional reform process showed anything, it is that Kitambi Mwalimo Digore was right: land is bigger than law. The reform might not remedy all the problems raised in it, such as the basic ethics of mortgaging, or the grievances between people who concentrate on farming and those who concentrate on herding—issues that seem somehow to have been squeezed from the draft constitution as debate and redrafting continued. But it represented at least a determined effort, and perhaps something like a prayer, with all the seriousness and the reach for ultimacy that are expressed in a word like "rights."

However worthy the cause, and however unusual the effort of six hundred delegates achieving a remarkable articulateness—in what, for many, was their second or third language—it was by no means a foregone conclusion that a written constitution in an equatorial African country, demarcated by outsiders, can reign supreme. Less certain still was it that a written legal-political document could capture the depth, the intricacy, and the culturally multifaceted nature of human attachments to land, with all their debatable or hazily understood cultural, emotional, and agronomic implications. The hearings were perhaps the best that a group this size could produce before the hardest choices had to be made, and a "permanent" legal document might be set down and ratified. Then would start the inevitable processes of translation, interpretation, and revision. It was anyone's guess how long such a document might endure before being overpowered by conquest, amended beyond recognition, or simply honored in the breach like so many national and colonial laws whose authors and implementers purport to cover multiethnic polities and span a range of cultures. But it was a try, a hope, and a rite of collective renewal.

CHAPTER 10

Conclusion

Property, Improperty, and the Mortgage

Land is life. . . . Every person must possess land because nobody was
born in the air.
—SYLVANUS ONYAMBU OGARI

"Reform, reform. Aren't things bad enough already?" So said
Arthur Wellesley, the first Duke of Wellington, in 1832, as England was just undergoing its second big wave of land enclosures, and before
any European had reached the great lake that is the innermost source of the
Nile.[1] If Africa's adventures in property reform have taught us anything since
then, it is that the grander theories of European or North American social
philosophy seldom apply well or neatly, either as frameworks for analysis or
as prescriptions for policy, on that continent astride the Equator. The evolutionary theories being tried out in African "property rights" are old ones,
long antedating Spencer and Darwin, or Maine and Morgan, or Marx and
Engels. But they have drifted in and out of fashion, catching the imagination
of particular peoples in particular eras. The colonial expansionist fervor that
swept Britain and several other western European countries in the Victorian
era was grounded in, but also produced and shaped, particular ideologies
about human evolution and civilization, and about the possibilities of markets, governments, laws, and written records. Some of these ideas were taken
up again and pushed forward in the wave of modernizationist theories and
ambitious social reform programs launched in Africa after the second world
war and continuing into our times.

The Kenyan land tenure reform, the first nationwide attempt in Africa
but not the first attempt in the continent's history to individualize or privatize landholding, offers an instructive test case of a 1950s-style modernization

scheme based on nineteenth-century evolutionist ideas. This bold scheme has been not just a program to title land; it has been part of a broader attempt to rationalize a peasantry, quell social dissent, boost an economy, modernize a way of life, and build a nation. The land tenure reform, however, has been a slow and difficult process. The basic registration of holdings remains unfinished after half a century. Where it was completed early on, it has taken decades for its results to begin to come into focus, and important questions still remain unanswered. The very slowness of the program's progress, and the difficulty of obtaining reliable data on its outcome, are evidence in themselves that the idea doesn't fit African cultural, social, or ecological realities well.

Especially hard to swallow, for rural Kenyans and other East Africans, has been the aspect of the new property regime that I have called the freehold-mortgage doctrine and process. Based on a logic so clear and compelling on the surface—that farm development requires credit, that credit requires collateral (or security), that collateral is made possible by individual land titles, and that these are best registered by state government—the process of making land available for exchange and alienation by pledge and mortgage makes large categories of persons more vulnerable than ever to dispossession and impoverishment.

The Luo people, living in an area of middling agricultural potential and high and rising population densities, illustrate characteristically African debates about the acceptability of the freehold-mortgage process and of the land tenure reform and financial interventions that it conjoins. While Luo cannot be called a typical African people—there *is* no such people—they are certainly in a typically African predicament, and enough of their way of life is shared by other equatorial and tropical African societies to make them worthy of serious attention. Perhaps, in delving into a particular case like theirs, we may even learn something more general about us all.

I hope to have shown in this volume that land tenure, finance, and symbolism have much to do with each other in a rural African setting. They connect most directly in issues of pledging, mortgaging, and selling land with homes and graves, which may have spirits perceived by many to be active around those places. The Kenyan national experiment in individual land titling has proceeded under the assumption that freehold title will allow farmers to use their lands for new loans to develop their farms. But where land is settled by lineage, and ancestral graves justify land claims, the freehold-mortgage process now being tried runs afoul of hard cultural facts.

Recurring Ethical Doubts About the Mortgage

Pledging and mortgaging are old ideas and practices in some parts of the world, but seemingly always somehow disputed or variously understood even there. Land pledging for money is discussed in Hammurabi's Code (hard to date; c. 1600–1900 B.C.) and certainly occurred in the Athenian city-state. It pretty clearly went on in Britain by the time of the Norman Conquest in 1066. But land mortgages as understood today, deadlined pledges with a permanent right for creditors to take over the land upon default, did not become conventional in England or America until well into industrial times.

Even in industrial (and postindustrial) times Euro-American intellectual tradition has never satisfied itself that *financial borrowing and lending* are good. Issues of interest and usury have been hotly debated over many centuries, and wherever there is lending, there are resentments about lenders who are rightly or wrongly perceived to take unfair advantage of their borrowers.

Nor are western Europeans and North Americans entirely satisfied that *private property in land* is to be desired. At all times has there been tension between conflicting views on this—since Rousseau contradicted Locke, since Aristotle debated Plato before them . . . and probably since long before that.

And certainly there is no general agreement yet that the *connection between credit and private property in land* (as in pledging) is a good idea. Far less, even, have we agreed that *mortgaging* (or deadlined pledging) is fair or just. The practice has only rather recently become acceptable in common law, after a long history filled with twists and turns, stubborn anachronisms of terminology and classification, and reversed decisions. Whatever the prevailing trends of opinion, both grand social theory and popular culture have long contained both strong admiration for the power of collateralized capital, and strong critiques of the mortgage and those who practice it.

All people have conflicting loyalties. Dominant Euro-American writers on finance and fiduciary custom in the past two centuries have paid more attention to questions of justice and freedom (often perceived as mainly male concerns) than to those of connectedness and continuing life of their ancestors, as spirits or divinity. But how humans approach these have more than a little bearing on whether humans cohere, and on whether they find places and acquiesce to others' presence on shared ground.

I have suggested that the concepts of financial credit and of private property in land are analytically separable but tightly interlinked in European and American social philosophy and in African scholarship affected by it. Pledging and mortgaging are their clearest intersection. A number of the most in-fluential schemas in social philosophy, mainstream or radical, have depicted "primitive" property as communal, and "civilized" property as individual and alienable. They have made out private property and the spread of money, credit, and the mortgage system to be central and interconnected aspects of the dissolution of kinship and of the rise of territorial entities including the state, for better or worse.

It has always proved hard for commentators on this process to avoid moral judgment. Many are the authors who write about credit without ex-plicit mention of debt, and vice versa. Theorists who most feared the spread of international financial capital have often been those who most feared pri-vate property in land; tacitly, economic philosophers have thus seemed to divide into camps for and against a mortgage system. More often than not, scholarship on these subjects has been undergirded with evolutionary pre-sumptions about primitiveness and civilization, and rooted in fundamen-tal questions about how closely humans resemble (other) animals. Or with analogies to human personal growth and development, likening people in "undeveloped" economies to children. Occasionally it is tinged with racism, and frequently it is charged with normative judgments about social justice.

Interestingly, some of the most pointed criticisms of the "mainstream" assumptions come from right within the agencies most closely identified with them (as in the work of J. D. Von Pischke or Shem Migot-Adholla at the World Bank, writing on rural finance and land titling, respectively). Conversely, some of the most convinced modernization theorists in my ex-perience are not hegemonists seated in the centers of wealth and power, but impoverished and disempowered people in East African farm hamlets. Theories pop up in surprising places, but it has been part of our task to lend a humbler, more grounded perspective to set against grand theories. Another part of the task now is to sort out property from impropery — including the "legitimate" property with something morally or ethically dubious about it — and to dust off historic experience, the "gold in it," to adapt to contem-porary contexts.

Entrustment and Belonging

Never was there an enduring system of truly individualistic or communal land tenure, despite much written on both. "The individual" and "society" as absolutes often mean rather less to people in Luo country than they do to Euro-American economists and social philosophers (though there are exceptions). Luo, like real people everywhere, seek some balance between self-interest and sociability, and ways to combine these ends. But the weighting of the different parts of "society" — who counts? — is never stable, always open to debate.

In East Africa one finds different mixtures of individual and communal principles, and of public and private tenure, wherever one looks. In the Luo country, as elsewhere, no single principle ever governed access to land, or rights and duties in it. Luo have always obtained land in many different ways. First settlement and clearing; descent, marriage, adoption, co-residence, and burial and reburial of kin; encroachment and conquest; labor, investment, swapping, loan, and outright purchase have all served, or been argued, to justify human attachments to land. But wherever landholding is concerned, there is an issue of entrustment, for landholding isn't just property or ownership but, in a different way of thinking, custody.

The African input is particularly instructive because it reminds us of long-term continuities and of loyalties connecting the living and the dead. In refusing to let *lineal* obligations get eclipsed by *lateral* ones — or to let "status" get eclipsed by "contract," in Morgan's terms — people like rural Luo have shown a way of coming to terms with the limits of our own wisdom. If we cannot easily hold onto or preserve the land we are on, we may find strength in remembering that others have come before us and yet others will follow. If humans make up the continuing life of their ancestors, perceived as spirits or conduits to divinity, these may in turn help humans cohere, and to find and accept their places on shared ground.[2]

In Luoland as anywhere, not every value has been expressible in monetary terms. Patrimonial land with houses, graves, and hoed or plowed fields may slide in and out of commodity-hood, but it is never *just* a commodity. Its monetary value hardly captures its sentimental value, a value partly governed by the intimacy of persons with overlapping claims in it. The same may be said of Luo cattle, involved as they are in widespread webs of entrustment in marriage. Cattle have a cash value and are also transferred in bridewealth, but a payment in cattle can never be entirely substituted with payment in cash (regardless of amount), and many Luo will tell you there is no marriage without it. Land and animals, in the Luo country, are culturally shielded from obligations incurred in cash. One who lends money had better not expect the borrower to sell cattle or land to repay it, for qualitatively these just aren't commensurable. Some trusts top others.

Entrustment and obligation do not mean just an expectation of reciprocity. There are other forms. Many Luo perceive many of life's most important debts as obliging not just whoever contracted them, but also, or instead, heirs or descendants. Some debts and obligations are thus incurred passively, and some outlast individual lives. One discharges them not by repaying their lenders, but only by passing on the benefits to someone else, continuing a flow. Birth and death don't clear the balance sheet. Intergenerational entrustments and obligations carry right through.[3]

Land custody, among Luo, is an intergenerational entrustment, with its heritable obligation. To sell or gamble away inherited land (as by mortgage) for one's personal gain is strictly antisocial. It breaks a flow. Instead, one must care for the land and pass it along, or if selling or exchanging it, somehow share and socialize the proceeds. School fee assistance today is treated as another intergenerational entrustment. These are things one is expected to return *or* pass along sometime, somehow, to someone who counts as kith or kin.

Limits of Individualism

Humans, Luo seem to tell us, aren't just individuals who make and break their own contracts. Shorter-term, contractual, reciprocal loans sometimes conflict with longer-term, passively incurred, or serial entrustments. A farmer with a generations-old bridewealth debt may not feel at liberty to repay a two-year-old crop loan, deal or no deal. Serial entrustments can supersede dyadic contractual ones. Heritable obligations make human collectivities; and Luo, like other people, sometimes resist seeing these negated in a day's, a year's, or even a life's work. The Luo people (and others in the lake basin) show no clear movement from "status" to "contract," in Maine's terms. Instead these principles interweave.

Branching (or "segmentary") lineages, typical of Luoland and some of its surrounds, are *not* the atavistic residue of a prehistoric way of life. They are better understood as recurrent cognitive and cultural models, and as contemporary inventions and re-creations too or instead, serving useful political and economic as well as social purposes for their members. They are particularly useful as adaptations to high-density agrarian settlement, and it is here that they find perhaps their clearest expression in eastern Africa and in the world. As arable land becomes scarce, it becomes relatively harder for new generations to found their rural homes away from kin. Continually rising densities don't stop movement—indeed they force labor migration, temporary or permanent—but keeping a rural home among family, lineage mates, or clansmen never gets any less important.

Belonging is fundamental. A wuon lowo or japiny, "man of the [or this] country" is distinguished from a jadak (again, "one who stays," or "dweller"—that is, someone in place only temporarily). The process is not just economic, but cultural and political as well; and the distinction between wuon lowo and jadak depends not just on land transfer but on residence and symbolic category membership too.

The symbolic dimensions may change, but only slowly; they do not just wither away as a result of changing circumstances or regulations. The symbolism of landholding in the Luo case, I have suggested, ties closely into sexuality as well as seniority. Just as young women are deemed in a sense visitors in their natal homes, so are jodak in a way like women: subordinate in status because of their temporary, insecure, or ambiguous belonging among a lineage or clan and on its land. Something like this analogy seems to lurk in the background, though it may not be made entirely conscious or explicit: wuon lowo is to jadak as male is to female or neuter. If a jadak asserts maleness or dominance—for instance, by erecting a roof spire pole (osuri) above the center of a house, by thrusting himself to the center of public meetings, or by inviting other immigrants to live on and use the land as jodak—he is likely to incur comment or active resistance from the hosts.[4]

Of course, birth and a placenta buried at home are not the only way of establishing or demonstrating attachment to land. Labor is another. And this, in equatorial Africa, is something even young children do. Much of their play is work, and vice versa; and their contribution to family livelihood is real and great. If labor creates rights, as John Locke, Charles Kingsley Meek, and others have argued, then children in Africa have rights to land, just as their mothers do who have moved there and taken over as both farm laborers and farm managers. Planting and building, as the young grow older, help solidify claims further. Finally, nothing anchors a claim to belonging, in East African understandings, better than burying one's dead at home.

Settlement in lineages, under rising densities, involves increasing attention to ancestral graves and home remains as justifications for land occupation and use. These are focal points of land disputes. Kinship doesn't just include; it excludes too. It tells some people that they have no hope for claims on equal footing with those who belong.

A rising emphasis on *graves* conflicts with a rising emphasis on *money* as justification for access to land. Graves are a symbol of familial and even ethnic attachment to fixed places; money symbolizes social power obtained anywhere, easily moved, and easily lost. Graves imply known antecedents; money doesn't. Graves are for belongers, money can be for strangers. Foreign lenders and state financiers, by marshalling a large bureaucratic apparatus to support contractual agreements like mortgages and irredeemable sales, have tried to reset the priorities, and to put "contract" over "status," but have not really succeeded. Luo people and others in the lake basin have refused to let them break the longer flow.

Change With Reform and Without

It need not take a state tenure reform to get changes in land tenure. By the time Luo and other Kenyans faced the issue of a government-organized individualization in the mid-twentieth century, they had already seen many changes in landholding and land use. Rising population densities, cash cropping, and labor migrations had altered the shapes and sizes of fields and eliminated buffer zones between. New money from both cash cropping and labor migration had altered land values and, more basically, given land cash value where it may not have had it before. Land rentals and sales, if forbidden by custom (as 1950s anthropologists, missionaries, and locals claimed they were), were nonetheless occurring, sometimes disguised as loans. To this limited extent, the suppositions of some economic evolutionists were indeed being borne out. Other parts of the continent were seeing comparable tenure changes. Even if the changes were part of a broader pattern, they were *not* steady, inexorable, or irreversible. But colonial powers in a time of emergency wanted to speed them up and make them so.

Africa's first experiment in nationwide land titling for individual free-hold tenure, long debated but launched in 1954, continues today in Kenya. Titling land as private, individual property both solves some problems and causes others. It brings many unintended consequences.

The process drags. It opens old disputes between kin and neighbors, and it invites new ones — particularly between land borrowers and lenders, or between their offspring or heirs — as some or all realize the possibility that what gets recorded might be permanent. It becomes clear that there are degrees of entrustment, measured in time. Those entrusted to borrow or move onto land temporarily may not have been entrusted to stay longer, or may not now, under more crowded conditions, be entrusted or allowed to stay and take on full status as equals.

A process of adjudication and titling, by altering the nature of land claims, also alters the nature of land disputes. The same process can settle boundary disputes but later open up new disagreements as land use rights and land titles begin to be traded independently of each other.

Titling is never just a neutral recording exercise; it always changes the rights and duties it records. The best-informed and best-connected people tend to end up with the biggest and best land. These aren't necessarily the best or most diligent farmers, nor are their heirs or assignees. The assumption of planners like the authors of the Swynnerton Plan, that titling will allow the more efficient farmers to gain larger holdings and the whole economy to benefit, would seem to have been based more on received wisdom and blind faith than on a rounded consideration of the possible outcomes over time.

In different cultural contexts one finds very different presumptions about land, finance, and the mortgage. Secured lending has been long known in Luoland, but not land collateral for money loans, and not land mortgages. These ideas, so commonplace, so ordinary seeming, so second nature to urban North Americans, are ones rural Luo broadly deem unnatural and unfair.

Several things make mortgaging so alien to common Luo ideas of propriety. These include its riskiness, its pivoting on individual decisions, and the permanency of land loss. In an agrarian setting in equatorial Africa, where so much of livelihood depends on farming (despite a history of labor migration), and where dicey rainfall, new crops and technology, unreliable markets, and general political instability fill farming with such uncertainty, it is simply too risky to let an individual bet the farm on several successive years of steady harvests, even with any likely off-farm remittances to supplement them. Too much has to go right.

A land titling program like Kenya's, even if advertised to farmers mainly as a way of giving them access to credit, as Kenya's was, doesn't by itself bring much more of it within their reach, as we can now say confidently with hindsight. Institutional lenders know well (or learn quickly) that there will be little they can do with a land title if many of the neighbors around the land are kin, friends, or clients of the dispossessed. Where land is settled in branching lineages, as it tends to be in the Luo country and adjacent areas of western Kenya, this is all the more true. The relatives always have ways of getting even with whoever tries to occupy or use the land (not least witchcraft, for those who can perform or hire it). And if they don't, some would say, spirits attached to them will.

"First-Class Ruination": A Sacred Trust Under Threat?

Ancestral spirits may seem to some foreign financiers trivial concerns, or just backward superstitions. But no one who has lived for long in western Kenya can ignore their presence in many local minds, a presence of which there are daily reminders all around. Place names contain the names of the dead who lived there, and people themselves are identified by the lineage and clan names of their forebears, bearing their names. Graves are there, right outside houses (or for unmarried women deceased, right outside the homestead enclosure entrances, on the left). Many sorts of fortune and misfortune are attributed to the actions of spirits, and to their interaction with the living. Persons who act differently from others—who run naked, speak in tongues, or foam at the mouth—are not locked away out of sight, but remain active in their communities, living testimony to the power of spirits to alter human experience and destiny. Missionaries or no missionaries, schools or no schools, perceptions of spirits in most East African minds are unmistakable. Spirits, continually reembodied in language, homestead design, and so on, are part of Luo culture in every sense (or what Marcel Mauss, Pierre Bourdieu, and others, including Michael Dietler and Ingrid Herbich, would call Luo *habitus*), as they are part of culture in a wider region of tropical Africa. They are not going away without others' coming along to replace them.

Having living and dead kin around the land makes it hard to take away. Lenders in western Kenya know that extracting a land title does not guarantee them repayment for their loans. So they don't readily lend on this basis. Most require something else besides: a salary to attach, a co-signature or two, a hefty bribe, or maybe all of these. Or they get bludgeoned into lending by electioneering politicians. When issuing such loans, they know it's likely that the recipients chosen for them will be too influential and well protected themselves ever to have to repay.

Creditors who represent organizations of strangers, to Luo, are at a strong disadvantage anyway. Luoland is in important ways a country of personal loyalties, and some of the hardest practicalities of local lives operate through known connections. Luo and their neighbors are *not* (I hasten to add) without universalistic ideals of human family too, as Luo Christian dogma (and some Luo Islamic too) ostensibly promotes. But the prevailing idiom and the strongest strains of honor, respect, cooperation, and obedience follow kinship, friendship, neighborhood, or other particular human attachments. In Luoland, we remember from Cohen and Atieno Odhiambo's words, "the stranger is an alien, possibly an enemy." Being a financial creditor doesn't fix that.

Patrimonial land is a sacred trust, or something like one — connecting the living with each other, with the dead and unborn, and with the places on the landscape where graves and buried placentas anchor their being. Unsurprisingly, popular sentiment seems to be that the trust cannot fairly be mixed up with farm loan collateral. The pledger's stake will always be higher than the pledgee's, though his or her power to affect the outcome of the transaction may not be. When the Agricultural Finance Corporation or commercial bank representatives arrive with police in their vehicles, or when buyers show up after a foreclosure auction, it is not seen as a natural conclusion to a contract, far less a "repossession." It is deemed a raid.

It is clear enough that the presence of ancestral graves and other traces on the land, and the great importance attached to these, can make the mortgaging system problematic for just about anyone concerned. It causes problems for borrowers and their kin and dependents because they risk dispossession and deracination–what Will Carleton called "first-class ruination" — and for lenders because they risk losing their loans. After auctions, it causes problems for land repurchasers because they risk becoming targets of violence. It also scares politicians because it adds to the numbers of angry, mobile people who might contribute to excitable mobs. All this seems to be so particularly in areas of relatively dense settlement, the ones where rural-rural mobility is most constricted and where lineage and clan loyalties tie most tightly into particular places on the land. The combined fears and misgivings can grind the mortgage system (if not perhaps the titling system and the lending system that combine to form it) to a slowdown, and even for periods–especially just before elections — to a complete halt.

It is also clear enough that a mortgage system can divide families by bringing about new disputes over control of title. And history and logical inference both suggest too that over the large aggregate and the longer term, it can, in district commissioner Peter McEntee's words, "drive a wedge" between social classes, not least by leading to dispossession and forced removals. Their quiet disappearance is, in Carleton's term, the "hidden sorrow," for not only may these people turn itinerant, but only some will wish to be reminded of their stories long enough to tell them. Persons who lose their places may end up moving or staying in town, country, or in between — where they may or may not find enough to live on.

One might well wonder whether both these things can be true: whether a mortgage system can on the one hand grind to a slowdown — and on the other still split up families; cause dispossession, uprooting, and the disorientation that can come with it; and bring about a wider, secular division between classes. The question is a good one, and I strongly suspect its answer is yes. The second, subtler sort of outcome is just likely to take longer — maybe generations longer — if the first holds true. But that does not necessarily make it impossible. It is apt to proceed from beyond the edges of patrimonial land: the places of recent settlement, the plots recently purchased, the lands around second homes — and see then how long it will take to threaten the "real" homes. In the Luo country this means the ones with the placentas, ancestral graves, and heavily manured animal enclosures where the tobacco grows that Luo have long used to get in touch with the ancestors. And depending on what agents of the nation designate and respect as monuments, it may even mean the rock outcroppings where the heroes died and the legends have them turned to stone. Whether mortgaging, ill-considered swapping, and forced or hasty sale will eventually threaten all these lands and homes or just some of them is anyone's guess.

Titling land affects lives in far more ways than just by affecting financial credit. It can affect decisions to fertilize, to enclose, to subdivide, to buy or sell, to migrate. Many of its effects are still unknown; most are hard to measure.

But three things are clear. One is that the land title registers in western Kenya and other parts of the continent where titling has been carried out are full of fiction — or at least have their own separate reality. Land sellers and land lenders have little reason to register their transactions with the national government; buyers too know that it is likely to cost them bribes and repeat visits, and open them to dealings with town clerks and lawyers whose motives they have no reason to trust. So most don't. But land continues to change hands as personal and family needs change, and as the generations turn over. Titles change hands separately. Titleholders and real users often are not the same people. Registers obsolesce quickly.

Also clear is that the imposition of a new tenure regime does not expunge the one that came before it. Written titles don't obviate witnesses. Signatures and thumbprints don't take automatic precedence over graves, abandoned bomas, and old furrows. Land registries in Luoland don't replace lineages and *jodong' gweng'*. Instead they add a new layer of evidence; a new set of tools for competition; and new channels of legal recourse for the bold, the schooled, or the well connected.

Third, state land titles are *not* to be equated with security of tenure. Particularly not where states are new, artificial-seeming, and rather brittle in constitution and leadership. Coming on top of an alternate and resilient system of claims, rights, and duties, new titles can end up raising land tenure security or lowering it. In any case, raising it for one usually means lowering it for someone else—even and especially for a titleholder's close kin, and women and children in particular, who may have little effective say over whether a holder sells or mortgages away a title to the land *they* work and live on. Mortgaging threatens not just the mortgager, but others too. *Freehold means freelose.*

Human-land attachments, in short, are not something one can easily re-form from one "system," like capitalism or socialism, to another—no matter how strong anyone's ideological commitment to a desired new order, or how compelling the sticks and carrots the reformers may wield. Human ideas about belonging are subtler, deeper, more vital than that.

The Freehold-Mortgage Doctrine Revisited

We are now in a position to reexamine the set of theoretical assumptions of many developers and property reformers as spelled out in the introduction. Let us take the theory piece by piece.

1. *Assumption:* To raise agricultural productivity, farmers need more inputs and new technology. *Critique:* Few would argue against production or productivity in itself. But why those people classed as farmers should be expected to raise productivity in the first place is far from certain. Some might benefit more from being able to move, or send others partly on their behalf, to other parts of the world where there is more production or easier access to (or consumption of) what is produced. New or imported farming

technology may rise faster in price, or swing more widely in price, than the goods produced. Increased use of manufactured farm inputs often carries its own costs to environment and public health, as through fertilizer and pesticide runoff. Finally, higher productivity is not always good for producers; it may sometimes lead to price collapses through temporary oversupply.

2. *Assumption:* Many farmers are too poor to save or to afford the inputs and new technology themselves. *Critique:* This assumption has been open to challenge in rural African communities. Where a new technique clearly raises productivity, someone is likely to try to procure it by saving or other means. Even in some of the world's poorest rural communities, there is often an economic or technological elite whose members are able to experiment most easily, who feel immune from criticism, or who can demonstrate the benefits of a new input or technique to others, wittingly or not.

Also, where financial markets function smoothly, borrowing is usually more expensive than saving. If a farmer is "too poor to save," isn't he or she too poor to borrow?

3. *Assumption:* Farmers therefore need loans from better-endowed people until they can afford to finance their own needs. *Critique:* This and the foregoing contentions presume that farmers are just farmers, and are going to use "farm loans" just for farming, and reinvest the proceeds in the same. This is decidedly not what has usually happened in tropical African settings. Instead, rural people have readily siphoned resources from one "sector" of economic activity into another, or used them for purposes only partly or indirectly economic in nature, such as marriage, schooling, health-seeking, trade, or casual or ceremonial entertainment. Farmers are people too, and they have their own ideas about what's urgent. Some are also heavily under the social or political influence of elders, patrons, chiefs, or persons to whom they may hold prior obligations.

The assumption that poor people need more loans not only ignores what debts and obligations they may already have (and these can be considerable, as seen in *The Nature of Entrustment*). It also neglects the political and psychological costs of borrowing and indebtedness. These, especially demoralization, may hurt production (among other things) in themselves, though their effects are indirect and hard to measure.

4. *Assumption:* Loans require collateral to ensure their repayment. *Critique:* Merely having access to collateral does not necessarily encourage lenders to lend (or, for that matter, borrowers to borrow). Most in tropical African settings like Luoland seem to require incentives or guarantees be-

yond it. Where land is titled, surrendering a title becomes a necessary but not sufficient condition for borrowing. Nor does collateral necessarily help ensure repayment once loans are issued.

There are many alternate ways of ensuring loan repayment. Careful selection of borrowers by character is one. Salaries and investments, if any, may be attached instead of tangible property, and third-party guarantees may help. Under certain circumstances, peer group pressure among borrowers (who may also be joint savers) can produce full loan repayment. This principle, evident in local contribution clubs like rotating saving and credit associations, seems to work best with persons roughly equal in status (for instance, all market women or all junior salaried employees of the same organization). It also works most smoothly with nonagricultural incomes and expenditures because of seasonal covariance problems. Where farming is subject to a boom–bust annual cycle, financial club flows may intermit seasonally.[5]

5. *Assumption:* The best collateral is land, because it is immovable. *Critique:* Whether land makes an acceptable collateral depends entirely on history and cultural context. In societies like the Luo with lineages (or other kin groups) reflected in settlement patterns, scattered homesteads, and graves used as markers, only some land may realistically be usable as loan collateral, and other land politically impossible or explosive to attach and distrain. Where children have grown up working on land, they grow up with all the more reason to care about it. In societies like Kenya's, where land has been historically a subject of intense ethnic, racial, and class strife, attaching land to loans may conjure up many old resentments or fuel misunderstandings.

6. *Assumption:* Land ought therefore to be negotiable—that is, transferable for monetary or other consideration. *Critique:* Most land, even in inland equatorial Africa, is already negotiable in some way or another. Making land *more* negotiable is a major social, cultural, economic, and political undertaking likely to have implications reaching far beyond farming and finance. It is hard to do quickly or efficiently in itself, because it involves someone's having to sort out long-standing, overlapping claims in land. Even where land becomes ostensibly freely negotiable, social inhibitions, including physical threats, may keep land markets strictly local. Land markets imply migration. At best, this may help produce a healthy social mixture and a dynamic economy; at worst, it can contribute to mass resentments and even (as in the western Kenyan "land clashes") ethnically pitched violence.

7. *Assumption:* The way to make land transfers easier, and to keep track

of them, is to issue titles of land ownership (or else deeds of transactions), registered with the national government. *Critique:* This assumption is subject to several possible objections. First, merely registering land titles does not by itself induce those who use or transfer the land to use their titles or to transfer the titles with it. Instead, in areas like western Kenya, we have seen separate markets emerging in land and titles, and much confusion and double dealing. It is wrong to assume that a new imposed system of owning land or validating claims in it will expunge the system(s) already in place. Finally, there is little reason to suppose a priori that a state government bureau (as against, say, local chiefdoms, self-help groups, voluntary associations, companies, churches, and so on) should be the ultimate authority over land, or that there should be any single such authority. National governments in tropical Africa have proved brittle, contested arenas of power and confrontation. Their ruling regimes have often proved authoritarian, kleptocratic, ethnically and regionally partisan, politically and economically manipulable by insiders and outsiders, . . . and in many countries, short-lived. They may, in any case, simply enjoy little public trust.

In all, the logical sequence that may seem so smooth on the surface hardly proves watertight where real people are concerned.

Clashes of Cultures over Mortgaging

Human attachments to land in the Luo country have much about them that is both social and sacred, and ever more so. They can determine social standing and spiritual connection. They are intimately connected to genealogy—both the patriliny for which Luo are well known, and the matrilineal and affinal ties that play subtler but no less important roles in allocating persons to fields and herds and vice versa. They are, by the same token, all bound up with a status system (not exactly class or caste, but bearing something in common with both) that divides early settlers from latecomers. Graves are a crucial part of this multisided nexus between humans and land. Ancestral spirits are perceived as ever involved in temporal affairs around those graves, if not also elsewhere. Financiers or purchasers who think they can yank away land from defaulting borrowers will inevitably clash with those borrowers *and* with their neighboring kin. Violence about belonging (already seen both in isolated incidents and in systematically organized ethnic purges in western Kenya) is always a possibility. The mortgage system has not worked, will not work, in Luoland, or in many densely settled parts of agrarian East Africa where lineage matters to settlement.

Many Luo have been deeply and increasingly concerned about the encroachment of the cash land market, and of the freehold-mortgage process, into their lives and homes. It is hard for them or anyone else to know how it will all end up. A process of land dispossession can be slow and gradual, and hard to isolate from other processes like rural-rural migration or mechanization. It may appear not to come from anywhere in particular. So it is hard to know just how, when, and where to make sure it doesn't happen. Inadequate research has been done on the process and popular responses to it to allow confident generalization or prediction. But there are signs that Luo are far from alone, in tropical farming settings, in their skeptical, ambivalent response to the freehold-mortgage process, and to the political philosophy of possessive individualism that it seems to represent.

It isn't that the parts are so bad, as rural Luo have sometimes pointed out. There's nothing inherently wrong, arguably, with land titling in itself. Nor with credit: for loans, from near or far, are something everybody needs sometimes. But the *conjunction* of individual land titling and farm credit in the freehold-mortgage process is what makes both parts together so hazardous, and personal, family, and community fortunes so volatile.

Tying together land tenure and financial credit, the freehold-mortgage process can help or hurt the titled mortgagors. The mortgage can be a useful expedient for some people with *steady, predictable incomes,* such as those that reliable manufacturing industry or other employment can provide in settings with reliable input supplies and markets. The mythology or structure of understandings surrounding the mortgage (Benjamin Franklin's "time is money," for example) is in large part a product of the industrial revolution. It can also be, as Max Weber and R. H. Tawney have both observed, a concomitant of religious transformation (whether as cause, effect, or parallel result of other factors). It may best fit an urban and peri-urban context with reliable transport and market infrastructure and multiple income opportunities.

By contrast, the freehold-mortgage process can be particularly dangerous for *agriculture,* particularly rain-fed agriculture, and rural people heavily dependent on it. It is especially hazardous where farming is most unreliable, markets fluctuating, health and strength at risk, bargaining power weak, or terms of trade disadvantageous—and in contemporary rural Africa it is all of these. Much manufacturing industry has more predictable returns than most rain-fed farming. This makes mortgages safer for such industry than for most farming.

The basic principle is simple enough. Loan interest typically accrues in a linear or parabolic fashion. Farm yields and earnings do not. They fluctuate up and down, and they may stay down for years. Lenders may or may not agree to reschedule (stretch out) collection. Sooner or later farmers are likely to get caught. This does not necessarily mean that the mortgage system will work well wherever rainfall is steadier. The case of high, fertile, well-watered Kisii gives the lie to this supposition. Here, evidently because of extreme crowding among other things, the defaults, litigation, and violence seem to have been just as intense as they are downhill in the agriculturally dicier Luo country.

There are other reasons, too, why the freehold-mortgage system seems to have been going awry. Seemingly most anywhere, people overestimate their own capacity to use and repay loans, and overexpose themselves. There is too much we cannot predict. Not all rural equatorial Africans have the store of generations-old cautionary legendry of the sort that might, through early learning, help protect potential borrowers from lenders in longer industrialized settings and longer monetized economies.[6] Imitation and the euphoria of boom times may prompt overinvestment. Or contrariwise, extreme or sudden poverty may shorten time horizons like a fisheye lens, making immediate needs loom larger and distant threats recede. Or it may prompt desperate action, or recourse to sacrifice or prayer, for remedy.

Urban-based financiers, and to an extent rural ones too, threaten to dislocate and impoverish farmers (particularly unlettered ones) through the mortgage and countless other legal-financial devices whenever boom times turn to bust. In East Africa it has happened to big farmers as well as small, "white" as well as "black." (It happened to prosperous Rift Valley settlers in the Great Depression, for instance.) It has happened in other parts of the world where the mortgage has caught on. These things we know.

Comparisons, Counterfactuals

Other things we do not know as well, but some of them are no less important for it. In this section and the next, we indulge in a bit of speculation, beginning by peering down a road not taken. What would have happened over the second half of the twentieth century had Kenya's government left its people's land unsurveyed, unadjudicated, and untitled? Would the rural populace, many of whom were migrating back and forth to cities, have kept tenure evolving toward some sort of private, saleable, mortgageable property on their own? Some of the best available answers are to be found in other African comparisons. Like any comparison worth making, though, they have their points of fit and misfit.

There is reason to suppose that individual claims over land might have continued to strengthen as population grew denser. Ugandan banana and coffee farmers in densely settled Ankole, studied by Simon Heck, present an interesting case. From the 1920s, and perhaps earlier, occasional land purchasing by chiefs was noted in the Ankole country, which was mostly untouched by the earlier *mailo* land titling program. After the second world war, as coffee growing expanded, new money flowed in, and demand for land rose, land purchase and sale became more common. In the 1970s and '80s, the effective collapse of state government in Uganda left local communities to their own devices, and in the 1980s, many farmers began selling bits of their holdings piecemeal to meet cash needs, and to address temporary problems in their family and homestead development cycles. Rural people appear to have devised their own form of written sales contracts, with the sanction of their own local associations. They required local eyewitnesses to their signing, and even though carbon paper, signatures, and thumbprints were used, the contracts were considered invalid without witnesses' oral support, and a public libation was called for to seal a deal. Banyankole thus used writing not to replace an indigenous form of oral testimony but to supplement it. Rural Banyankole devised and refined their system of contracts even though, and partly *because*, they had no functioning state government attempting to manage land matters (Heck 1998, esp. Ch. 7). Local neighborhood associations filled a power vacuum that the collapse of the state and the military had left. They promoted their own land market. In many other cases too, in Africa south of the Sahara, rural people with limited access to lawyers, courts, or government registries—or reason to avoid them—have devised their own local forms of written contracts and witnessing for regulating their own land dealings (Benjaminsen and Lund 2003).

If, in the western Kenyan case, a land market kept arising without titling, would agriculture have flourished in Kenya as it did from the 1950s to the 1980s? This question is especially hard to answer. Comparing titled and untitled lands for productivity takes measuring yields on fields likely to be intercropped, and sometimes farmed by more than one person or family. It takes comparing plots whose farmers are naturally experimenting on their own with mixed varieties and cultivation methods—and who have different characters in the first place. It takes observing family and field histories over time, and watching as the titling process temporarily heats up boundary squabbles then replaces them with disputes about who bought and sold what. Only an accumulation of research will answer it.

The best one can do is compare the Kenyan areas titled early and those titled late. This task is not easy in itself and can produce misleading results, since the tenure reform started in the higher, better-watered, more fertile areas (notably in the Gikuyu and Gusii countries), and broadly proceeded downhill to where farming is harder, less rewarding, and less reliable. The early-settled areas were getting the best agricultural extension and infrastructure—the densest road networks and best marketing facilities—with foreign funding. Not surprisingly, the areas titled first seemed by the late 1970s and early 1980s to be the most productive agriculturally.[7] What role the titling itself played in accounting for the differences is hard to disaggregate.

Alternatively, one might attempt to compare the agricultural histories of Kenya and other countries that did not embark on such ambitious tenure reforms. Here a related set of problems arises to muddy the test. Kenya was a favorite recipient of international agricultural "aid" in equatorial Africa through to the early 1980s (partly because the donors and lenders favored the tenure reform and other market-oriented policies in themselves). Uganda and Tanzania, as abutting countries around the lake, might seem to offer the most obvious points of comparison. But Uganda was undergoing a period of state terrorism and state collapse from the late 1960s to the early 1980s, while Tanzania was undergoing a heavy-handed socialist revolution, with "villag-ization," involving much forced resettlement and stiff popular resistance to it. Neither nation received anything close to the amount of foreign "aid" and investment Kenya did in this period (though Tanzania did attract significant Scandinavian, Chinese, and other assistance).

Northern Rhodesia/Zimbabwe, a country with many surface parallels to Kenya, might seem to offer another point of comparison, but its explicit racial segregation policies and international ostracism over several decades complicates the picture. Zimbabwe's is a story of two starkly contrasting populations: one with land-titled, state-subsidized, mechanized, and highly productive farming on large estates largely cleared of their earlier inhabi-tants—and the other dispossessed of most of its land and left on crowded, untitled "communal lands" with poor soils and scarce local economic oppor-tunity of any kind. Much of this characterizes Kenya too, but Zimbabwe's class and racial divisions have been even starker. A secular economic decline in the years of the socialist-leaning Robert Mugabe regime, and waves of government-condoned "spontaneous" resettlement (call it reclamation or invasion) by land-deprived Shona, Ndebele, and others onto formerly "white"-controlled large farms and ranches, contributed to a general insecurity unique to Zimbabwe in the late 1990s and early 2000s. Just as in the case of Kenya's resettled areas, though, land titles have hardly protected those whose lands were to be invaded.

All these cases, the ones that would seem to offer the closest comparisons with Kenya, have their own historical particularities that confound the sort of comparisons that would lead to a clear picture of the road not taken in Kenya, or to general conclusions about optimal tenure policies. Comparisons farther afield become strained too as different ecological conditions, settlement patterns, and colonial legacies come into play.[8]

To sum up, Kenya's agricultural scene was far from static at the time the tenure reform was undertaken and land selling and mortgaging became legitimate under the state. By the time the attempted reform began in the 1950s, individuals appeared to be asserting personal claims over used and unused land more strenuously than in the past, but not without local debate and administrative uncertainty about the adaptability of custom. There is no easy comparison—inside Kenya or out—to show how far the land use or productivity of Luoland or Kenya might have evolved differently without titling.[9] Whether the act of land titling and the increasingly fictitious land registers resulting together produce net gains in agricultural investment and productivity, or how long these might last if so, remains extremely hard to tell.

If dispossession continues—as land grabbing by unscrupulous politicians and the coalitions they represent, as violent raids by gangs of angry youth or militias, or as a subtler, slower process of dispossession and displacement through mortgaging, and through sell-offs in times of distress or reckless loss of self-control, how far might it go? This is hard to say, again, but what evidence we have from around Africa and elsewhere suggests it can go far indeed. Kenya's land grabbing by politicians and friends has been dramatic enough already, as we have seen and as others have documented further.[10] Research on Cameroon's grassfields and other parts of that country has made it clear that some of the most effective ways politicians and civil servants can grab land in quite new markets is by framing their actions in terms of traditionally accepted values.[11] The history in Darfur, southern Sudan, also at the turn of the twenty-first century has made clear enough to the world what racially and religiously charged territorial routing can look like, if not so easily what it can feel like. As for the more gradual effects of titling and mortgaging, one may need to look a little farther away for more time perspective. Colin Murray's historical study of Tswana and Sotho people in Thaba Nchu, a farming area within South Africa's Orange Free State, affords a century-long view. It depicts in unique, grueling detail the family and neighborhood sagas of gradually forced relocation in which titling and mortgaging play no small part—beginning well before the cementing of apartheid as national policy in that country (1992). As Murray shows, it need not be a simple, categorical dispossession, since some previously advantaged rural people can and do benefit from loan money to convert their children, through education, into a different, more urban-based kind of elite—something happening in Kenya too (1992). But since the land loss can scatter the losers (to poorer lands, to peri-urban slums, to wherever they have kin or friends to help them adjust), their stories can be hard to round up and pass along. Land dispossession destroys its own traces.

Farther away from equatorial Africa, we recall the wider American mortgaging saga referred to in Chapter 2, in its generalities and its specificities. Specifically among the people who did not have long experience with literacy and lawyers, and financiers—or at least not good experience—were American Indians (or Native Americans, or First People). A turning point for them came with the General Allotment Act (also called the Dawes Severalty Act) in 1887. The granting of transferable (though not freely salable) individual titles in reservation land, to persons unaccustomed to such a form of property in the past—and surrounded by ambitious homesteaders, ranchers, and prospectors who outnumbered them in lawyers—led to mortgaging and lease-offs that stripped away some two-thirds of the Indian reservation lands (that is, of that which remained after the so-called excess was thrown open to non-Native settlers) within thirty years. Between their time and ours have come the foreclosures of the Dust Bowl and Depression era and other less dramatic episodes. At the moment this book went to press, the mortgage market was seeming to more than a few financial analysts to pose a serious threat to the general economy in the United States and abroad—causing widespread dispossession and evictions—because of the overextension of easy credit to borrowers retrospectively deemed uncreditworthy (collectively referred to as the "subprime market"). The panic, reaching rich and poor alike, came about because even mortgage foreclosure, with all the pain and hardship it causes its victims (whatever they may have done or not done to deserve it), evidently does not save the day for the banks and other lenders, or for others depending on them.[12]

None of these few stories can be done justice here in their complexity (and sometimes hidden ironies), but they do amount to warnings—severally and together—of processes that may occur too slowly to look like emergencies to policy makers or to the general public over the time they happen. They are not inevitable outcomes—just possible ones, and even likely ones unless careful stock is taken of historic trends and the limits of the ability of individual humans to make spot decisions as individuals about landholding over generations. If freehold means freelose too, the mortgage is one mechanism.

. . . and Hypotheticals

For the reader who wishes, or whose imagination permits, something now about the outer reaches of our knowledge. Below are a few aspects of attachment that no brief study like this one can pretend to cover thoroughly, but that merit mention nonetheless. They are included to invite readers from different disciplines and occupations, to invite their participation in future study, and maybe with that to connect more dots. Or (to return to our original metaphor): if the subject of land is a common grazing ground for the disciplines, it is also one where each can doubtless drop something easy for another to disparage by epithet, but subtly valuable that will fertilize the soil. We begin with one or two speculations about causes and effects, continue to offer some generalizations that are tempting but still a little hard to make, and then move to the vexed question of ways forward.

Why not start with the sexy bit? Access to land, or control over it, implies access to and sometimes control over people too. There is a sexual and reproductive dimension in all this, as I have suggested and as any historian or primate ethologist can tell you. It is hardly by mere coincidence that kings, chiefs, emperors, land barons, gang leaders, and sundry alpha males have so often had so many females to mate with (as spouses, concubines, paramours, or rape victims); sired so many offspring; and contributed so much—for better or worse—to the gene pools of posterity.[13] The processes may be obscure or unspeakable at times, the causes and effects varyingly circular and complex, the interpretations open to sexism and gender struggles. But the fact that territory, sexuality, and reproduction connect in one way or another has never been much of a secret anywhere and is hardly open to question.

Whether we are talking about instinct or learning, when discussing territoriality and belonging, is a debate without end.[14] But it is a false choice. Humans are far from alone among vertebrates in displaying competition over land — or cooperation in coalitions either, for that matter. If we share as many tendencies as we do with reptiles and birds, we can hardly have thought it all up out of whole cloth as a purely human, purely cultural construct. We sense and learn with what our genes allow us to sense and learn with, and conversely, our learning and experience conditions, in subtle ways, what our genes can make up in the physical constitution of our brains and their neurological pathways. The influences between biology and learned culture go back and forth in ways we are just beginning to discover. Nor does biology always create the universals and culture the local particulars, as so commonly assumed. It can work the other way around too. Human reproduction and selection, through genetic endowment, can certainly generate much variety (for instance, in strength, maturation speed, resilience, or cunning) that cultural rules sometimes simply deny (for instance, through rites of transition, linguistic classification, standardized occupational training, or categories for taxation or regulation).

One who does not wish to speculate on causes might still wish to speculate on effects. Some important questions remain without definitive answers here, though I have tried to offer what feel for them I can. One has to do with whether individual or private land titling contributes to soil conservation and raises crop productivity. There is credible evidence around that it can, but less sure is under what circumstances, how consistently, and (the part most often neglected) *for how long*. The "able or energetic" landholder, given new opportunities through a land market, does not always convey abilities or energy to assignees or heirs.

Another key question is whether, or how steadily and inexorably, land so titled becomes concentrated into fewer hands. It seems it often does so concentrate, but such a trend can conceal some ironic wrinkles as larger landholders with new leeway for selling sell off parts of land they are not using. No author or discipline knows the total effects of all this for sure—at least for the interior of Africa — despite the seeming urgency of the questions and the number of authors always coming up who claim to have gathered compelling evidence one way or the other. Even after many years of attention to land matters (with bright economists and ecologists often at hand, no less), I shan't make firm or blanketing generalizations on these trends, and I caution the reader against those who do.

Whether mortgaging of farmland ought to be warned against in education campaigns, or in popular cautionary stories that do their own work, or subjected to some sort of ban (as in Islamic law, in its theory; or in Chinese secular law) or official disincentive in this setting or that depends of course on perspective as well as on local cultural context. I cannot claim the authority to say much more. Official bans may not be a realistic idea in many parts of the world, and sometimes they have perverse effects. Draconian measures sometimes backfire, like land reforms that have started out with a leveling ideology but ended up worsening the distribution of holdings through the workings of special connections and favors. Or like bans on money lending that end up raising interest rates in unregulated markets. Half measures, like allowing land to be used to secure loans but not with a deadline (that is, pledging but not mortgaging), or allowing options for eventual land buyback, are familiar compromise answers around Africa and elsewhere.

At the very least, anyone who engages in a mortgage in a rain-fed farming area, especially one with unreliable crop markets, ought to be well informed of the terms and well warned of the hazards. So ought his or her kin, dependents, neighbors, and others with partial or potential claims on the land. As an ethical if not also practical matter, anyone who does the lending or foreclosing ought to be respectful of sacred or personally meaningful sites, mindful of the presence and needs of kith and kin around, and prepared to be lenient with repayment rescheduling and interest forgiveness. And no one should count on absolute protection, or enduring wisdom, from unknown authorities. Anyone anywhere should expect the terms and conventions of mortgaging, and the authorities attempting to regulate it, to keep on changing—just as they have done for centuries in Britain and in other parts of the world where the idea is that old. It seems the idea is just too fraught for stability.

The point to remember on these questions of evolution, and about directions for the future, is that biologically programmed inclinations, such as they may be, need not mean inevitability. If by chance or by natural selection we are born with a tendency to territorial defensiveness or aggression, it is yet possible, and arguably our duty, to overcome it with moral actions and institutions: to surmount, or compensate for, mean genes with kind minds — or at least fair, tolerant, and respectful minds. Under the dangers now posed by the weapons and threatening germs becoming so widely available, we had better.

That brings us back to the question whether an invisible social bond is as real as a piece of sisal twine. Whether we are talking about the link between person and land, between person and person, or between the living, dead, and unborn, the answer to this is in the eye of the beholder, and in the tangible effects of human decency. But without the ties that bind, or at least the shared illusion or parallel perception of them, the world will not be such a nice or safe place.

Certain, in any case, is that belonging and territoriality can be explored and pursued at any scale, indoors or out: from the size of a square on a checkerboard, to space in a bed or bedroom, to a continent or a planet with planted flag. Whether it will all extend to the stars (say, maybe as radio broadcast zones) — is anyone's guess. If there should turn out to be creatures out there who have survived all this, we could use some of their wisdom about how to get along. But most of us were not born in the air, as Sylvanus Onyambu Ogari in Kenya reminds us. We down here are on our own with no one to listen to, and to accommodate, but each other as humans and living beings, and each other's ideals and beliefs. That is enough.

Property, Inequality, and Sovereignty

Of the many hopes and fears surrounding the titling of land as private property, most come down to two sorts. On the one hand are dreams of secure tenure, higher productivity, and incentives for conservation. On the other are fears of an eventual concentration of holdings into fewer hands, with the nightmares of confinement or dispossession, of dislocation, and of their ensuing effects on health and civil order. When Rousseau published in 1755 that essay on the origins of human inequality, which became so famous and influential, he identified private property in land as a taproot of what he considered the problem that not only divided society but also infected human morality and misdirected human achievement. His starting point was mainly speculative, as he admitted. His vision of the solitary man in the state of nature was based on only travelers' tales of property-less societies in the Americas, received notions from earlier authors like Hobbes and Locke, and dim memories of childhood stays in Swiss mountain villages. So his account of the human story began as dreamy legend. But it took on a flavor increasingly realistic as it went on to describe the rise of human competition, class and state formation, and property law with vested interests behind it.

In equatorial African settings where land is being titled now as private property, we can reevaluate theories and quasi-histories like Rousseau's with more realistic starting premises. We now know that economic inequality long antedated official title in land. Never was there a time of total social equality, and maybe there never will be. But it seems that a process of privatizing or individualizing landholding, to the extent it succeeds, can indeed prepare the way to widen class rifts, if only through gradual, piecemeal dispossession and displacement. This is as likely to be true in Kenya as in other parts of the world where titling and mortgaging have occurred.

Inequalities in land access, wealth, and power can feed on themselves. On this point, if not on every other, Henry George was right; and the evidence in rural Africa is as abundant as it is in San Francisco, New York, or London. Farming people who have too little land to rotate fields or crops exhaust their soils by overuse. Having to hire themselves, their children, or their animals out to better-off neighbors, or migrate away to work, in crucial periods in the farming season threatens their herding and schooling and cuts into their harvests. Poverty's ratchet forces them to oversell their crops cheaply after harvest and buy them back more expensively before the next, while those who can afford to speculate on those crops by doing the reverse, or have the vehicles to do the transport, can profit. It also tempts or forces the strapped to over-borrow on unfavorable terms, or so to sell off less-used pieces of land to waiting neighbors or to speculators based in towns and cities. In cases of disputes, the better-off have more to offer in fees or bribes in court cases — and they always seem to have more witnesses. When, in ways like these, the rich do indeed get richer and the poor poorer, these are not disconnected facts.

We find in the Luo country and Kenya, however, that landholding does not necessarily *remain* the sole or even main basis of inequality, even among people equal in (say) race-, gender-, or age-based status. Rural landholders sell and mortgage land for children's school fees, they use their crop loans for additional wives, they use their farming proceeds to get out of farming. Land and farming remain the fallback, and the graves in family homesteads remain the symbolic anchors of individual and family identity. People want attachment to land, but they want to be able to leave it sometimes too.

The notion of a social contract in a territorial polity presumes its parties to have, or to have had, some choice about whether to consent to it in the first place. To Thomas Hobbes, the choice may be a very limited one by the time nations or empires are established. One body politic conquers another, and offers its members a choice between dying or surviving on the victorious sovereign's terms. To Hobbes, the agreement to accept the victor's terms counts as a social contract.

Many, though, would reject this chillingly minimalist definition of "contract" and insist that that the vanquished have some other living option. Two possibilities spring to mind: that they be able to replace the ruler(s) with another (or others), or that they be able and free to move away.

The first was what John Locke insisted in his second treatise on government. Locke, like Hobbes, liked the idea of a social contract, but considered the people, not the monarch or assembly, to be the proper sovereign. The second condition—that citizens or subjects be able and free to move away— was never successfully championed by any authority known to me until the United Nation's Universal Declaration of Human Rights, in 1948, just after what many call the second world war. By this time, though, the entire world had been claimed by nation-states. It had happened in a process Jean-Jacques Rousseau had aptly described in his essay on the origins of human inequality: once one nation forms, others must form to defend themselves against it. And it had all ended up the way Rousseau later, in his work on the "social contract," showed he dreaded: the units were too large for all voices to be directly heard in government.

This was the world at the turn of the millennium. Anyone who wished not to live under a nation-state's rules and rulers had a hard time finding anywhere to go. Even Antarctica had been cut up like a pie, all slices claimed by nation-states. Arguably, even the most democratic countries had developed a condition that Alexis de Tocqueville found objectionable in the America he admired, and warned the world against: tyranny by the majority.

Within tropical Africa, things were more restricted still. Because of the size and scale of nation-states, or because of the methods of their ostensible sovereigns, many citizens or subjects felt powerless to change their constitutions or rulers. Rulers were deposed by coups d'état. Elections were rigged or brutally manipulated. Former power holders were executed, minorities or opposition leaders intimidated. Under conditions like these, citizens or subjects may well insist they need an exit option: some land where they can go without having to live under a nation-state. But this, at the turn of the millennium, they scarcely had—short of venturing, as in sci-fi, to Atlantis or to the stars.

If no direct or effective representation, *and* no exit option, then no social contract with the nation-state. Rather than any such "contract," the situation in tropical African settings more closely resembled the one described by David Hume in denouncing that very idea. Most rulers or their predecessors had begun as usurpers. Among those who had not, many remained in power by deftly keeping opposition leaders divided against themselves, or by "disappearing" them. Subjects obeyed sovereigns out of mere coercion or long-acquired habit.

A place on the land—a place to belong among others—is something people fight for. If it was true in antiquity, as Max Weber claimed, that "nearly all social struggles . . . were essentially for the ownership and use of land," much the same could be said of the world at the turn of the present millennium.[15] Africa's hallmark form of land tension and strife, sometimes simplified and exaggerated by mass media abroad, is expressed as interethnic violence, just as southern Asia's seems most often expressed as religious, and South America's as class, conflict. But in truth, each of these regions has *all* these dimensions in its land struggles, and Kenya's episodes in the late twentieth and early twenty-first centuries showed them all clearly.

Beneath the ethnic purges and waves of witchcraft accusations, in Kenya just as in Rwanda, lies discomfort with tightly confined lands, as well as with broader economic and political conditions. Whether living in former "reserves" or in demarcated resettlement areas, most wanted more and better land, and many needed it. They wanted to be able to make their own choices about whether to remain on the land or travel and sojourn away, about whom their neighbors would be, and about the regime of property within which they would live. They wanted to be able to devise and implement their own forms of tenure security—and a deeper sense of belonging—beside or beyond promises from brittle states, or their predatory or evanescent rulers.

Where claims to sovereignty over land matters become oppressive—as when government authorities impose draconian resettlement schemes, use titling as a pretense for their own land grabbing, or foment or condone ethnic purging—the options for relaxing the grip of the nation-state would seem to boil down to three. One is that local and regional entities within nations might be allowed more autonomy. Federalism, *majimbo*, might be one such solution. It is one that only people within an African nation can arrange, and there are models abroad for their doing so if they choose. This is, though, a solution with some warnings in it for local minorities who might lose whatever state protection they have enjoyed.

Second, the importance of the nation-state might be diminished in the world by other means, from outside. Of these, one is the development of more associational cross-webbing (for instance, through civic, medical, and religious organizations, twinning of communities, and so on) across borders. Another means is the establishment of centralized, supranational authorities more powerful than those currently in existence (the United Nations, the Organization for African Unity, and so on). This latter approach would seem less safe than the one preceding—the less centralized, overlapping webbing—since all the abuses of power that occur in the leadership of nations might just as easily go wrong in any broader or global government.

A third and final option is arranging to permit freer movement of African people themselves—between countries and between continents. This means confronting racism and xenophobia, in southern and northern Africa and overseas, with all their deep and tangled roots. That is a tall order, but one as important as any.

Nature, Culture, and Property, in Myth and Symbol

Social theorists' imaginations about property and progress are hard to contain. It seems somehow to have been difficult for Euro-American, African, or other writers on Africa to discuss that continent's integration into nations and world markets without also referring to more abstract teleological conditions like nature and culture, savagery and civilization, provincialism and cosmopolitanism. It seems to have been hard, too, to think about legal, economic, or political integration without making morally charged judgments about the good or ills of change.

Nor, it appears, is it easy to ponder *property* without at some point making the same sorts of judgments. Nearly wherever one looks, discourse on changing balance between individual and collective rights and duties is tinged with overtones of good and bad, or of primitivity and sophistication. We *can* think without making these judgments, but we never seem to do so for long.

It is as if, at the extreme, we all judged ourselves and each other, wittingly or not, by likeness or unlikeness to some baseline standard of savagery, some unseen borderline between human and animal.[16] How much we are like and unlike other species, other orders of being, seems to be a fundamental and recurring human concern.

Property and economic matters slide right into it as issues of civilization and modernity. The evolutionistic schemas of Jean-Jacques Rousseau, Adam Smith, Henry Maine, Lewis Henry Morgan, and others who saw the development of private property as a move away from our early animality and savagery (and judged it for better or worse) are *not* just quaint curiosities of a bygone era. The ideas were implicit in Lord Lugard's sweeping remark about landholding, sale, and mortgage, that "natural evolution, leading up to individual ownership, may . . . be traced in every civilization known to history." They were there behind Roger Swynnerton's and his subordinates' blueprint for Kenya's land tenure and agriculture, stating that private property's effects in concentrating landholdings into fewer hands is "a natural step in the evolution of a country." In Nairobi, London, or Washington, evolutionary words about private property and civilization much like theirs can still be heard—ridiculous sounding or not.

At some level, social theorists have been pretty reductionist in thinking and communicating about possession and property. We have kept coming down to very crude ways of thinking about belonging and ownership, and about credit and debt. We do it, for instance, by structures of binary opposition (like Ferdinand Tönnies' *gemeinschaft*, and *gesellschaft*), linear continua (Robert Redfield's folk-urban continuum), chains or ladders of being (like ibn Khaldûn's, Shakespeare's, or Rousseau's early variants of evolutionism), or by stages (as in Karl Marx's schema of precapitalist, capitalist, socialist, and communist, or Walt Rostow's pro-market "stages of economic growth"). We do it also by projecting kinship onto land and community, as when Luo interpreter Jairo Owino stated to the Kenya Land Commission, "The land is our mother." But are all these cognitive structures and rhetorical devices *too* crude—and does the nature of our minds allow us any choice?

The imagery and rhetoric of progress or development, with their combined implications of maturity, civilization, and sophistication, exert a powerful influence over human political and economic culture, and nowhere does this resonate more powerfully—more explosively—than inland tropical Africa. People cut off by geography and history from centers of power and wealth; people in warm climates where the known ancestors wore few clothes and needed few tools; people humiliated and demeaned by conquest and colonial occupation; people denied the incomes, passports, and visas to travel like all the missionaries, consultants, and tourists they see come and go; people depicted in press and on screen as spear-toting savages; people in newly imposed, shaky nations whose leaders daily warn them against tribalism . . . sometimes welcome reassurance that they too are fully human, fully capable of civilization, of growing up. Others more confident about it, who yet know that their fathers or grandfathers who ventured into town, mine, or plantation were dubbed "houseboy" into old age, have been sensitized to slighting innuendo, as to bee stings.

Such is the sway of this imagery of progress that economic and social reformers, both inside Africa and out, seem to have done things in the name of development that they might not do otherwise. Don't we all at times? We venture grand gestures of charity, we cast votes for visionaries, we gamble. We lower to each other, or climb watchfully onto, rope ladders no one has really tested, or tested so long ago no one can remember who slipped off.

In their responses to land tenure reform, African people may have something to teach Europeans and Americans about these people's own societies too. The capitalist and socialist ideologies, and experiments in social engineering, that Africans have so successfully parried, resisted, chopped up, and transmuted since early colonial times may not, in the end, be so well suited either to the peoples and lands that have called them their own. By taking apart foreign-introduced programs, adopting some pieces and rejecting others, rural African people have perhaps suggested what we all must do: to devise together our own local cultural mixtures of rights and duties, of self-interest and sociability, of freedom and connectedness.

Notes

Chapter 1: Introduction

Epigraph. Karl Polanyi (1957, 178).

1. These materially embodied divisions become, in the term Marcel Mauss in the 1920s (1967) and Pierre Bourdieu in the 1970s (1977) adapted from older Roman usage, part of our *habitus* or (in another term of Bourdieu's) "structuring structure" that perpetuates itself as ways of thinking and acting, routinely combined. (In the English tradition, Anthony Giddens's concept of "structuration" is comparable.) See also Dietler and Herbich (1998) for a Luo and western Kenyan application to be discussed.

2. A World Bank mission in 1962, on the eve of Independence, stated, "A sound system of tenure is the key to agricultural development. . . . Registered title is essential to the full development of agricultural land. It provides an incentive to improvement and it furnishes the security needed in order to obtain the loans required for development" (cited in L. D. Smith 1976, 128). In the World Bank in the early 1990s, a small number of critics opposed the spread of land titling programs south of the Sahara. One was Shem Migot-Adholla, a western Kenyan by birth.

3. The *Kenya Development Plan, 1974–78,* set it out again: "The land adjudication and registration programme is now larger than ever before and this expansion has been regarded as a prerequisite for faster agricultural development. The security of title which it provides makes farmers more willing to undertake long-term farm improvements, while it enables them to obtain agricultural credit more easily through pledging their land as security" (Kenya 1966–89, II:216).

4. The Kenya Ministry of Economic Development's *South Nyanza District Development Plan, 1979–83,* said similarly, "Land registration is not yet completed in numerous areas with a deleterious effect upon the availability of credit" (p. 16). Some western Kenyan scholars, probably a minority, have accepted the line at times. Writing specifically about the Lake Victoria Basin, a University of Nairobi geographer recommended in

1979, "Land consolidation should be completed and title deeds issued in order to enable farmers to get loans" (Obara 1979, 36).

5. For more on Kenya's political-economic slide as generally perceived in the late twentieth century, see Widner (1992), Ogot and Ochieng' (1995), Throup and Hornsby (1998). Some economists deem the trend to have begun reversing from the century's turn to the time of the December 2007 election and the ensuing civil crisis.

6. This section, included for context, recapitulates some points further discussed in *The Nature of Entrustment* (Shipton 2007). Separately: the population figure here comes from the Kenya national census. Its accuracy is sometimes questioned on the grounds that population figures are subject to manipulation for political and economic reasons.

7. Entrustment is a wider category than loan or credit, since it can refer to a gift or other transfer made upon condition other than a direct return—for instance, a cow to be held by the recipient until used in a marriage payment to a third party. Entrustment can also, of course, have non-economic meanings, as with a secret.

8. More is said about research methods in Shipton (2007) and in the forthcoming volume on credit between cultures.

Chapter 2: Sand and Gold

1. Quoted in Meek (1946, 243). Arthur Young, after two centuries perhaps still Britain's most famous agronomist, is also credited with this other bit of hyperbole: "Give a man the secure possession of a bleak rock, and he will turn it into a garden; give a man a nine years' lease on a garden, and he will convert it into a desert." Original written sources for both remain obscure, though he wrote dozens of books on agronomy and political economy. (Perhaps he never wrote them down.) Early Kenyan colonists finessed—or fudged—the issue by importing from Britain the 999-year lease. Only parts of the rocks and deserts have bloomed so far, with 900 years to go. Some Kenyans whose forebears were edged aside are losing patience. See Chapter 8.

2. A mortgage, from the old French *mort*, dead, and *gage*, a pledge, implies a chronological deadline by which, if a loan goes unrepaid, a transfer of property pledged as collateral becomes permanent. See Glanville (1932, 6–12); S. R. Simpson (1976, 132–33); also Denman (1958, 147) on other uses of the related French terms *mortgage* and *vifgage*. The Latin *vivum vadium* and *mortuum vadium*, according to Glanville, referred in about 1187 to whether the interim profits from pledged land went to reduce the debt (if so, the pledge was "alive"; if not, it was sinful and usurious in the church but not outlawed by the royal courts).

3. Edelman and Haugerud (2005) discuss many uses and abuses of "modernization" and "globalization," and the articles they excerpt clear much fog in social science theory.

4. Weber's broad-brush sweep of ancient Eurasian land and property relations and their social cultural foundations (1998) still holds up remarkably well, not least on Mesopotamia. He or his translators stretch his knowledge, however, in applying the term "mortgage" in some contexts (e.g., p. 93). Probably the fullest recent and specific treatments of land tenure and "privatization" from ancient Mesopotamia to the Medi-

terranean are two collections coedited by Michael Hudson and Baruch Levine (1996 and 1999).

5. For detailed analysis of early medieval English land tenure tradition leading up to and beyond the 1066 Norman conquest, F. W. Maitland's late nineteenth-century writings (in Maitland 1897, Pollock and Maitland 1952) remain hard to beat for authority or prose style. Fleming's treatment a century later (1998) incorporates more recent findings and thinking on the period, especially on William the Conqueror's Domesday Book and, no less important, the inquest behind it as a formative stage in itself in the history of English law. Bill Maurer, using some of the same English sources I have used, also notes "the morbid root of mortgages" (2006, 19).

6. After consulting dozens of sources on British and commonwealth law of land and finance, and after asking several historian specialists, I have been surprised not yet to find an adequate general history of the mortgage for social- or cultural-historical purposes. Among the nearest things, Denman (1958), Pollock and Maitland (1952), S. R. Simpson (1976), and Spies (1970), while all now dated, remain good surveys on land tenure for starters. Among classic earlier sources on different periods, the names William Blackstone, Henry de Bracton, Ranulf de Glanville, and Thomas Littleton recur again and again; their works often turn out more engaging than dry. Macfarlane's cultural histories of Britain (1978, 1987), like Fustel de Coulanges' classic work (reprinted 1980) on the Roman legacy and France, provide broader reflections, and spirited polemics, on what the authors deem the rise of individualism under specific conditions. In other veins, statute books and how-to manuals on conveyancing for lawyers and realtors are many, but these usually leave open to guesswork real custom in practice.

7. See B. Moore (1966) and Neeson (1993) for two of many available treatments of enclosure in Britain. Work by Pauline Peters (1994, 2002) draws parallels from Botswana and elsewhere, emphasizing class formation. To see how the enclosure and dispossession stories play out among Maya in Guatemala, and what new forms they have taken there, see Grandia (forthcoming).

8. If English or French land law presents complication because of the long *time* period over which it has evolved, North American land law presents complexity because of the enormity of the *space* and diverse topography covered (as manifest in varied codes and practices from state to state). Africa has something of *both*, with a richer mix of languages to complicate things further. But a striking proportion of its statutory law is copied verbatim from European law books—and accordingly, often, unknown or ignored by most people in town and country alike.

9. The 1925 laws included a Law of Property Act, Settled Land Act, Trustee Act, Administration of Estates Act, Land Charges Act, and Land Registration Act. By and large, they favored fee simple (Britain's closest thing to absolute ownership) and easy transfer, and disfavored feudalistic service requirements: part of a postwar drive for rebuilding and economic growth.

10. From a model mortgage deed found in a respected 1982 British legal manual (Burn 1982, adapted from the *Encyclopaedia of Forms and Precedents,* 4th ed., 14:166).

11. A. Simpson (1961, 132–34, 225–29) offers a history of the mortgage within a broader history of property in British law from medieval times to the twentieth century.

He notes that the mortgage was never given legal recognition as such until 1925 but always masqueraded as other things in common law (p. 225).

12. On Muslims and home mortgages in urban and suburban America, see Maurer (2006). Like many studies of Islamic custom elsewhere, this one makes it clear that not all religious laws are followed to the letter or spirit, and that some elaborate institutions have evolved, amid much debate and some anxiety, for their circumvention. Key moral issues, here as around the world, are "interest" and uneven sharing of knowledge of risk between borrowers and lenders.

13. In the large literature on the General Allotment Act (or Dawes Severalty Act), some of the central sources covering the essentials are Wilcolm Washburn's book (1975) and several by Francis Paul Prucha. In addition to allowing private titling, the act allowed the selling off to "non-Indian" settlers of "Indian" land officially deemed the excess.

14. Stam et al. (1991), Peoples et al. (1992). Singer and Mason (2006, 142, 313 n. 15), basing their claim on a compilation of data from the U.S. Department of Agriculture and other sources, state, "The proportion of the population living on farms in the U.S. has fallen from nearly 40 percent in 1900 to less than 2 percent today." (By way of comparison, they add that the 1.2 million remaining full-time farmers are fewer than the people in prison.)

15. Described in more detail in Watkins (1993).

16. Barlett (1993), Dudley (2000); see also Chibnik (1987), Rosenblatt (1990).

17. Carleton's "The Tramp's Story" is part of his ballad *"The Festival of Industry"* (in Carleton 1882). Verses reproduced: pp. 128, 131.

18. To hear something of the farming woman's story of husband failure in western Kenya, mincing no words about husband recklessness or drinking (though not always tied to mortgaging), see Abwunza (1997), Francis (2000), or Chapter 9 herein.

19. The unusual bankruptcy laws of the United States, passed in a succession of acts (the first several repealed) since 1800 and extensively amended in the 1930s and 1978, have made it easier for persons or firms in debt to remain or start over in business without fully repaying.

20. Some of Hobbes's most important and influential ideas on social order and disorder can be traced further still to the work of Thucydides on the Peloponnesian Wars, which Hobbes had translated before writing *De Cive*. Two crucial episodes were the Athenian plague and the Corcyrean civil war, both of which Thucydides had portrayed as socially atomizing.

21. Most, but not all, seventeenth- and eighteenth-century European social philosophers accepted the idea of an original social contract. One who did not was David Hume, who preferred to point to force and to habit as the roots of governments, including ones that protected private property.

22. Nothing corresponding to the phrase "noble savage" so often attributed to Rousseau will be found in his work in fact. He (or she?) can, however, be found so designated in the earlier English poetry of John Dryden, and in Rousseau's early works appears the image of the primordial savage, although not so brutish and nasty as Hobbes's.

23. Quoted in Maine (1986), with the attribution of Blackstone's "2nd book and 1st chapter."

24. Since Smith's *Lectures on Jurisprudence* come to us only through the notes of his students, however, it is unclear how much of the stadial evolutionary theory comes from him or them. What we know for sure is that it was in the air.

25. On the French side, meanwhile, no one leaned harder on stadial theories of social development than Georges-Louis Leclerc, Comte de Buffon (1707–1788).

26. One who wants to trace the roots of evolutionism back many centuries before Darwin may find many clear elements of it in authors as diverse as Jean-Jacques Rousseau in France and Geneva, ibn Khaldûn in North Africa and southern Spain, Lucretius in Rome, and probably Epicurus in Greece before him.

27. Sexist, too. Spencer came to think only males had powers of higher abstraction.

28. From Spencer's last (1904) revision to *First Principles,* the opener to his multi-volume *Synthetic Philosophy,* republished the year after his death.

29. Among influential neo-evolutionist works that echo Spencer are Robert Wright's. Much of *Nonzero,* for instance, reads almost as if Spencer had written it. See esp. Ch. 8, which offers comparable body-society analogies. Here money appears as nerve signaling (through price communication), though, rather than as blood.

30. See especially Hegel's 1821 *Philosophy of Right,* especially the First Part, which treats property, credit, and (briefly) the pledge and its particular form, the mortgage, under "abstract right" (Hegel 1967, para. 80, pp. 62–64). Abstractions and universals he deemed more the province of men than of women, because of their different educations (para. 166, addition 107, p. 263). These of course are topics of hot dispute in East Africa as elsewhere today.

31. Elsewhere in his Algerian reports Tocqueville, while defending French colonialism in Africa, decried slavery and religious imperialism.

32. That is, no one theory contains all the traits that define the class, and no trait is found in all the theories of the class. But each of the theories may share enough strands (however combined) with others so that you feel you know one when you see one. Anthropologists call this kind of class "polythetic." Needham (1975) borrowed the "polythetic" or "polytypic" idea from Wittgenstein (1958) and from the eighteenth-century French biologist Michel Adanson.

33. See Long (1977) and Robertson (1984) for concise summaries of modernization theories related to economic development, and Etzioni and Etzioni-Harvey (1964) for diverse examples from several social sciences.

34. The "tragedy of the commons" thesis for which Hardin has become known can in fact be traced as far back as Thucydides' *History of the Peloponnesian War:* "They devote a very small fraction of time to the consideration of any public object, most of it to the prosecution of their own objects. Meanwhile each fancies that no harm will come to his neglect, that it is the business of somebody else to look after this or that for him; and so, by the same notion being entertained by all separately, the common cause imperceptibly decays" (Book I, sec. 141). For the same idea, see Aristotle's *Politics* (Book II, Ch. 3, 1261b), and closer to our times, economist Ludwig Von Mises (1949, ch. 23, sec. 6).

35. See Ostrom (1990), and Peters (1994) on Botswana in particular. Daniel Bromley has been another main contributor to the debates. Hardin later qualified his theory somewhat, acknowledging a distinction between "managed commons" and "open access,"

while extending his theory in other directions. Acheson (2006) sums up anthropologists' contributions to "common property" debates, which continue unabated at the time of this writing.

36. Originally framed as a reaction against a revolutionary guerrilla movement in Peru, the Sendero Luminoso (or Shining Path), de Soto's work, equally visionary in tone and flavor, attracts both strong praise and strong criticism, on theoretical and methodological grounds. Home and Lim's collection (2004), based on research in several peri-urban African settings and Trinidad, attacks de Soto in turn—without espousing revolutionary doctrine. This source by land surveyors and others, which came to my attention as this study was heading to press, offers case findings from around cities that complement a number of my rural findings rather well. A part of de Soto's argument that my experience confirms, though, is his finding that poor people commonly want to save.

37. From his *Capital, Vol. 3*, published posthumously in 1894 (1976, 830).

38. In *The Laws,* Plato prescribed that in his utopian society the buying and selling of land would be banned for fairness. Plato's student Aristotle, in *Politics,* opted, in his own utopia, for land privately owned but publicly worked.

39. If the "critical" theorists are devoted less space here than the "mainstream" ones who have gone before, it is not to suggest they are less right or ultimately important. It is instead because they have been less *consistently* influential in Kenyan policy making, and because some of their terms and ideas are already introduced.

40. Rousseau never proposed violent revolution, though his work has certainly inspired more than one, including of course France's in 1789. Nor did he ever propose a permanent return to a primeval condition—a point many miss. Instead, he favored returning just long enough to redirect society along more moral lines than he thought it had charted.

41. Too few appreciate how much Marx borrowed from Adam Smith, commonly viewed as his nemesis. The reader might be interested to place *The Wealth of Nations* and *Capital* on the table side by side to see how many of the same terms and concepts recur—on prices, supply and demand, or the mind-dulling effect of specialized labor. Not least for our topic is the problem of big hereditary landownership and land poverty, especially after enclosure—a situation both authors lamented and despised as unfair.

42. As in note 37 above.

43. Engels's saying refers to Molière's play *Georges Dandin, ou le mari confondu* (George Dandin, or the Confused Husband), and its title character, a rich peasant.

44. See Isichei (2002) for a collection of such vampire stories. Blood-taking medics are not immune to such accusations either, as P. Wenzel Geissler has elsewhere described Luo rumors.

45. Henry George's ideas have been championed in recent years by the Lincoln Institute of Land Policy, operating nationally and internationally from Cambridge, Massachusetts.

46. Fabians took their name from Roman general Quintus Fabius Maximus "Cunctator" (the Delayer), known for his patient, subtle war of attrition against Hannibal. For

a description of Fabians' influence in West African land and finance, see Cowen and Shenton (1991). Their influence on East Africa has never been adequately described.

47. Polanyi's work influenced that of many economic anthropologists (including Paul Bohannan) and anthropological economists (including George Dalton). Bohannan and others did much sensitive work on African kinship and land tenure (see, e.g., Bohannan 1963), and on markets, though not always in a way that conjoined the first two with the last as an anthropological study of mortgaging might do.

48. Susan George, one of the most outspoken critics of the World Bank and its government allies north and south, invokes military strategy in writing in the 1980s of "the debt weapon" used in "low-intensity conflict" on behalf of "a crazed economy that operates on behalf of a select few" (1988, 5,9, 234–35).

49. Von Pischke (1977), Von Pischke et al. (1983), Bates (1981, 50, 56), Hart (1982), Adams et al. (1984).

Chapter 3: Luo and Others

Epigraph. Christopher Ehret (1976, 17–18).

1. In this study I have changed the names of individuals interviewed and neighbors in western Kenya, to protect their privacy (except for the acknowledgments or a few instances where specifically requested to mention real names). For the same reason, the names of the most local neighborhoods or communities where they live have also been changed; but the names of larger, encompassing ones (for instance, Kanyamkago, Kagan, Uyoma, and Isukha, most of which were indigenous local polities), and of towns like Awendo and Migori, are real. Districts and smaller units have subdivided periodically.

2. According to Fr. Joseph Crazzolara's unusually detailed oral histories, the furthest point of origin was southeast of Wan and south of the Bahr-el-Ghazal, that is, somewhere in the area of 7 degrees north latitude and 30 degrees east longitude (1951, 31). No one has much evidence to contradict him.

3. Sources on Luo origins based largely on oral histories include Hobley (1902), Evans-Pritchard (1965), Crazzolara (1950, 1951, 1954), Ayany (1989), Malo (1953), Ogot (1967), Ochieng' (1975), and Cohen and Atieno Odhiambo (1989), among others.

4. Christopher Ehret's reconstructed linguistic histories (1971, 1976), and Blount and Curley's on the Luo tongue in particular (1970)—all relying in part on classification by Joseph Greenberg—remain among the standards. But linguists change their categories from time to time. Some are currently questioning the usefulness of the term "Bantu," which has been used to cover most of the languages of the southern half of Africa.

5. The timing here comes from Herring (1976, 101); B. A. Ogot's histories are also valuable.

6. See, for instance, Thomson (1887, 482); Colville (1895, 24); Johnston (1904); Roscoe (1915, 227, 291).

7. Some deem the first such walled settlements in present-day Kenya to have been in a place now called Ligala, in Samia, a way station in southerly migration for the Jok

group of Luo speakers (Cohen and Atieno Odhiambo 1989, 14). As the authors note, *goyo ligala,* or striking a new foundation, is still the term used for a establishing a new homestead. For more on the stone enclosures, see Chittick (1965).

8. This is, strictly speaking, what the smaller Luo homesteads still are today, since women commonly marry in from diverse places of origin, and since some homesteads also include other in-laws or fostered or unrelated members.

9. The defensive hedges may not be disappearing for good. State government failure to curtail cattle raiding, particularly around ethnic border zones, gives them new purpose.

10. As these are the topics of a fuller description elsewhere (Shipton 2007) and another to come, only enough need be said here to make the chapters that follow comprehensible.

11. Discussed further in Shipton (2007, ch. 4).

Chapter 4: An Earthly Anchorage

Epigraph. From Cohen and Atieno Odhiambo (1989, 25). As they note, burying the placenta, *biero,* around the homestead, among familiars, is deemed to give one strength. Home, in a Luo understanding, is also where one's forebears are buried.

1. These dichotomies refer back to Henry Maine, Lewis Henry Morgan, and Ferdinand Tönnies. Along with kinship and territory, some would add age organization (as in age sets or age grades) as a third major mode of sociopolitical organization in eastern Africa. Among Luo, age stratification and sequencing are more subtle than among some neighboring peoples including Kuria, Maasai, Gusii, Nandi, or Tiriki. Among some of these, circumcision rituals have been major public events, and "warrior" age grades famous. But when examined more deeply, age and seniority turn out no less important among Luo.

2. Obviously, and as noted earlier, these two possibilities—contrasted here mainly for heuristic purposes—do not exhaust the repertoire of ways of organizing a society. Networks and open-ended categories (sexes, classes, etc.) are as important to Luo as to anyone.

3. Discussed further in Shipton (1984). A deepening and sharpening of lineage and clan ties is not the only possible consequence of rising competition for land and other resources. In some cases, as among Sukuma, Nyamwezi, and others living south of Nyanza, territorial polities not based so much on kinship have also sharpened their boundaries and their land laws. Much depends on what kind of social organization a society had before land became scarcer.

4. Of course, population growth (for better or worse) has many causes not discussed in detail here. These can include new methods of perinatal health care. They can also include poverty, but not by any simple, irreversible formula.

5. See Glazier (1985) on Mbeere, in central Kenya, for a discussion of how deepened, broadened lineages have been used in court cases requiring the mobilization of many witnesses.

6. *Oganda* also translates to "large bean." Some believe the term is applied to the

human unit because of the idea that multiple clans within an oganda resemble beans within a pod.

7. Evans-Pritchard (1965, 212) wrote, "There was nothing that can be considered a political office in a Luo tribe. The *ruoth* was an influential person, but no more": a wealthy person, often a member of the dominant clan in an oganda, to whose home others came to discuss important things. Southall (1952) accepts this view. Others, however, have criticized it, notably B. A. Ogot, who claims to be able to trace hereditary "*ruoth*-ship" back as much as ten generations in some ogendni (1963, 252; 1967, 154, 171–72, and passim). See also Hobley (1903, 359), Northcote (1907, 60), Gordon Wilson (1968, 1), Whisson (1961, 6–7; 1964, 23–4), Ocholla-Ayayo (1976, 196ff.), Cohen and Atieno Odhiambo (1989, ch. 2). There was clearly much variation in size and structure from one Luo oganda to another by early colonial times, and it is not clear that Luo were ever fully agreed about which aggregations counted as ogendni and which did not.

8. Buffer zones may be reappearing, in places, as a result of "ethnic cleansing" campaigns since the 1990s.

9. This topic is being treated in a separate work in progress on Luo sequencing and seniority. See also Dietler and Herbich (1998) and Herbich and Dietler (1993)—their observations on this topic from north of the Winam Gulf resonate well with my own from the south.

10. See diagrams, Ocholla-Ayayo (1980, d. 1, p. 159) and Dietler and Herbich (1998, 258).

11. All wives from the third on are referred to as *rero* (sometimes spelled *reru*).

12. Compare Lang'o *anyeko,* co-wife (Driberg 1923, 411) and Acholi *nyek.*

13. Gordon Wilson (1968, 40–42); see also Dakeyne (1962, 185), Dietler and Herbich (1998).

14. Schwartz (1995) ruefully reports learning that as an adult but unmarried woman, she would, according to Luo tradition, have been buried outside her hosts' homestead, by the latrine, if her life ended in Luo country.

15. For fuller discussions of the S. M. Otieno burial case, Ojwang and Mugambi (1989), Cohen and Atieno Odhiambo (1989, 133–40; 1992).

16. Schwartz (2000, esp. 449); see also Lienhardt (1975, 213) on the "reciprocity of enmity and aggression."

17. Compare nation, from the Latin *natio.*

18. Compare the Luo *dhoot* with the Nuer *thok dwiel,* which also means doorway and descent group (Evans-Pritchard 1940, 247). A picture of a Luo doorway with a hen and chick, on the cover of Cohen and Atieno Odhiambo (1989), carries a double meaning.

19. Compare Eng. "ramage" (from L. *ramus,* branch), a useful term now passed out of style in anthropology.

20. By segmentation anthropologists conventionally refer to subdivision, sometimes implying that the process repeats in later generations (some call this "polysegmentation").

21. Here, for instance, are a few attempts that, if compared, show their discrepancies of scaling. Mboya (1978, 31), native to Karachuonyo, breaks down Luo traditional territorial and social organization, in decreasing order of size, into *piny* [or *oganda*] (a "tribe"

or federation of clans), *dhoot* (pl. *dhoudi*), *gweng'* (pl. *gwenge*), *anyuola, pacho, dala* (pl. *mier*) (homestead). Gordon Wilson, in 1961, came up with this lineup in his manual of Luo law and custom: *oganda* ("tribe"), *dhoot* (five to ten generations, real or fictitious common ancestor), *libamba* (pl. *libembni*) (four to seven generations, real or fictitious common ancestor), *keyo* or *hosi* (three to five generations, common ancestor), *kokakwaro* (three or more generations, common grandfather or group of grandfathers who are full brothers), *jokadayo* (three generations, common grandmother or grandmothers are linked co-wives [say, in *nyar ot* relationship]), *jokawuoro* (two or more generations, common father or fathers whose mothers were linked co-wives), and *jokamiyo* (two or more generations, common mother or mothers who are linked co-wives) (Gordon Wilson 1968, 5). Emin Ochieng' Opere, when interviewed by me in Kanyamkago in 1982, listed *kendo* (lit. fireplace or marriage—three to four generations), *anyuola* (three to six or more generations), *jokakwaro* (lit. people of one grandfather—again, sliding from three to six or more generations), *keyo* (branch or strip, can be deeper or larger than *anyuola*), and *dhoot* (clan—eight to fifteen generations). To give an idea of variability, however, one of his uncles spoke at the same time of a *kendo* (and a *keyo* too) as being up to ten generations deep.

22. To anthropologists, conventionally, a clan differs from a lineage in not necessarily having a known number of generations, or a full chain of known, nameable links connecting them. But Luo Anglophones conventionally use "clan" to refer to lineages of any size and scale, whether all the genealogical links be known or not.

23. Still fairly obscure, for instance, are the roles of the war leader (*osumba*) and peace maker (*ogaye*), both of whose functions were made obsolete—at least temporarily—by colonial government.

24. See, e.g., Rodney Needham (1971), David Schneider (1984), Harold Scheffler (2001).

25. The debates on this issue are, in different idiom and among other things, about what philosophers have called "free will"—and debated among themselves for at least two millennia.

26. At one extreme, Adam Kuper (1982) and some followers have even suggested (for a while) that the concepts of lineage and descent group are outmoded anthropological fictions that should be done away with. But others, for instance Harold Scheffler (2001), have sought to restore the old concept, rallying to defend anthropologists who used it carefully for particular African contexts. And "postmodernist" scholars in the 1980s and 1990s, keen to criticize their own kind, made much of lineage models in attacking the structural functionalism of 1930s to 1960s anthropology. As I suggest elsewhere, disabusing ourselves of the idea that status ascription means primitivity is a first step to getting beyond such debates.

27. See Barnes's 1962 critique on "African Models in the New Guinea Highlands,," for instance. Elsewhere (Shipton 1984) I briefly discuss a broader literature on African lineage models on Pacific islands; Scheffler (2001) offers a more recent bibliography.

28. Much of the attention has focused on the celebrated cases of the Nuer (or Nath) in southern Sudan, most famously studied by Edward Evans-Pritchard (1940, 1951), and the Tallensi in northern Ghana, covered in Meyer Fortes's almost equally famous work

(1945). That decades of anthropologists chose the Nuer people as an archetypal example of "segmentary" (or ramifying) lineages is a bit unfortunate, since they are not a great example of these. The more southerly, also Nilotic-speaking Luo in Kenya and some of their Bantu-speaking neighbors there are far clearer ones. Indeed, after Evans-Pritchard visited the Nuer in Sudan in the early 1930s, but before he published his book on them in 1940, he had sojourned in the Luo country in Kenya in 1936. And I suspect it was at least as much the Luo and lake basin Kenyan pattern of lineages and clans more clearly visible on the ground, as the murkier Nuer one of more diffused residence patterns, that he had foremost in mind when he wrote his famous first Nuer book. But that is only speculation.

29. "Descent theory," with its emphasis on "vertical" or intergenerational associations, is sometimes contrasted with "alliance theory," with its emphasis on "horizontal," affinal ones, and some anthropologists have pegged their names to one or the other. In East African contexts, at least, such theorists seem like people walking on one leg.

30. Ioan Lewis (1965) and others have drawn similar distinctions. Succession to office is a further criterion more relevant to some other societies. Even within a single criterion, one finds variation: in Luo inheritance, for instance, land that moves patrilineally and cooking or water storage pots that move matrilineally. On the broader point that not all the criteria need coincide, think of the many Jewish people who like to trace their faith and heritage matrilineally but have come to pass along names through the patriline.

31. The foundational study distinguishing African patrilineal "descent" and highland New Guinean "cumulative patrifiliation" is Barnes (1962)—an article written on shipboard and left unreferenced, leaving us at sea for the whos, wheres, and whens. Richard Werbner, Jane Guyer, and others sharing in Barnes's (Mancunian and Rhodes-Livingstonian) tradition have carried on comparing those regions, cleating down more specifics. The now standard study on Amhara Ethiopian land and kinship is Hoben's (1973.)

32. Scheffler argues, for instance, that among Nuer, Tiv, Tallensi, and Gusii, patrifiliation is "necessary and sufficient" for inclusion in a group, such that "each group includes all and only the offspring of its male members and, if it is presumed to have had a unique founding ancestor, all and only his patrilineal descendants." By comparison, among Swat Pathan and people in parts of China and India, patrifiliation is "necessary but not sufficient" for group membership; while among Enga, Chimbu, Melpa, Siane, and Mende in highland New Guinea, patrifiliation is "sufficient but not necessary" for group membership (Scheffler 2001, 26–27). Some of the eastern Africa–western Pacific comparisons are discussed elsewhere, less extensively, in terms of kinship and land (Shipton 1984).

33. This presumes bridewealth has been paid—a condition seldom fulfilled all at once, and indeed, in some contemporary unions, neglected altogether.

34. Humans in Luoland, like most anywhere, *do* tinker at times with their genealogies. They offer a master class, for harmony, in Blount (1975).

35. See, e.g., Gordon Wilson (1961, 6), Ocholla-Ayayo (1976, 122, 126, 129).

36. *Dala*, now the more common term, is probably of Bantu origin.

37. Some dhoudi (for instance, one in which I have been made a fictive member)

have established, through migration, transplanted branches, or colonies grown pretty independent of each other, in more than one part of Luo country.

38. Discussed in Cohen and Atieno Odhiambo (1989, 92–95); see also Ocholla-Ayayo (1979, 180–85), Shipton (2007).

39. Evans-Pritchard (1965, 211) appears mistaken on this point, as does Audrey Butt, who takes her information straight from him (1952, 110). Cf. Southall (1952, 19–20), Fearn (1961, 33), Gordon Wilson (1961, 19–20, 67ff.), Ocholla-Ayayo (1976, 125). It may be that by 1936, when Evans-Pritchard arrived, secondary and tertiary buffer zones had already been filled in.

40. Southall (1952, 21–22, 26–27); Ocholla-Ayayo (1976, 117, n. 16). See also Evans-Pritchard (1965, 210–211) on Luo homicides, and Gordon Wilson (1967; 1968, 3); Whisson (1964, 30).

41. A male killer's clanmates might expect him not only to undergo ritual purification and to avoid mystical affliction (*chira*), but also to dig the grave of a clansman killed, to marry his wives, and to raise children in his name.

42. W. E. Owen in KLC (1934b, 2196–97); Gordon Wilson (1961, 3).

43. Whisson (1961, 7) and Lonsdale (1968) treat the privileged colonial education of chiefs and their sons.

44. LeVine (1962b) posited a correlation between the living proximity of co-wives and witchcraft accusations among them, comparing information on the Kenya Luo and the neighboring Gusii and Kipsigis. He found that the Luo, among whom co-wives live closest to each other, had the highest rate of witchcraft accusations.

45. Compare Evans-Pritchard on Nuer: "Just as a man is a member of a tribal segment opposed to other segments of the same order and yet also a member of the tribe which embraces all these segments, so also he is a member of a lineage opposed to other lineages of the same order and yet also a member of the clan which embraces all these lineages, and there is a definite correspondence between these two sets of affiliations, since the lineage is embodied in the segment and the clan in the tribe" (1940, 240–41). And: "Nuer consider that lineage cleavage arises from a fundamental cleavage in the family between *gaatgwan,* children of the father, and *gaatman,* children of the mother. Where there are two wives and each has sons, the lineage bifurcates from this point. A lineage bifurcation is a polygamous family writ large . . . the tiny twigs we see in the gol, household, grow into the great branches of the lineages" (p. 247). Recall that Evans-Pritchard had already lived and researched among Luo when he wrote *The Nuer* and the other two volumes of his Nuer trilogy.

46. Gordon Wilson (1961, 35; see also his 1967 article), Evans-Pritchard (1965, 213), Southall (1952, 6, 20), Ocholla-Ayayo (1976, 121).

47. Ayot (1979, ch. 10), on Luo and Suba.

48. In 1981, during my first stay in Nyanza, the Kenya government, finding its courts overwhelmed with land disputes, restored new powers to land elders for handling land cases.

49. This is the kind of expansion that Paul Bohannan (1954), in the Tiv case, termed "expansion" rather than "disjunction." Ogot (1967, 110, 169) contrasts the Luo pat-

tern with that of the Padhola of Uganda, who, having less constricted land by the late nineteenth or early twentieth century, tended to fragment their lineages more readily. As Ocholla-Ayayo put it, "people of the same clan should occupy continuous areas" to minimize fighting (1976, 126), but whether their doing so really has this effect is harder to say.

50. See, for instance, Ominde (1963), Hauge (1974, 26–27); see also diagrams and discussions in Southall (1952, 26), Gordon Wilson (1961, 19–24).

51. Roscoe (1915, 277); KLC (1934b, 2292–94 [Jairo], 2401 [Scheffer]); see also Whisson (1964, 23). For more on Luo sacrifice, see Shipton (2007, ch. 9).

52. Even in 1907, South Nyanza district commissioner G. A. S. Northcote described the population there as painfully litigious (Northcote 1907, 65–66), and the rates of land suits kept rising throughout the colonial period (Whisson 1962a, 27; 1962b, 5; 1964, 81n; de Wilde 1967, 151; see also Evans-Pritchard 1965, 225; Sytek 1966, 3). Gusii in particular have been known for litigiousness, in part because of their dense settlement—not, I have suggested, just a voluntary condition.

53. In the 1980s and '90s, as the great women's movement begun in the late 1960s in Europe and America became better established, a new wave of feminist and revisionist scholarship hit East African studies. Not content to accept a model of social structure and process that relegated women to the margins, revisionists—more often than not women themselves—looked for new signs of female power, authority, and influence. Some scholars concentrated on Luo religious traditions and inventions surrounding the Virgin Mary, as in the Legio Maria offshoot of Roman Catholicism (Schwartz 1989). Some concentrated on churches founded and (at first) led by women, such as the Roho (Spirit) churches (Hoehler-Fatton 1996). Others scaled down their focus to concentrate on the matrifocal family and household, as distinguished from the larger, often multi-house homestead, as the key units of human aggregation and of analysis (Holmes 2000). Yet others concentrated on women's experiences as young wives and mothers in their marital homes, and on their relations with their mothers-in-law and other women there (Francis 2000).

54. Evans-Pritchard (1951, 156), Southall (1952, 5–7),

55. Cohen and Atieno Odhiambo (1989, 13), Holmes (2000, 223–24); see also Ayot (1979, 166–67) on Luo-Suba. Uxorilocal, the reverse of virilocal, means postmarital residence in or around the wife's (rather than husband's) natal home and kin.

56. People spoke of such unions without marriage dues as a novelty and an expedient adaptation to poverty or to scarcity of animals. But whether they were indeed more frequent than in the past, and when or whether any such trend might reverse, are hard to tell if one takes account of elders' nostalgia and possibly distorted memories.

57. According to Potash (1986b, 58), between 1973 and 1975, of thirty-eight widows she interviewed in what she called the "levirate" (actually widow inheritance or take-over), thirty-four remained in the husband's home. She found that widows were not considered to have the right to return to their natal homes (p. 45).

58. On "invented tradition," see Hobsbawm and Ranger (1983), and for the same on western Kenya Cohen and Atieno Odhiambo (1989, 28); Holmes (2000).

59. For more on lineages as tools of territorial expansion, see Sahlins (1961), Shipton (1984), Glazier (1985); see also Mackenzie (1998, 76 and passim).

Chapter 5: Birthright and Its Borrowing

Epigraph. Peter Taylor (1986, 1).

1. Evans-Pritchard (1965, 224), Whisson (1962a, 2), Ogot (1967, 38–39), Ocholla-Ayayo (1976, 17).

2. Spear and Waller (1993) on Maasai; Little (1992) on Njemps Kalenjin.

3. On the Wilson manual, "'This,' observed a departing administrative officer to his successor, 'is your Bible for land cases'" (quoted in Whisson·1964, 86). Gordon Wilson, though, states that he intended it more as a point of departure than as a code of laws to be set in stone (1961, 10).

4. Inheritance of movable things and persons is treated in *The Nature of Entrustment*, Ch. 8 (Shipton 2007).

5. Luo may well debate this, although I have not encountered such a case.

6. Millikin (1906, 55) suggests the distribution varied with numbers of cattle paid by the father in bridewealth for the marriages of the sons in question. Dundas (1913) and Roscoe (1915, 280) say the distribution among sons is just up to the father. Gordon Wilson (1961, 40 ff.) and Ocholla-Ayayo (1976, 120–21) leave mixed impressions about equality and inequality in inherited holdings. Whisson's observations (1964, 86–87) most closely resemble my own: that portions are expected ideally to be pretty equal but very often end up very unequal, especially when the quality of land is taken into account.

7. Inheritance of movable things is discussed further in Shipton (2007).

8. The quotation comes from a Luo's testimony before the Kenya Land Commission in 1932 (Kenya Land Commission 1934a, 2166; hereafter KLC).

9. The autochthon/alien distinction in Luoland is also a central topic in a work in preparation on Luo sequencing.

10. A *wuon lowo* is sometimes also called *wuon piny* (master of the country) or *wuon puodho* (master of the field or garden). *Wuon piny* is sometimes used to refer to a member of a host *oganda*. Much has been written about Luo weg lowo, weg piny, and jodak, but not always with consistent terminology. See Kenya Land Commission (1934b, 2295–99, 2401, and passim); P. Mboya (1938, 58); Evans-Pritchard (1965, 215–16); Gordon Wilson (1961), which includes summaries of court cases; Whisson (1961; 1964, 42 and passim); Ocholla-Ayayo (1976, 100, 126–28, 210, and passim); Odenyo (1973); Pala Okeyo (1977, 106–15); Shipton (1984); Holmes (2000). See also the work of historians Lonsdale (1964, 58), Ogot (1967, 163), Hay (1972, 102), and Butterman (1979, 42). Kenny (1982) analyzes legendry about the role of the stranger among Suba in the Lake Victoria Basin.

For the record, ch. 6 of the *South Nyanza District Socio-Cultural Profile*, "Land Rights," was misattributed to S. G. Mbogoh, having been written by me. Apparently by clerical error in final production, several of the other chapter and author names were also mixed around. Chapter 5, "Production Systems and Labour," which I wrote, appeared under Mbogoh's name albeit with a mysteriously altered conclusion; and ch. 10, "Provision of Shelter," was erroneously attributed to my name.

11. For evidence of the easier movement through land clientage in the past, see Gordon Wilson (1961, 29) and Whisson (1964, 94).

12. For native/stranger distinctions in different tongues, see Wagner (1956, 78–81) on Maragoli and other Luhya; Mayer (1949, 28), Mayer and Mayer (1965, 74), and Håkansson (1988, 35, 83) on Gusii; Cory (1947, esp. 78) on Kuria; Kenny (1982) on Suba and others; Sorrenson (1967, 11) on Gikuyu. For a broader but personalized view of autochthons and aliens (including Europeans who slide between) in Kenya and East Africa such as only fiction can provide, see (pseudonymous) Louisa Dawkins's ethnographic novel *Natives and Strangers.*

13. The remainder in our subsample broke down as follows: 24 percent said they had bought their land, 2 percent said they had rented it, 1 percent were landless, and 12 percent gave more complex or unclassifiable answers. The last seemingly included some current or former jodak. Johnson's breakdown among Luo-Suba in 1976 (1980a, 309n) was as follows: 53 percent inherited, 36 percent purchased, 10 percent taken freely, and 3 percent given. See also Paterson (1980a, 1011) for a breakdown on the Luhya of Bunyore, and Okoth-Ogendo (1976, 185) on the Gusii and Kikuyu.

14. For more details on the position of the jadak, see Butterman (1979, 43), KLC (1934b, 2287), Gordon Wilson (1961, 57), and Ocholla-Ayayo (1976, 128).

15. It is not hard to imagine some sort of eventual feminist protest, perhaps with (who knows?) some new symbol on the rooftop, and maybe a breach or inversion of the old Luo taboo (*kwer*) against females climbing on roofs. This prohibition is something that some Luo have hitherto associated with the sanction of *chira*, the deadly mystical affliction and wasting illness feared to strike the infractor or kin any time, even generations later. Another approach is simply demanding title to land, as many women have begun doing.

16. Such a series of immigrants was evident to me in Kanyamkago, where the original Luo settlers were later joined over the twentieth century by others from Uyoma and then by Luhya speakers from Maragoli who partly assimilated. Those from Uyoma moved informally from jadak toward, or into, wuon lowo or wuon piny status, at least with respect to the lastcomers.

17. Gordon Wilson (1968, 56, see also 57–62). Note the loose, questionable translation of jodak as "tenant."

18. For broader discussions of diversification as a strategy for livelihood under conditions of political and economic uncertainty, see Francis (2000) on western Kenya, Haugerud (1995) on central Kenya, and Berry (1993) on Africa comparatively.

19. Surveyors in the Kenya Agricultural Sample Census found in 1960–61, on the eve of independence, that in Central Nyanza, 62 percent of holdings (of homesteads) were "fragmented," yielding an average of 2.84 isolated parcels per holding. Forty-two percent had four or more (De Wilde 1967, 127). This degree of "fragmentation" in Luoland geographer R. B. Dakeyne deemed "extreme" (1962, 185).

20. See Bentley (1987) for worldwide comparisons on land "fragmentation" and its purposes.

21. Discussed in the forthcoming volume on credit across cultures.

22. This consolidationist pressure goes along with straight rows, right angles, "villag-

ization," and so on, as part of what James Scott has called "high modernism" in bureaucratic law and administration (1998).

23. Most in my experience in Kanyamkago, a relatively newly settled area cleared of tsetse flies after the second world war, farm no more than three or four separated plots.

24. This section summarizes findings reported and documented in more detail in Shipton (1984).

25. High population density, competition for land, and ecological pressure on it often coincide, but not necessarily, since trade, industry, and other activities can take pressure off farming, herding, or other material exploitation.

26. Kenny (1977, 282); see also Ayot (1979, p. 176 and Chs. 9, 10); and Johnson (1980) on Suba "Luo-ization."

27. See, e.g., the memos to the Kenya Land Commission by Anglican Archdeacon Walter Edwin Owen (KLC 1934b, 2198) and the Native Catholic Union of Central Kavirondo (KLC 1934b, 2147); and Gordon Wilson (1961, 75–80), De Wilde (1967, 130), Maini (1967, 17), Ocholla-Ayayo (1976, 37).

28. Evans-Pritchard (1950, esp. p. 86); see also Shipton (2007, 167–72).

29. Whether, by community, Oginga Odinga meant lineage, clan, or oganda is unclear. Gordon Wilson (1961, 30) described how an individual or group might invite agnatic kin onto land near the edge of their holding, but jodak well within it, to keep them confined.

30. Dundas (1913, 55), KLC (1934b, 2229); Fearn (1961, 34).

31. See, e.g., the cases related by Jairo Omondi to the Kenya Land Commission in 1932 (KLC 1934b, 2294).

32. Hailey (1957, 785), Gordon Wilson (1961, 75–76, 78–79), Whisson (1964, 95).

33. Whisson (1964, 95), Johnson (1980); see also Shipton (2007, ch. 5). See also Robertson (1987) for comparisons and theoretical discussion of share contracting in Africa south of the Sahara.

34. See Parkin (1978) on urban ethnic unions in Nairobi; Hoehler-Fatton (1996) on churches.

Chapter 6: The Thin End

1. Probably the most comprehensive summaries of colonial titling programs available on Africa are the ones by Bruce (1998), and Riddell and Dickerman (1986). See also Dickerman (1987), Simpson (1978), Cheater (1983), Downs and Reyna (1988), Shipton (1989b), and Palmer 1997. The most thoroughly documented case history in the wider literature on tropical Africa is that of the *mailo* titling in Uganda. See Mukwaya (1953), West (1972), and Hanson (2003) for three book-length historical treatments. The last of these emphasizes the deterioration of sentiments of mutual responsibility (locally spoken of in terms connoting love) between kings, chiefs, and their subjects, as colonial rulers co-opted local ones and symbiotic relations yielded to one-way "upward" exploitation. Lucy Mair's applied anthropological writings beginning in the 1940s on Africa south of the Sahara (collected in Mair 1969), Malengreau's summary on francophone central

Africa (1947), and Obol-Ochola's collection on East African tenure and reforms (1969) sum up concisely a range of local tenure reform programs in other African countries (see especially Okec 1969 on parts of Uganda beyond the mailo area). These noted little to encourage and much to discourage further private titling initiatives, while leaving open some big questions for further research.

2. Cowen and Shenton (1991) describe the long and involved debates between bankers and colonial administrators on the question of mortgages in early twentieth-century Ghanaian and Nigerian history, showing from primary sources that the administrators remained mainly concerned, rightly or wrongly, with protecting potential borrowers from over-indebtedness. (A parallel history remains to be written on Kenya.) The history they recount makes it clear what a mistake it can be to conceive of the imperial voice, opinion, or project as unified. As noted elsewhere herein, the history of Kenyan missionaries, settlers, and government administrators shows much the same.

3. At Marinde, 20 September 1932. Kenya Land Commission (hereafter KLC), original evidence, Bk. 14. Syracuse film no. 1925, reel 11, p. 85.

4. Kenya Land Commission, original evidence, Vol. XIV, Central Kavirondo. Syracuse film no. 1925, reel 10.

5. Undated memo to KLC, original evidence, Vol. XIV, Central Nyanza Section. Syracuse film no. 1925, reel 10.

6. 9 September 1932. KLC, original evidence, Vol. XIV, Central Nyanza. Syracuse film no. 1925, reel 10. Oviti cautioned, in conclusion, that "a European begins in a small way and spreads everywhere."

7. 9 September 1932, to KLC, at Marenyu. KLC, original evidence. Syracuse film no. 1925, reel 11.

8. KLC, original evidence, Bk. 14. Syracuse film no. 1925, reel 11, pp. 85–87.

9. KLC, original evidence, Bk. 14. Syracuse film no. 1925, reel 11, pp. 85–87.

10. Nyanza Province *Annual Report*, 1932. KNA, AR/1275. Syracuse film no. 2801, reel 33.

11. KLC, original typescript of *Evidence*, Vol. XIV, Central Kavirondo. Syracuse Film no. 1925, reel 10.

12. KLC, original typescript of *Evidence*, Vol. XIV, South Kavirondo, p. 3. Syracuse Film no. 1925, reel 10.

13. A well-placed Luhya, with the Maragoli name of G. H. Kerre, reported to Nairobi in 1949, "Long-term loans of [i.e., on] security of land: This is a very complex and dangerous social and economic problem. . . . It is also a dangerous policy to mortgage your land, as a great burden will be placed on the farmer to repay the capital and this will violate the assumed principle of land ownership in North Nyanza, i.e. the unalienable right to land by tribal inheritance. African land tenure in Nyanza Province does not permit a person to lose his land for failure to repay a loan. However, it is possible that long-term loans may be made to African farmers on security other than tribal land" [crop liens, he suggested, being "probably the most satisfactory method"]. Kerre, Secretary of Local Native Council, North Nyanza District, to the Member for Agricultural and Natural Resources, in Nairobi, 2 August 1949. KNA 3/1794 (ADM. 7/5/2), Syracuse

reel 256, sec. 10. In the same file, the Provincial Native Courts Officer reported to the Nyanza Provincial Commissioner on 27 August 1949, "We are fortunate in this Province that there is no general agricultural indebtedness, though a few cases have occurred where large sums of money have passed between individuals on the alleged security of land—for example, the case of the Maragoli trader, Zuberi lending nearly 800 to the Tiriki Chief Paul Amian on the alleged security of Chief Paul's land in Tiriki . . . [a case, he added gratuitously] where the money appears to have been squandered."

14. E. P. Oranga, Assistant Agricultural Officer, Central Nyanza District, to Senior Agricultural Officer, Nyanza Province, 28 June 1949. KNA 3/1794 (Adm. 7/5/1), Syracuse reel 256, sec. 10, p. 57. Emphasis in original. The report was made as the administration was beginning to gather grass-roots sentiments about possibilities of land titling and farm credit for the Ingham Committee on Agricultural Credit to Africans.

15. The pledging of daughters and other humans, and Oranga's brief report on it, are discussed in the companion study *The Nature of Entrustment* (Shipton 2007, ch. 6).

16. After the first colonial decades, "African" had gradually replaced the arguably more pejorative-sounding "native" as the descriptor of choice among officials for written purposes. That they had race and not just geographic origins in mind is clear enough from context in many instances. (Caucasian immigrants from South Africa, for example, seldom got counted as "African.") The quotation marks are sometimes dropped herein to avoid tedium or undue sanctimony.

17. Sir Malcolm Darling, memorandum, "The Finance of the Cultivator," for Kenya Colonial Economic Advisory Committee. In Ingham et al. (1950, 72–78). His views were somewhat more complex still than indicated, and more two-sided. The quotation refers to "short-term" credit. Darling's view of "long-term" credit for "progressive" farmers was quite different: "For long-term credit the best [security] is land, and the land should be held in individual ownership under a clear title which can be easily ascertained, and it must be free of any restriction which will make foreclosure and sale difficult" (p. 77).

18. This brief sketch on early government lending to "African" farmers touches only on aspects involving land mortgaging. A fuller story, encompassing official lending without the use of land as collateral, is part of the third study in this set, on credit between cultures. Government loans of either sort directly affected only a tiny proportion of indigenous farmers until after the second world war, when ambitious plans for lending that had been drawn up in the depressed years of the 1930s got pumped up with new funding and floated, along with new loans from private banks and other sources.

19. Some private money lending had been ostensibly controlled under the Pawn-brokers Act of 13th October, 1913 (*Laws of Kenya*, revised, Cap. 529). Controls would later be extended to other private lenders under the Money-lenders Ordinance of 1st January, 1933 (*Laws of Kenya*, revised, Cap. 528), whose main stipulation was a ceiling on interest rates at 48 percent annually (Sec. 15, para. 1). Both laws were copied almost verbatim out of British law, and lightly revised versions remain in force today. My observations suggest high-interest rural moneylending to be more common in some other parts of rural Africa, for instance in the Gambia, than in rural western Kenya. In the Gambian setting they are the subject of frequent cross-cultural misunderstandings.

20. Kenya, *Annual Report* (1931, 7); Okoth-Ogendo (1978, 232–36).

21. In one auction in 1930, in the start of the Depression when the public banks were not yet established, forty-four settler farms were gaveled off (and twenty-two more offered) at Kibos, Solai, Athi, Kijabe, Naivasha, Nyeri, Nanyuki, and Laikipia. Other land auctions that year were held at Nakuru, Thomson's Falls, Kisumu, Nyeri, Kitale, and Kibwezi Townships (Kenya Colony, *Annual Report,* 1930). By this time there were four commercial banks in Kenya: the National Bank of India, Ltd. (based in London); the National Bank of South Africa, Ltd. (based in Pretoria); the Standard Bank of South Africa, Ltd. (based in London); and the Bank of India, Ltd. (based in Bombay).

22. The enormous literature on Mau Mau and the Gikuyu and cognate groups at its center ties most directly into the topic of displacement, land dispossession, and early tenure "reform" in many places, notably in Sorrenson (1967), Kershaw (1997), and Mackenzie (1986, 1993, 1998). Other influential histories include those of Tabitha Kanogo (1987), David Throup (1987), David Anderson (2005), and Caroline Elkins (2005). Jean Davison (1996) provides rare transcribed reminiscences by women. On the moral quandaries, ambiguities, and ironies, nothing tops (James) Ngugi wa Thiong'o's historical novel *A Grain of Wheat.*

23. For a perspective on Mau Mau favored by some "hard core" settlers, expressing concerns about threats to farms and homes, see Ruark (1955).

24. The Mumbo movement, and the sacrifices and entrustments involved, are discussed further in Shipton (2007, Ch. 9) and sources cited there.

25. C. E. Mortimer, Member for Health and Local Government, circular to all Provincial Commissioners, 29 October 1947. KNA 3/1792 (ADM. 23/2/2/4/47), Syracuse reel 256.

26. Letter of September (no day), 1948. KNA 3/1794 (VET 26/3/5/180), Syracuse reel 256.

27. North, Central, and South Kavirondo were being renamed North, Central, and South Nyanza, respectively, in 1948.

28. Letter from C. M. Deverell, Secretary, Development and Reconstruction Authority (in the Secretariat), to the Commissioner, African Land and Settlement, 16 July 1948. KNA 3/1794 (Adm. 7/5/2/), Syracuse reel 256.

29. C. H. Williams, District Commissioner, North Nyanza, to Provincial Commissioner, Nyanza, 17 May, 1949. KNA 3/1794 (AGR. 7/1/1, Vol. II). Syracuse film 2800, reel 256. The Member for Agriculture and Natural Resources estimated in 1951 that a rate of 8 percent would have been needed to cover costs—KNA 3/2533 (L.B./3/2/2/1), Syracuse film no. 2800, reel 257.

30. The incarnations of the board included the African Settlement Board, African Settlement and Land Utilization Board, African Land Development Board (ALDEV), Land Development Board (Non-Scheduled areas), and Board of Agriculture (Non-Scheduled areas). See also pp. 161–63.

31. KNA 3/1794 (CNC.A 10/2/19). Syracuse reel 256, sec. 10.

32. The memo added the rather high-handed recommendation that titled "farms" be indivisible in inheritance, unlike "customary" landholdings.

33. Ingham et al. (1950). The committee's members, appointed by P. M. Gordon, Member for Agriculture and Natural Resources, were J. H. Ingham, E. J. A. Leslie, D. O'Hagan, T. L. Hately, C. L. Todd, P. C. Chambers, and E. W. Mathu.

34. Ingham et al. (1950, 12, 14, 17–18, 24).

35. Ingham et al. (1950, 1).

36. D. O'Hagan was Native Courts Officer, E. J. A. Leslie was Registrar of Co-operative Societies.

37. The authors perceived that some large Kenyan peoples (including Luhya) deemed purchased land salable, but inherited land unsalable. Beliefs surrounding such "source-purpose linkages" in Luo and other African cultures are examined in Shipton (1989a).

38. 15 August 1951. Kenya National Archives 3/2971 (LND. 16/4/A). Syracuse film no. 2800, reel 362, sec. 10.

39. Swynnerton was commissioned to the task on 14 October 1953, by a letter from F. Cavendish-Bentinck, the Member for Agriculture and Natural Resources (KNA/ AGR 32/2), through the Director of Agriculture, after a meeting on 24 September with provincial commissioners. He submitted the plan on 8 December 1953, to Cavendish-Bentinck, who sent it on to Britain's secretary of state for the colonies. When first published in May 1954, it had gained government basic approval.

40. The Plan's second main thrust, along with land titling, was to promote "Africans'" growing lucrative cash crops earlier forbidden to them. The planners' deliberations are discussed in Thurston (1984).

41. The report instructed the government to raise the maximum loan from the ALDEV (Agriculture and Livestock Development Board) from £100 to £200 (p. 55). Commit £200,000 to a new "Loan (or Land) Bank" for African farmers, it said, and once titling gets into stride, establish a fund an order of magnitude larger: £2 million (p. 55). The Plan noted that only £11,000 out of £30,000 committed to ALDEV lending in the previous three years had actually been borrowed (p. 55). But that did not seem to matter.

42. The pros and cons of fragmented holdings, some subtle, are discussed in Bentley (1987) and Shipton (1989b).

43. Report of the Working Party on African Land Tenure (1957–58, pp. 26–27); Sorrenson (1967, 191).

44. Like the Ingham report before it, the Swynnerton Plan strongly supported the cooperative movement as a credit channel, though not necessarily for mortgaging: "It is most important to establish a strong co-operative organization. . . . Co-operative societies should be used to the fullest extent in the issue and collection of loans to farmers" (pp. 26, 27). But Swynnerton and his report's ghostwriters clearly saw that all was not well in the co-ops even then: "lack of foresight, of a sense of urgency and of application to detail at present prevail. . . . In recent years in Kenya there has been a large development of agricultural producers' organizations which have frequently lacked stability because of inexperienced or irresponsible committees or management" (p. 26). Foreigners in Kenyan agricultural development have persisted in optimistically gambling on the improvement of organizations they have perceived as weak or corrupt. Agencies and the government

have kept lending through cooperatives before these have proved themselves, often leading to eventual letdown on one or more sides. See Deschamps et al. (1989). The theme is also important in the forthcoming third volume of this trilogy, where cooperatives and their successes and failures are discussed in some depth.

45. Even as the Swynnerton Plan was getting implemented before Kenya's Independence in 1963, some in the administration still feared land mortgaging might be dangerous to the small-scale farmer. The Working Party on African Land Tenure in 1958 drafted a Registration Bill with a procedure to keep mortgagers from losing land directly to moneylenders and remaining in debt to them. In the case of a default, the mortgagee would have to serve notice, wait over three months, and put land up for sale before being allowed to take over the land. In the case of no sale, foreclosure would cancel the debt. But all this provided farmers slim protection from land losses. They would soon devise their own ways to try to protect themselves, as discussed in the chapters to follow.

46. Development planning born of crisis is a central theme of A. F. Robertson's sweeping summary and analysis (1984).

Chapter 7: The Ghost Market

1. Portions of this chapter are adapted from Shipton (1988). Among the many other available treatments on the land tenure "reform" and its consequences in this and other parts of the country are works by Sytek (1966), Sorrenson (1967), R. Wilson (1971), Okoth-Ogendo (see esp. 1976, 1978), Pala Okeyo (1980), Mkangi (1983), Glazier (1985), Coldham (1978a, b; 1979), Haugerud (1983, 1989), Greene (1987), Fleuret (1988), Mackenzie (1998), Lesorogol (2008), Shipton (1992), and Shipton and Goheen (1992).

2. The symbolic resistance to land sales was apparent in perceptions and practices concerning what Luo called *pesa makech*, or bitter money, money with the taint of an immoral act (see Shipton 1989a). Money gained from selling land, and inherited land in particular, was expected likely to bring harm to the seller, possibly afflicting one or more close kin or descendants in addition or instead.

3. Sytek's 1966 study recounts as narrative history the tenure debates in Luoland from the issuance of the Swynnerton Plan until after Independence in 1963. See also Okoth-Ogendo (1978) and, on the Gikuyu (Kikuyu) country, Sorrenson (1967).

4. For perspective, 14 percent of homestead heads in our sample there were listed by my assistants as being women. But this is not a hard-and-fast figure, since homestead headship depends on definition (one factor in which must be a question of intermittent male residence) and on perception. In some ways the proportion of female heads was probably considerably higher. In the 1979 national census, 52 percent of the district's resident population were female (1:209). Okoth-Ogendo (1976, 177), Pala Okeyo (1977, 177), and Coldham (1978b, 100) have also found that after titling, about 6 percent or less of the land titles in various parts of Kenya studied were in women's hands. Pala Okeyo gives special attention to the registration's apparently harmful consequences for women. See also Mackenzie (1986, 1993, 1998) on Gikuyu (Kikuyu) and Fleuret (1988) on Taita.

5. See the brief discussion of Luo "widow inheritance" in Shipton (2007) and for

fuller discussion of Luo and other African widows, see Potash (1986a, b). In Ankole and Buganda, in southern Uganda, Bikaako and Ssenkumba have found widows' land claims to depend heavily on how long they had been married, whether they had borne children, and the sex of these. Having male children's interests to look after was a widow's best hope for being left in charge of land. The authors noted what they deemed new fluidity, though, in favor of wives and girl children in some cases (Bikaako and Ssenkumba 2003, 251–52).

6. Informants recalled that many Maragoli had left as registration drew near, partly under pressure from a wuon lowo chief, but that many returned after his death.

7. Jodak/wuon lowo ties are still being formed by land loans after registration. They do not, however, usually include compulsory labor as some may have done in the past; labor a jadak does for a wuon lowo is now more likely to be paid.

8. Being a finite resource, land normally gains value with time as population grows. Hence, arguably, a long-term land loan repaid in full would carry added value returned.

9. Compare Moock (1976, 212) on Maragoli Luhya.

10. Okoth-Ogendo (1981a,176) found in the Kisumu District sugar belt that the incidence of land disputes was lowest in the oldest-registered areas.

11. Compare R. Wilson (1971, 20–21) on Kisii and Nyeri Districts.

12. On rising disputes over sold land early in the registration, see also Glazier's detailed account of tenure reform among Mbeere of Embu District (1985, 232–33). Changes in dispute resolution procedures make the incidence of disputes hard to measure statistically. Lesorogol (2008) treats titling dilemmas for Samburu herders.

13. R. Wilson (1971, 10–11) on Kisii (and Nyeri); Okoth-Ogendo (1978, 500) on Kisii; Paterson (1984, 64, 77, 80, 124) on East Bunyore in Kakamega District. Cf. Hill (1982, passim) on the sluggish land market in extremely densely settled parts of Hausaland in Nigeria.

14. Some, of course, preferred *not* to keep relatives around them, as Cohen and Atieno Odhiambo (1989) noted of rising Luo individualists who moved away to settlement schemes in the Nyanza "sugar belt."

15. My finding on the mainly local nature of the rural Luo land market in most areas, with few sales or other transfers occurring over long distances, parallels Haugerud's (1989) on the Embu country in central Kenya. State-organized resettlement schemes have been exceptional in this regard, attracting immigrants from around and about into their designated spaces and allotments.

16. See, for instance, Swynnerton (1955, 9), Whisson (1964, 100–101), Wanjigi (1972, 179), Simpson (1976, passim), and Streeten (1981, 125).

17. On the workings of the land control boards, see Kenya, Ministry of Lands and Settlement (1969) and R. Wilson (1972). See also Okoth-Ogendo (1976–78, 1:166–7, 180–81), Coldham (1978b), and Simpson (1976, ch. 24). My own observations of the Migori board were made mainly in 1982. Some have since included more women.

18. Also observed earlier by Okoth-Ogendo (1976, 174) elsewhere in Kenya.

19. Collier and Lal (1980, 10), Shipton (1988, 115–18), Haugerud (1989). Haugerud's and my figures suggest that land buyers have been generally wealthier and better

integrated into a cash economy than land sellers. See also Downs and Reyna (1988) for broader discussions of land concentration.

20. A classic modern statement on the poverty ratchet (a principle familiar since Marx's *Capital* and before) is Chambers (1983). Kitching's treatise (1980), among other available works, applies an idea like this specifically to rural central and western Kenya.

21. Of 102 informants (here representing homesteads) in our Kanyamkago sub-sample who reported on the issue, 21 percent reported having sold some land by 1982; at least 16 percent had done so since titling was completed. By comparison, 13 percent said they had bought land, again mostly since registering. Five percent of the 108 homestead groups were unclassifiable for purchases and sales. Probably some farmers had bought or sold but did not report having done so.

22. Transaction fees vary on a graduated scale according to the land parcel's size and price, but the minimum total fees in South Nyanza (Shs. 325) in 1982 equaled the cash wages of sixty-five days' casual farm labor (!), and the real costs could rise several times this high. Farmers commonly understate real sale prices to cut down fees.

23. The government has tried to incorporate local elders nationwide into its own machinery for land administration. Most notable has been the Magistrates Jurisdiction (Amendment) Act, passed 31 December 1981, empowering elders under district officers to hear land disputes formerly taken to the courts.

24. See, on Kenya, Coldham (1979, 618), R. Wilson (1972, 132), Haugerud (1983, 76–77), and Paterson (1984, 70). See also West (1972, 173–74 and passim) on *mailo* holdings in Buganda, Okec (1969) on other parts of Uganda, Simpson (1976, 637) on parts of southern Sudan, Cheater (1983) on parts of Zimbabwe, Palmer (1997) on eastern and southern Africa country by country, and Riddell and Dickerman (1986) and Bruce (1998) on Africa country by country.

Chapter 8: Nothing More Serious

Epigraph. The anonymous Cameroonian is quoted in Geschiere and Jackson (2006a, 6).

1. Parts of this chapter are adapted from Shipton (1992).

2. For a brief history of ALDEV and the rest of the series of AFC predecessors, see Cone and Lipscomb (1972, 91–96). Loans to Europeans were handled separately by the Land Development Board (Scheduled Areas) (from 1957), which became the Board of Agriculture (Scheduled Areas) in 1960. Lending for the scheduled and non-scheduled areas was merged under the Central Agricultural Board in 1963.

3. Established under the Agricultural Finance Corporation Act of 1969 (Laws of Kenya, Cap. 323), the AFC has some seasonal crop lending, including, since the 1980s, some seasonal crop lending unsecured by collateral.

4. Under pressure from the World Bank and other international agencies, the Kenya government officially deregulated interest rates in October 1991. Few financial institutions responded dramatically, however. The managers of the AFC, for one, refused to raise interest for fear of high-level government sanction.

5. By 1991 the AFC had forty-nine branches and three sub-branch offices for

Kenya's forty-one districts, most of the offices situated in cities and towns. Most of my firsthand information on farmers' responses to the AFC comes from that time; this discussion may not accurately reflect more recent history. Use of cellular phones is one major change that undoubtedly has an effect on the communications.

6. The 1964–86 data come from Grosh (1987, 57) and Kenya, Ministry of Economic Planning; Central Bureau of Statistics, *Statistical Abstract*, 1990 (p. 160); 1991 claim from Kenya *Weekly Review*, 20 September 1991 (p. 24).

7. Sources: AFC; World Bank Regional Mission in Eastern Africa (hereafter RMEA).

8. World Bank RMEA; AFC. Loans averaged about K.Sh. 6,000, an amount the donors acknowledged was appropriate only for larger farms than most in Nyanza.

9. In the World Bank's Third Smallholder Agricultural Credit Project (1977–81), which cost about U.S. $40 million (K.Sh. 330 million), an international and national attempt was made to expand the volume of lending to small- and medium-scale cultivators. This expansion severely overburdened the administrative capacity of the AFC. By the best available estimates, the third project issued just over 19,000 loans. The Bank then proceeded to finance the Fourth Smallholder Agricultural Credit Project, under which the AFC reported issuing some 25,000 to 30,000 more loans, from 1983 to 1989. This "Credit IV" program lent the government about U.S. $35 million (about K.Sh. 630 million in 1988 terms) ostensibly meant for the AFC's re-lending to farmers and its institutional strengthening.

10. Sources: *Kenya Population Census*, 1979, vol. 2, pp. 2–4; Agricultural Finance Company, Kenya, *Statistical Digest*, 1990, p. 11.

11. Shipton (1988, 118–19, 129) sums up the gender distribution of land titles.

12. No one inside or outside the organization knows the frequency or aggregate amounts of payments made under the table. Borrowers' reports of these payments are more likely to be accurate than lenders', since the latter have more to lose from being discovered, but neither are wholly reliable.

13. See Paulson (1984), Marende (1978). The latter provides a Marxist critique of the AFC lending operations as observed in Vihiga Division, Kakamega District.

14. Marende (1978), Grosh (1987, 65–66); Benjamin Polack, personal communication. Nothing was made any easier for AFC operations, of course, by the famous car bomb blast on 7 August 1998, that destroyed the U.S. embassy across the street from AFC headquarters, causing untold personal loss and suffering within the AFC and severely damaging the offices and records.

15. A reform in one of the world's largest credit banks, the Bank Ratyang Indonesia (BRI), in the 1980s exemplifies an experiment with the opposite approach of lending money without attempting to control the use of funds.

16. By the end of 1984, 2,680 sq. km. (49 percent) of 5.459 km. available for smallholder registration had been titled in South Nyanza District. Sixty-four percent of the registrable 7,629 sq. km. in the then three Luo-speaking districts had been titled (Kenya, Ministry of Economic Planning, *Statistical Abstracts*, 1990, p. 5).

17. Paulson (1984, 109, 178–79); see also Grosh (1987, 61–65).

18. Kenya *Weekly Review*, 12 February 1988, p. 32.

19. The sampled districts were Nakuru, Uasin Gishu, Kakamega, Machakos and Kitui (two covered by one office), and Embu. These districts vary greatly in their population densities and landholding sizes, but average land sizes of AFC borrowers in these districts together probably exceed those of borrowers in Nyanza Province.

20. According to the Migori AFC branch manager's estimate in 1991, about 99 percent of loan applications at his branch were approved, but inquirers whom his staffers encouraged to the point of application had fallen from about 75 percent to about 25 percent in the few years preceding.

21. Or at least these were the amounts the latter *recorded* taken. AFC loans have gradually increased in amounts as the shilling has lost value. In the year preceding my last visit, nearly every AFC borrower approved through the Migori branch had borrowed Shs. 50,000 (U.S. $1,785 in late 1991), the maximum allowed under the "small-scale" credit category.

22. A few, however, had received still larger amounts from commercial banks.

23. In their naiveté or optimism about their own abilities to use their loans well, the mortgaging farmers were not too different from their counterparts in (say) Massachusetts.

24. Paulson (1984, 161, emphasis mine); see also Von Pischke (1977); Marende (1978); Grosh (1987, 61–63).

25. Paulson (1984, 152). She did find, however, that in 1981–82, when the AFC was forbidden to foreclose on mortgages, repayment dropped sharply (p. 161). Reports on AFC repayment rates differ, but it appears that AFC land-tied schemes for small-scale farms had repayment rates of about 70 to 80 percent by the end of 1982 (source: World Bank RMEA). Separate cooperative programs achieved rates of only 20 to 25 percent without land security, though in areas where loans were tied to permanent crops like coffee the rates were much higher, sometimes well into the 90–100 percent range. From about early 1983, the AFC severely restricted lending to farmers without land titles, and the World Bank pressed the government to stiffen collateral requirements. But the AFC's repayment rates continued falling for the next decade.

26. Lawrance (1966) discusses lending procedures of commercial bank branches in Kenya from the late 1950s to mid-1960s.

27. The big three banks also had about 348 of the nation's 428 branches, including sub-branches and mobile banks (commonly a four-wheel drive vehicle with driver, teller, and armed guard) (Mullei and Ng'elu 1990, 269). Many of the sub-branches and mobile units did not lend.

28. As of the end of 1983, 16 percent of commercial bank agricultural loans outstanding in Kenya, or about K.Sh. 610 million, were classed as being for farms of up to fifty hectares (source: World Bank). Of course, within this farm size range, larger, more "progressive," and better-situated farmers took a large share. About 81 percent of the agricultural loans were for durations of two years or less. In addition to this direct lending, the commercial banks do lend to the cooperatives, and thus indirectly to farmers.

29. See Cowen and Shenton (1991) again on colonial government constraints to lending in British West Africa.

30. E.g., Marco Surveys (1965); Gerhart (1975, 38). In the latter's survey of 360

western Kenyan farmers classed as smallholders, not one mentioned commercial banks when asked about possible sources of credit open to them.

31. Loans to women's groups in recent years have not normally required collateral but have relied instead on peer pressure. This subject is discussed in Shipton (2007) and in the forthcoming volume on credit between cultures.

32. The tendency was noted earlier by P. Moock in 1973 (p. 199), among others.

33. David and Wyeth (1978, 12 and passim), and Collier (1984, 1015); both on Nyanza, Western, Rift, Valley Eastern, and Central Provinces combined. See also Lawrance (1966, 125) for an earlier report.

34. For more general information on commercial bank lending in Kenya, Uganda, and Tanzania, see the sources listed in Killick et al. (1984, 64-73) and, for Kenyan information more up to date, the Central Bank of Kenya's quarterly reports.

35. As counted in South Nyanza District land registry records. Fifteen of the twenty-five were from commercial banks, eight from the AFC, and two from the South Nyanza Trade Development Joint Board.

36. Data compiled from the then South Nyanza District land registry, Homa Bay. Excluded are loans that might have been made against the physical transfer of title deeds and illegally unreported to the land registry. Creditor claims arising from such mortgages would be hard to enforce.

37. Compare Staudt (1985, xiv), on part of Kakamega District in 1974-75: there, while only 2 percent of those in jointly managed farms received loans, another 12 percent applied for them or could describe the application process accurately, as opposed to only 1 percent of female farm managers who could do so.

38. The following information on land-secured loans is based mainly on interviews with land mortgagers, with their neighbors and relatives, and with AFC officials in Nyanza Province; and on secondary sources.

39. Some AFC officials have found Gusii generally to be even more sensitive on the issue than Luo. The Gusii have had a lineage system of land rights much like that of the Luo but live at higher densities. In some newly settled or resettled areas of western Kenya, where farmers are less likely to have kin living right around, lenders find it easier to seize defaulters' land.

40. See Southall (1952), Gordon Wilson (1961), Whisson (1964), Evans-Pritchard (1965), and Shipton (1984) for discussions and bibliographies. Cattle are similarly conceived as a permanent family asset belonging at once to the dead, the living, and the unborn. They too make poor loan collateral.

41. See Sorrenson (1967), among many other sources on Gikuyu (Kikuyu) lands and the revolt.

42. AFC interest rates have been partly subsidized. For seasonal credit, they ranged from 9 to 11 percent from 1977 to 1980, and up to 14 percent in 1983. Top commercial bank rates by 1983 were about 16 percent. Sources: AFC, World Bank RMEA. But Luo small-scale farmers tended, as noted earlier, to have had little experience with, or understanding of, interest charges. Those who did could perceive that farm loans were cheaper than industrial and other kinds of credit, hence an outflow of resources from agriculture into other "sectors" of the economy (cf. Okoth-Ogendo 1976, 175-76).

43. Of 652 parcels of land that the AFC advertised for sale in 1979, only thirty-six (6 percent) were reported sold by public auction. Sixty-nine (11 percent) of them were bought or kept by the AFC itself for lack of bidders at auctions. In the remaining 547 cases (84 percent) the auctions would appear to have been postponed or called off. Sources: AFC, World Bank RMEA.

44. In September 1980, a time of food shortage and general political uncertainty in Kenya, a presidential speech implying that the AFC had been harassing farmers prompted the AFC to suspend loan recovery work for thirteen months. It was only when a new long rainy-season harvest had been reaped in Kenya, and worries of political unrest had been (temporarily) allayed, that collection work began again. In 1991 presidential standing orders prevented financial institutions from auctioning land without having been through the cumbersome procedure of provincial administration clearance. By the year's end the district headquarters were overwhelmed with AFC and bank applications for permissions to act and spending much of their time arbitrating reschedulings.

45. An example in international lore is the 1991 Walt Disney adventure film of Nils Gaup, *Shipwrecked,* in which the entire drama of a Norwegian boy Haakan Haakansen's going to sea as a cabin boy in the 1850s is set into motion by a town financier's callous refusal to reschedule collection on the mortgaged rural family home after Haakan's father's injury on the same ship. The film, aimed at young viewers, is a cautionary tale about the ruthlessness not only of pirates at sea but also of moneylenders at home. Countless summer camp dramas contain similar admonitory lessons about amoral or immoral rentiers and mortgage lenders.

46. For fuller discussion of the famous S. M. Otieno case, see Ojwang and Mugambi (1989), Cohen and Atieno Odhiambo (1989, pp. 133–40; and 1992).

47. The account from an international investigation mission to Kenya, authored mainly by Binaifer Nowrojee and promptly published in 1993, made waves with a powerful indictment of politicians' complicity in "state-sponsored ethnic violence" over land in resettled areas in the run-up to the 1992 elections (Africa Watch 1993; see also Human Rights Watch 1994). Médard (1999) and Oucho (2002) both offer politico-geographic analysis of the clashes, the latter with some unashamedly partisan opinions mixed in. The early and mid-1990s were a time when journalists and others were testing their limits under wide new freedoms but still experiencing occasional government harassment. The news reporting of the period in Kenya was relatively vivid, and sometimes boldly and sharply critical of national authorities, particularly in Kenya's *Daily Nation* newspaper and *Weekly Review* but also at times in the daily *Standard.* The *Kenya Times* more consistently toed the KANU ruling party line. Oucho's book includes a directory of relevant articles, chronologically organized. See also Kenya (1992) for a parliamentary committee report. Mueller (2008) traces political roots of Kenyan violence over decades.

48. For more on the Million Acre Resettlement Scheme and other later such programs and their outcomes, see Abrams (1979), Leo (1984), Médard (1999), Kanyinga (1998, esp. on the coastal areas), and Oucho (2002). In its early years most analysts considered the Million Acre scheme to have been smoothly run and relatively successful.

49. The forthcoming companion volume on credit between cultures relates these to other farm loan repayment issues. Here the move to more spacious or fertile lands may

be offset by the farmers' inexperience in new microclimates or with new markets, and surely sometimes too by lack of trust among new neighbors—as well as by the hardships and disorientation of resettling itself.

50. This distinction between "permanent" resettlers from central Kenya and "part-time" straddlers from Western Kenya I owe to Oucho (2002). It rings true to other information available to me, though the line surely blurs.

51. Kenya *Weekly Review*, 8 November 1991, p. 3. According to Mohammed Yusuf Haji, 310 original bona fide owners had increased to 589.

52. But other areas of the country were no less under contention. In November 1991, as the land clashes were getting under way in western Kenya, the names Hon. Mwai Kibaki and Lucy Muthoni Kibaki appeared in the newspaper in an unaccustomed place. (Kibaki was former vice president and current minister for health.) The Kibakis reportedly found their (possibly mortgaged?) land on the Mombasa beach together heading for the auction block—until, by whatever means, they were able to get them pulled off just the week of the scheduled auction (Kenya *Standard*, 6 November 1991, p. 33). A month later, Dr. James Ouko, a former university lecturer from Kisumu with land in Kitale, found himself appealing to President Daniel arap Moi to keep the Agricultural Finance Corporation from selling 250 of his 600 acres to "a parastatal boss" unnamed (Kenya *Daily Nation*, 14 December 1991, p. 5). I cannot presume to offer any judgmental opinion on these reported cases.

53. Further evidence of the general political and economic insecurities of the time may be found in Gusii country. During the aid-fund drought and the run-up to the same 1992 election when the "land clashes" were flaring up elsewhere, Gusii country experienced a dramatic spate—it can be called an epidemic—of persecution of persons perceived as witches, usually women, by young men in gangs. See Ogembo (2006).

54. This is not to say no cultural differences or racial or cultural stereotypes remained in local minds from earlier times. For a compilation, remembered or newly voiced when recorded after Independence, see Sytek's (1972) smorgasbord of savory and unsavory stereotypes between Luo and other ethnic groups in western Kenya and farther away. (It is part of Northwestern University's broader Cross-cultural Study of Ethnocentrism.) For a variety of theories on ethnocentrism and ethnic stereotyping more generally, from several disciplines, see LeVine and Campbell (1972).

55. Nor would it be right to infer that more ethnic mixture is always more dangerous. Although it would stretch beyond my information to say so with confidence, it would seem that the areas with two or just a few predominant ethnic groups (as locally distinguished) represented were just as volatile as, or more than, those with many groups well mixed around.

56. Africa Watch (1993, 19). Notably scarce, in descriptions of these homemade arsenals, are devices like East Asian martial arts devices (so commonly seen in Kung Fu movies and the like, in western Kenya as across the continent), or American hoodlum gear like chains or brass knuckles. Lethal as they might have been, they would have confused the self-consciously "tribalist" symbolism.

57. Note that "savaging it up" for terror in combat is *not* an exclusively or even mainly African pattern. Participants in the Boston Tea Party, other American revolu-

tionaries, and soldiers in Vietnam and Iraq did it. Ground soldiers and warriors most anywhere do it. Even athletes do it, with "warpaint" under their eyes on football fields.

58. Africa Watch (1993, 90–91). Figures quoted by Human Rights Watch in a July 1994 newsletter set the numbers displaced since October 1991 at between 260,000 (a February 1994 UN Development Programme estimate) and 304,833 (an October 1993 National Council of Churches of Kenya estimate based on food relief registration). Contrast a report read by Jackson Kolweo, a minister of state in the Office of the President, to a largely incredulous parliament in early May 1993, giving figures of only 365 killed and 7,113 displaced ("Uproar over Clash Figures," Kenya *Weekly Review*, 14 May 1993, p. 13). The magazine called these last figures "grossly understated" (p. 14).

59. That few forced migrants returned to the resettled areas by 2002 is the distinct impression of Oucho (2002); that most had not returned by mid-2007 is the impression left by recent Web postings of the Kenya Land Alliance and by the verbiage of the Draft National Land Policy discussed in the next chapter.

Chapter 9: Bigger than Law

1. Klopp (2002, 2006) offers insight into the land interests of particular senior politicians in the period. Such information in Kenya can be hard to obtain reliably and is always extremely sensitive.

2. The draft constitution's twenty chapters treated these topics: sovereignty, the republic, national values, citizenship, rights, representation, the legislature, the executive, the judiciary, devolution, land and property, the environment, public finance, public service, defense and national security, leadership and integrity, constitutional commissions, amendments, interpretations, and the expected transition to the new constitutional order.

3. The account that follows is based on the first plenary meeting's verbatim report. It is not meant to be complete, but merely to suggest the wide range of issues covered, to add more voices—in some cases ones from kinds of people seldom heard and poorly represented—and to give some idea how issues touched upon elsewhere in this study appeared to Kenyans from different walks of life at the dawn of the twenty-first century.

4. Classic texts on controlled "rites of rebellion"—a hallmark of the Rhodes-Livingstone Institute and, in Britain, the Manchester University school of anthropology in the late colonial years—include Max Gluckman's in 1956 (1963) and Victor Turner's in 1969 (1995). See Angelique Haugerud's study of the Kenyan *baraza*, or public political assembly (1995), for an extended treatment of similar themes, of variously contained voicing of opposition and a related phenomenon, the scripted ritual charade of approval—in that country's socio-political life.

5. I refer, of course, to Arnold Van Gennep's *The Rites of Passage* in 1908 (1960), which gave this broad class of activities their name as such and divided them into phases of separation, transition, and reincorporation. Different kinds of passage rites, as he noted, can place the emphasis on different phases, or aspects, among these three.

6. These were not, of course, the only debatables. Far from it. Here are just a few of the many others that might have been noted: the languages to be used in communications

and documents about land; the capping of landholding sizes or of the duration of absentee landlordship; the legality of land sale, and of sharecropping and other share contracting; the limits of leases; land taxation; the nature and timing of compensations (in cash or kind) to land losers in confiscation; the claims of widows, widow-inheritors, and quasi-married or separated persons; the roles of elders and of oral history and tradition; the recognition of ancestral graves and homestead remains; and the role of witchcraft and witchcraft accusations and persecutions. As it happened, several of these issues would surface on their own.

7. Some delegates with more local concerns spoke of land confiscations for mines; sugar and tea plantations ("nucleus estates"); churches, mosques, and temples; and re-settlement schemes.

8. Most spoke in English, a minority spoke in Swahili, and some spoke in mixtures of the two. If anyone spoke in any of Kenya's many other languages with no interpreter, their words were not recorded.

9. Charles Keter Cheruiyot, MP and "District Delegate" from Belgut and Kericho District, stated a male point of view: "When I grew up, my great grandfather told me that in our culture you could never be a man if you don't have land" (p. 38).

10. Like some other delegates, Ogari complained of the bribes or years of delay nec-essary for dealing with the "very corrupt" Land Department to get "lost" files found and a title in hand. He complained too of elders' having to travel to Nairobi in land dispute cases, saying cases should be settled "at almost village level. These are the people who know the history of the land and . . . the people who are in dispute" (pp. 54–55).

11. Founded in 1999 and registered as a trust in 2001, the KLA described itself in 2007 as "a non-profit-making and non-partisan umbrella network of civil society orga-nizations and individuals advocating for Formulation and Implementation of land and natural resource policies and institutional reforms in Kenya" (www.kenyalandalliance .or.ke, last accessed 6 June 2007). Its trustees numbered thirteen and its members ninety-three. Nearly all of both had recognizably Kenyan names, identifiable with a variety of ethnic groups. The funders acknowledged in KLA documents in 2007, but not there held responsible for its views, included the British Department for International De-velopment (DFID), the Danish International Development Agency (DANIDA) and the Danish Association for International Cooperation–Kenya (MS-Kenya), and Oxfam, among others.

12. The Draft National Land Policy as cited here is the one marked on its cover as March 2007 and published in the Kenya *Daily Nation* on 19 April 2007. Another sixty-one-page undated version, evidently from 2004 and directly issued by the National Land Policy Secretariat, remained on that body's Web site as of 13 July 2007. The March draft awaited presentation to Parliament for debate and passage into law through a proposed unified Land Act.

13. The "absolute sanctity" to be eliminated evidently refers to Laws of Kenya, Chapter 300 (1985 revision), Pt. III, 27, on "absolute ownership"; and 28, on such rights being "not liable to be defeated except as provided in this Act." Nor, now, could so many old wrongs be so easily repeated, if the draft became accepted policy or law. The gov-ernment would "rationalize" freehold by "repealing the principle of absolute sanctity of

first registration under the Registered Land Act" (3.3.3.1, para. 76, item ii). Non-citizens would not now be allowed freehold tenure, but only leases; and shorter ones at that than before—a topic to which we return momentarily.

14. Ideals included, to appeal to a broad political spectrum, were "equitable access for subsistence, commercial productivity and settlement," "intra-and inter-generational equity," "secure land rights," effective regulation, efficient management, "vibrant land markets," and transparent and democratic administration (DNLP 1.5.1).

15. "Minority" groups—for instance, forest foragers—would be inventoried and protected (3.6.6).

16. The draft policy also specified that freehold tenure, as provided for under the Registration of Titles Act (Cap. 281), the Land Titles Act (Cap. 282), or the Government Lands Act (Cap. 280), would be merged with "absolute proprietorship" as provided for under the Registered Land Act (Cap. 300) to eliminate the difference and the confusion it caused (DNLP 3.3.3.1).

17. Pastoralists—people whose way of life is based on livestock raising—were recognized in the draft plan as seldom before, and portrayed as having different tenure needs from other rural people. They require some unspecified "alternative methods of registration" allowing for "flexible and negotiated cross boundary access to water, pastures and salt licks among clans, groups and communities for mutual benefit to facilitate the migratory nature of pastoralism" (3.6.3, para. 180). This provision is more progressive and sensitive than many land tenure policies in Africa have been. It comes, of course, at a time when many "pastoralist" people have been heading out of pastoralism and into farming, trading, or computing. And few were ever unambiguously definable as pastoralists anyway, since they also traded and otherwise followed mixed or shifting strategies of livelihood. But this special provision does show some new official sensitivity to important differences in ways of life.

18. Found on the Web site of Michael Norton-Griffiths, at http://www.mng5 .com/papers/klfOverview.pdf, last accessed 13 July 2007. Norton-Griffiths was a spokesman for some Kenyan residents of long standing and former head of a small Langata-based ecological research company called EcoSystems Limited, specializing in low-level aerial surveys by small propeller planes on land use, animal population, and vegetation, using grid sampling and producing computerized databases in the early years of personal computing. His data on Kenya, some of which I have used on other occasions, indicated a correlation between land titling and higher crop productivity, though earliness of titling in agronomically favored areas complicates the issue, making it much harder to draw conclusions about its effects. By 2007 Norton-Griffiths identified himself as a "Consultant in Landuse Economics" and was active in national and area range and wildlife management affairs as well as broader land policy. His site linked to several papers by him containing overlapping messages and similar wording, some distinctive phrases of which newly appeared in the April 2007 version of the Draft National Land Policy and are presumably traceable to the influence of his strong critique. One of those is, "It is not possible for every person to own land since land is a finite resource" (DNLP 3.3.3, para. 71)—a proposition that logically would presuppose either infinite population or a specific minimum on holding sizes.

19. For instance, a few ethnic group names kept appearing in the Kenya Land Alliance publications. And many indeed kept appearing in those of the Human Rights Watch and Oxfam, two groups that pride themselves on independence from any national government controls—and thus something like sovereignty over their respective subject matter.

20. But ethnic groups like Luo, Gikuyu, or Luhya never have such clear boundaries. Would Kenyans need eventually to resort to some measure like "blood quantum" (fraction of ancestry)? The question is not moot. Germans in the early twentieth century had tried it for Aryans and Jews, with disastrous results. The United States and American Indian tribal governments had tried it from the 1930s on to distinguish natives from non-native Americans—and continue to do try to make it work to the time of this writing. Would Kenyans be willing to face all the definitional disputes, uncertainties, and resentments attendant? An administrative nightmare loomed, not to mention the worst.

21. A clause on this had been added and deleted too; it was softened back to a vague one on "putting in place measures to determine appropriate land sizes according to use and productivity of land" (DNLP, March 2007, 3.4.2.1, para. 117).

22. The clause about "all natural resources" to be vested in the people, the citizens of Kenya, as a whole appeared in the rejected draft constitution (3.4.3.1, para. 127). Some critics focused on this as a provision they deemed Marxist. Common ownership would have meant a radical change indeed for Kenyan law. The March 2007 draft backed down to a softer phrasing in "sharing of benefits," these being left undefined (3.3.4.1).

23. The issue of encroachment was specified precisely in early drafts, but not later ones. It is of interest not least because such encroachment is an issue of human and cultural rights for persons deemed "indigenous"—and opens the thorny issue of whether one mode of livelihood (foraging, herding, farming) makes anyone more "indigenous" than anyone else—and thus opens issues of prehistory and debated speculation about creation and evolution. It is also an issue of redistribution—just one not necessarily organized from officialdom.

24. A clause stating that they must be compensated before, not just after, being moved (when experience across Kenya, Africa, and indeed the world had showed it might come too little or not at all), came into the draft constitution (6.58.3.b) but did not reappear in the later March 2007 draft policy.

25. It was during the period of debate about the Kenyan constitutional reform that the Massachusetts state legislature made world news by determining that homosexual unions could legally count as marriage. This may have influenced the removal of the clause.

26. No mention about the disposition of remains of the dead, or of their possible rights, appears in the last land policy draft at the time of this writing. Only the faintest "ghost" of recognition remained in a vaguer statement that "land is a cultural heritage which should therefore be conserved for future generations" (3.1, para. 28).

27. To be sure, the March 2007 version of the Draft National Land Policy did in one section propose to "decentralize land registries" (3.5.7, para. 163), but whether this meant any control beyond the mere storage of and access to records (written or electronic) was left unclear. The new emphasis on "community," and thus on ethnic groups, tem-

pered the centralizing tendencies to an extent. So did the endorsement of separate rules for pastoralist people. But then again, the draft policy even as such still left leeway for the "community" of any ruling regime to expand in its numbers and claims (as Kalenjin "community" had done in the Moi years). In this way, again, it could allow persons in power to grab land of their ostensible "communities" for themselves.

28. Not at least since the French revolution, when the indiscriminate mowing down of royalty, noble aristocracy (feudalistic landlords), clergy, and other elites ended up clearing the field for Napoleonic totalitarianism. This lesson, drawn by Alexis de Tocqueville (1983), has been acknowledged by historians of different political stripes.

Chapter 10: Conclusion

Epigraph. Silvanus Onyambu Ogari, quoted by Constitution of Kenya Review Commission (2003, 55).

1. Sometimes punctuated "Reform? Reform? Aren't things bad enough already?" the Duke of Wellington's words were a comment on the proposed 1832 electoral reform act, tangential here. Separately: The subtitle of this chapter is one I have also used for a different paper on an overlapping set of topics.

2. Not that it cannot work the other way around. Often—too often— competition and strife are justified by reference to *different* deities or spirits presumed as intolerant as those doing their bidding.

3. This topic is covered more fully in *The Nature of Entrustment* (Shipton 2007).

4. While it is tempting to say a male jadak in such cases risks less opprobrium than a female, I cannot say this for sure. I think it as likely that being a female jadak, structurally doubly disadvantaged (like a female sharecropper or slave in other contexts), may ironically serve a woman's advantage when she wants to speak out. It might make her boldness stand out.

5. These issues of financial contribution clubs are treated in more detail in the forthcoming volume on credit between cultures.

6. Cautions about usurers in, say, Dante, Dostoyevsky, or Dickens faintly resonate in the movies, where the hero saves a struggling widow or disabled father from dispossession by an avaricious financier by going off on a bold and dangerous adventure, triumphing over adversity, and finally coming home with the money to pay off the mortgage.

7. Based on aerial photographic data prepared for the Lake Basin Development Authority by EcoSystems Ltd., Nairobi, and kindly provided to me by that organization.

8. Ivory Coast (Côte d'Ivoire), with a pro-market regime like Kenya's, did not attempt a nationwide titling program when Kenya did in the late twentieth century. Ivory Coast based its rural economies on a very different set of crops (notably cocoa) and depended more heavily on forest farming. Ivory Coast (or more properly, some in it) prospered in the 1960s and '70s to the degree that many called its story an economic miracle, then lost that momentum in the 1980s and '90s, while Kenya did too. In neither country did a land tenure policy ensure a lasting rural prosperity.

9. Readers wishing a set of analyses with many statistics, but similarly discouraging or inconclusive findings about the agricultural benefits of land titling, are referred to

Bruce and Migot-Adholla (1993), a study funded by the World Bank. See also Riddell and Dickerman's country-by-country survey of the continent (1986), and Palmer's of its eastern and southern parts (1997).

10. See Klopp (2006) on Kenyan land grabs by the well connected in the 1990s and early 2000s.

11. Goheen (1996). See also Fisiy (1992) and Firmin-Sellers and Sellers (1999) for other comparable Cameroonian findings with critical or at least ambivalent perspectives on rural titling.

12. "Subprime" in this usage is not to be confused with the "prime lending rate" of the U.S. Federal Reserve Bank. It means something more like suboptimal.

13. For some firsthand observations of territorial and reproductive strategies among species that Anglophones rather self-centeredly deem primates, see Wrangham and Peterson (1996), Waal (2000). For broader and somewhat more speculative discussions relating findings like theirs to human evolutionary psychology, see Wright (1994, 2001). That socially dominant males of the species deemed primates seem so often to reproduce disproportionately more than most subordinate ones, by having access to more females, does not of course mean that there are not some individuals or categories at the bottom end of one social, economic, and political scale or another who find ways to reproduce prolifically.

14. Malmberg (1980) offers a literature review, still as comprehensive as any, of research on human territoriality, including comparisons with other vertebrate species. (When faced with nature/nurture decisions, or what have been so called, he comes down more often than not on the side of nature, but he gives a good taste of both sides.) Missing from it, though, are two simultaneous waves of research and opinion from the late twentieth and early twenty-first centuries: sustained participant-observational research on apes and monkeys, and postmodernist critiques of the presumptions of science and scientism.

15. Weber (1998, 343).

16. Or perhaps instead, for some, it is measuring the progress of our civilizations by our distance from some imagined borderline that separates humans from divinity. One Luo song, transcribed by Cohen and Atieno Odhiambo (1989, 120), contains the line *Polo k'larie ndalo*, which loosely translates, "There are no land disputes in Heaven."

Bibliography

Abrahams, R. G. 1967a. *The Peoples of Greater Unyamwezi, Tanzania.* Ethnographic Survey of Africa, East Central Africa 17. London: International African Institute.

———. 1967b. *The Political Organization of Unyamwezi.* Cambridge: Cambridge University Press.

———. 1991. *A Place of Their Own: Family Farming in Eastern Finland.* Cambridge: Cambridge University Press.

Abrams, P. D. 1979. *Kenya's Land Resettlement Story.* Nairobi: Challenge Publishers.

Abwunza, Judith. 1997. *Women's Voices, Women's Power: Dialogues of Resistance from East Africa.* Peterborough, Ontario: Broadview.

Acheson, James. 2006. "Institutional Failure in Resource Management." *Annual Review of Anthropology* 35:117–34.

Adams, Dale W., Douglas H. Graham, and J. D. Von Pischke. 1984. *Undermining Development with Cheap Credit.* Boulder, Colo.: Westview.

Africa Watch. 1993. *Divide and Rule: State-Sponsored Ethnic Violence in Kenya.* New York, Washington, D.C., Los Angeles, London: Human Rights Watch.

Agricultural Finance Company, Kenya. 1990. *Statistical Digest.* Nairobi: A.F.C.

Allan, William. 1965. *The African Husbandman.* London: Oliver and Boyd.

Anderson, David. 2002. *Eroding the Commons: The Politics of Ecology in Baringo, Kenya, 1890s–1963.* Oxford, Nairobi, and Athens, Ohio: James Currey, E. A. E. P., and Ohio University Press.

———. 2005. *Histories of the Hanged: The Dirty War in Kenya and the End of Empire.* New York: W. W. Norton.

Apthorpe, Raymond. 1969. "Land Law and Land Policy in Eastern Africa." In James Obol-Ochola, ed., *Land Law Reform in East Africa, pp. 115–25.* Kampala: The National Trust.

Aristotle. 1962. *The Politics*. Trans. T. A. Sinclair. Harmondsworth: Penguin.

Ayany, Samuel. G. 1989. *Kar Chakruok mar Luo* (On the Origins of the Luo). Kisumu: Lake Publishers. Orig. pub. 1952.

Ayot, Henry Okello. 1979. *A History of the Luo-Abasuba: From A.D. 1760–1940*. Nairobi: Kenya Literature Bureau.

Barlett, Peggy. 1993. *American Dreams, Rural Realities: Family Farms in Crisis*. Chapel Hill: University of North Carolina Press.

Barnes, John A. 1962. "African Models in the New Guinea Highlands." *Man* 62(2):5–9.

Barrows, R., and Michael Roth. 1990. "Land Tenure and Investment in African Agriculture: Theory and Evidence." *Journal of Modern African Studies* 28(2):265–97.

Bassett, J. T. 1993. "The Land Question and Agricultural Transformation in Sub-Saharan Africa." Introduction to J. T. Bassett and D. E. Crummey, eds., *Land in African Agrarian Systems*. Madison: University of Wisconsin Press.

Bassett, J. T., and D. E. Crummey, eds. 1993. *Land in African Agrarian Systems*. Madison: University of Wisconsin Press.

Bates, Robert. 1981. *Markets and States in Tropical Africa*. Berkeley: University of California Press.

———. 1983. *Essays on the Political Economy of Rural Africa*. Cambridge: Cambridge University Press.

Beattie, John H. M. 1957. "Nyoro Kinship." *Africa* 27:317–40.

Benjaminsen, Tor, and Christian Lund, eds. 2003. *Securing Land Rights in Africa*. London: Frank Cass.

Bentley, Jeffrey. 1987. "Economic and Ecological Approaches to Land Fragmentation: In Defense of a Much-Maligned Phenomenon." *Annual Review of Anthropology* 16:31–67.

Berry, Sara. 1984. "The Food Crisis and Agrarian Change in Africa: A Review Essay." *African Studies Review* 27(2):59–112.

———. 1985. *Fathers Work for their Sons: Accumulation, Mobility and Class Formation in an Extended Yòrubá Community*. Berkeley: University of California Press.

———. 1993. *No Condition is Permanent: The Social Dynamics of Agrarian Change in Africa*. Madison: University of Wisconsin Press.

Besteman, Catherine. 1994. "Individualisation and the Assault on Customary Tenure in Africa: Title Registration Programmes and the Case of Somalia." *Africa* (Journal of the International African Institute) 64(4):484–515.

———. 1999. *Unravelling Somalia: Race, Violence, and the Legacy of Slavery*. Philadelphia: University of Pennsylvania Press.

Besteman, Catherine, and Lee V. Cassanelli, eds. 1996. *The Struggle for Land in Southern Somalia: The War Behind the War*. Boulder, Colo.: Westview.

Biebuyck, Daniel, ed. 1963. *African Agrarian Systems*. London: Oxford University Press.

Bikaako, Winnie, and John Ssenkumba. 2003. "Gender, Land and Rights:

Contemporary Contestations in Law, Policy and Practice in Uganda."
In L. Muthoni Wanyeki, ed., *Women and Land in Africa: Culture, Religion and Realizing Women's Rights*, pp. 232–78. London: Zed Books.

Blackstone, Sir William. 1930. *Commentaries on the Laws of England*. Vol. 2: *Of the Rights of Things*. Chicago: University of Chicago Press. Orig. pub. 1765–69.

Blount, Ben. 1975. "Agreeing to Agree on Genealogy: A Luo Sociology of Knowledge." In Ben G. Blount and Mary Sanches, eds., *Sociocultural Dimensions of Language Use*, pp. 117–36. New York: Academic Press.

Blount, Ben G., and Elise Padgug Blount. n.d. *Luo-English Dictionary*. Nairobi Institute of African Studies, University of Nairobi. Occasional Publication.

Blount, Ben, and R. T. Curley. 1970. "The Southern Luo Languages: A Glottochronological Reconstruction." *Journal of African Languages* 60(1):1–18.

Bohannan, Paul. 1954. "The Migration and Expansion of the Tiv." *Africa* (Journal of the International African Institute) 24(1):2016.

———. 1963. "'Land,' 'Tenure,' and 'Land-tenure.'" In Daniel Biebuyck, ed., *African Agrarian Systems*, pp. 101–15. Oxford: Oxford University Press.

Bond, B. W. 1934. "Notes on What I Believe to Be Approximately the Luo System of Land Tenure." In Kenya Land Commission, *Evidence and Memoranda* (Col. 91), pp. 2285–88. London: HMSO.

Bourdieu, Pierre. 1977. *Outline of a Theory of Practice*. Cambridge: Cambridge University Press. Orig. pub. 1972.

Broch-Due, Vigdis, and Richard A. Schroeder, eds. 2000. *Producing Nature and Poverty in Africa*. Uppsala, Sweden: Nordic Africa Institute.

Bruce, John, ed. 1998. *Country Profiles of Land Tenure: Africa 1996*. LTC Working Paper 130. Madison: Land Tenure Center, University of Wisconsin.

Bruce, John, and Shem Migot-Adholla. 1993. *Searching for Land Tenure Security in Africa*. Washington, D.C.: World Bank.

Burn, E. H. (and Geoffrey Cheshire). 1982. *Cheshire and Burn's Modern Law of Real Property*. London: Butterworth.

Butt, Audrey. 1952. *The Nilotes of the Anglo-Egyptian Sudan and Uganda*. Darryl Forde, ed., *Ethnographic Survey of Africa: East Central Africa* Part IV. London: International African Institute.

Butterman, Judith M. 1979. *Luo Social Formations in Change: Karachuonyo and Kanyamkago, c. 1800–1945*. Ph.D. dissertation, Syracuse University.

Cassanelli, Lee V. 1982. *The Shaping of Somali Society: Reconstructing the History of a Pastoral People*. Philadelphia: University of Pennsylvania Press.

Chambers, Robert. 1983. *Rural Development: Putting the Last First*. London: Longman.

Cheater, Angela P. 1983. "Formal and Informal Rights to Land in Zimbabwe's Black Freehold Areas: A Case-Study from Msengezi." *Africa* (Journal of the International African Institute) 52(3):77–91.

Chibnik, Michael, ed. 1987. *Farm Work and Fieldwork: American Agriculture in Anthropological Perspective*. Ithaca, N.Y.: Cornell University Press.

Chittick, Neville. 1965. "A Note on Stone-built Enclosures in South Nyanza, Kenya." *Man* (65):152–53.

Chrétien, Jean-Pierre. 2003. *The Great Lakes Region of Africa: Two Thousand Years of History.* New York: Zone Books.

Clarke, Grace A. n.d. *Luo-English Dictionary.* Kendu Bay, Kenya: East African Publishing House.

Cohen, David William, and E. S. Atieno Odhiambo. 1989. *Siaya: The Historical Anthropology of an African Landscape.* London: James Currey; Nairobi: Heinemann Kenya; Athens, Ohio: Ohio University Press.

———. 1992. *Burying SM: The Politics of Knowledge and the Sociology of Power in Africa.* Portsmouth, N.H., and London: Heinemann and James Currey.

Cohen, John M. 1980a. "Land Tenure and Rural Development in Africa." In Robert H. Bates and Michael F. Lofchie, eds., *Agricultural Development in Africa: Issues of Public Policy,* pp. 349–400. New York: Praeger.

Coldham, Simon. 1978a. "Land Control in Kenya." *Journal of African Law* 22(1):63–77.

———. 1978b. "The Effect of Registration upon Customary Land Rights in Kenya." *Journal of African Law* 22(2):91–111.

———. 1979. "Land Tenure Reform in Kenya: The Limits of Law." *Journal of Modern African Studies* 17(4):615–27.

Collier, Paul. 1984. "Why Poor People Get Rich: Kenya 1960–79." *World Development* 12(10):1007–18.

Collier, Paul, and Deepak Lal. 1980. "Poverty and Growth in Kenya." World Bank Staff Working Paper 389. Washington, D.C.: World Bank.

Colville, Sir Henry. 1895. *The Land of the Nile Springs.* London: Edward Arnold.

Cone, Winston, and J. F. Lipscomb. 1972. *The History of Kenya Agriculture.* Nairobi: University Press of Africa.

Constitution of Kenya Review Commission (CKRC). 2003. "Plenary Proceedings, Presentation of Draft Bill, Chapter 11 (Land and Property Rights), Held at Bomas of Kenya on 27th May 2003." Nairobi.

Constitution of Kenya Review Commission (CKRC), Kenya National Constitutional Conference. 2004 (March 15). "The Draft Constitution of Kenya 2004." Nairobi.

Consultative Group for International Agricultural Research (CGIAR), International Potato Center, 2006. Kenya land map, http://www.cipotato.org/DIVA/data/DataServer.htm, accessed May 31, 2006.

Cory, Hans. 1947. "Land Tenure in Bukuria." *Tanganyika Notes and Records* 23:70–79.

———. 1953. *Sukuma Law and Custom.* London: Oxford University Press.

———. 1955. *Sheria na Kawaida za Wanyamwezi* (Nyamwezi Law and Custom). Dar es Salaam, Tanganyika: Government Printer.

Coulanges, Fustel de. 1980. *The Origin of Property in Land.* London: George Allen and Unwin.

Cowen, Michael P., and R. W. Shenton. 1991. "Bankers, Peasants, and Land in British West Africa 1905–37." *Journal of Peasant Studies* 19(1):26–58.

Crazzolara, J.P. 1950, 1951, 1954. *The Lwoo*, Part I: *Lwoo Migrations*. Part II: *Luo Traditions*. Part III: *Clans*. Verona: Museum Combonianum.

Dakeyne, R. B. 1962. "The Pattern of Settlement in Central Nyanza, Kenya." *Australian Geographer* 8(4):183–91.

Darling, (Sir) Malcolm Lyall. 1947. *The Punjab Peasant in Prosperity and Debt*, 4th ed. Bombay: Oxford University Press. Orig. pub. 1925.

David, Martin, and Peter Wyeth. 1978. *Kenya Commercial Bank Loans in Rural Areas: A Survey*. University of Nairobi: Institute of Development Studies, Working Paper 342A.

Davison, Jean, ed. 1988. *Agriculture, Women, and Land: The African Experience*. Boulder, Colo.: Westview.

———. 1996. *Voices from Mutira: Lives of Kikuyu Women*. Boulder, Colo.: Lynne Rienner.

Dawkins, Louisa (pseudonym). 1985. *Natives and Strangers*. Boston: Houghton Mifflin.

Deininger, Klaus. 2003. *Land Policies for Growth and Poverty Reduction: A World Bank Policy Research Report*. Oxford and Washington, D.C.: Oxford University Press and the World Bank.

Denman, D. R. 1958. *Origins of Ownership: A Brief History of Land Ownership and Tenure in England from Earliest Times to the Modern Era*. London: George Allen and Unwin.

Deschamps, Jean-Jacques, Peter Castro, Michael Caughlin, Peg Clement, and Dick Howes. 1989. "Impact Evaluation of Kenya Agriculture Sector I Project." Washington, D.C.: Development Alternatives; and Binghamton, N.Y.: Institute for Development Anthropology.

Dickerman, Carol W. 1987. *Security of Tenure and Land Registration in Africa: Literature Review and Synthesis*. LTC Paper 137. Madison: Land Tenure Center, University of Wisconsin.

Dietler, Michael, and Ingrid Herbich. 1998. "*Habitus*, Techniques, Style: An Integrated Approach to the Social Understanding of Material Culture and Boundaries." In Miriam T. Stark, ed., *The Anthropology of Social Boundaries*, pp. 232–29. Washington, D.C.: Smithsonian Institution Press.

Downie, Leonard Jr. 1975. *Mortgage on America*. New York: Praeger.

Downs, Richard E., and S. P. Reyna. 1988. *Land and Society in Contemporary Africa*. Hanover, N.H.: University Press of New England.

Driberg, Joseph H. 1923. *The Lango: A Nilotic Tribe of Uganda*. London: T. Fisher Unwin.

Dudley, Kathryn Marie. 2000. *Debt and Dispossession: Farm Loss in America's Heartland*. Chicago: University of Chicago Press.

Duly, Leslie Clement. 1968. *British Land Policy at the Cape, 1795–1844: A Study of Administrative Procedures in the Empire*. Durham, N.C.: Duke University Press.

Dundas, K. R. 1913. "The Wawanga and Other Tribes of the Elgon District, British East Africa." *Journal of the Royal Anthropological Institute* 43:19–75.

Durkheim, Emile. 1964. *The Division of Labor in Society,* trans. George Simpson. New York: Free Press. Orig. pub. 1893.

East Africa Protectorate. 1913–14. *Annual Report.* London: Author.

Edelman, Marc, and Angelique Haugerud, eds. 2005. *The Anthropology of Development and Globalization: From Classical Political Economy to Contemporary Neoliberalism.* Oxford, U.K., and Malden, Mass.: Blackwell.

Ehret, Christopher. 1971. *Southern Nilotic History: Linguistic Approaches to the Study of the Past.* Evanston, Ill.: Northwestern University Press.

———. 1976. "Aspects of Social and Economic Change in Western Kenya, c. A.D. 500–1800." In B. A. Ogot, ed., *Kenya Before 1900,* pp. 1–20. Nairobi: East African Publishing House.

Elkins, Caroline. 2005. *Imperial Reckoning: The Untold Story of Britain's Gulag in Kenya.* New York: Owl Books.

Engels, Friederich. 1972. *The Origin of the Family, Private Property, and the State.* New York: International Publishers. Orig. pub. 1884.

Ensminger, Jean. 1997. "Changing Property Rights: Reconciling Formal and Informal Rights to Land in Africa." In John N. Drobak and John V. C. Nye, eds., *Frontiers of the New Institutional Economics,* pp. 165–98. New York: Academic Press.

Etzioni, Amitai, and Eva Etzioni-Harvey. 1964. *Social Change.* New York: Basic Books.

Evans-Pritchard, Edward E. 1940. *The Nuer.* Oxford: Oxford University Press.

———. 1950. "Ghostly Vengeance among the Luo of Kenya." *Man* 50(133):86–87.

———. 1951. *Kinship and Marriage among the Nuer.* Oxford: Clarendon Press.

———. 1965. "Luo Tribes and Clans." In Edward E. Evans-Pritchard, *The Position of Women in Primitive Societies and Other Essays in Social Anthropology,* pp. 205–27. London: Free Press. Orig. pub. 1949.

Fay, Derick, and Deborah James, eds. 2008. *"Restoring What Was Ours": The Rights and Wrongs of Land Restitution.* London: Routledge-Cavendish.

Fearn, Hugh. 1961. *An African Economy: A Study of the Economic Development of the Nyanza Province of Kenya, 1903–1953.* London: Oxford University Press.

Feder, Gershon, and Klaus Deininger. 1999. "Land Institutions and Land Markets." Working Paper. Washington, D.C.: World Bank.

Feder, Gershon, Tongroj Onchan, Yongyuth Chalamwong, and Chira Hongladarom, 1988. *Land Policies and Farm Productivity in Thailand.* Baltimore: Johns Hopkins University Press, for the World Bank.

Ferguson, James. 1990. *The Anti-Politics Machine: "Development," Depoliticization, and Bureaucratic Power in Lesotho.* Cambridge: Cambridge University Press.

Fine, John V. A. 1951. *Horoi: Studies in Mortgage, Real Security, and Land Tenure in Ancient Athens. Hesperia Supplements,* vol. 9. Athens: American School of Classical Studies at Athens.

Finley, Moses. 1952. *Studies in Land and Credit in Ancient Athens, 500–200 B.C.: The Horos Inscriptions.* New Brunswick, N.J.: Rutgers University Press.

Firmin-Sellers, Kathryn, and Patrick Sellers. 1999. "Expected Failures and Unexpected Successes of Land Titling in Africa." *World Development* 27(7):1115–28.

Fisiy, Cyprian. 1992. *Power and Privilege in the Administration of Law: Land Law Reforms and Social Differentiation in Cameroon.* Leiden: African Studies Center.

Fleming, Robin. 1998. *Domesday Book and the Law: Society and Custom in Early Medieval England.* Cambridge: Cambridge University Press.

Fleuret, Anne. 1988. "Some Consequences of Tenure and Agrarian Reform in Taita, Kenya." In R. E. Downs and S. P. Reyna, eds., *Land and Society in Contemporary Africa,* pp. 136–58. Hanover, N.H.: University Press of New England.

Fortes, Meyer. 1945. *The Dynamics of Clanship among the Tallensi.* London: Oxford University Press.

Fourie, Clarissa. 2004. "Land Readjustment for Peri-Urban Customary Tenure: The Example of Botswana." In Robert Home and Hilary Lim, eds., *Demystifying the Mystery of Capital: Land Tenure and Poverty in Africa and the Caribbean,* pp. 31–49. London and Portland, Ore.: Cavendish.

Francis, Elizabeth. 2000. *Making a Living: Changing Livelihoods in Rural Africa.* London: Routledge.

Furness, Eric L. 1975. *Money and Credit in Developing Africa.* London: Heinemann.

Gennep, Arnold van. 1960. *The Rites of Passage.* Chicago: University of Chicago Press. Orig. pub. 1908.

George, Henry. 1938. *Progress and Poverty.* New York: Robert Schalkenbach Foundation. Orig. pub. 1879.

George, Susan. 1988. *A Fate Worse than Debt.* New York: Grove Weidenfeld.

Gerhart, John. 1975. *The Diffusion of Hybrid Maize in Western Kenya.* Mexico City: International Maize and Wheat Improvement Center.

Geschiere, Peter, and Stephen Jackson, eds. 2006a. *Autochthony and the Crisis of Citizenship. African Studies Review* 49(2), special issue.

———. 2006b. "Autochthony and the Crisis of Citizenship: Democratization, Decentralization, and the Politics of Belonging" (Introduction). *African Studies Review* 49(2):1–7.

Gilbert, Jérémie. 2006. *Indigenous Peoples' Land Rights Under International Law: From Victims to Actors.* Ardsley, N.Y.: Transnational Publishers.

Girard, René. 1972. *Violence and the Sacred,* trans. Patrick Gregory. Baltimore: Johns Hopkins University Press.

Glanville, Ranulf de (attrib.). 1932. *Tractatus de Legibus et Consuetudinibus Regni Angliae,* ed. G. E. Woodbine. New Haven: Yale University Press. Orig. pub. c. 1187.

Glazier, Jack. 1985. *Land and the Uses of Tradition among the Mbeere of Kenya.* Lanham, Md.: University Press of America.

Glickman, Maurice. 1974. "Patriliny Among the Gusii and Luo of Kenya."
    American Anthropologist 76:312–18.
Gluckman, Max. 1963. *Custom and Conflict in Africa*. Oxford: Basil Blackwell.
    Orig. pub. 1956.
————. 1965. *The Ideas in Barotse Jurisprudence*. New Haven: Yale University
    Press.
Goheen, Miriam. 1988. "Land Accumulation and Local Control: The
    Manipulation of Symbols and Power in Nso, Cameroon." In Richard E. Downs
    and S. P. Reyna, eds., *Land and Society in Contemporary Africa*, pp. 281–301.
    Hanover, N.H.: University Press of New England.
————. 1996. *Men Own the Fields, Women Own the Crops: Gender and Power in the
    Cameroonian Grassfields*. Madison: University of Wisconsin Press.
Goheen, Miriam, and Parker Shipton, eds. 1992. *Rights over Land: Categories
    and Controversies*. Special issue of *Africa* (Journal of the International African
    Institute) 62(3).
Goldenberg, David. 1982. *We Are All Brothers: The Suppression of Consciousness
    of Socio-Economic Differentiation in a Kenya Luo Lineage*. Ph.D. thesis, Brown
    University. Ann Arbor, Mich.: University Microfilms.
Goody, Jack. 1977. "Population and Polity in the Voltaic Region." In J. Friedman
    and M. J. Rowlands, eds., *The Evolution of Social Systems*. London: Duckworth.
Grandia, Liza. Forthcoming. *Unsettling: The Repeated Dispossessions of the Q'eqchi'
    Maya and New Frontiers of Enclosure*.
Greene, Joy. 1987. "Evaluating the Impact of Consolidation of Holdings,
    Individualization of Tenure, and Registration of Title: Lessons from Kenya."
    LTC Paper 129. Madison: Land Tenure Center, University of Wisconsin.
Greene, Sandra. 2002. *Sacred Sites and the Colonial Encounter: A History of
    Meaning and Memory in Ghana*. Bloomington and Indianapolis: Indiana
    University Press.
Griffith-Charles, Charisse. 2004. "Trinidad: 'We Are Not Squatters, We Are
    Settlers.'" In Robert Home and Hilary Lim, eds., *Demystifying the Mystery
    of Capital: Land Tenure and Poverty in Africa and the Caribbean*, pp. 99–119.
    London and Portland, Ore.: Cavendish.
Grosh, Barbara. 1987. "Performance of Financial Parastatals in Kenya, 1964–84."
    Working Paper 449, Institute of Development Studies, University of Nairobi.
Gulliver, Phillip H. 1958. *Land Tenure and Social Change among the Nyakyusa*. East
    African Studies 11. Kampala: East African Institute of Social Research.
Hailey, William Malcolm, First Baron. 1957. *An African Survey*. London: Oxford
    University Press, for Royal Institute of International Affairs. Orig. pub. 1938.
Håkansson, Thomas. 1988. *Bridewealth, Women, and Land: Social Change among
    the Gusii of Kenya*. Stockholm: Almqvist and Wiksell.
Hanson, Holly. 2003. *Landed Obligation: The Practice of Power in Buganda*.
    Portsmouth, N.H.: Heinemann.
Hardin, Garrett. 1968. "The Tragedy of the Commons." *Science* 162:1243–48.

Hart, Keith. 1982. *The Political Economy of West African Agriculture*. Cambridge: Cambridge University Press.

Hauge, Hans-egil. 1974. *Luo Religion and Folklore*. Oslo: Universitetsforlaget.

Haugerud, Angelique. 1983. "The Consequences of Land Tenure Reform Among Smallholders in the Kenyan Highlands." *Rural Africana* 15–16:65–89.

————. 1989. "Land Tenure and Agrarian Change in Kenya." *Africa* (Journal of the International African Institute) 59(1):61–90.

————. 1995. *The Culture of Politics in Modern Kenya*. Cambridge: Cambridge University Press.

Hay, Margaret Jean. 1972. *Economic Change in Luoland: Kowe, 1890–1945*. Ph.D. thesis, University of Wisconsin.

————. 1982. "Women as Owners, Occupants and Managers of Property in Colonial Western Kenya." In M. J. Hay and Marcia Wright, eds., *African Women and the Law: Historical Perspectives*, pp. 110–23. Boston: Boston University African Studies Center.

Hegel, Georg. 1967. *Hegel's Philosophy of Right*, trans. and ed. T. M. Knox. London, Oxford, and New York: Oxford University Press. Orig. pub. 1821.

Herbich, Ingrid, and Michael Dietler. 1993. "Space, Time and Symbolic Structure in the Luo Homestead: An Ethnoarchaeological Study of 'Settlement Biography' in Africa." In Juraj Pavúk, ed., *Actes du XIIe Congrès International des Sciences Préhistoriques et Protohistoriques*, Bratislava, Czechoslovakia, September 1-7, 1991, Vol. I, pp. 26–32. Nitra: Archaeological Institute of the Slovak Academy of Sciences.

Herring, Ralph. 1976. "The Influence of Climate on the Migrations of the Central and Southern Luo." In B. A. Ogot, ed., *Ecology and History in East Africa*. *Hadith* 7, pp. 77–107. Nairobi: Kenya Literature Bureau.

Herring, R. S., D. W. Cohen, and B. A. Ogot. 1984. "The Construction of Dominance: The Strategies of Selected Luo Groups in Uganda and Kenya." In Ahmed Ida Salim, ed., *State Formation in Eastern Africa*, pp. 126–61. Nairobi, London, and Ibadan: Heinemann Educational Books.

Herz, Barbara Knapp. 1974. *Demographic Pressure and Economic Change: The Case of Kenyan Land Reforms*. Ph.D. thesis, Yale University.

Hill, Polly. 1982. *Dry Grain Farming Families: Hausaland (Nigeria) and Karnataka (India) Compared*. Cambridge: Cambridge University Press.

Hobbes, Thomas. 1984. *De Cive*, English version. Oxford: Oxford University Press. Orig. pub. 1641.

————. 1998. *Leviathan*. Oxford: Oxford University Press. Orig. pub. 1651.

Hoben, Allan. 1973. *Land Tenure Among the Amhara: The Dynamics of Cognatic Descent*. Chicago: University of Chicago Press.

————. 1988. "The Political Economy of Land Tenure in Somalia." In Richard Downs and S. P. Reyna, eds., *Land and Society in Contemporary Africa*, pp. 192–220. Hanover, N.H.: University Press of New England.

Hobley, C. W. 1902. "Nilotic Tribes of Kavirondo." In *Eastern Uganda: An*

Ethnological Survey. Royal Anthropological Institute Occasional Papers, no. 1, 26–35.

———. 1903. "Anthropological Studies in Kavirondo and Nandi." *Journal of the Anthropological Institute of Great Britain and Ireland* 33:325–59.

Hobsbawm, Eric, and Terence O. Ranger, eds. 1983. *The Invention of Tradition*. Cambridge: Cambridge University Press.

Hobson, John Atkinson. 1937. *Property and Improperty*. London: Gollancz.

Hoehler-Fatton, Cynthia. 1996. *Women of Fire and Spirit: History, Faith, and Gender in Roho Religion in Western Kenya*. Oxford and New York: Oxford University Press.

Holmes, Jane Teresa. 2000. *A Home for the Kager: Negotiating Tribal Identities in Colonial Kenya*. Ph. D. thesis, University of Virginia.

Home, Robert. 2004. "Outside de Soto's Bell Jar: Colonial/Postcolonial Land Law and the Exclusion of the Urban Poor." In Robert Home and Hilary Lim, eds., *Demystifying the Mystery of Capital: Land Tenure and Poverty in Africa and the Caribbean*, pp. 11–29. London and Portland, Ore.: Cavendish.

Home, Robert, and Hilary Lim, eds. 2004. *Demystifying the Mystery of Capital: Land Tenure and Poverty in Africa and the Caribbean*. London and Portland, Ore.: Cavendish.

Hudson, Michael, and Baruch Levine, eds. 1996. *Privatization in the Ancient Near East and Classical World*. Peabody Museum Bulletin 5. Cambridge, Mass.: Peabody Museum of Archaeology and Anthropology, Harvard University.

———, eds. 1999. *Urbanization and Land Ownership in the Ancient Near East*. Peabody Museum Bulletin 7. Cambridge, Mass.: Peabody Museum of Archaeology and Anthropology, Harvard University.

Human Rights Watch. 1994. "Multipartyism Betrayed in Kenya." *Newsletter* 6, no. 5. New York: Human Rights Watch.

Humphrey, Norman. 1947. *The Liguru and the Land: Sociological Aspects of Some Agricultural Problems in North Kavirondo*. Nairobi: Government Printer.

Huxley, Elspeth. 1960. *A New Earth: An Experiment in Colonialism*. London: Chatto and Windus.

Hyden, Goran. 1983. *No Shortcuts to Progress: African Development Management in Perspective*. Berkeley: University of California Press.

Ingham, J. H., E. J. A. Leslie, D. O'Hagan, T. L. Hately, C. L. Todd, P. C. Chambers, and E. W. Mathu. 1950. Colony and Protectorate of Kenya: *Report of Committee on Agricultural Credit for Africans*. Nairobi: Government Printer.

International Labour Organization (ILO). 1972. *Employment, Incomes, and Inequality in Kenya*. Geneva: ILO.

Isichei, Elizabeth. 2002. *Voices of the Poor in Africa: Moral Economy and the Popular Imagination*. Rochester, N.Y.: University of Rochester Press.

Johnson, Steven Lee. 1980. *Production, Exchange, and Economic Development Among the Luo-Abasuba of Southwestern Kenya*. Ph.D. thesis, Indiana University. Ann Arbor, Mich.: University Microfilms.

Johnston, Sir Harry. 1904. *The Uganda Protectorate*, vol. 2. London: Hutchinson and Co.

Juma, Calestous, and J. B. Ojwang, eds. 1996. *In Land We Trust: Environment, Private Property and Constitutional Change*. Nairobi and London: Initiatives Publishers and Zed Books.

Juul, Kristine, and Christian Lund, eds. 2002. *Negotiating Property in Africa*. Portsmouth, N.H.: Heinemann.

Kangwa, John. 2004. "Zambia: 'Having a Place of Your Own' in Kitwe." In Robert Home and Hilary Lim, eds., *Demystifying the Mystery of Capital: Land Tenure and Poverty in Africa and the Caribbean*, pp. 121–43. London and Portland, Ore.: Cavendish.

Kanogo, Tabitha. 1987. *Squatters and the Roots of Mau Mau, 1905–1963*. Athens, Ohio: Ohio University Press.

Kanyinga, Karuti. 1998. *The Land Question in Kenya: Struggles, Accumulation and Changing Politics*. Ph.D. thesis. Roskilde, Denmark: Roskilde University.

Kenny, Michael. 1977. "The Relation of Oral History to Social Structure in South Nyanza District, Kenya." *Africa* (Journal of the International African Institute) 47:276–88.

——. 1982. "The Stranger from the Lake: A Theme in the History of the Lake Victoria Shorelands." *Azania* 17:1–26.

Kenya. *Annual Reports*. Nairobi: Government Printer.

Kenya. *Laws of Kenya*. Nairobi: Government Printer.

Kenya. 1966–89. *Kenya Development Plans* for 1966–70, 1974–78, 1979–83, 1989–93. Nairobi: Government Printer.

Kenya. 1992. *Report of the Parliamentary Select Committee to Investigate Ethnic Clashes in Western and Other Parts of Kenya*. Nairobi: Government Printer.

Kenya, Central Bureau of Statistics. 1979, 1989, 1999 *Population Census*. Nairobi: Government Printer.

Kenya, Economics and Statistics Division. 1962. *African Agricultural Sample Census 1960–1*. Nairobi: Government Printer.

Kenya, Ministry of Economic Planning; Central Bureau of Statistics. *Economic Surveys*. Annual. Nairobi: Government Printer.

Kenya, Ministry of Economic Planning. 1979. *South Nyanza District Development Plan, 1979–1983*. Nairobi: Government Printer.

——. *Kenya Statistical Abstracts*. Annual. Nairobi: Government Printer.

Kenya, Ministry of Lands and Settlement. 1969. *The Land Control Act, 1967: A Handbook for the Guidance of Land Control Boards*. Nairobi.

Kenya, Working Party on African Land Tenure. 1958. *Report, 1957–1958*. Nairobi: Government Printer.

Kenya Land Commission. 1934a. *Evidence and Memoranda*. United Kingdom Colonial Office (Col. 91). London: HMSO.

——. 1934b. *Report*. United Kingdom Colonial Office (Cmd. 4556). London: HMSO.

Kenya Landowners Federation. 2007. "Overview of the Draft National Land

Policy (DNLP)." http://www.mng5.com/papers/klfOverview.pdf; accessed July 13, 2007.

Kenya National Land Policy Secretariat. 2007a. "Kenya Draft National Land Policy: The Formulation Process." *Daily Nation* [Kenya], April 19, 2007.

———. 2007b. "Draft National Land Policy." Nairobi: Ministry of Lands. http://www.ardhi.go.ke/onflydocuments/Draft%20NLP.pdf; accessed July 13, 2007.

Kershaw, Greet. 1997. *Mau Mau from Below*. Athens, Ohio: Ohio University Press.

Kikiro, Amos, and Calestous Juma, eds. 1991. *Gaining Ground: Institutional Innovations in Land-Use Management in Kenya*. Nairobi: African Center for Technology Studies.

Killick, Tony, et al., eds. 1984. *The IMF and Stabilization: Developing Country Experiences*. London: Heinemann Educational Books.

Kisumu Native Chamber of Commerce. 1934. Memorandum to Kenya Land Commission. Kenya Land Commission. *Evidence and Memoranda*, 2144-7. United Kingdom Colonial Office (Col. 91). London: HMSO.

Kitching, Gavin. 1980. *Class and Economic Change in Kenya*. New Haven: Yale University Press.

Klopp, Jacqueline. 2002. Can Moral Ethnicity Trump Political Tribalism? The Struggle for Land and Nation in Kenya. *African Studies* 61(2):269–94.

———. 2006. "Kenya's Internally Displaced: Managing Civil Conflict in Democratic Transition." In Dorina A. Bekoe, ed., *East Africa and the Horn: Confronting Challenges to Good Governance*, pp. 59–80. Boulder, Colo.: Lynne Rienner.

Kuper, Adam. 1982. "Lineage Theory: A Critical Retrospect." *Annual Review of Anthropology* 11:71–95.

La Fontaine, Jean. 1959. *The Gisu of Uganda*. Ethnographic Survey of Africa, Eastern Central Africa 10. London: International African Institute.

Lawrance, J. C. D. 1966. Kenya Mission on Land Consolidation and Registration, *Report, 1965–1966*. Nairobi: Government Printer.

Leakey, Louis S. B., and Walter Edwin Owen. 1945. *A Contribution to the Study of the Tumbian Culture in East Africa*. Corydon Museum, Occasional Paper no. 1 (March).

Leakey, Louis S. B., Walter Edwin Owen, and M. D. Leakey. 1948. *Dimple-Based Pottery from Central Kavirondo, Kenya Colony*. Corydon Museum, Occasional Paper no. 2 (May).

Leo, Christopher. 1984. *Land and Class in Kenya*. Toronto: University of Toronto Press.

Lesorogol, Carolyn K. 2008. *Contesting the Commons: Privatizing Pastoral Lands in Kenya*. Ann Arbor: University of Michigan Press.

LeVine, Robert A. 1962a. "Wealth and Power in Gusiiland." In Paul Bohannan and George Dalton, eds., *Markets in Africa*, pp. 520–36. Evanston, Ill.: Northwestern University Press.

———. 1962b. "Witchcraft and Co-Wife Proximity in Southwestern Kenya." *Ethnology* 1(1):39–45.

————. 1964. "The Gusii Family." In R. F. Gray and P. H. Gulliver, *The Family Estate in Africa*. London: Routledge and Kegan Paul.

LeVine, Robert A., and Donald T. Campbell. 1972. *Ethnocentrism: Theories of Conflict, Ethnic Attitudes, and Group Behavior*. New York: John Wiley and Sons.

LeVine, Robert A., and Barbara LeVine. 1966. *Nyansongo: A Gusii Community in Kenya*. New York: John Wiley.

Lewis, Ioan M. 1965. "Problems in the Comparative Study of Unilineal Descent." In Michael Banton, ed., *The Relevance of Models for Social Anthropology* (A. S. A. Monograph 1), pp. 87–112. London: Tavistock.

————. 1981. *Somali Culture, History, and Social Institutions: An Introductory Guide to the Somali Democratic Republic*. London: London School of Economics and Political Science.

————. 1999. *A Pastoral Democracy: A Study of Pastoralism and Politics Among Northern Somalia of the Horn of Africa*. London: International African Institute, Lit Verlag, and James Currey. Orig. pub. 1961.

Leys, Colin. 1975. *Underdevelopment in Kenya*. London: Heinemann.

Lienhardt, Godfrey. 1975. "Getting Your Own Back: Some Themes in Nilotic Myth." In John Beattie and Godfrey Lienhardt, eds., *Studies in Social Anthropology*, pp. 213–37. Oxford: Clarendon.

Lim, Hilary. 2004. "Inheritance, HIV/AIDS and Children's Rights to Land." In Robert Home and Hilary Lim, eds., *Demystifying the Mystery of Capital: Land Tenure and Poverty in Africa*, pp. 51–72. London and Portland, Ore.: Cavendish.

Little, Peter D. 1992. *The Elusive Granary: Farmers, Herders, and the State in Northern Kenya*. Cambridge: Cambridge University Press.

————. 2003. *Somalia: Economy Without State*. Bloomington: Indiana University Press.

Little, Peter D., and Michael Watts, eds. 1994. *Living Under Contract: Contract Farming and Agrarian Transformation in Sub-Saharan Africa*. Madison: University of Wisconsin Press.

Liversage, V. 1945. *Land Tenure in the Colonies*. Cambridge: Cambridge University Press.

Locke, John. 1952. *The Second Treatise of Government*. New York: Liberal Arts Press. Orig. pub. 1690.

Long, Norman. 1977. *Introduction to the Sociology of Rural Development*. London: Tavistock.

Lonsdale, John. 1964. *A Political History of Nyanza, 1883–1945*. Ph.D. thesis, Cambridge University.

————. 1968. "Some Origins of Nationalism in East Africa." *Journal of African History* 9(1):119–46.

————. 1971. "Rural Resistance and Mass Political Mobilization Amongst the Luo." Commission Internationale d'Histoire des Mouvements Sociaux et des Structures Sociales, *Mouvements Nationaux d'Indépendance et Classes Populaires aux XIXe et XXe Siècles en Occident et en Orient*, Tome II. Paris: Armand Colin.

Lonsdale, John, and Bruce Berman. 1992. *Unhappy Valley: Conflict in Kenya and Africa*. 2 vols. London: James Currey.

Lugard, F. J. D. 1965. *The Dual Mandate in British Tropical Africa*. London: Frank Cass & Co. Ltd. Orig. pub. 1922.

Macfarlane, Alan. 1978. *The Origins of English Individualism*. Oxford: Basil Blackwell.

———. 1987. *The Culture of Capitalism*. Oxford: Basil Blackwell.

Machyo, B. Chango. 1969. "Land Tenure and Economic Development." In James Obol-Ochola, ed., *Land Law Reform in East Africa*, pp. 96–114. Kampala: National Trust Adult Education Centre.

Mackenzie, Fiona. 1986. "Local Initiatives and National Policy: Gender and Agricultural Change in Murang'a District, Kenya." *Canadian Journal of African Studies* 20(3):377–401.

———. 1993. "A Piece of Land Never Shrinks: Reconceptualizing Land Tenure in a Smallholding District, Kenya." in T. J. Bassett and D. E. Crummey, eds., *Land in African Agrarian Systems*, pp. 194–221. Madison: University of Wisconsin Press.

———. 1998. *Land, Ecology and Resistance in Kenya, 1880–1952*. Portsmouth, N.H.: Heinemann, for the International African Institute.

MacPherson, Crawford Brough. 1962. *The Political Theory of Possessive Individualism: Hobbes to Locke*. Oxford: Clarendon Press.

———, ed. 1978. *Property: Mainstream and Critical Positions*. Toronto: University of Toronto Press.

Maine, Henry Sumner. 1986. *Ancient Law*. Tucson: University of Arizona Press. Orig. pub. 1861.

Maini, Krishan M. 1967. *Land Law in East Africa*. Nairobi: Oxford University Press.

———. 1969. *A Guide to Registration of Title Practice*. Nairobi: East African Literature Bureau.

Mair, Lucy. 1969. *Anthropology and Social Change*. London School of Economics Monographs on Social Anthropology, no. 38. London and New York: Athlone and Humanities Press.

Maitland, Frederic William. 1897. *Domesday and Beyond: Three Essays in the Early History of England*. Cambridge: Cambridge University Press.

Malcolm, Donald Wingfield. 1953. *Sukumaland: An African People and Their Country*. London: Oxford University Press, for the International African Institute.

Malengreau, Guy. 1947. "De l'accession des indigènes à la propriété foncière individuelle." *Zaïre* (February): 235–70, 399–434.

Malmberg, Torsten. 1980. *Human Territoriality*. The Hague: Mouton.

Malo, Shadrack. 1953. *Dhoudi Mag Central Nyanza*. Nairobi: Eagle Press.

Manji, Ambreena. 2006. *The Politics of Land Reform in Africa: From Communal Tenure to Free Markets*. London and New York: Zed Books.

Manners, Robert A. 1972. "The Kipsigis of Kenya: Culture Change in a 'Model'

East African Tribe." In Julian Steward, ed., *Three African Tribes in Transition*, pp. 207–360. Urbana, Chicago, London: University of Illinois Press. Orig. pub. 1967.

Marco Surveys Ltd. (for Kenya Ministry of Labour and Social Services). 1965. *A Baseline Survey of Factors Affecting Agricultural Development in Three Areas of Kenya (Samia, Kabondo, Bomet)*. Nairobi: Marco Surveys Ltd.

Marende, Kenneth Otiato. 1978. *The Role of Credit in Kenya's Agricultural Industry: A Case Study of the AFC (with special Reference to Vihiga Division)*. L.L.B. thesis, University of Nairobi.

Marshall, Alfred. 1929. *Money, Credit and Commerce*. London: Macmillan. Orig. pub. 1923.

Marx, Karl. 1906. *Capital* (Vol. 1): *A Critique of Political Economy*, ed. Frederick Engels. New York: Random House. Orig. pub. 1867.

———. 1963. *The Eighteenth Brumaire of Louis Bonaparte*. New York: International Publishers. Orig. pub. 1852.

———. 1976. *Capital* (Vol. 3): *The Process of Capitalist Production as a Whole*, ed. Frederick Engels. New York: International Publishers. Orig. pub. 1894.

Maurer, Bill. 2006. *Pious Property: Islamic Mortgages in the United States*. New York: Russell Sage Foundation.

Mauss, Marcel. 1967. *The Gift: Forms and Functions of Exchange in Archaic Societies*. New York: W.W. Norton. Orig. pub. 1925.

Mayer, Philip. 1949. "The Lineage Principle in Gusii Society." International African Institute Memorandum 24. London: Oxford University Press.

———. 1951. *Two Studies in Applied Anthropology in Kenya*. Colonial Research Studies 3. London: HMSO.

Mayer, Philip, and Iona Mayer. 1965. "Land Law in the Making." In Hilda Kuper and Leo Kuper, eds., *African Law*. Berkeley: University of California Press.

Mbogoh, S. G. (misattrib.) 1986a. "Production Systems and Labour." In Kenya Ministry of Economic Planning and Development, and University of Nairobi, Institute of African Studies, *District Socio-Cultural Profiles Project: South Nyanza District*, pp. 28–37. Nairobi.

———. (misattrib.) 1986b. "Land Tenure." In Kenya Ministry of Economic Planning and Development, and University of Nairobi, Institute of African Studies, *District Socio-Cultural Profiles Project: South Nyanza District*, pp. 38–50. Nairobi.

Mboya, Paul. 1938. *Luo: Kitgi gi Timbegi*. Kisumu and Nairobi: Anyange Press and East African Standard.

———. 1978. *"Richo Ema Kelo Chira"* (booklet). Nairobi: East African Publishing House.

McEntee, Peter D. 1960. "Improved Farming in the Central Nyanza District, Kenya Colony." *Journal of African Administration* 12(2):68–73.

Médard, Claire. 1999. *Territoires de l'Ethnicité: Encadrement, Revendications et Conflits Territoriaux au Kenya*. Doctoral thesis, University of Paris I (Pantheon-Sorbonne).

Meek, Charles Kingsley. 1946. *Land Law and Custom in the Colonies.* London: Oxford University Press.

Migot-Adholla, Shem Edwin. 1977. *Migration and Rural Differentiation in Kenya.* Ph.D. thesis, University of California at Los Angeles.

Millikin, A. S. 1906. "Burial Customs of the Wa-Kavirondo of the Kisumu Province." *Man* 6:54–55.

Mises, Ludwig Von. 1949. *Human Action: A Treatise on Economics.* New Haven: Yale University Press. Orig. pub. in 1940 as *Nazionalöconomie: Theorie des Handelns und Wirtschaftens.*

———. 1981. *The Theory of Money and Credit.* Trans. H. E. Batson. Indianapolis: Liberty Classics. Orig. pub. 1934.

Mkangi, G. C. 1983. *The Social Cost of Small Families and Land Tenure Reform: A Case Study of the Wataita of Kenya.* New York: Pergamon.

Molebatsi, Chadzimula. 2004. "Botswana: 'Self-Allocation,' 'Accommodation,' and 'Zero Tolerance' in Mogoditshane and Old Naledi." In Robert Home and Hilary Lim, eds., *Demystifying the Mystery of Capital: Land Tenure and Poverty in Africa and the Caribbean,* pp. 73–97. London and Portland, Ore.: Cavendish.

Moock, Joyce L. 1976. *The Migration Process and Differential Economic Behaviour in South Maragoli, Western Kenya.* Ph.D. thesis, Columbia University.

Moock, Peter Russell. 1973. *Managerial Ability in Small-Farm Production: An Analysis of Maize Yields in the Vihiga District of Kenya.* Ph.D. thesis, Columbia University.

Moore, Barrington Jr. 1966. *Social Origins of Dictatorship and Democracy: Lord and Peasant in the Making of the Modern World.* Boston: Beacon.

Moore, J. E. 1971. "Rural Population Carrying Capacities for the Districts of Tanzania." Research Paper 18. University of Dar es Salaam: Bureau of Resource Assessment and Land Use Planning.

Moore, Sally Falk. 1978. *Law as Process: An Anthropological Approach.* London: Routledge.

———. 1986. *Social Facts and Fabrications: "Customary" Law on Kilimanjaro, 1880–1980.* Cambridge: Cambridge University Press.

———. 1998. "Changing African Land Tenure: Reflections on the Incapacities of the State." *European Journal of Development Research* 10(2):33–49.

Morgan, Lewis Henry. 1964. *Ancient Society.* Cambridge: Harvard University Press. Orig. pub. 1877.

Moritz, Mark, ed. 2006. "Introduction: Changing Contexts and Dynamics of Herder-Farmer Conflicts Across West Africa." *Canadian Journal of African Studies,* Special Issue 40(1):1–40.

Mueller, Susanne. 2008. "The Political Economy of Kenya's crisis." *Journal of Eastern African Studies* 2(2):185–210.

Mukwaya, A. B. 1953. *Land Tenure in Buganda.* Dar es Salaam, Kampala, Nairobi: Eagle Press.

Mullei, Andrew K., and Joshua M. Ng'elu. 1990. "Evolution, Structure and performance of Kenya's Financial System." *Savings and Development* 3(14):265–83.

Murray, Colin. 1992. *Black Mountain: Land, Class and Power in the Eastern Orange Free State, 1880s to 1980s.* Washington, D.C.: Smithsonian Press.

Nabudere, Dani Wadada. 1989. *The Crash of International Financial Capital and Its Implications for the Third World.* Harare: Southern Africa Political Economy Series (SAPES) Trust.

Nakabayashi, Nabuhiro. 1981. "The Clan System and Social Change in Modern Isukha." In Nobuhiro Nagashima, ed., *Themes in Socio-Cultural Ideas and Behaviour Among the Six Ethnic Groups of Kenya,* pp. 12–42. Kunitachi, Tokyo: Hitotsubashi University.

National Council of Churches of Kenya. 1992. *The Cursed Arrow: Organized Violence against Democracy in Kenya.* Nairobi.

Native Catholic Union of Kavirondo. 1934. Memorandum. In Kenya Land Commission, *Evidence and Memoranda* (Col. 91), 3:2147. London: HMSO.

Needham, Rodney. 1971. "Remarks on the Analysis of Kinship and Marriage." In R. Needham, ed., *Rethinking Kinship and Marriage,* pp. 1–34. London: Tavistock.

———, ed. 1973. *Right and Left: Essays on Dual Symbolic Classification.* Chicago: University of Chicago Press.

———. 1975. "Polythetic Classification." *Man* (new series) 10:349–67.

Neeson, J. M. 1993. *Commoners: Common Right, Enclosure and Social Change in England, 1700–1820.* Cambridge: Cambridge University Press.

Ngugi wa Thiong'o (James Ngugi). 1967. *A Grain of Wheat.* London and Portsmouth, N.H.: Heinemann.

Njonjo, Charles (Chairman). 2002. *Report of the Commission of Enquiry into the Land Law System of Kenya.* Nairobi: Government Printer.

Northcote, G. A. S. 1907. "The Nilotic Kavirondo." *Journal of the Royal Anthropological Institute* 38:58–66.

Nyamu-Musembi, Celestine. 2002. "Are Local Norms and Practices Fences or Pathways? The Example of Women's Property Rights." In Abdullahi A. An-Na'im, ed., *Cultural Transformation and Human Rights in Africa,* pp. 126–50. London: Zed Books.

Nzioki, Akinyi. 2002. "The Effect of Land Tenure on Women's Access and Control of Land in Kenya." In Abdullahi A. An-Na'im, ed., *Cultural Transformation and Human Rights in Africa,* pp. 218–60. London: Zed Books.

Obama, Barack. 2004. *Dreams of My Father: A Story of Race and Inheritance.* New York: Three Rivers Press. Orig. pub. 1995.

Obara, Dunstan. 1979. "Cotton Production in the Lake Victoria Basin of Kenya." Nairobi: University of Nairobi, Institute of Development Studies.

Obol-Ochola, James, ed. 1969. *Land Law Reform in East Africa.* Kampala: The National Trust, Adult Education Centre.

Ochieng', William Robert. 1974. *An Outline History of Nyanza up to 1914.* Nairobi: East African Literature Bureau.

————. 1975. *The First Word: Essays on Kenya History*. Nairobi: East African
Literature Bureau.

Ocholla-Ayayo, A. B. C. 1976. *Traditional Ideology and Ethics among the Southern
Luo*. Uppsala, Sweden: Scandinavian Institute of African Studies.

————. 1979. "Marriage and Cattle Exchange among the Nilotic Luo." *Paideuma*
25: 173–93.

————. 1980. *The Luo Culture: A Reconstruction of the Material Patterns of a
Traditional African Society*. Wiesbaden: Franz Steiner Verlag.

Odenyo, Amos O. 1973. "Conquest, Clientage and Land Law among the Luo."
Law and Society Review 7:767–78.

Odgaard, Rie. 2003. "Scrambling for Land in Tanzania: Process of Formalisation
and Legitimisation of Land Rights." In Tor A. Benjaminsen and Christian
Lund, eds., *Securing Land Rights in Africa*, pp. 71–88. London and Portland,
Ore.: Frank Cass.

Odinga, Oginga. 1967. *Not Yet Uhuru*. London: Heinemann.

Ogembo. Justus. 2006. *Contemporary Witch-hunting in Gusii, Southwestern Kenya*.
Lewiston, N.Y.: Edwin Mellen Press.

Ogot, Bethwell A. 1963. "British Administration in the Central Nyanza District of
Kenya, 1900–60." *Journal of African History* 4(2):249–73.

————. 1967. *Peoples of East Africa: History of the Southern Luo*. Vol. 1, *Migration
and Settlement, 1500–1900*. Nairobi: East Africa Publishing House.

————. 1999. "Kingship and Statelessness among the Nilotes." In B. A. Ogot,
Reintroducing Man into the African World, pp. 55–72. Kisumu: Anyange Press.
Orig. pub. 1964.

Ogot, B.A., and W.R. Ochieng', eds. 1995. *Decolonization and Independence in
Kenya, 1940–93*. London, Nairobi, and Athens Ohio: James Currey, East
African Educational Publishers, and Ohio University Press.

Ojany, F. F., and R. B. Ogendo. 1987. *Kenya: A Study in Physical and Human
Geography*. Nairobi, Dar es Salaam, and Kampala: Longman.

Ojwang, Jackton Boma, and J. N. K. Mugambi. 1989. *The S. M. Otieno Case:
Death and Burial in Modern Kenya*. Nairobi: Nairobi University Press.

Okec, S. 1969. "Pilot Schemes for the Registrations of Land Titles in Uganda." In
James Obol-Ochola ed., *Land Law Reform in East Africa*, pp. 255–64. Kampala:
The National Trust, Adult Education Centre.

Okoth-Ogendo, H. W. O. 1976. "African Land Tenure Reform." In Judith Heyer,
J. K. Maitha, and W. M. Senga, eds., *Agricultural Development in Kenya: An
Economic Assessment*, pp. 152–85. Nairobi: Oxford University Press.

————. 1978. *The Political Economy of Land Law: An Essay in the Legal
Organisation of Underdevelopment in Kenya, 1895–1974*. D.S.L. thesis, Yale
University.

————. 1981a. "Land Ownership and Land Distribution in Kenya's Large-Farm
Areas." In Tony Killick, ed., *Papers on the Kenyan Economy*, pp. 329–37.
Nairobi: Heinemann.

————. 1981b. "Land Policy and Agricultural Production in Kenya: The Case of the Nyanza Sugar Belt." In H. W. O. Okoth-Ogendo, ed., *Approaches to Rural Transformation in Eastern Africa*, pp. 164–84. Nairobi: Bookwise.

————. 1986. "The Perils of Land Tenure Reform: The Case of Kenya." In J. Artezen, L. Ngcongco, and S. Turner, eds., *Land Policy and Agriculture in Eastern and Central Africa*, pp. 79–92. Tokyo: United Nations University.

————. 1989. "Some Issues of Theory in the Study of Tenure Relations in African Agriculture." *Africa* (Journal of the International African Institute) 59(1):6–17.

————. 1991a. "Agrarian Reform in Sub-Saharan Africa. An Assessment of State Responses to the African Agrarian Crisis and Their Implications for Agricultural Development." In T. J. Bassett and Donald E. Crummey, eds., *Land in African Agrarian Systems*, pp. 247–73. Madison: University of Wisconsin Press.

————. 1991b. *Tenants of the Crown: Evolution of Agrarian Law and Institutions in Kenya*. Nairobi: African Centre for Technology Studies (ACTS) Press.

Ominde, Simeon H. 1963. *Land and Population in the Western Districts of Nyanza Province, Kenya*. Ph.D. thesis, University of London.

————. 1981. *Land and Population Movements in Kenya*. London, Nairobi, and Ibadan: Heinemann.

Onalo, P. L. 1986. *Land Law and Conveyancing in Kenya*. Nairobi: Heinemann Kenya.

Orvis, S. 1997. *The Agrarian Question in Kenya*. Gainesville: University of Florida Press.

Ostrom, Elinor. 1990. *Governing the Commons: The Evolution of Institutions for Collective Action*. Cambridge: Cambridge University Press.

Oucho, John. 2002. *Undercurrents of Ethnic Conflict in Kenya*. Leiden: E. J. Brill.

Owen, Walter Edwin, Archdeacon. 1934. Sworn Statement and Memorandum to the Kenya Land Commission. In Kenya Land Commission, *Evidence and Memoranda* (Col. 91), 3:2190–2204. London: HMSO.

Pala Okeyo, Achola. 1977. *Changes in Economy and Ideology: A Study of the Joluo of Kenya (With Special Reference to Women)*. Ph.D. thesis, Harvard University.

————. 1980. "Daughters of the Lake and Rivers: Colonization and the Land Rights of Luo Women in Kenya." In Mona Etienne and Eleanor Leacock, eds., *Women and Colonization: Anthropological Perspectives*, pp. 186–213. New York: Praeger.

————. 1983. "Women's Access to Land and their Role in Agriculture and Decision-Making on the Farm: Experiences of the Joluo of Kenya." *Journal of Eastern African Research and Development* 13:69–87. Orig. pub. 1978.

Palmer, Robin. 1997. *Contested Lands in Southern and Eastern Africa: A Literature Survey*. Oxford: Oxfam.

Palmeri, Paolo, and Chase Sterne. 2006. *AIDS and Land Tenure in Africa: Two Case Studies in Mozambique and Tanzania*. Padua: CLEUP (Coop. Libreria Editrice Università di Padova).

Parkin, David J. 1972. *Palms, Wine, and Witnesses: Public Spirit and Private Gain in an African Farming Community*. San Francisco: Chandler.

————, ed. 1975. *Town and Country in Central and Eastern Africa*. London: Oxford University Press, for International African Institute.

————. 1978. *The Cultural Definition of Political Response: Lineal Destiny among the Luo*. London: Academic Press.

Paterson, Douglas B. 1980. "Coping with Land Scarcity: The Pattern of Household Adaptations in One Luhya Community." University of Nairobi, Institute for Development Studies, Working Paper 360.

————. 1984. *Kinship, Land and Community: The Moral Foundations of the Abaluhya of East Bunyore (Kenya)*. Ph.D. dissertation, University of Washington. Ann Arbor, Mich.: University Microfilms International.

Paulson, Jo Ann. 1984. *The Structure and Development of Financial Markets in Kenya: An Example of Agricultural Finance*. Ph.D. thesis, Stanford University.

Peoples, Kenneth L., David Freshwater, Gregory D. Hanson, Paul T. Prentice, and Eric P. Thor, 1992. *Anatomy of an American Agricultural Credit Crisis: Farm Debt in the 1980s*. Lanham, Md.: Rowman and Littlefield.

Peters, Pauline. 1994. *Dividing the Commons: Policy and Politics in Botswana*. Charlottesville: University Press of Virginia.

————. 2002. "The Limits of Negotiability: Security, Equity and Class Formation in Africa's Land Systems." In Kristine Juul and Christian Lund, eds., *Negotiating Property in Africa*, pp. 46–66. Portsmouth, N.H.: Heinemann.

Phillips, Arthur. 1945. *Report on Native Tribunals, Colony and Protectorate of Kenya*. Nairobi: Government Printer.

Pischke, J. D. Von. 1977. *The Political Economy of Farm Credit in Kenya*. Ph.D. thesis, University of Glasgow.

Pischke, J. D. Von, Dale W. Adams, and Gordon Donald, eds. 1983. *Rural Financial Markets in Developing Countries: Their Use and Abuse*. Baltimore: Johns Hopkins University Press, for the World Bank.

Plato. 1976. *The Laws*, trans. Trevor J. Saunders. Harmondsworth: Penguin.

Platteau, Jean-Philippe. 1996. "The Evolutionary Theory of Land Rights as Applied to Sub-Saharan Africa: A Critical Assessment." *Development and Change* 27:29–86.

Polanyi, Karl. 1957. *The Great Transformation: The Political and Economic Origins of Our Time*. Boston: Beacon. Orig. pub. 1944.

Pollock, Frederick, and F. W. Maitland. 1952. *The History of English Law Before the Time of Edward I*. 2nd ed., 2 vols. Cambridge: Cambridge University Press. Orig. pub. 1895.

Potash, Betty, ed. 1986a. *Widows in African Societies: Choices and Constraints*. Stanford, Calif.: Stanford University Press.

————. 1986b. "Widows of the Grave: Widows in a Rural Luo Community." In Betty Potash, ed., *Widows in African Societies: Choices and Constraints*, pp. 44–65. Stanford, Calif.: Stanford University Press.

Proudhon, Pierre Joseph. 1849. *Qu'est-ce que la propriété?* Paris: Dondey-Dupré.

Prunier, Gérard. 1998. *The Rwanda Crisis: History of a Genocide*. London: C. Hurst. Orig. pub. 1995.

Redfield, Robert. 1947. "The Folk Society." *American Journal of Sociology* 52:293–308.

Riddell, James C., and Carol Dickerman. 1986. *Country Profiles of Land Tenure: Africa 1986.* LTC Paper 127. Madison: Land Tenure Center, University of Wisconsin.

Robertson, A. F. 1984. *People and the State: An Anthropology of Planned Development.* Cambridge: Cambridge University Press.

———. 1987. *The Dynamics of Productive Relationships: African Share Contracts in Comparative Perspective.* Cambridge: Cambridge University Press.

Roscoe, John. 1915. *The Northern Bantu: An Account of Some Central African Tribes of the Uganda Protectorate.* London: Frank Cass.

Rosenblatt, Paul C. 1990. *Farming Is in Our Blood: Farm Families in Economic Crisis.* Ames: Iowa State University Press.

Roth, Michael, Harold Lemel, John Bruce, and John Unruh. 1987. "An Analysis of Land Tenure and Water Allocation Issues in the Shalambood Irrigation Zone, Somalia." Madison: Land Tenure Center, University of Wisconsin.

Rousseau, Jean-Jacques. 1967a. "Discourse on the Origin and the Foundation of Inequality Among Mankind" (Discours sur l'origine et les fondements de l'inégalité parmi les hommes), anon. trans. In J.-J. Rousseau, *The Social Contract and Discourse on the Origin of Inequality*, ed. Lester G. Crocker, pp. 175–258. New York: Washington Square Press. Orig. pub. 1755.

———. 1967b. *The Social Contract* (Du contrat social), trans. Henry J. Tozer. In J.-J. Rousseau, *The Social Contract and Discourse on the Origin of Inequality*, ed. Lester G. Crocker, pp. 5–150. New York: Washington Square Press. Orig. pub. 1762.

Ruark, Robert. 1955. *Something of Value.* Garden City, N.Y.: Doubleday.

Sahlins, Marshall. 1961. "The Segmentary Lineage: An Organization of Predatory Expansion." *American Anthropologist* 63:322–45.

Saint-Exupéry, Antoine de. 1943. *The Little Prince.* New York: Harcourt, Brace and World.

Scheffer, Fr. 1934. "Land Tenure amongst the Luo." In Kenya Land Commission, *Evidence and Memoranda* (Col. 91), 3:2400–2401.

Scheffler, Harold W. 2001. *Filiation and Affiliation.* Boulder, Colo.: Westview.

Schneider, David. 1984. *A Critique of the Study of Kinship.* Ann Arbor: University of Michigan Press.

Schneider, Harold. 1974. *Economic Man: The Anthropology of Economics.* New York: Free Press.

Schwartz, Nancy. 1989. *"World Without End: The Movements and Meanings in the History, Narratives, and "Tongue-Speech" of Legio Maria of African Church Mission among Luo of Kenya.* Ph.D. thesis, Princeton University.

———. 1995. "Contested Spaces, Contested Places: Anthropology's Necrology and the Rewriting of Lives in Western Kenya." Paper presented at the 38th Annual Meeting of the African Studies Association, Orlando, Florida, 3–6 November.

————. 1997. "'Thick Participation,' Plural Healing Systems, and Death and Reburial Controversies: A Case Study from Western Kenya." Paper presented at the 40th Annual Meeting of the African Studies Association, Columbus, Ohio, 12–16 November.

————. 2000. "Active Dead or Alive: Some Kenyan Views About the Agency of Luo and Luyia Women Pre-and Post-Mortem." *Journal of Religion in Africa* 30(4):433–67.

Scott, James C. 1998. *Seeing Like a State: How Certain Schemes to Improve the Human Condition Have Failed.* New Haven: Yale University Press.

Seidman, Ann. 1986. *Money, Banking and Public Finance in Africa.* London: Zed Books.

Shaw, Malcolm. 1986. *Title to Territory in Africa: International Legal Issues.* Oxford: Clarendon.

Shipton, Parker. 1984. "Strips and Patches: A Demographic Dimension in Some African Landholding and Political Systems." *Man* (new series) 19:613–34.

————. 1988. "The Kenyan Land Tenure Reform: Misunderstandings in the Public Creation of Private Property." In R. E. Downs and S. P. Reyna, eds., *Land and Society in Contemporary Africa,* 91–135. Hanover, N.H.: University Press of New England.

————. 1989a. *Bitter Money: Cultural Economy and Some African Meanings of Forbidden Commodities.* American Ethnological Society Monograph 1. Washington, D.C.: American Anthropological Association.

————. 1989b. "How Private Property Emerges in Africa: Directed and Undirected Land Tenure Reforms in Densely Settled Areas South of the Sahara." Report to Bureau of Program and Policy Coordination, U.S. Agency for International Development.

————. 1990. "African Famines and Food Security: Anthropological Perspectives." *Annual Review of Anthropology* 19:353–94.

————. 1992. "Debts and Trespasses: Land, Mortgages, and the Ancestors in Western Kenya." In M. Goheen and P. Shipton, guest eds., *Rights Over Land: Categories and Controversies.* Special Issue of *Africa* (Journal of the International African Institute), 62(3):357–88.

————. 1994. "Land and Culture in Tropical Africa: Soils, Symbols, and the Metaphysics of the Mundane." *Annual Review of Anthropology* 23:347–77.

————. 1995. "Luo Entrustment: Foreign Finance and the Soil of the Spirits in Kenya." *Africa* 65(2):165–96.

————. 2003. "Legalism and Loyalism: European, African, and Human 'Rights.'" In Bartholomew Dean and Jerome M. Levi, eds., *At the Risk of Being Heard: Identity, Indigenous Rights, and Postcolonial States,* pp. 45–79. Ann Arbor: University of Michigan Press.

————. 2007. *The Nature of Entrustment: Intimacy, Exchange, and the Sacred in Africa.* New Haven: Yale University Press.

Shipton, Parker, and Miriam Goheen. 1992. "Understanding African Landholding: Power, Wealth and Meaning." Introduction to M. Goheen and

P. Shipton, guest eds., *Rights over Land: Categories and Controversies*. Special Issue of *Africa* (Journal of the International African Institute) 62(3):307–25.

Simmel, Georg. 1982. *The Philosophy of Money*, trans. Tom Bottomore and David Frisby. Boston, London, Melbourne, and Henley: Routledge. Orig. pub. 1900.

Simons, Anna. 1995. *Networks of Dissolution: Somalia Undone*. Boulder, Colo.: Westview.

Simpson, A. W. B. 1961. *An Introduction to the History of Land Law*. Oxford: Oxford University Press.

Simpson, Stanhope Rowton. 1976–78. *Land Law and Registration*. 2 vols. Cambridge: Cambridge University Press.

Singer, Peter, and Jim Mason. 2006. *The Ethics of What We Eat*. Emmaus, Pennsylvania: Rodale.

Smith, Adam. 1976. *The Theory of Moral Sentiments*, ed. D. D. Raphael and A. L. Macfie. Oxford, U.K.: Clarendon. Orig. pub. 1759, last rev. 1790; reprinted in 1984 by Liberty Fund, Indianapolis.

———. 1978. *Lectures on Jurisprudence*, ed. R. L. Meek, D. D. Raphael, and P. G. Stein. Indianapolis: Liberty Fund. Orig. pub. 1762–63.

———. 1981. *An Inquiry into the Nature and Causes of the Wealth of Nations*, ed. R. H. Campbell and A. S. Skinner. Indianapolis: Liberty Fund. Orig. pub. 1776.

Smith, L. D. 1976. An Overview of Agricultural Development Policy. In Judith Heyer, J. K. Maitha, and W. M. Senga, eds., *Agricultural Development in Kenya*. Nairobi: Oxford University Press.

Sorrenson, M. P. K. 1967. *Land Reform in the Kikuyu Country*. London: Oxford University Press.

Soto, Hernando de. 1989. *The Other Path: The Invisible Revolution in the Third World*. New York: Harper.

———. 2000. *The Mystery of Capital: Why Capitalism Triumphs in the West and Fails Everywhere Else*. New York: Perseus.

Southall, Aidan. 1952. "Lineage Formation among the Luo." International African Institute Memorandum 26, pp. 1–43. London: Oxford University Press.

———. 1956. *Alur Society*. Cambridge: Heffer.

———. 1970. "Rank and Stratification among the Alur and Other Nilotic Peoples." In Arthur Tuden and Leonard Plotnicov, eds., *Social Stratification in Africa*, pp. 31–46. New York: Free Press.

Spear, Thomas, and Richard D. Waller, eds. 1993. *Being Maasai: Ethnicity and Identity in East Africa*. London and Athens, Ohio: James Currey and Ohio University Press.

Spencer, Herbert. 1892–98. *Principles of Sociology*. Vols. 6–8 of *A System of Synthetic Philosophy*. London: Williams and Norgate.

———. 1904. *First Principles*, 6th ed., revised. Vol. 1 of *A System of Synthetic Philosophy*. London: Williams and Norgate. Orig. pub. 1851.

———. 2008. "The Social Organism." Extract in R. Jon McGee and R. L. Warms, *Anthropological Theory*, pp. 11–27. New York: McGraw Hill. Orig. pub. in *Westminster Review*, 1860.

Spies, Emerson George. 1970. "Mortgage." *Encyclopaedia Britannica* 15:865–66.

Stam, Jerome M., S. R. Koenig, S. E. Bentley, and H. E. Gale, Jr. 1991. *Farm Financial Stress, Farm Exits, and Public Sector Assistance in the Farm Sector in the 1980s.* U.S. Department of Agriculture Economic Research Service, Agricultural Economic Report no. 645.

Stamp, Patricia. 1991. "Burying Otieno: The Politics of Gender and Ethnicity in Kenya." *Signs: Journal of Women in Culture and Society* 16(4):808–45.

Staudt, Kathleen. 1985. *Agricultural Policy Implementation: A Case Study from Western Kenya.* West Hartford, Conn.: Kuramian Press.

Stemler, A. B. L., et al. 1975. "Caudatum Sorghums and the Speakers of the Chari-Nile Languages in Africa." *Journal of African History* 16(2):161–83.

Stevenson, R. F. 1968. *Population and Political Systems in Tropical Africa.* New York: Columbia University Press.

Streeten, Paul. 1981. *Development Perspectives.* London: Macmillan.

Swynnerton, R. J. M. 1955. "A Plan to Intensify the Development of African Agriculture in Kenya." Nairobi: Department of Agriculture, Government Printer. Orig. pub. 1953.

Sytek, William. 1966. "A History of Land Consolidation in Central Nyanza, 1956–1962." East African Institute of Social Research Conference Papers, Makerere University College.

———. 1972. *Luo of Kenya.* Ethnocentrism Series. New Haven: Human Relations Area Files.

Tawney, Richard Henry. 1921. *The Acquisitive Society.* London: G. Bell and Sons.

Taylor, B. K. 1962. *The Western Lacustrine Bantu.* Ethnographic Survey of Africa, East Central Africa 13. London: International African Institute.

Taylor, Christopher C. 1999. *Sacrifice as Terror: The Rwandan Genocide of 1994.* Oxford, U.K.: Berg.

Taylor, Peter. 1986. *A Summons to Memphis.* New York: Vintage.

Thomson, Joseph. 1887. *Through Masai Land.* London: Samson Low & Co.

Throup, David. 1987. *Economic and Social Origins of Mau Mau.* London and Columbus: James Currey and Ohio University Press.

Throup, David, and Charles Hornsby. 1998. *Multi-Party Politics in Kenya: The Kenyatta and Moi States and the Triumph of the System in the 1992 Election.* Oxford: James Currey; and Athens, Ohio: Ohio University Press.

Thucydides. 1910. *History of the Peloponnesian Wars,* trans. Richard Crawley. New York: E. P. Dutton.

Tocqueville, Alexis de. 1983. *The Old Régime and the French Revolution.* New York: Doubleday. Orig. pub. 1856.

———. 2001. *Writings on Empire and Slavery,* ed. and trans. Jennifer Pitts. Baltimore: Johns Hopkins University Press.

Tönnies, Ferdinand. 1957. *Community and Society (Gemeinschaft und Gesellschaft),* trans. Charles P. Loomis. East Lansing: Michigan State University Press. Orig. pub. 1887.

Tosh, J. 1978. *Clan Leaders and Colonial Chiefs in Lango.* Oxford: Clarendon Press.

Turner, Victor. 1995. *The Ritual Process*. Chicago: Aldine. Orig. pub. 1969.

Van Hekken, P. M., and H. U. E. Van Velzen. 1972. *Land Scarcity and Rural Inequality in Tanzania*. The Hague: Mouton.

Vasthoff, Josef. 1968. *Small Farm Credit and Development: Some Experiences in East Africa with Special Reference to Kenya*. Munchen: Weltforum Verlag; London: C. Hurst & Co.; and New York: Humanities Press.

Waal, Frans De. 2000. *Chimpanzee Politics: Power and Sex among Apes*, revised ed. Baltimore: Johns Hopkins University Press.

Wagner, Günter. 1949, 1956. *The Bantu of North Kavirondo* (2 vols.). London: Oxford University Press, for International African Institute.

Walsh, Janet. 2003. "Double Standards: Women's Property Rights Violations in Kenya." Report. New York: Human Rights Watch.

Wanjigi, J. Maina. 1972. "Agriculture and Land Tenure in Kenya." In W. T. W. Morgan, ed., *East Africa: Its Peoples and Resources*, 2nd ed., pp. 177–88. Nairobi: Oxford University Press.

Wanyeki, L. Muthoni, ed. 2003. *Women and Land in Africa: Culture, Religion and Realizing Women's Rights*. London: Zed Books.

Washburn, Wilcomb. 1975. *The Assault on Tribalism: The General Allotment Law (Dawes Act) of 1887*. Philadelphia: J. B. Lippincott.

Watkins, T. H. 1993. *The Great Depression: America in the 1930s*. Boston: Back Bay Books (Little, Brown).

Weber, Max. 1998. *The Agrarian Sociology of Ancient Civilizations*. London and New York: Verso. Orig. pub. 1896, 1909 (parts), 1924 (whole).

———. 2002. *The Protestant Ethic and the Spirit of Capitalism*, trans. and ed. S. Kalberg. Los Angeles: Roxbury. Orig. pub. 1904–1905.

Welbourn, F. B., and B. A. Ogot. 1966. *A Place to Feel at Home: A Study of Two Independent Churches in Western Kenya*. London: Oxford University Press.

West, Henry W. 1972. *Land Policy in Buganda*. Cambridge: Cambridge University Press.

Whisson, Michael G. 1961. "The Rise of Asembo and the Curse of Kakia." *Conference Papers*. East African Institute of Social Research, Makerere University College, Kampala.

———. 1962a. "The Journeys of the JoRamogi." *Conference Papers*, East African Institute of Social Research, Makerere University College, Kampala, July.

———. 1962b. "The Will of God and the Wiles of Men: An Examination of the Beliefs Concerning the Supernatural Held by the Luo with Particular Reference to their Functions in the Field of Social Control." *Conference Papers*, East African Institute of Social Research, Makerere University College, Kampala, July.

———. 1964. *Change and Challenge: A Study of the Social and Economic Changes Among the Kenya Luo*. Nairobi: Christian Council of Kenya.

Widner, Jennifer. 1992. *The Rise of a Party-State in Kenya: From "Harambee!" to "Nyayo!"* Berkeley: University of California Press.

Wilde, John C. de. 1967. "Kenya: Central Nyanza District." In John C. deWilde,

Experiences with Agricultural Development in Tropical Africa, vol. 2. Baltimore: Johns Hopkins University Press.

Wilson, Godfrey. 1938. *The Land Rights of Individuals among the Nyakyusa.* Rhodes-Livingstone Paper 1. Manchester: Manchester University Press. Orig. pub. 1932.

Wilson, Gordon M. 1967. "Homicide and Suicide among the Joluo of Kenya." In Paul Bohannan, ed., *African Homicide and Suicide.* New York: Atheneum. Orig. pub. 1960.

———. 1968. *Luo Customary Law and Marriage Laws [and] Customs.* Nairobi: Government Printer. Orig. pub. 1961.

Wilson, Monica. 1950. "Nyakyusa Kinship." In A. R. Radcliffe-Brown and Daryll Forde, eds., *African Systems of Kinship and Marriage.* London: Oxford University Press, for International African Institute.

———. 1963. "Effects on the Xhosa and Nyakyusa of Scarcity of Land." In Daniel Biebuyck, ed., *African Agrarian Systems.* London: Oxford University Press.

Wilson, Rodney J. A. 1971. "The Economic Implications of Land Registration in Kenya's Smallholder Areas." Nairobi: University of Nairobi, Institute for Development Studies, Staff Paper 91.

———. 1972. "Land Control in Kenya's Smallholder Farming Areas." *East African Journal of Rural Development* 5(1–2):123–46.

Wipper, Audrey. 1977. *Rural Rebels: A Study of Two Protest Movements in Kenya.* Oxford: Oxford University Press.

Wittgenstein, Ludwig. 1958. *Preliminary Studies for the "Philosophical Investigations," Generally known as the Blue and Brown Books.* Oxford: Blackwell.

World Bank. 1989. *Sub-Saharan Africa: From Crisis to Sustainable Growth.* Washington, D.C.: World Bank.

———. 2006. Poverty Map, Nyanza Province, Kenya. http://www.worldbank.org/research/povertymaps/kenya/ch4.9.pdf, accessed May 31, 2006.

———. *World Development Reports* (annual). New York: Oxford University Press, for the World Bank.

Wrangham, Richard, and Dale Peterson. 1996. *Demonic Males: Apes and the Origins of Human Violence.* Boston and New York: Mariner (Houghton Mifflin).

Wright, Robert. 1994. *The Moral Animal: Why We Are the Way We Are: The New Science of Evolutionary Psychology.* New York: Vintage.

———. 2001. *Nonzero: The Logic of Human Destiny.* New York: Vintage.

Yudelman, Montague. 1964. *Africans on the Land: Economic Problems of African Agricultural Development in Southern, Central, and East Africa, with Special Reference to Southern Rhodesia.* Cambridge, Mass.: Harvard University Press.

Index

Terms in the Luo language (DhoLuo) are translated in parentheses; KiSwahili terms are distinguished with the abbreviation "Sw." Numbers in italics indicate figures.

Abdi, Sophia, 208
absentee landlords, setting time limits on, 210
acting, in relation to being, xii
Adams, Dale, 55
AFC. *See* Agricultural Finance Corporation
Africa: allowing freer movement of people from, 252; avoiding assumptions about, 37, 38; debt of countries in, 55; first nationwide attempt in, to title property, 10–11; landholding in, related to communal or individual rights, 70–71; mortgages in, 2; society combining principles of kinship and territorial polity, 85; theories about improving farming and economies in, 8–9
African Courts, 102
African Land Development Board, 161, 163
African Land Utilization and Settlement Authority, 140
African Settlement and Land Utilization Board, 161
afterbirth, placement and burial of, 90, 198, 229
age relations, land titling and, 151
Agricultural Betterment Funds, 139
Agricultural Finance Corporation (AFC), 161–71, 177
Algeria, mortgaging in, 43
alliance theory, 265n29
America, North, farm finance in, 30–31, 33. *See also* Indians, American

ancestors: importance of, in East Africa, 33; perceptions of, 5–6, 218, 232
ancestor worship, attempts at discouraging, 94–95
ancestral homelands, importance of, to farm economy, 176
Ancient Society (Morgan), 49–50
animals: in livelihood, 64; and property, 39–40; in redistributing plant energy, 71–72; used as loan security, 135
Ankole (Uganda), 241
Annan, Kofi, 194
anthropology, modernization in, 46
anyuola (descent group type), 96–97, 263–64n21
apprentice farming, 106
Asiyo, Juni, 160, 179
Athens, ancient, land and loans in, 27, 51
Atieno Odhiambo, E. S., 65, 288n16
attachment, ideologies of, in general, 7–8, 238–39
auctions. *See* land auctions
autochthon/immigrant relationship, 29, 114–18, 152–53, 229, 269n12, 276n7

Babylonia, records of loans and debts in, 26
bankruptcy, laws of, 258n19
Baran, Paul, 54
Barclay's Bank, 171

senting entrustment in titling body, 200; resulting in insecurity, 181, 200; rethinking, 199, 237–38, 246; tensions raised by, 151–53; unknown effects of, 234

land transfer reporting, refused or neglected, 156–57

large-scale loans, from AFC, 165–66

Lawrance Mission on Land Consolidation and Registration in Kenya, 148–49

laws, rationalization for, 37

leasehold, 214, 256n1; Fabians' favoring of, 53

Lectures on Jurisprudence (Smith), 38

legibility, political, 56

Leslie, E. J., 141

LeVine, Robert, 266n44, 282n54

Leviathan (Hobbes), 35

Leys, Colin, 54

libamba (descent group type), 263–64n21; land rights within, 100

Liberia, attempting land adjudication program, 130–31

ligala (settlement, new home), 261n7

Limitation Act, 118, 184

Lincoln Institute of Land Policy, 260n45

lineage: as adaptation to contemporary conditions, 20, 128; branching (segmentary), 99, 108, 228–29; disagreements about, 98–100; relativity of, 103–5

lineage mates, overlapping rights of, 142

Lipton, Michael, 55

Little Prince, The (Saint-Exupéry), 1

Littleton, Thomas, 257n6

livelihood: diversification of, 38, 118–19; stadial theories of, 38–39

livestock. *See* animals; cattle

living, clashing with nonliving, over mortgages, 6

Lloyd, William Forster, 47

loans: funds diverted for other purposes, 168–70; methods of ensuring repayment, 237; traditional security, 134–35; without mortgages, 199–200

Local Native Councils, 139, 141

Locke, John, 36, 37, 229, 248, 250

Low, P., 142–43

Lugard, Frederick J. D., 45–46, 253

Luhya, 95; land usage and political organization among, 122–23; native/stranger distinctions among, 269n12; rarity among, of borrowing against land, 134; in the resettlement zones, 184, 185, 186; similarities with Luo, 199; in 2007–8 crisis, 190

Luo: adjusting strategies of livelihood, 64; alcohol consumption of, 68; altering their environments, 64–65; ancestors of, 60, 62–63, 72; ancestral homeland of, 3; anti-authoritarianism of, 98; being and becoming, 60–66; burial placements for the dead, 94–96; cardinal principle of land ownership for, 124–25; cash crops of, 67–68; changing view of land, 6–7, 66, 109–10, 150; characteristics of, 7, 13–16, 59; coping with foreign financial intervention, 11–12; culture of, 14, 16, 59–60, 67, 69; current challenges to patriarchy, bridewealth, and widow inheritance, 125–26; deemphasizing herding, 64; defining social identities for, x; denouncing idea of registering and mortgaging land, 132; de-specializing and de-integrating, 38; development plans in, reflecting freehold-mortgage doctrine, 9–10; diffuse authority and prestige structures of, 89; dispute settlement among, 104; dogma of, 233; eclectic agrarian lifestyle of, 66–70; education among, 14; elders recounting migration, *74;* extreme decentralization of, 126–27; favoring lineal over lateral inheritance, 126; fencing of fields, as recent practice, 66; fortified settlements of, 65; genealogical seniority among, 93–94; graves as sacred places for, 5, 63–64; growing attachment of, to fixed sites, 64; hierarchy among, 114–16; history of transferring land among, 124; homesteads of, 101; increased importance of female-centered households and churches, 105; increasing emphasis on agriculture, 110; increasingly convinced that they are settled in Nyanza, 109–10; individuals and families limiting seasonal access to lands, 66; information on land tenure, sources of, 87; initial resistance to land titling program, 150; intergenerational land transfers of, 111–14; intimacy for, xii; involved in urban migration, 126; jealousy among lineage segments, 103; landholding themes of, 103; land passing between brothers, 111–12; land tenure for, 71; layout of fields outside homestead enclosures, 93; living without central political regime, 88; loans to districts, 163; looking up to influential political leaders, 88–89; multi-house homestead, *75;* opposed to Kenya's agricultural credit plans, 142–43; participation of, in land titling process, 150–51; patriliny, 13–

Swahili, 15
Swazuri, Mohamed, 205, 206
Swynnerton, Roger J. M., 143–44
Swynnerton Plan, 118, 131, 141, 142, 219;
citing purposes for reforming landholding,
149; intentional creation of landed and
landless classes, 144, 145–46, 155; making
land titling and mortgages official Kenyan
policy, 143–46; political stabilization as its
hidden agenda, 146; supporting cooperative movement, 274–75n44; widely varied
responses to, 150
symbolism, in land matters, 5, 106, 107, 117,
127, 224, 229

Taliban (gang, in Kenya), 192
Tallensi, 85, 264–65n28
Tanzania, 188, 242
Tawney, R. H., 239
taxation, 90, 214–15
Taylor, Peter, 114
tenure, common, 40
tenure/estate, 29
tenure, individualized, DNLP's criticism of,
216. *See also* land tenure
territorial circumscriptions, 44
territoriality, 140, 248, 288n14. *See also* land
tenure
terroir (French, multiple meanings), 22
Tetu, Lorna Timanoi, 208–9
Thaba Nchu, 244
thim (wilderness), 89
Tinderet, 185
titling. *See* land titling
Tocqueville, Alexis de, 43, 250
Togo, land registration in, 131
Tönnies, Ferdinand, 253
*Tractatus de Legibus et Consuetudinibus Regni
Angliae* (Treatise on the Laws and Customs
of the English Kingdom) (Glanvil), 27
tragedy of the commons, 47
"Tramp's Story, The" (Carleton), 32
Transfer of Property Act of 1882, 137
transnational authorities, 252
truth commission, call for, 206
Tswana, 244
tyranny by the majority, 250

ugali (Swahili, food form), 67
Uganda, 131, 242. See also *mailo*
Ugarit, land ownership in, 26

Union of South Africa, early land titling program in, 131
United Nations Universal Declaration of
Human Rights, 250
United States: bankruptcy laws in, 258n19;
mortgages in, 2; Native Americans' mortgaging experience in, 244; present mortgage
crisis in, 244–45
United States Agency for International Development (USAID), 170–71, 182
untouchables (protected borrowers), 165
urban bias, 55
Uyoma, 17

values, expressed in non-monetary terms,
227–28
verbal language, reliance on, 21–22
Victoria, 1–2
village, alternately translated, 98
villagization, 56
violence, between ethnic groups in intersettled
lands, 180–81, 185–89
violence, surrounding foreclosures, 175–76,
179
virilocality, 14
Von Pischke, J. D., 55, 226
vulnerable groups, addressed under DNLP,
215

Wangoi, Sarah, 196
war, effect of, on property rights, 41. *See also*
violence
wealth: inequalities in, related to city's age, 52;
proximity of, to poverty, 52–53
Wealth of Nations, The (Smith), 38, 260n41
Webb, Beatrice, 53
Webb, Sidney, 53
Weber, Max, 25, 239, 251, 256n4
Wellesley, Arthur (Duke of Wellington), 223
Westernization, 25
Whisson, Michael, 87, 110, 114, 119
widows: denied land after death of husbands,
209; inheritance of, 275–76n5; treatment
of, 91–92
Wilson, Gordon, 87, 93, 104, 111, 117–18
witchcraft, guarding against, 69, 282n53
wives and co-wives: linked, 93; terms for
multiple, 92. *See also* kinship; polygamous
families; woman-woman marriage
woman-woman marriage, 112
women: farm work of, *77;* heading ministries